T0210481

Lecture Notes in Computer Science 9522

Commenced Publication in 1973
Founding and Former Series Editors:
Gerhard Goos, Juris Hartmanis, and Jan van Leeuwen

More information about this series at http://www.springer.com/series/7410

Ion Bica · David Naccache
Emil Simion (Eds.)

Innovative Security Solutions for Information Technology and Communications

8th International Conference, SECITC 2015
Bucharest, Romania, June 11–12, 2015
Revised Selected Papers

 Springer

Editors
Ion Bica
Military Technical Academy
Bucharest
Romania

David Naccache
Departement d Informatique
Ecole Normale Superieure
Paris
France

Emil Simion
Advanced Technologies Institute
    and University Politehnica of Bucharest
Bucharest
Romania

ISSN 0302-9743   ISSN 1611-3349 (electronic)
Lecture Notes in Computer Science
ISBN 978-3-319-27178-1   ISBN 978-3-319-27179-8   (eBook)
DOI 10.1007/978-3-319-27179-8

Library of Congress Control Number: 2015956125

LNCS Sublibrary: SL4 – Security and Cryptology

This Springer imprint is published by SpringerNature
The registered company is Springer International Publishing AG Switzerland

Foreword

The present volume is the outcome of the 8th International Conference on Security for Information Technology and Communications that comes in a long series of successful events starting in 2008. This conference series was founded to foster novel and exciting research in this area and to help generate new directions for further research and development.

Information and Communications Technologies (ICT) encourage globalization, exchange of information, and the proliferation of cyber space. The advantages of using these technologies are immense but, alongside opportunities, a broad range of issues and drawbacks have limited to some extent the full extraction of benefits from ICT use. One of the main issues with ICT today is *security*, which has to deal with the flourishing of a myriad electronic attacks, malware, vulnerabilities, and intrusions in the domain of information and communications technologies.

For seven years, SECITC has brought together computer security researchers, cryptographers, industry representatives, and graduate students. One of SECITC's primary goals is to gather researchers from different communities and provide a forum allowing for the informal exchanges necessary for the emergence of new scientific collaborations. Special attention was devoted to young researchers, master and Ph students, with scientific interests in the field of information security, cyber defense, cryptography, and communications and network security.

The initial concept of SECITC arose from a teaching and research collaboration between the two co-founder universities, Military Technical Academy and Bucharest University of Economic Studies, which was meant to highlight the increasing importance of computer and information security. This was followed by discussions with a number of fellow cyber security researchers. Their enthusiastic encouragement persuaded the co-founder universities to move ahead with the daunting task of creating a high-quality conference.

The organization of a conference like SECITC requires the collaboration of many individuals. First of all, we would like to thank the authors and the keynote speakers for graciously accepting our invitation. We express our gratitude to the Program Committee members and external reviewers for their efforts in reviewing the papers, engaging in active online discussion during the selection process, and providing valuable feedback to authors. Last but not least, we would like to thank the two co-chairs of the conference, Prof. David Naccache and Dr. Emil Simion for their special effort to ensure the scientific high quality of our conference.

November 2015   Victor-Valeriu Patriciu

Preface

This volume contains the papers presented at SECITC 2015, the 8th International Conference on Security for Information Technology and Communications (www.secitc.eu), held during June 11–12, 2015, in Bucharest.

There were 34 submissions and each submitted paper was reviewed by at least three Program Committee members. The committee decided to accept 15 papers, and the program also included three invited guest speakers.

For seven years SECITC has been bringing together computer security researchers, cryptographers, industry representatives, and graduate students. The conference focuses on research on any aspect of security and cryptography. The papers present advances in the theory, design, implementation, analysis, verification, or evaluation of secure systems and algorithms.

One of SECITC's primary goals is to bring together researchers belonging to different communities and provide a forum that facilitates the informal exchanges necessary for the emergence of new scientific collaborations. We would like to acknowledge the work of the Program Committee, whose great efforts provided a proper framework for the selection of the papers.

The conference was organised by Advanced Technologies Institute, Bucharest University of Academic Studies and Military Technical Academy.

May 2015

Ion Bica
David Naccache
Emil Simion

Organization

Program Committee

Ludovic Apvrille	Telecom ParisTech, France
Sambit Bakshi	National Institute of Technology Rourkela, India
Paulo Barreto	University of São Paulo, Brazil
Ion Bica	Military Technical Academy, Romania
Catalin Boja	Bucharest Academy of Economic Studies, Romania
Sanjit Chatterjee	Indian Institute of Science, India
Liqun Chen	Hewlett-Packard Laboratories
Xiaofeng Chen	Xidian University, China
Christophe Clavier	Université de Limoges, France
Jean-Sébastien Coron	University of Luxembourg, Luxembourg
Joan Daemen	STMicroelectronics
Naccache David	Ecole Normale Superieure, France
Eric Diehl	Sony Pictures
Itai Dinur	Ecole Normale Superieure, France
Bao Feng	HuaWei
Eric Freyssinet	IRCGN
Wang Guilin	IRCGN, Huawei International Pte. Ltd.
Helena Handschuh	Rambus – Cryptography Research
Xinyi Huang	Fujian Normal University, China
Malay Kishore Dutta	Amity School of Engineering and Technology, India
Jean-Louis Lanet	Inria-RBA, France
Tancrede Lepoint	CryptoExperts
Kostas Markantonakis	ISG-Smart Card Centre, Founded by Vodafone, G&D and the Information Security Group of Royal Holloway, University of London, UK
Alfred Menezes	University of Waterloo, Canada
Dan Page	University of Bristol, UK
Victor-Valeriu Patriciu	Military Technical Academy, Romania
Rene Peralta	NIST
Giuseppe Persiano	University of Salerno, Italy
Bart Preneel	Katholieke Universiteit Leuven - COSIC, Belgium
Reyhanitabar Reza	EPFL, Lausanne, Switzerland
Mark Ryan	University of Birmingham, UK
Peter Ryan	University of Luxembourg, Luxembourg

Pierangela Samarati	Università degli Studi di Milano, Italy
Damien Sauveron	XLIM, UMR University of Limoges/CNRS 7252, France
Emil Simion	Advanced Technologies Institute and University Politehnica of Bucharest, Romania
Rainer Steinwandt	Florida Atlantic University, USA
Willy Susilo	University of Wollongong, Australia
Mehdi Tibouchi	NTT Secure Platform Laboratories
Cristian Toma	Bucharest University of Economic Studies, Romania
Michael Tunstall	Rambus – Cryptography Research
Ingrid Verbauwhede	KU Leuven, ESAT/COSIC, Belgium
Qianhong Wu	Beihang University, China
Moti Yung	Google and Columbia University, USA
Lei Zhang	East China Normal University, China

Additional Reviewers

Apvrille, Axelle
Debiao, He
Donida Labati, Ruggero
He, Shuangyu
Lugou, Florian

Singelee, Dave
Sinha Roy, Sujoy
Wang, Ding
Wurcker, Antoine
Zhang, Yuexin

Invited Talks

Authenticated-Encryption: Security Notions, Designs and Applications

Reza Reyhanitabar

EPFL, Switzerland

Abstract. Practical applications of symmetric-key encryption usually aim for two complementary data security properties: confidentiality (privacy) and authenticity (integrity). Yet classical encryption modes such as CBC solely provide confidentiality; hence, are an inadequate tool of a very limited utility unless combined appropriately with an additional cryptographic primitive called a message authentication code (MAC).

An authenticated encryption (AE) scheme simultaneously provides confidentiality and authenticity. The historically popular generic composition paradigm to build an AE scheme by combining two separate primitives, one to ensure confidentiality and another to guarantee authenticity, is neither most efficient nor most robust to implementation errors. This motivated the emergence of dedicated AE designs. AE has been studied for over a decade, yet remains a highly active and interesting area of research as evidenced by the currently running CAESAR competition by the cryptographic community. The competition aims to boost public discussions towards a better understanding of AE designs and to identify a portfolio of next-generation AE schemes by 2017.

In this talk we will explore the historical development of AE as a cryptographic goal and different methods to achieve this goal. I will start by explaining some of the failed attempts to use encryption-with-redundancy mechanisms; for example, the CBCC scheme (CBC encryption with the XOR of the message blocks as the checksum). Then I will talk about the emergence of AE as a formally defined security notion in its own right in 2000. We will explore the generic composition paradigm to achieve the AE goal. I will then look at the evolution of dedicated AE designs, offering better efficiency and usability compared to generic composition, from the introduction of RPC, IAPM, XCBC and OCB in 2001 to the currently running CAESAR competition with 57 algorithms as its first-round submissions.

Importance of useable AE to practice, and to some extent, difficulty of getting it right, is evident from the number of standards in which different AE constructions have been specified (such as IEEE 802.11i, NIST SP 800-38D, ANSI C12.22, and ISO/IEC 19772:2009) as well as widely-deployed standard protocols that employ AE schemes (such as IPsec, SSH, SSL/TLS). Finally, we will look at these standards.

Keywords: Authenticated encryption · Security notions · Provable security · Generic composition · Dedictaed AE designs · CAESAR competition.

New Results on Identity-Based Encryption from Quadratic Residuosity

Ferucio Laurenţiu Ţiplea[1] and Emil Simion[2]

[1] Department of Computer Science, "Al.I.Cuza" University of Iaşi,
700506 Iaşi, Romania
fltiplea@info.uaic.ro
[2] Advanced Technologies Institute, Bucharest, Romania,
ati@dcti.ro

Abstract. This invited talk surveys the results obtained so far in designing identity-based encryption (IBE) schemes based on the quadratic residuosity assumption (QRA). We begin by describing the first such scheme due to Cocks, and then we advance to the novel idea of Boneh, Gentry and Hamburg. Major improvements of the Boneh-Gentry-Hamburg scheme are then recalled. The recently revealed algebraic torus structures of the Cocks scheme allows for a better understanding of this scheme, as well as for new applications of it such as homomorphic and anonymous variants of it.

Identity-based encryption (IBE) was proposed in 1984 by Adi Shamir [10] who formulated its basic principles but he was unable to provide a solution to it, except for an identity-based signature scheme. Sakai, Ohgishi, and Kasahara [9] have proposed in 2000 an identity-based key agreement scheme and, one year later, Cocks [4] and Boneh and Franklin [1] have proposed the first IBE schemes. Cocks' solution is based on quadratic residues. It encrypts a message bit by bit and requires $2 \log n$ bits of cipher-text per bit of plain-text. The scheme is quite fast but its main disadvantage is the ciphertext expansion. Boneh and Franklin's solution is based on bilinear maps. Moreover, Boneh and Franklin also proposed a formal security model for IBE, and proved that their scheme is secure under the Bilinear Diffie-Hellman (BDH) assumption.

The Cocks scheme [4] is very elegant and per se revolutionary. It is based on the standard QRA modulo an RSA composite. The scheme encrypts one bit at a time. The bits are considered to be exactly the two values (i.e., -1 and 1) of the Jacobi symbol modulo an RSA modulus n, when applied to an integer non-divisible by n. Thus, if Alice wants to send a bit $b \in \{-1, 1\}$ to Bob, she randomly generates an integer t with the Jacobi symbol b modulo n, hides t into a new message $s = t + at^{-1} \bmod n$ obtained by means of Bob's identity a, and sends s to Bob. The decryption depends on whether a is a quadratic residue or not modulo n. As neither Alice nor Bob knows whether a is a quadratic residue or not, Alice repeats the procedure above with another integer t' whose Jacobi symbol modulo n is b, and sends $s' = t' - at'^{-1} \bmod n$ as well. Now, Bob

Work partially supported by the Romanian National Authority for Scientific Research (CNCS-UEFISCDI) under the project PN-II-PT-PCCA-2013-4-1651.

can easily decrypt by using a private key obtained from the key generator, because either a or $-a$ is a quadratic residue modulo n. It can be shown that the Cocks IBE scheme is IND-ID-CPA secure in the random oracle model under the QRA.

The main disadvantage regarding the efficiency of the Cocks scheme consists of the fact that it encrypts one bit by $2 \log n$ bits. A very interesting idea proposed by Boneh, Gentry and Hamburg [2] is to encrypts a stream of bits by multiplying each of them by an Jacobi symbol randomly generated. The generation of these new Jacobi symbols are based on the equation $ax^2 + Sy^2 \equiv 1 \bmod n$. Any solution to this congruential equation leads to two polynomials f and g with the property that $g(s)$ and $f(r)$ have the same Jacobi symbol modulo n, for any square root s of S and any square root r of a. Therefore, g can be used to encrypt one bit, while f can be used to decrypt it. If the solutions of the above congruential equation can be obtained by a deterministic algorithm, then the decryptor knows how to decryt the ciphertext. Therefore, in order to send an ℓ-bit message to Bob, Alice has to solve 2ℓ equations as above (two equations for each bit, one for Bob's identity a and the other one for $-a$), while the decryptor needs to solve only ℓ equations. The ciphertext size is $2\ell + \log n$ bits. Some improvements at the sender side reduces the number of equations to be solved by the encryptor to $\ell + 1$.

An important improvement of the Boneh-Gentry-Hamburg (BGH) scheme was proposed later by Jhanwar and Barua [7]. The improvement works in two directions: improve the time complexity of the algorithm to solve equations $ax^2 + Sy^2 \equiv 1 \bmod n$, and reduce the number of equations to be solved. The first improvement is based on a careful analysis of the solutions of the equation $ax^2 + Sy^2 \equiv 1 \bmod n$. Thus, an efficient probabilist algorithm is developed to randomly generate solutions of such an equation. The second improvement is based on a composition formula according to which two solutions can be combined in some way to obtain a new solution. Therefore, to encrypt an ℓ-bit message, only $2\sqrt{\ell}$ equations need to be solved. Unfortunately, the probabilistic nature of the algorithm by which solutions are obtained leads to a ciphertext larger than in the case of the BGH scheme, namely $2\ell + 2\sqrt{\ell} \log n$ bits. The Jhanwar-Barua (JB) scheme was revisited in [6], where some errors were corrected; unfortunately, the security was not sufficiently argued as it was later remarked in [5]. Moreover, [5] also proposes an improvement by which the number of equations needed to be solved by Alice is reduced to $2 \log \ell$. The ciphertext size is also reduced to $2\ell + 2(\log \ell)(\log n)$ bits.

It is well-known that the Cocks scheme is not anonymous [2]. Several researchers tried to extend this scheme to offer identity anonymity; usually, such extensions are based on creating lists of ciphertext so that the identity becomes hidden in the lists. This approach gives rise to very large ciphertexts. It was also a believe that the Cocks scheme does not have homomorphic properties. A very recent result [8] rehabilitates the Cocks scheme with respect to these two weaknesses. Joye [8] identified the algebraic structure of the Cocks ciphertexts: he proved that these are squares in a torus like structure, and form a quasi-group. The underlying group law is the operation needed on ciphertexts to show that the Cocks scheme is homomorphic when the operation on clear messages is the multiplication. Therefore, the Cocks scheme offer homomorphic properties. Another important consequence obtained in [8] is about the anonymity of the Cocks scheme. It was shown that a different way of computing the ciphertext, without expansion, leads to identity anonymity.

A very interesting question is whether high order Jacobi symbols can be used in the Cocks scheme in order to encrypt more than one bit at a time. A first attempt to do that is the one in [3]. Unfortunately, the only secure scheme proposed in [3] suffers from massive ciphertext expansion.

References

1. Boneh, D., Franklin, M.K.: Identity-based encryption from the Weil pairing. In: Proceedings of the 21st Annual International Cryptology Conference on Advances in Cryptology, pp. 213–229. CRYPTO 2001. Springer-Verlag, London, August 2001
2. Boneh, D., Gentry, C., Hamburg, M.: Space-efficient identity based encryption without pairings. In: Proceedings of the 48th Annual IEEE Symposium on Foundations of Computer Science, pp. 647–657. FOCS 2007. IEEE Computer Society, Washington, DC, USA (2007)
3. Boneh, D., LaVigne, R., Sabin, M.: Identity-based encryption with e^{th} residuosity and its incompressibility. In: Autumn 2013 TRUST Conference. Washington, DC, October 2013. Poster Presentation
4. Cocks, C.: An identity based encryption scheme based on quadratic residues. In: Proceedings of the 8th IMA International Conference on Cryptography and Coding, pp. 360–363. Springer-Verlag, London, December 2001
5. Țiplea, F.L., Simion, E., Teșeleanu, G.: An improvement of Jhanwar-Barua's identity-based encryption scheme. Technical report (2015)
6. Elashry, I., Mu, Y., Susilo, W.: Jhanwar-Barua's identity-based encryption revisited. In: Au, M., Carminati, B., Kuo, C.C. (eds.) Network and System Security. LNCS, vol. 8792, pp. 271–284. Springer International Publishing (2014)
7. Jhanwar, M.P., Barua, R.: A variant of Boneh-Gentry-Hamburg's pairing-free identity-based encryption scheme. In: Inscrypt, pp. 314–331 (2008)
8. Joye, M.: On identity-based cryptosystems from quadratic residuosity (2015)
9. Sakai, R., Ohgishi, K., Kasahara, M.: Cryptosystems based on pairing. In: Symposium on Cryptography and Information Security. SCIS2000, January 2000
10. Shamir, A.: Identity-based cryptosystems and signature schemes. In: Proceedings of CRYPTO 84 on Advances in cryptology, pp. 47–53. Springer-Verlag New York, New York (1985)

Efficient Techniques for Extracting Secrets from Electronic Devices

Marios Choudary

University Politehnica of Bucharest
marios.choudary@cs.pub.ro

Summary

Smartcards, such as those provided to their customers by many banks across the world, use a microcontroller to encrypt or decrypt data, in order to authenticate a person (e.g. verify a PIN) or a transaction (e.g. generate an electronic transaction certificate), based on a secret key stored in the microcontroller. However, the physical implementation of a microcontroller *leaks* information via a *side-channel*, such as the power-supply current or electromagnetic emanations. This leakage may allow an attacker to recover the secret key of a microcontroller, and use that to generate valid certificates for unlawful commercial transactions. To reduce this threat, microcontrollers used in the smartcards provided by banks have several layers of countermeasures to limit the amount of side-channel information available to an attacker. But, to develop efficient countermeasures, and to have a correct assessment of the level of security provided by such smartcards, it is important to have a good understanding of the potential of side-channel attacks.

Along the search for better cryptosystems during the two World Wars, to encrypt messages over a particular communication channel, the military discovered the possibility of "listening" to the main communication channel by means of another, unintentional, channel, known as the *side-channel*. As Kuhn [11, Section 1.1.1] and Markettos [12, Section 2.11.1] describe in more detail, there were many such cases during the past century. Among the first known cases, during the First World War, the Germans were able to retrieve the communications of enemy troops, by analysing the earth return-current of the single-wire telegraph system used by those troops [1]. Another important case, this time involving a cryptosystem, was the side-channel analysis performed by British intelligence on the French embassy in London, around 1960–1963 [14]. MI5 and GCHQ scientists used a broad-band radio-frequency tap on the communication line used by the French embassy to transmit information, encrypted using a *low-grade* cipher, in the hope of obtaining partial information of the plaintext, that may *leak* into the channel. It turned out that they were indeed able to retrieve the plaintext of the communication encrypted using the low-grade cipher. Furthermore, they were also able to retrieve a secondary signal, corresponding to the plaintext of a *high-grade* encrypted communication, which leaked somehow (e.g. via electromagnetic cross-talk) into the low-grade channel.

While the previous attacks showed that it was possible to use side-channel leakage, such as the signal recovered by the British intelligence, to recover the plaintext message, the publication of side-channel attacks against the cryptosystem itself, e.g. to recover the secret key, came much later. Probably the first such publication was the paper by Paul Kocher in 1996 [10], describing the use of timing information to determine the private-key used by the RSA cryptosystem. Kocher's *timing attack* exploited the fact that the time needed to perform the modular multiplication and exponentiation operations, used by the RSA cryptosystem, depended on the value of the private key bits.

Two years later, in 1998, Kocher, Jaffe and Jun published another side-channel attack, known as *Differential Power Analysis* (DPA) [9], which exploited the monitored power consumption of a microcontroller executing DES encryptions, to determine the secret key used with DES. This publication marked a very important point in history, since a cryptosystem such as DES, which was considered secure against all known cryptanalytic attacks, and was even designed to resist the *differential cryptanalysis* attacks discovered by Biham and Shamir [2] after its publication, could be easily broken (i.e. we could recover the secret key), when implemented on a physical device accessible to an attacker. This had important consequences for the pay-TV industry, and later for the banking industry as well, who provided their customers with a microcontroller (in the form of a smartcard), in order to authenticate them, by using their smartcard to perform some encryption using a cryptosystem such as DES. After the publication of DPA, this technique has also been used with the electromagnetic emissions of microcontrollers [8], [13], and was also immediately analysed for the case of AES [3].

In 2002, Suresh Chari, Rao Josyula and Pankaj Rohatgi presented a very powerful method, known as the *Template Attack* [4], to infer secret values processed by a microcontroller, by analysing its power-supply current, generally known as its *side-channel leakage*. This attack uses a profiling step to compute the parameters of a multivariate normal distribution from the leakage of a training device, and an attack step in which these parameters are used to infer a secret value (e.g. cryptographic key) from the leakage of a target device. This has important implications for many industries, such as pay-TV or banking, that use a microcontroller executing a cryptographic algorithm to authenticate their customers.

In this presentation I shall provide an introduction in this interesting field of side-channel attacks, including the Differential Power Analysis and Template attacks. Then, I shall briefly discuss some of my research on obtaining efficient implementations of the Template attack that can push its limits further, by using multivariate statistical analysis techniques to: *a*) determine almost perfectly an 8-bit target value, even when this value is manipulated by a single LOAD instruction [6]; *b*) cope with variability caused by the use of either different devices or different acquisition campaigns [7]; *c*) speed-up the profiling phase of template attacks, resulting in the most efficient kind of template attacks [5].

References

1. Bauer, A.O.: Some aspects of military line communications as deployed by the german armed forces prior to 1945. In: The History of Military Communications, Proceedings of 5th Annual Colloquium (1999)
2. Biham, E., Shamir, A.: Differential cryptanalysis of DES-like cryptosystems. J. Cryptol. **4**(1), 3–72 (1991)
3. Chari, S., Charanjit, J., Rao, J., Rohatgi, P.: A cautionary note regarding evaluation of AES candidates on smart-cards. In: NIST AES Round 1 (1999)
4. Chari, S., Rao, J., Rohatgi, P.: Template attacks. In: Cryptographic Hardware and Embedded Systems. CHES 2002. LNCS, vol. 2523, pp. 51–62. Springer, Berlin (2003)
5. Choudary, M.O., Kuhn, M.G.: Efficient stochastic methods: profiled attacks beyond 8 bits. In: CARDIS 2014. LNCS, vol. 8968. Springer, Berlin (2014)
6. Choudary, O., Kuhn, M.G.: Efficient template attacks. In: Smart Card Research and Advanced Applications. CARDIS 2013, pp. 253–270. LNCS, vol. 8419. Springer, Berlin (2013). http://eprint.iacr.org/2013/770/
7. Choudary, O., Kuhn, M.G.: Template attacks on different devices. In: Workshop on Constructive Side Channel Analysis and Secure Design. CODADE 2014, pp. 179–198. LNCS, vol. 8622. Springer, Heidelberg (2014). http://eprint.iacr.org/2014/459/
8. Gandolfi, K., Mourtel, C., Olivier, F.: Electromagnetic analysis: concrete results. In: Cryptographic Hardware and Embedded Systems. CHES 2001, pp. 251–261. LNCS, vol. 2162. Springer, Berlin (2001)
9. Kocher, P., Jaffe, J., Jun, B.: Differential power analysis. In: Advances in Cryptology. CRYPTO 1999. LNCS, vol. 1666, pp. 789–789. Springer, Berlin (1999). First published in 1998. http://www.cryptography.com/public/pdf/DPA.pdf
10. Kocher, P.C.: Timing attacks on implementations of Diffie-Hellman, RSA, DSS, and other systems. In: Advances in Cryptology. CRYPTO 1996, pp. 104–113. LNCS, vol. 1109. Springer, Berlin (1996)
11. Kuhn, M.G.: Compromising emanations: eavesdropping risks of computer displays. Technical Report UCAM-CL-TR-577. University of Cambridge, Computer Laboratory, December 2003. http://www.cl.cam.ac.uk/techreports/UCAM-CL-TR-577.pdf
12. Markettos, A.T.: Active electromagnetic attacks on secure hardware. Technical Report UCAM-CL-TR-811. University of Cambridge, Computer Laboratory, December 2011. http://www.cl.cam.ac.uk/techreports/UCAM-CL-TR-811.pdf
13. Quisquater, J.J., Samyde, D.: ElectroMagnetic Analysis (EMA): measures and counter-measures for smart cards. In: Smart Card Programming and Security, pp. 200–210. LNCS, vol. 2140. Springer, Berlin (2001)
14. Wright, P., Greengrass, P.: Spycatcher: The candid autobiography of a senior intelligence officer. Dell (1988)

Secure and Trusted Application Execution on Embedded Devices

Konstantinos Markantonakis, Raja Naeem Akram,
and Mehari G. Msgna

Information Security Group, Smart Card Centre, Royal Holloway,
University of London, UK
{k.markantonakis, r.n.akram,
mehari.msgna.2011}@rhul.ac.uk

Abstract. Embedded devices have permeated into our daily lives and significant day-to-day mundane tasks involve a number of embedded systems. These include smart cards, sensors in vehicles and industrial automation systems. Satisfying the requirements for trusted, reliable and secure embedded devices is more vital than ever before. This urgency is also strengthened further by the potential advent of the Internet of Things and Cyber-Physical Systems. As our reliance on these devices is increasing, the significance of potential threats should not be underestimated, especially as a number of embedded devices are built to operate in malicious environments, where they might be in the possession of an attacker. The challenge to build secure and trusted embedded devices is paramount. In this paper, we examine the security threats to embedded devices along with the associated prevention mechanisms. We also present a holistic approach to the security and trust of embedded devices, from the hardware design, reliability and trust of the runtime environment to the integrity and trustworthiness of the executing applications. The proposed protection mechanisms provide a high degree of security at a minimal computational cost. Such an agnostic view on the security and trust of the embedded devices can be pivotal in their adoption and trust acquisition from the general public and service providers.

A Number-Theoretic Error-Correcting Code

Eric Brier[1], Jean-Sébastien Coron[2], Rémi Géraud[1,3],
Diana Maimuţ[3], and David Naccache[2,3]

[1] Ingenico
28-32 boulevard de Grenelle, 75015, Paris, France
{eric.brier, remi.geraud}@ingenico.com
[2] Université du Luxembourg
6 rue Richard Coudenhove-Kalergi, 1359 Luxembourg, Luxembourg
{jean-sebastien.coron, david.naccache}@uni.lu
[3] École normale supérieure
Département d'Informatique
45 rue d'Ulm, 75230, Paris Cedex 05, France
{remi.geraud, diana.Maimut, david.naccache}@ens.fr

Abstract. In this paper we describe a new error-correcting code (ECC) inspired by the Naccache-Stern cryptosystem. While by far less efficient than Turbo codes, the proposed ECC happens to be more efficient than some established ECCs for certain sets of parameters.

The new ECC adds an appendix to the message. The appendix is the modular product of small primes representing the message bits. The receiver recomputes the product and detects transmission errors using modular division and lattice reduction.

Contents

Security Technologies for ITC

Invited Talks

Secure and Trusted Application Execution on Embedded Devices

Konstantinos Markantonakis, Raja Naeem Akram[✉], and Mehari G. Msgna

Information Security Group, Smart Card Centre, Royal Holloway,
University of London, Egham, UK
{k.markantonakis,r.n.akram,mehari.msgna.2011}@rhul.ac.uk

Abstract. Embedded devices have permeated into our daily lives and significant day-to-day mundane tasks involve a number of embedded systems. These include smart cards, sensors in vehicles and industrial automation systems. Satisfying the requirements for trusted, reliable and secure embedded devices is more vital than ever before. This urgency is also strengthened further by the potential advent of the Internet of Things and Cyber-Physical Systems. As our reliance on these devices is increasing, the significance of potential threats should not be underestimated, especially as a number of embedded devices are built to operate in malicious environments, where they might be in the possession of an attacker. The challenge to build secure and trusted embedded devices is paramount. In this paper, we examine the security threats to embedded devices along with the associated prevention mechanisms. We also present a holistic approach to the security and trust of embedded devices, from the hardware design, reliability and trust of the runtime environment to the integrity and trustworthiness of the executing applications. The proposed protection mechanisms provide a high degree of security at a minimal computational cost. Such an agnostic view on the security and trust of the embedded devices can be pivotal in their adoption and trust acquisition from the general public and service providers.

Keywords: Smart cards · Fault attacks · Runtime attacks · Hardware security · Runtime security · Trusted platform · Trusted execution · Trojans · Counterfeit products

1 Introduction

Embedded devices provide a computing environment that is miniaturised to fit in as part of a much larger systems. For example, a smart phone, modern car and aircraft might have number of embedded devices interconnected with each other to perform associated tasks. The deployment of embedded devices is steadily increasing and the advent of the Internet of Things (IoTs) and Cyber Physical Systems (CPS) will make them closely integrated into almost every aspect of our lives.

© Springer International Publishing Switzerland 2015
I. Bica et al. (Eds.): SECITC 2015, LNCS 9522, pp. 3–24, 2015.
DOI: 10.1007/978-3-319-27179-8_1

These embedded devices must provide highly reliable and deterministic services – some of which might even be crucial to the health and safety of an individual or a community. Examples of such deployments can be the embedded devices used in the health sector, vehicles and industrial systems. Therefore, such devices have to not only provide efficient and reliable services in difficult operational environments but also provide a degree of security and trustworthiness. The level of security and trustworthiness is obviously dictated by the nature of the overall system that the embedded devices are going to integrate with.

Having computational and in certain cases operational restrictions, embedded devices not only have to protect against software based attacks, but also hardware modifications and a combination of the both. Furthermore, such devices are mostly deployed in operational environments where they are easily accessible to the malicious users. Therefore, being small, less powerful and adhering to very stringent performance and economical costs — they are still required to be reliable, secure and trusted. These are the major challenges that embedded devices have to meet.

In addition to the security and reliability of such devices, another important aspect is the genuineness of the device. The genuineness problem has two aspects, which are raised due to the increased demand in outsourcing of the chip/device fabrication to (external/foreign) foundries. These foundries can inject hardware Trojans to the original design of the device. In addition, the foundry can also create counterfeit devices. Therefore, any organisations receiving these devices need to have a high assurance and capability to validate that these devices are legitimate and not tampered with. We term this is a problem of genuineness of the embedded devices.

In this paper, we will investigate the state-of-the-art of the threat and security in the embedded computing field along with examining proposals that cover the embedded device's security, trust and genuineness.

2   Embedded Computing's Security Challenges

In this section, we try to briefly answer two questions, firstly why security and reliability is essential for the embedded devices, and secondly what security threats are posed to embedded devices.

2.1   Rationale for Security Considerations

In the last few decades, embedded devices have proliferated into almost every computing and industrial system. A most common example of the embedded device with which most of the public might be familiar with is "smart cards". These devices are issues to individual users by organisations, so the individuals can access the organisation's services in a secure and reliable manner. Environments these smart cards are deployed in include mobile telecommunication, banking and access control, to name a few. We appreciate further that failure to the respective organisations services might result in potential monetary, reputation and even physical harm in certain cases.

Another example to understand the necessity of the security and reliability of embedded devices can be in automotive industry. Security of the Electronic Control Unit (ECU) plays a crucial role to ensure the safety and reliability of the car. These ECUs are embedded devices used to control different (crucial) operations in a car. In modern cars, there can be 70 ECUs [33] and if any of them can be compromised, the safety of the car and passengers may be at risk.

Embedded devices are tiny electronic chips that perform multitude of tasks in high-tech systems. These devices are present in electronic equipment ranging from microwave oven to high-speed railway systems, nuclear plants, and aeroplanes etc. A failure of a single device has the potential to damage the overall system. Such failures can lead to disastrous consequences, as revealed by the U.S. Senate Committee on Armed Services that identified suspected components in the CH-46 Sea Knight helicopter, C-17 military transport aircraft, P-8A Poseidon sub hunter and F-16 fighter jet [10]. Multi-million dollar defence equipment reliability might be compromised by a $2 insecure and counterfeit embedded device. As estimated by the Semiconductor Industry Association (SIA) in 2013, the cost of counterfeit embedded devices is at US $7.5 billion per year [11]. The problem is by no means localised only affecting certain areas but a global issue. There are number of high profile cases [10] that came to light that identified sub-standard embedded devices in military equipment because of stringent safety testing. In commercial environments, the problem is perceived to be higher in magnitude than the military.

From the discussion in this section we can conclude that not only the security and reliability of these embedded devices is crucial but also the genuineness. In subsequent sections we will discuss different threats posed to the embedded systems.

2.2   Threat Model for Embedded Devices

In this section, we discuss the threat model in relation to the embedded devices. Embedded devices can be in the hands of an adversary; therefore, he or she has the potential to attack the devices in every conceivable way ranging from hardware intrusions to introducing malicious applications/code. From an adversary's point of view, he or she might target:

1. Hardware platform.
2. Permanent data (saved in the devices, which can include cryptographic keys).
3. Runtime data.
4. Control flow of the program (i.e. to interfere with the execution of an application).

The above list of potential targets is just a subset of attributes that an adversary might try to focus on during his or her attack. It is by no means an exhaustive list and should be taken as an example of potential targets.

2.3   Hardware Attacks

In these types of attacks, an adversary tries to alter the silicon design of an embedded device. This attack requires a high level of knowledge of the hardware design and specialised equipment that could be used to change the circuit on the silicon. However, these attacks are very powerful as it would be extremely challenging for any software based protection mechanism to provide protection against them.

Furthermore, another facet of the hardware attacks includes the malicious changes to chip design during the manufacturing stage. In this case, when the manufacturing of the devices is outsourced, the foundry can potentially introduce malicious designs that act as hardware Trojans.

As countermeasures to these attacks, the chip designer can include:

1. Smaller circuitry: Reducing the size makes physical attacks more difficult.
2. Hiding the bus: Glue logic and placing bus lines on lower layers of the circuitry of the chip.
3. Scramble bus lines: Communication buses can be scrambled in static, chip-specific or session-specific manner. The scrambling of the communication buses is carried out in order to make the function of individual silicon connections in a communication bus not apparent to the adversary (hidden).
4. Tamper-resistance: Placing sensors to detect physical perturbation and kill the device as a result.

2.4   Attacks on Persistent Storage

Data stored in persistent memory can include sensitive information, including passwords, Personal Identification Number (PIN), and cryptographic keys. In addition to data, proprietary application code and/or algorithm might also be stored on the persistent memory. Therefore, the persistent memory is like a treasure trove for an adversary. There are several potential ways an adversary can read the persistent storage that might include:

- Reading the memory via directly tapping into the storage locations and/or communication buses.
- Exploiting a potential bug/vulnerability in the sandboxing mechanism of the runtime environment, which might lead to a malicious application reading the entire persistent memory.
- Using side channel leakages to infer the data.

As a security designer, to protect against potential attacks on the persistent storage, set of comprehensive security countermeasures are required that might include:

1. Encrypted storage/communication buses: To avoid data being read from storage or during transit, the data should be encrypted while in storage and over the communication bus using a hardware based key.
2. Memory read: Allowing only selected instruction in a given condition to access such data and then check their conditions.
3. Side channel protection: Implementing side channel protection techniques that hide the presence of data from the side channel footprint.

2.5 Attacks on Runtime Data

During the execution of an application, several data structures are generated that facilitate the execution. These might include intermediate computation results, function call parameters, return addresses and un/conditional statement parameters. These data structures might contain valuable information for an adversary to compromise the application. Modification to the runtime data can change the behavior of the application execution.

Modification to the runtime data is usually carried out by injecting a fault during the execution of the application. The aim of an adversary during a fault attack is to disrupt the correct execution of an application by introducing errors. These errors are usually introduced by physical perturbation of the hardware platform on which the application is executing. By introducing errors at a precise instruction, an adversary can circumvent the security measures implemented by the runtime environment. Possible types of faults an adversary can produce are described as below:

1. Precise bit error: In this scenario, an adversary has total control over the timing and locations of bits that needs to be changed.
2. Precise byte error: This scenario is similar to the previous one; however, an adversary only has the ability to change the value of a byte rather than a bit.
3. Unknown byte error: An adversary has no control on the timing and byte that it modifies during the execution of an instruction.
4. Unknown error: In this scenario, an adversary generates a fault but has no location and timing control.

From the above list of fault models, the first model adversary can be considered the most powerful. However, for a smart card environment the second scenario (i.e. precise byte error) is the most realistic one. Due to the advances in the smart card hardware and counter-measures against fault attacks (i.e. especially for cryptographic algorithms) it is difficult to have total control of timing and locations of bits to flip [46]. Furthermore, fault attacks require knowledge of the underlying platform and application execution pattern [28]. This is possible to achieve by side-channel analysis [36]. In most processors runtime data is processed as stack items; therefore their protection also works around the stack.

Countermeasures to the attacks on the runtime data include but are not limited to:

1. Stack canaries is a method where the processor inserts canary values into the stack and then check them during operation. If they are changed then there is an attack otherwise execution continues [27].
2. Separation of data and return address stack in this work the authors propose a segregation of the stack memory used for return addresses and other stack items. Then enforce instruction based access to the return addresses [31].
3. Verifying the integrity of an instruction before executing it. A trade-off between the security and the computational cost that the countermeasure adds.

4. Code signing: Verify it before loading it to the processor. However, this doesnt protect the program against runtime attacks. One of the solutions proposed to protect the instructions at runtime is to add an integrated module into the design that hashes the executed instructions and verifies their signature on the fly.

2.6 Notion of Trust and Trustworthiness

The definition of trust, taken from Merriam Webster's online dictionary[1] states that trust is a "belief that someone or something is reliable, good, honest, effective, etc."

Based on this, we generically define digital trust as "a trust based either on past experience or evidence that an entity has behaved and/or will behave in accordance with the self-stated behaviour." The self-stated purpose of intent is provided by the entity and this may have been verified/attested by a third party. The claim that the entity satisfies the self-stated behaviour can either be gained through past interactions (experience) or based on some (hard) evidence like validatable/verifiable properties certified by a reputable third party (i.e. Common Criteria evaluation for secure hardware [2]). This definition is not claimed to be a comprehensive definition for digital trust that encompasses all of its facets. However, this generic definition will be used as a point of discussion for the rest of the paper.

In the real world, trust in an entity is based on a feature, property or association that is entailed in it. In the computing world, establishing trust in a distributed environment also follows the same assumptions. The concept of trusted platforms is based on the existence of a trusted and reliable device that provides evidence of the state of a given system. How this evidence is interpreted is dependent on the requesting entity. Trust in this context can be defined as an expectation that the state of a system is as it is considered to be: secure. This definition requires a trusted and reliable entity called a Trusted Platform Module (TPM) to provide trustworthy evidence regarding the state of a system. Therefore, a TPM is a reporting agent (witness) not an evaluator or enforcer of the security policies. It provides a root of trust on which an inquisitor relies for the validation of the current state of a system.

The TPM specifications are maintained and developed by an international standards group called the Trusted Computing Group (TCG)[2] Today, TCG not only publishes the TPM specifications but also the Mobile Trusted Module (MTM), Trusted Multi-tenant Infrastructure, and Trusted Network Connect (TNC). With emerging technologies, service architectures, and computing platforms, TCG is adapting to the challenges presented by them.

---

[1] Website: http://www.merriam-webster.com/dictionary/trust.

[2] Trusted Computing Group (TCG) is the culmination of industrial efforts that included the Trusted Computing Platform Association (TCPA), Microsoft's Palladium, later called Next Generation Computing Base (NGSCB), and Intel's LaGrande. All of them proposed how to ascertain trust in a device's state in a distributed environment. These efforts were combined in the TCG specification that resulted in the proposal of TPM.

2.7   Trust in Execution Environment

In this section we briefly introduce some of the proposals for a secure and trusted application execution and data storage.

ARM TrustZone. Similar to the MTM, the ARM TrustZone also provides the architecture for a trusted platform specifically for mobile devices. The underlying concept is the provision of two virtual processors with hardware-level segregation and access control [7,48]. This enables the ARM TrustZone to define two execution environments described as Secure world and Normal world. The Secure world executes the security- and privacy-sensitive components of applications and normal execution takes place in the Normal world. The ARM processor manages the switch between the two worlds. The ARM TrustZone is implemented as a security extension to the ARM processors (e.g. ARM1176JZ(F)-S, Cortes-A8, and Cortex-A9 MPCore) [7], which a developer can opt to utilise if required (Fig. 1).

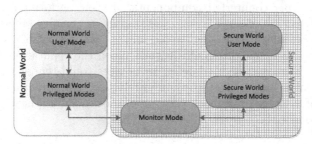

Fig. 1. Generic architectural view of ARM TrustZone

GlobalPlatform Trusted Execution Environment (TEE). The TEE is GlobalPlatform's initiative [4,6,9] for mobile phones, set-top boxes, utility meters, and payphones. GlobalPlatform defines a specification for interoperable secure hardware, which is based on GlobalPlatform's experience in the smart card industry. It does not define any particular hardware, which can be based on either a typical secure element or any of the previously discussed tamper-resistant devices. The rationale for discussing the TEE as one of the candidate devices is to provide a complete picture. The underlying ownership of the TEE device still predominantly resides with the issuing authority, which is similar to GlobalPlatform's specification for the smart card industry [3].

3   Trust in the Underlying Hardware

In the early days of computing systems security was almost virtually associated with the software. However, the commercial and economic conditions of late have forced hardware manufacturers to outsource their production process to countries with cheaper infrastructure cost. While this significantly reduces the integrated circuit production cost, it also makes it much easier for an attacker to compromise their supply chain and replace them with unoriginal or malicious ones. Such items could be counterfeits or hardware Trojans. This threat to the IC supply chain is already a cause for alarm in some countries [12,39]. For this reason, some governments have been subsidising few high-host local foundries for producing ICs used in military applications [30]. However, this is not affordable solution for most of the developing countries.

Counterfeits. Counterfeiting at a global stage covers almost everything that is made or manufactured, from spare parts to clothing to prescription drugs. In contrast to other counterfeit items, the ramifications of a counterfeit IC device failure in an electronic system are more than just inconvenience or a minor loss of money. According to [26], the number of counterfeit incidents has increased from 3,868 in 2005 to 9,356 in 2008. These incidents can have the following ramifications; (a) original IC providers incur an irrecoverable loss due to the sale of often cheaper counterfeit components, (b) low performance of counterfeit products (that are often of lower quality and/or cheaper older generations of a chip family) affects the overall efficiency of the integrated systems that unintentionally use them; this could in turn harm the reputation of authentic providers, and (c) unreliability of defective devices could render the integrated systems that unknowingly use the parts unreliable; this potentially affects the performance of weapons, airplanes, cars or other crucial applications that use the fake components [37].

Hardware Trojans. Hardware Trojans are malicious circuitry implanted in an IC. The malicious circuit can be inserted for different reasons, such as stealing sensitive information, IP reverse engineering or spying on the user. One way of implanting a Trojan into an IC is by compromising the supply chain of ICs and adding the Trojan mask into the original design. Trojan circuits are designed to be very difficult, nearly impossible, to detect by purely functional testing. They are designed to monitor for specific but rare trigger conditions; for instance specific bit patterns on received data or the bus. Once triggered the actions of the Trojan could be leaking secrets, creating glitches to compromise the security of larger electronic equipments or simply disabling the circuit. For example, a simple yet deadly Trojan in RSA [45] could be to inject a fault into the CRT inversion step during RSA signature computation that could lead to the compromise of the RSA keys [24].

3.1   Countermeasure

Counterfeit ICs and hardware Trojans could be designed to be hard to detect by purely functional testing. However, in the real world ICs leak information about their internal state unintentionally. This leakage comes as a power consumption or electromagnetic emissions caused by a varying electric current flowing through the IC's circuitry. This leakage can be recorded and analysed to adequately detect counterfeits and hardware Trojans. For instance in [47], a gate-level passive hardware characterisation of an IC was proposed to identify defective ICs. However, the gate-level characteristics are dependent on ageing, temperature and supply voltage instability. The authors use the negative bias temperature instability model proposed in [25] to calculate the original characteristics of aged ICs. In another proposal [13], power consumption of a device was proposed for detecting hardware Trojans implanted in ICs. In this paper process variation noise modelling (constructed using genuine ICs) is used for detecting ICs with Trojan circuits through statistical analysis. In this section we discuss how same leakage can be used to verify the integrity of control flow jumps and instructions integrity before the IC is integrated into a security critical environments.

We implemented these techniques on the ATMega164 processor. This processor has 130 instructions used for transferring data, performing arithmetic and logic operations. To simplify the experiment we removed redundant instructions. The processor is powered up by a +5V power supply and running at a 4 MHz clock speed. Leroy WaveRunner 6100A [38] is used to measure the power traces.

Control Flow Verification. An application is a combination of basic blocks. A basic block is a linear sequence of executable instructions with only one entry point and one exit point [22]. After executing one basic block the processor jumps into another basic block based on the branching instruction executed at the end of the current basic block. In this paper we refer to basic blocks as states.

To reconstruct the state sequence that a device followed during the execution of a program from its side channel leakage we modelled the device as a *Hidden Markov Model* (*HMM*) [29,43]. A *Markov Model* is a memoryless system with a finite number of hidden states. It is called memoryless because the next state depends only on the current state. In such a model the states are not directly observable. However, there has to be (at least) one observable output of the process that reveals partial information about the state sequence that the device has followed. Figure 2, illustrates a *Markov Process* with five hidden states (i.e. A to E).

To build the HMM of our test program we collected 1000 traces for each state and computed all the necessary parameters. We have also pre-computed the possible valid control flow jumps of the program. At runtime we collected the power consumption of the program without any prior information which path the device followed to execute the program. From the trace we recovered the control flow jumps using the HMM and Viterbi algorithm [34]. We repeated this experiment multiple times and successfully verified the control flow jumps. Details of the technique and experiment results are presented in [41].

Verifying Integrity of Executed Instructions. The first step in our verification is the construction of instruction-level side channel templates using few identical processors. During verification, the verifying device records the processor's power consumption waveform while executing the application and extracts

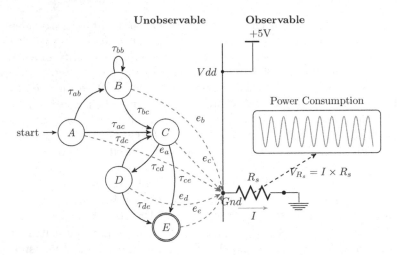

Fig. 2. A Markov model representing a device executing a program with five states (A, B, C, D and E). The power consumption is the observable output that reveals partial information about the state sequence of the device.

the executed instructions by matching it against the pre-constructed templates. The extracted information together with the pre-computed signatures are then used to verify the integrity of the software component using *RSA signature screening* algorithm [23].

As shown in the diagram (Fig. 3), the embedded system has the embedded parameter calculator (EP-C), embedded processor and the application package which includes the application executable and the basic block signatures. The EP-C is a special module that calculates the product of two large numbers. It can be implemented in hardware or software; although, hardware would be preferable for performance reasons. The embedded processor is the core that executes the software component of the embedded system (application executable). After the execution of every basic block the EP-C updates its parameter (EP) by multiplying it with the basic block's signature.

The verifying device has the templates, the instruction classifier, the verifier parameter calculator (VP-C) and the software integrity verifier. The templates are constructed ahead of time using identical processors and then installed into the verifying device's non-volatile memory. How these templates are installed into the verifying device is beyond the scope of this paper. The instruction classifier uses these templates to extract the executed instructions from the processor's power consumption waveform (W). The power consumption waveform is measured as a voltage drop across a shunt resistor connecting the embedded processor's ground and the verifying device's ground voltage. The VP-C uses the output of the classifier to compute the verifying device's parameter. Finally, the software integrity verifier uses the output of the EP-C and VP-C to verify the software using *RSA signature screening* algorithm. Details of the template construction, instruction classification and software integrity verification processes are discussed [42].

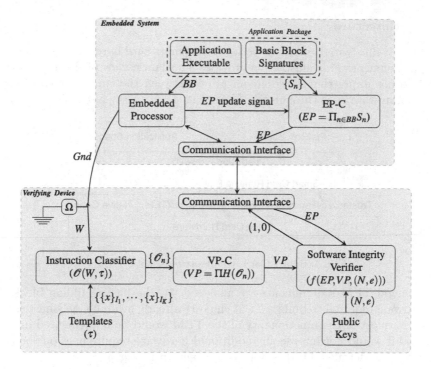

Fig. 3. Software integrity verification block diagram

The templates of selected instructions are created from 2500 traces collected by executing the instructions using different conditions; such as data processed, memory locations and registers. Finally, using these templates we successfully verified the integrity of executed instructions of a sample PIN verification program. Full detail of the verification techniques and experimental results are presented in [42].

4   Trusted Platform and Execution for Embedded Devices

The Trusted Computing Group is currently looking into the concept of trusted platform for embedded devices. Although, there is no specification made public at the time of writing this paper. However, we have proposed a similar trusted platform for smart cards and we will be discussing it in subsequent sections.

4.1   Trusted Environment and Execution Manager (TEM)

This section discusses the architecture of a Trusted Environment & Execution Manager (TEM) specifically for smart cards, and highlights how the TEM differs from a typical TPM not only in architectural but also in operational context.

4.2   Architecture

The TEM is illustrated as a layer between the smart card hardware and the run-time environment. This illustration provides a semantic view of the architecture and does not imply that all communication between the runtime environment and the hardware goes through the TEM (Fig. 4).

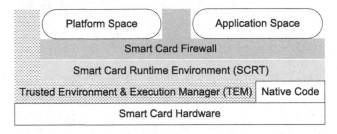

Fig. 4. Smart Card Architecture in with TEM

If general TPM requirements are analysed [5], the basic building blocks in the hardware required to build a TPM chip are already available on smart cards. Therefore, most of the functionality of the TEM would be implemented in soft-ware and it would not impose any additional hardware requirement on the host platform. The detailed TEM architecture is shown in Fig. 5.

Figure 5 depicts native code and smart card hardware as complementary com-ponents of the TEM. This is because the TEM does not need separate hardware for its operations. It will utilise the existing services provided by the smart card hardware. To avoid duplicating the code, the TEM uses the native code imple-mentation of cryptographic services like encryption/decryption, digital signature and random number generation.

Interface. The interface manages communication with external entities that can either be on-card or off-card entities. Any request that the interface receives is interpreted: if it is a well-formed request and the requesting entity is authorised to do so, then the interface will redirect the request to the intended module in the TEM. The interface during the interpretation of the request will enforce the access policy of the TEM as defined by the access control module (discussed in subsection 'Access Control' of Sect. 4.2). To manage these relationships with the authorised entities, the TEM should have a mechanism to establish the relation-ship in the first place. Therefore, at the time of installation of an application, a binding (symmetric key) is generated between the downloaded application and the TEM. For all subsequent communications, the application would use this key when requesting the TEM [16]. The protocol that establishes this binding is managed by the interface and the binding is stored in the key/certificate manager and corresponding access privilege in access control module.

Attestation Handler. During the application installation process, both an application and a smart card platform would need to verify each other's current state to gain assurance of their trustworthiness. An application can only request attestation for either itself or the respective platform. It cannot request attestation for other applications on the smart card concerned. However, to facilitate the application sharing mechanism [14] an application can issue an authorisation token. The attestation handler will then provide the attestation of the token-issuing application to the requesting application [15].

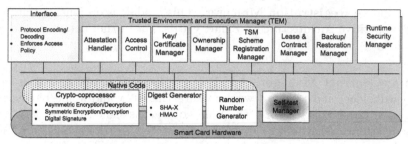

Fig. 5. Trusted Platform Module for Smart Card Architecture

Access Control. At the time of application installation, the Service Provider (SP) involved would request attestation of the card platform. However, no information regarding any of the other applications installed on the card would be provided to the SP at this stage. Once the application is installed, it can request attestation only for itself and not for any other applications. These restrictions are required to avoid privacy issues like application scanning attacks [15].

Key & Certificate Manager. The key & certificate manager manages the keys and certificates that a TEM stores in the non-volatile memory (EEPROM [44]). Contrary to the general TPM architecture, there are no migratable keys in the TEM. The TEM signature key pair and certificate is the permanent key and certificate (it can be considered as the endorsement key in the general TPM architecture). Besides managing the keys and certificates, it also generates them. Therefore, it is a combination of key generation and non-volatile memory components of the general TPM.

The key & certificate manager stores the evaluation certificates which are provided by the respective applications. Therefore, when an application requests attestation, the TEM does not return the hash value of the application. In fact, it returns an evaluation of whether the current state complies with the state for which the evaluation certificate was issued. Therefore, the decision whether an application is trustworthy or not is actually made by the TEM. If the evaluation fails, then depending upon the application or platform policy it might either block the application or delete it (and inform the cardholder and respective SP).

Ownership Manager. This component manages the ownership of a smart card. When a smart card is acquired by a user either from a card manufacturer or a card supplier, it is under the default ownership of the card manufacturer/supplier. The user then initiates the ownership acquisition process that requires the user to provide personal information (i.e. name and date of birth) and their Card Management Personal Identification Number (CM-PIN). The TEM will then generate a signature key pair specific to the cardholder along with a certificate that will also include the user information. Although this key is assigned to the cardholder, it will be protected by the TEM.

TSM Scheme Registration Manager. This module is optional and it facilitates Competitive Architecture for Smart Cards. For further details please refer to [17].

Lease & Contract Manager. An SP would lease its application to a smart card (cardholder) and the card would assure that it would abide by the SP's Application Lease Policy (ALP) The lease contract is signed by the TEM with the user's signature key and as these keys are stored/restrict access only to the TEM, the signing and storage of the contracts are on the TEM. The cardholder can retrieve these contracts after providing the CM-PIN if he/she needs to. Similarly, individual applications can also retrieve their own contracts from the TEM repository.

Backup/Restoration Manager. A cardholder may download multiple applications onto her smart card. If she loses her smart card, she will lose access to all of the applications (and related services). One possible approach can be to acquire a new card and then manually install all the applications again. However, another approach could be that a user creates a backup of the installed applications and restores the backup to a new smart card, if required. This backup mechanism is credential-based (a token issued by the SPs and not the actual application) and it is stored securely at a remote location [19]. When users lose their smart cards, they only need to get a new smart card and then initiate the restoration process, which will take each credential from the backup and initiate the application download process with respective SPs. The restoration process can also request the respective SPs to block (revoke the lease) their application(s) installed on the stolen/lost device.

Self-Test Manager. For security validation, the TEM implements a validation mechanism that is divided into two parts: tamper-evidence and reliability assurance. Smart cards are required to be tamper-resistant devices [44] and for this purpose card manufacturers implement hardware-based tamper protections. The tamper-evidence process verifies whether the implemented tamper-resistant mechanisms are still in place and effective. The reliability assurance process, on the other hand, verifies that the software part of the smart card that is crucial for its security and reliability has not been tampered with.

A TEM tamper-evidence process should provide the properties listed below:

1. Robustness: On input of certain data, it always produces the associated output.

2. Independence: When the same data is input to a tamper-evidence process on two different devices, it outputs different values.
3. Pseudo-randomness: The generated output should be computationally difficult to distinguish from a pseudo-random function.
4. Tamper-evidence: An invasive attack to access the function should cause irreversible changes, which render the device unusable.
5. Assurance: The function can provide assurance (either implicitly or explicitly) to independent (non-related) verifiers. It should not require an active connection with the device manufacturer to provide the assurance. The assurance refers to the current hardware and software state as it was at the time of third party evaluation.

For the TEM tamper-evidence process there are several candidates including: active (intelligent) shield/mesh [44]; Known Answer Test (KAT) [1], hardwired HMAC key, attestation based on PRNG [35]; and Physically Unclonable Function (PUF) [32]. Two algorithms that provide tamper-evidence and reliability based upon PUF and PRNG based validation mechanisms are discussed in [20,21] respectively.

Runtime Security Manager. The purpose of the runtime security manager is to enforce the security counter-measures defined by the respective platform. To enforce the security counter-measures, the runtime security manager has access to the heap area (e.g. method area, Java stacks) and can be implemented as either a serial or a parallel mode.

A serial runtime security manager will rely on the execution engine of the Java Card Virtual Machine (JCVM) [8] to perform the required tasks. This means that when an execution engine encounters instructions that require an enforcement of the security policy, it will invoke the runtime security manager that will then perform the checks. If successful the execution engine continues with execution, otherwise, it will terminate. A parallel runtime security manager will have its own dedicated hardware (i.e. processor) support that enables it to perform checks simultaneously while the execution engine is executing an application. Having multiple processors on a smart card is technically possible [44]. The main question regarding the choice is not the hardware, but the balance between performance and latency (Fig. 6).

Performance, as the name suggests, is concerned with computational speed, whereas latency deals with the number of instructions executed between an injected error and the point at which it is detected. For example, if during the execution of an application 'A', at instruction A4 a malicious user injects an error, which is detected by the platform security mechanism at instruction A7 of the application, the latency is three (i.e. $7 - 4 = 3$). A point to note is that the lower the latency value the better the protection mechanism, as it will catch the error quickly. Therefore, theoretically we can assume that a serial runtime security manager will have low performance but also a low latency value, while a parallel runtime security manager will have a good performance measure but a higher latency value.

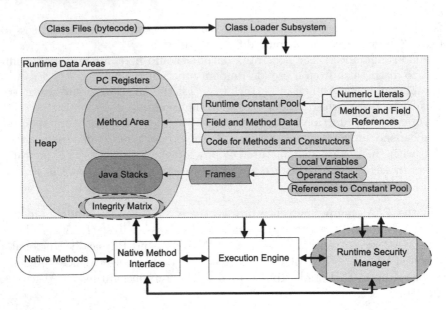

Fig. 6. Runtime Security Manager Integration with Java Card Runtime Environment

It is obvious that the implementation of additional components like runtime security managers will also incur additional economic costs (i.e. increase in the price of a smart card. The security measures that could be enforced are:

1. Operand Stack Integrity: In this we XOR the value pushed on to the operand stack with the top value of the integrity stack and the results are pushed back on to the integrity stack. When a value is popped from the operand stack, we will XOR the popped value from the top value in the integrity stack (where n is the top value of the stack). If the result is same as the value $n-1$ in the integrity stack, the execution continues, if not, then it is interrupted by the runtime security manager.
2. Control Flow Analysis: Authorised execution flows are generated oncard at the time of application installation. Later when application is executing, only the authorised execution flow is allowed to go ahead. Any violation would render the application blocked and may lead of it being deleted from the device.
3. Bytecode Integrity: Each basic block of an application code has an associated integrity value. When the basic block is fetched to the runtime memory, the integrity value is verified.

Preliminary Results. For evaluation of proposed counter-measures, we have selected four sample applications. Two of the applications selected are part of the Java Card development kit distribution: Wallet and Java Purse. The other two applications are the implementation of our proposed mechanisms that include the offline attestation algorithm [20] and STCP$_{SP}$ protocol [18].

4.3   Latency Analysis

As discussed before, latency is the number of instructions executed after an adversary mounts an attack and the system becomes aware of it. Therefore, in this section we analyse the latency of proposed counter-measures under the concept of serial and parallel runtime security managers that are listed in Table 1 and discussed subsequently.

Table 1. Latency measurement of individual countermeasure

Counter-measures	Serial RSM	Parallel RSM
Operand stack integrity	$0+i$	$3+i$
Permitted execution path analysis	0	$3(C_n)$
Bytecode integrity	0	0

In case of the operand stack integrity, the serial runtime security manager finds the occurrence of an error (e.g. fault injection) with latency "$0+i$", where 'i' is the number of instructions executed before the manipulated value reaches the top of the operand stack. For example, consider an operand stack with values V_1, V_2, V_3, V_4, and V_5, where V_5 is the value on the top. If an adversary changes the value of V_3 by physical perturbation, then the runtime security manager will not find out about his change until the value is popped out of the stack. Therefore, the value of 'i' depends upon the number of instructions that will execute until the V_3 reaches the top of the operand stack and JCVM pops it out. Similarly, the latency value in case of the operand stack integrity for the parallel runtime security manager is "$3+i$", where '3' is the number of instructions required to perform a comparison on a pop operation. The latency value of the parallel runtime security manager is higher than the serial. This has to do with the fact that while parallel runtime security manager is applying the security checks the JCVM does not need to stop the execution of subsequent instructions.

Regarding the control flow analysis, the serial runtime security manager has a latency of zero where the parallel runtime security manager has latency value of "$3(C_n)$", where the value C_n represents the number of legal jumps in the respective execution flow set. The value '3' represents the number of instructions required to execute individual comparison.

A notable point to mention here is that all latency measurements listed in the Table 2 are based on the worst-case conditions. Furthermore, it is apparent that it might be difficult to implement a complete parallel runtime security manager. To explain our point, consider two consecutive jump instructions in which the parallel runtime security manager has to perform control flow analysis. In such situation, there might be a possibility that while the runtime security manager is still evaluating the first jump, the JCVM might initiate the second jump instruction. Therefore, this might create a deadlock between the JCVM and parallel runtime security manager - we consider that either JCVM should wait for the runtime security manager to complete the verification, or for the sake of performance the runtime security manager might skip certain verifications. We opt for the parallel runtime security manager that will switch to the serial runtime security manager mode - restricting the JCVM to proceed with next instruction until the runtime security manager can apply the security checks. This situation will be further explained during the discussion on the performance measurements in the next section.

4.4 Performance Analysis

To evaluate the performance impact of the proposed counter-measures we developed an abstract virtual machine that takes the bytecode of each Java Card applet and then computes the computational overhead for individual counter-measure. When a Java application is compiled the java compiler (javac) produces a class file. The class file is Java bytecode representation, and there are two possible ways to read class files. We can either use a hex editor (an editor that shows a file in hexadecimal format) to read the Java bytecodes or better utilise the javap tool that comes with Java Development Kit (JDK). In our practical implementation, we opted for javap as it produces the bytecode representation of a class file in human-readable mnemonics as represented in the JVM specification [40]. We used javap to produce the mnemonic bytecode representation; the abstract virtual machine takes the mnemonic bytecode representation of an application and searches for push, pop, and jump (e.g. method invokes) opcodes. Subsequently, we calculated the number of extra instructions required to be executed in order to implement the counter-measures discussed in previous sections.

Table 2. Performance measurement (percentage increase in computational cost)

Applications	Serial RSM	Parallel RSM
Wallet	+29 %	+22 %
Java purse	+30 %	+26 %
Offline attestation [21]	+27 %	+23 %
STCP$_{SP}$ [20]	+39 %	+33 %

To compute the performance overhead, we counted the number of instructions an application has and how long the application takes to execute on our test Java Cards (e.g. C1 and C3). After this measurement, we have associated costs based on additional instructions executed for each JCVM instruction and calculated as an (approximate) increase in the percentage of computational overhead and listed in Table 2.

For each application, the counter-measures have different computational overhead values because they depend upon how many times certain instructions that invoke the counter-measures are executed. Therefore, the computational over-head measurements in Table 2 can only give us a measure of how the performance is affected in individual cases - without generalising for other applications.

In this section we discussed the smart card runtime environment by taking the Java Card as a running example. The JCRE was described with its different data structures that it uses during the execution of an application. Subsequently, we discussed various attacks that target the smart card runtime environment and most of these attacks based on perturbation of the values stored by the runtime environment. These perturbations are called fault injection, which was defined and mapped to an adversary's capability in this chapter. Based on these recent attacks on the smart card runtime environment, we proposed an architecture that includes the provision of a runtime security manager. We also proposed various counter-measures and provided the computational cost imposed by these counter-measures. No doubt, counter-measures that do not change the core architecture of the Java virtual machine, will almost always incur extra computational cost. Therefore, we concluded in this chapter that a better way forward would be to change the architecture of the Java virtual machine. However, in the context of this paper we showed that current architecture can be hardened at the cost of a computational penalty.

5 Conclusions

In this paper, we have briefly highlighted the security, trust and genuineness requirements for the embedded devices. These devices are becoming ever present in our daily life and reliance on them is going to increase in coming years. Therefore, utmost efforts have to be invested into their security and reliability in order to provide a safe and efficient service to the users. In this paper, we discussed some of the threat vectors that an adversary can use to compromise these devices. Furthermore, we also discussed the associated countermeasures along with some state-of-the-art protection mechanism. In this paper, we have also detailed a few of our proposal to provide security, reliability, trust and genuineness. The field of embedded computing still faces a number of challenges, effectively making it an exciting domain for security research to investigate and be innovative.

References

1. FIPS 140–2: Security Requirements for Cryptographic Modules, May 2005. http://csrc.nist.gov/publications/fips/fips140-2/fips1402.pdf
2. Common Criteria for Information Technology Security Evaluation, Part 1: Introduction and General Model, Part 2: Security Functional Requirements, Part 3: Security Assurance Requirements, August 2006. http://www.commoncriteriaportal.org/thecc.html
3. GlobalPlatform: GlobalPlatform Card Specification, Version 2.2, March 2006
4. GlobalPlatform Device: GPD/STIP Specification Overview. Specification Version 2.3, GlobalPlatform, August 2007

5. Trusted Computing Group, TCG Specification Architecture Overview. revision 1.4, The Trusted Computing Group (TCG), Beaverton, Oregon, USA, August 2007. http://www.trustedcomputinggroup.org/files/resource_files/AC652DE1-1D09-3519-ADA026A0C05CFAC2/TCG_1_4_Architecture_Overview.pdf

6. GlobalPlatform Device Technology: Device Application Security Management - Concepts and Description Document Specification, April 2008

7. ARM Security Technology: Building a Secure System using TrustZone Technology. White Paper PRD29-GENC-009492C, ARM (2009)

8. Java Card Platform Specification: Classic Edition; Application Programming Interface, Runtime Environment Specification, Virtual Machine Specification, Connected Edition; Runtime Environment Specification, Java Servlet Specification, Application Programming Interface, Virtual Machine Specification, Sample Structure of Application Modules, May 2009. http://java.sun.com/javacard/3.0.1/specs.jsp

9. GlobalPlatform Device Technology: TEE System Architecture. Specification Version 0.4, GlobalPlatform, October 2011

10. Inquiry into Counterfeit Electronic Parts in the Department of Defense Supply Chain. Online, September 2012. http://www.levin.senate.gov/download/?id=24b3f08d-02a3-42d0-bc75-5f673f3a8c93

11. Winning the Battle Against Counterfeit Semiconductor Products. Online, August 2013. http://www.semiconductors.org/clientuploads/Product

12. Agency, D.A.R.P.: Darpa baa06-40, a trust for integrated circuits, May 2013. https://www.fbo.gov/index?s=opportunity&mode=form&id=db4ea611cad37648 14b6937fcab2180a&tab=core&_cview=1

13. Agrawal, D., Baktir, S., Karakoyunlu, D., Rohatgi, P., Sunar, B.: Trojan detection using IC fingerprinting. In: IEEE Symposium on Security and Privacy, SP 2007, pp. 296–310 (2007)

14. Akram, R.N., Markantonakis, K., Mayes, K.: Firewall mechanism in a user centric smart card ownership model. In: Gollmann, D., Lanet, J.-L., Iguchi-Cartigny, J. (eds.) CARDIS 2010. LNCS, vol. 6035, pp. 118–132. Springer, Heidelberg (2010)

15. Akram, R.N., Markantonakis, K., Mayes, K.: Application-binding protocol in the user centric smart card ownership model. In: Parampalli, U., Hawkes, P. (eds.) ACISP 2011. LNCS, vol. 6812, pp. 208–225. Springer, Heidelberg (2011)

16. Akram, R.N., Markantonakis, K., Mayes, K.: Cross-platform application sharing mechanism. In: Wang, H., Tate, S.R., Xiang, Y. (eds.) 10th IEEE International Conference on Trust, Security and Privacy in Computing and Communications (IEEE TrustCom 2011). IEEE Computer Society, Changsha, November 2011

17. Akram, R.N., Markantonakis, K., Mayes, K.: Building the bridges - a proposal for merging different paradigms in mobile NFC ecosystem. In: Xie, S. (ed.) The 8th International Conference on Computational Intelligence and Security (CIS 2012). IEEE Computer Society, Guangzhou, November 2012

18. Akram, R.N., Markantonakis, K., Mayes, K.: A secure and trusted channel protocol for the user centric smart card ownership model. In: 12th IEEE International Conference on Trust, Security and Privacy in Computing and Communications (IEEE TrustCom 2013). IEEE Computer Society, Melbourne (2013)

19. Akram, R.N., Markantonakis, K., Mayes, K.: Recovering from lost digital Wallet. In: Xiang, F.G.M., Ruj, S. (eds.) The 4th IEEE International Symposium on Trust, Security, and Privacy for Emerging Applications (TSP 2013). IEEE CS, Zhangjiajie, November 2013

20. Akram, R.N., Markantonakis, K., Mayes, K.: Remote Attestation Mechanism based on Physical Unclonable Functions. In: Zhou, C.M., Weng, J. (eds.) The 2013 Workshop on RFID and IoT Security (RFIDsec 2013 Asia). IOS Press., Guangzhou, November 2013

21. Akram, R.N., Markantonakis, K., Mayes, K.: Remote attestation mechanism for user centric smart cards using pseudorandom number generators. In: Qing, S., Zhou, J., Liu, D. (eds.) ICICS 2013. LNCS, vol. 8233, pp. 151–166. Springer, Heidelberg (2013)

22. Allen, F.: Control flow analysis. In: Proceedings of a Symposium on Compiler Optimization, pp. 1–19. ACM, New York, July 1970. http://doi.acm.org/10.1145/800028.808479

23. Bellare, M., Garay, J.A., Rabin, T.: Fast batch verification for modular exponentiation and digital signatures. In: Nyberg, K. (ed.) EUROCRYPT 1998. LNCS, vol. 1403, pp. 236–250. Springer, Heidelberg (1998)

24. Boneh, D., DeMillo, R.A., Lipton, R.J.: On the importance of checking cryptographic protocols for faults. In: Fumy, W. (ed.) EUROCRYPT 1997. LNCS, vol. 1233, pp. 37–51. Springer, Heidelberg (1997)

25. Chakravarthi, S., Krishnan, A., Reddy, V., Machala, C., Krishnan, S.: A comprehensive framework for predictive modeling of negative bias temperature instability. In: 42nd Annual 2004 IEEE International Reliability Physics Symposium Proceedings, pp. 273–282 (2004)

26. Commerce, U.D.O.: Defense industrial base assessment: Counterfeit electronics. Technical report, Bureau of Industry and Security, Office of Technology Evaluation, January 2010. http://www.bis.doc.gov/defenseindustrialbaseprograms/osies/defmarketresearchrpts/final_counterfeit_electronics_report.pdf

27. Cowan, C., Pu, C., Maier, D., Hintony, H., Walpole, J., Bakke, P., Beattie, S., Grier, A., Wagle, P., Zhang, Q.: Stackguard: automatic adaptive detection and prevention of buffer-overflow attacks. In: Proceedings of the 7th Conference on USENIX Security Symposium - Volume 7, SSYM 1998, pp. 5–5. USENIX Association, Berkeley (1998). http://dl.acm.org/citation.cfm?id=1267549.1267554

28. Éluard, M., Jensen, T.: Secure Object Flow Analysis for Java Card. In: CARDIS 2002: Proceedings of the 5th Conference on Smart Card Research and Advanced Application Conference, pp. 11–11. USENIX Association, Berkeley (2002)

29. Fink, A.: Markov Models for Pattern Recognition. Springer, Heidelberg (2008)

30. Force, D.S.B.T.: High performance microchip supply, May 2013. http://www.acq.osd.mil/dsb/reports/ADA435563.pdf

31. Frantzen, M., Shuey, M.: Stackghost: hardware facilitated stack protection. In: Proceedings of the 10th Conference on USENIX Security Symposium - Vol. 10. SSYM 2001, USENIX Association, Berkeley (2001). http://dl.acm.org/citation.cfm?id=1251327.1251332

32. Gassend, B., Clarke, D., van Dijk, M., Devadas, S.: Silicon physical random functions. In: Proceedings of the 9th ACM conference on Computer and Communications Security, CCS 2002, pp. 148–160. ACM, New York (2002)

33. Henniger, O., Apvrille, L., Fuchs, A., Roudier, Y., Ruddle, A., Weyl, B.: Security requirements for automotive on-board networks. In: 2009 9th International Conference on Intelligent Transport Systems Telecommunications, (ITST), pp. 641–646. IEEE (2009)

34. Forney, Jr., D.F.: The Viterbi Algorithm: a personal history. CoRR abs/cs/0504020 (2005)

35. Kennell, R., Jamieson, L.H.: Establishing the genuinity of remote computer systems. In: Proceedings of the 12th Conference on USENIX Security Symposium - Volume 12, pp. 21–21. USENIX Association, Berkeley (2003). http://portal.acm.org/citation.cfm?id=1251353.1251374
36. Kocher, P.C., Jaffe, J., Jun, B.: Differential power analysis. In: Wiener, M. (ed.) CRYPTO 1999. LNCS, vol. 1666, pp. 388–397. Springer, Heidelberg (1999)
37. Koushanfar, F., Sadeghi, A.R., Seudie, H.: EDA for secure and dependable cyber-cars: challenges and opportunities. In: 2012 49th ACM/EDAC/IEEE Design Automation Conference (DAC), pp. 220–228 (2012)
38. LeCroy, T.: Teledyne LeCroy website, February 2013. http://www.teledynelecroy.com
39. Lieberman, J.I.: The national security aspects of the global migration of the u.s. semiconductor industry, May 2013. http://www.fas.org/irp/congress/2003_cr/s060503.html
40. Lindholm, T., Yellin, F.: The Java Virtual Machine Specification, 2nd edn. Addison-Wesley Longman, Amsterdam (1999)
41. Msgna, M., Markantonakis, K., Mayes, K.: The B-side of side channel leakage: control flow security in embedded systems. In: Zia, T., Zomaya, A., Varadharajan, V., Mao, M. (eds.) SecureComm 2013. LNICST, vol. 127, pp. 288–304. Springer, Heidelberg (2013)
42. Msgna, M., Markantonakis, K., Naccache, D., Mayes, K.: Verifying software integrity in embedded systems: a side channel approach. In: Prouff, E. (ed.) COSADE 2014. LNCS, vol. 8622, pp. 261–280. Springer, Heidelberg (2014)
43. Rabiner, L.: A tutorial on Hidden Markov Models and selected applications in speech recognition. Proc. IEEE $77(2)$, 257–286 (1989)
44. Rankl, W., Effing, W.: Smart Card Handbook, 3rd edn. Wiley, New York (2003)
45. Rivest, R.L., Shamir, A., Adleman, L.M.: A method for obtaining digital signatures and public-key cryptosystems. Commun. ACM $21(2)$, 120–126 (1978)
46. Sere, A.A., Iguchi-Cartigny, J., Lanet, J.L.: Automatic detection of fault attack and countermeasures. In: Proceedings of the 4th Workshop on Embedded Systems Security, WESS 2009, pp. 71–77. ACM, New York (2009)
47. Wei, S., Nahapetian, A., Potkonjak, M.: Robust passive hardware metering. In: International Conference on Computer-Aided Design (ICCAD), 7–10 November 2011, pp. 802–809. IEEE (2011)
48. Wilson, P., Frey, A., Mihm, T., Kershaw, D., Alves, T.: Implementing embedded security on dual-virtual-CPU systems. IEEE Des. Test Comput. 24, 582–591 (2007)

A Number-Theoretic Error-Correcting Code

Eric Brier[1], Jean-Sébastien Coron[2], Rémi Géraud[1,3], Diana Maimuţ[3(✉)], and David Naccache[2,3]

[1] Ingenico, 28-32 boulevard de Grenelle, 75015 Paris, France
{eric.brier,remi.geraud}@ingenico.com
[2] Université du Luxembourg, 6 rue Richard Coudenhove-Kalergi,
1359 Luxembourg, Luxembourg
{jean-sebastien.coron,david.naccache}@uni.lu
[3] Département d'Informatique, École normale supérieure, 45 rue d'Ulm,
75230 Paris Cedex 05, France
{remi.geraud,diana.maimut,david.naccache}@ens.fr

Abstract. In this paper we describe a new error-correcting code (ECC) inspired by the Naccache-Stern cryptosystem. While by far less efficient than Turbo codes, the proposed ECC happens to be more efficient than some established ECCs for certain sets of parameters.

The new ECC adds an appendix to the message. The appendix is the modular product of small primes representing the message bits. The receiver recomputes the product and detects transmission errors using modular division and lattice reduction.

1 Introduction

Error-correcting codes (ECCs) are essential to ensure reliable communication. ECCs work by adding redundancy which enables detecting and correcting mistakes in received data. This extra information is, of course, costly and it is important to keep it to a minimum: there is a trade-off between how much data is added for error correction purposes (bandwidth), and the number of errors that can be corrected (correction capacity).

Shannon showed [13] in 1948 that it is in theory possible to encode messages with a minimal number of extra bits[1]. Two years later, Hamming [7] proposed a construction inspired by parity codes, which provided both error detection and error correction. Subsequent research saw the emergence of more efficient codes, such as Reed-Muller [8,10] and Reed-Solomon [11]. The latest were generalized by Goppa [6]. These codes are known as algebraic-geometric codes.

Convolutional codes were first presented in 1955 [4], while recursive systematic convolutional codes [1] were introduced in 1991. Turbo codes [1] were indeed revolutionary, given their closeness to the channel capacity ("near Shannon limit").

---

[1] Shannon's theorem states that the best achievable expansion rate is $1 - H_2(p_b)$, where H_2 is binary entropy and p_b is the acceptable error rate.

© Springer International Publishing Switzerland 2015
I. Bica et al. (Eds.): SECITC 2015, LNCS 9522, pp. 25–35, 2015.
DOI: 10.1007/978-3-319-27179-8_2

Results: This paper presents a new error-correcting code, as well as a form of message size improvement based on the hybrid use of two ECCs one of which is inspired by the Naccache-Stern (NS) cryptosystem [2,9]. For some codes and parameter choices, the resulting hybrid codes outperform the two underlying ECCs.

The proposed ECC is unusual because it is based on number theory rather than on binary operations.

2   Preliminaries

2.1   Notations

Let $\mathfrak{P} = \{p_1 = 2, \dots\}$ be the ordered set of prime numbers. Let $\gamma \geq 2$ be an encoding base. For any $m \in \mathbb{N}$ (the "message"), let $\{m_i\}$ be the digits of m in base γ *i.e.*:

$$m = \sum_{i=0}^{k-1} \gamma^i m_i \qquad m_i \in [0, \gamma - 1], \quad k = \lceil \log_\gamma m \rceil$$

We denote by $h(x)$ the Hamming weight of x, *i.e.* the sum of x's digits in base 2, and, by $|y|$ the bit-length of y.

2.2   Error-Correcting Codes

Let $\mathcal{M} = \{0,1\}^k$ be the set of messages, $\mathcal{C} = \{0,1\}^n$ the set of encoded messages. Let $\mathcal{P}$ be a parameter set.

Definition 1 (Error-Correcting Code). *An* error-correcting code *is a couple of algorithms:*

- *An algorithm μ, taking as input some message $m \in \mathcal{M}$, as well as some public parameters* params $\in \mathcal{P}$, *and outputting $c \in \mathcal{C}$.*
- *An algorithm μ^{-1}, taking as input $\tilde{c} \in \mathcal{C}$ as well as parameters* params $\in \mathcal{P}$, *and outputting $m \in \mathcal{M} \cup \{\bot\}$.*

The $\bot$ symbol indicates that decoding failed.

Definition 2 (Correction Capacity). *Let $(\mu, \mu^{-1}, \mathcal{M}, \mathcal{C}, \mathcal{P})$ be an error-correcting code. There exists an integer $t \geq 0$ and some parameters* params $\in \mathcal{P}$ *such that, for all $e \in \{0,1\}^n$ such that $h(e) \leq t$,*

$$\mu^{-1}\left(\mu\left(m, \text{params}\right) \oplus e, \text{params}\right) = m, \qquad \forall m \in \mathcal{M}$$

and for all e such that $h(e) > t$,

$$\mu^{-1}\left(\mu\left(m, \text{params}\right) \oplus e, \text{params}\right) \neq m, \qquad \forall m \in \mathcal{M}.$$

t is called the correction capacity *of $(\mu, \mu^{-1}, \mathcal{M}, \mathcal{C}, \mathcal{P})$.*

Definition 3. *A code of message length k, of codeword length n and with a correction capacity t is called an (n, k, t)-code. The ratio $\rho = \frac{n}{k}$ is called the code's* expansion rate.

3   A New Error-Correcting Code

Consider in this section an existing (n, k, t)-code $C = (\mu, \mu^{-1}, \mathcal{M}, \mathcal{C}, \mathcal{P})$. For instance C can be a Reed-Muller code. We describe how the new (n', k, t)-code $C' = (\nu, \nu^{-1}, \mathcal{M}, \mathcal{C}', \mathcal{P}')$ is constructed.

Parameter Generation: To correct t errors in a k-bit message, we generate a prime p such that:

$$2 \cdot p_k^{2t} < p < 4 \cdot p_k^{2t} \tag{1}$$

As we will later see, the size of p is obtained by bounding the worst case in which all errors affect the end of the message. p is a part of $\mathcal{P}'$.

Encoding: Assume we wish to transmit a k-bit message m over a noisy channel. Let $\gamma = 2$ so that m_i denote the i-th bit of m, and define:

$$c(m) := \prod_{i=1}^{k} p_i^{m_i} \bmod p \tag{2}$$

The integer generated by Eq. (2) is encoded using C to yield $\mu(c(m))$. Finally, the encoded message $\nu(m)$ transmitted over the noisy channel is defined as:

$$\mu(m) := m \| \mu(c(m)) \tag{3}$$

Note that, if we were to use C directly, we would have encoded m (and not c). The value c is, in most practical situations, much shorter than m. As is explained in Sect. 3.1, c is smaller than m (except the cases in which m is very small and which are not interesting in practice) and thereby requires fewer extra bits for correction. For appropriate parameter choices, this provides a more efficient encoding, as compared to C.

Decoding: Let α be the received[2] message. Assume that at most t errors occurred during transmission:

$$\alpha = \nu(m) \oplus e = m' \| (\mu(c(m)) \oplus e')$$

where the error vector e is such that $h(e) = h(m' \oplus m) + h(e') \leq t$.

Since $c(m)$ is encoded with a t-error-capacity code, we can recover the correct value of $c(m)$ from $\mu(c(m)) \oplus e'$ and compute the quantity:

$$s = \frac{c(m')}{c(m)} \bmod p \tag{4}$$

Using Eq. (2) s can be written as:

$$s = \frac{a}{b} \bmod p, \quad \begin{cases} a = \displaystyle\prod_{(m'_i=1) \wedge (m_i=0)} p_i \\ b = \displaystyle\prod_{(m'_i=0) \wedge (m_i=1)} p_i \end{cases} \tag{5}$$

---

[2] *i.e.* encoded and potentially corrupted.

Note that since $h(m' \oplus m) \leq t$, we have that a and b are strictly smaller than $(p_k)^t$. Theorem 1 from [5] shows that given t the receiver can recover a and b efficiently using a variant of Gauss' algorithm [14].

Theorem 1. *Let $a, b \in \mathbb{Z}$ such that $-A \leq a \leq A$ and $0 < b \leq B$. Let p be some prime integer such that $2AB < p$. Let $s = a \cdot b^{-1} \mod p$. Then given A, B, s and p, a and b can be recovered in polynomial time.*

As $0 \leq a \leq A$ and $0 < b \leq B$ where $A = B = (p_k)^t - 1$ and $2AB < p$ from Eq. (1), we can recover a and b from t in polynomial time. Then, by testing the divisibility of a and b with respect to the small primes p_i, the receiver can recover $m' \oplus m$ and eventually m.

A numerical example is given in Appendix A.

Bootstrapping: Note that instead of using an existing code as a sub-contractor for protecting $c(m)$, the sender may also recursively apply the new scheme described above. To do so consider $c(m)$ as a message, and protect $\bar{c} = c(c(\cdots c(c(m)))$, which is a rather small value, against accidental alteration by replicating it $2t+1$ times. The receiver will use a majority vote to detect the errors in $\bar{c}$.

3.1 Performance of the New Error-Correcting Code for $\gamma = 2$

Lemma 1. *The bit-size of $c(m)$ is:*

$$\log_2 p \simeq 2 \cdot t \log_2(k \ln k). \tag{6}$$

Proof. From Eq. (1) and the Prime Number Theorem[3].   □

The total output length of the new error-correcting code is therefore $\log_2 p$, plus the length k of the message m.

C' outperforms the initial error correcting code C if, for equal error capacity t and message length k, it outputs a shorter encoding, which happens if $n' < n$, keeping in mind that both n and n' depend on k.

Corollary 1. *Assume that there exists a constant $\delta > 1$ such that, for k large enough, $n(k) \geq \delta k$. Then for k large enough, $n'(k) \leq n(k)$.*

Proof. Let k be the size of m and k' be the size of $c(m)$. We have $n'(k) = k+n(k')$, therefore

$$n(k) - n'(k) = n(k) - (k + n(k')) \geq (\delta - 1)k - n(k').$$

Now,

$$(\delta - 1)k - n(k') \geq 0 \Leftrightarrow (\delta - 1)k \geq n(k').$$

---

[3] $p_k \simeq k \ln k$.

But $n(k') \geq \delta k'$, hence

$$(\delta - 1)k \geq \delta k' \Rightarrow k \geq \frac{k'\delta}{(\delta - 1)}.$$

Finally, from Lemma 1, $k' = O(\ln \ln k!)$, which guarantees that there exists a value of k above which $n'(k) \leq n(k)$. ☐

In other terms, any correcting code whose encoded message size is growing linearly with message size can benefit from the described construction (Fig. 1).

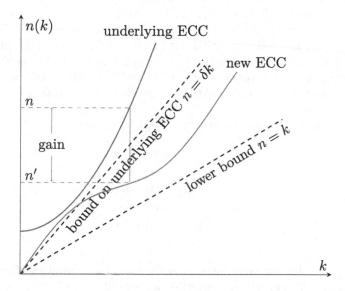

Fig. 1. Illustration of Corollory 1. For large enough values of k, the new ECC uses smaller codewords as compared to the underlying ECC.

Expansion Rate: Let k be the length of m and consider the bit-size of the corresponding codeword as in Eq. (6). The expansion rate ρ is:

$$\rho = \frac{|m| |\mu(c(m))|}{|m|} = \frac{k + |\mu(c(m))|}{k} = 1 + \frac{|\mu(c(m))|}{k} \tag{7}$$

Reed-Muller Codes. We illustrate the idea with Reed-Muller codes. Reed-Muller (R-M) codes are a family of linear codes. Let $r \geq 0$ be an integer, and $N = \log_2 n$, it can apply to messages of size

$$k = \sum_{i=1}^{r} \binom{N}{i} \tag{8}$$

Table 1. Examples of length n, dimension k, and error capacity t for Reed-Muller code.

n	16	64	128	256	512	2048	8192	32768	131072
k	11	42	99	163	382	1024	5812	9949	65536
t	1	3	3	7	7	31	31	255	255

Such a code can correct up to $t = 2^{N-r-1} - 1$ errors. Some examples of $\{n, k, t\}$ triples are given in Table 1. For instance, a message of size 163 bits can be encoded as a 256-bit string, among which up to 7 errors can be corrected.

To illustrate the benefit of our approach, consider a 5812-bit message, which we wish to protect against up to 31 errors.

A direct use of Reed-Muller would require $n = 8192$ bits as seen in Table 1. Contrast this with our code, which only has to protect $c(m)$, that is 931 bits as shown by Eq. 6, yielding a total size of $5812 + n(931) = 5812 + 2048 = 7860$ bits.

Other parameters for the Reed-Muller primitive are illustrated in Table 2.

Table 2. (n, k, t)-codes generated from Reed-Muller by our construction.

n'	638	7860	98304
k	382	5812	65536
$c(m)$	157	931	9931
$\mathrm{RM}(c(m))$	256	2048	32768
t	7	31	255

Table 2 shows that for large message sizes and a small number of errors, our error-correcting code slightly outperforms Reed-Muller code.

3.2   The Case $\gamma > 2$

The difficulty in the case $\gamma > 2$ stems from the fact that a binary error in a γ-base message will in essence scramble all digits preceding the error. As an example,

$$\underline{122002101220201}20100111202020_3 + 2^{30} = \underline{122002102211}2000112220110110_3$$

Hence, unless $\gamma = 2^\Gamma$ for some Γ, a generalization makes sense only for channels over which transmission uses γ symbols. In such cases, we have the following: a k-bit message m is pre-encoded as a γ-base κ-symbol message m'. Here $\kappa = \lceil k/\log_2 \gamma \rceil$. Eq. (1) becomes:

$$2 \cdot p_\kappa^{2t(\gamma-1)} < p < 4 \cdot p_\kappa^{2t(\gamma-1)}$$

Comparison with the binary case is complicated by the fact that here t refers to the number of *any* errors regardless their semiologic meaning. In other words, an error transforming a 0 into a 2 counts exactly as an error transforming 0 into a 1.

Example 1. As a typical example, for $t = 7$, $\kappa = 10^6$ and $\gamma = 3$, $p_\kappa = 15485863$ and p is a 690-bit number.

For the sake of comparison, $t = 7$, $k = 1584963$ (corresponding to $\kappa = 10^6$) and $\gamma = 2$, yield $p_k = 25325609$ and a 346-bit p.

4   Improvement Using Smaller Primes

The construction described in the previous section can be improved by choosing a smaller prime p, but comes at a price; namely decoding becomes only heuristic.

Parameter Generation: The idea consists in generating a prime p smaller than before. Namely, we generate a p satisfying :

$$2^u \cdot p_k^t < p < 2^{u+1} \cdot p_k^t \tag{9}$$

for some small integer $u \geq 1$.

Encoding and Decoding: Encoding remains as previously. The redundancy $c(m)$ being approximately half as small as the previous section's one, we have :

$$s = \frac{a}{b} \mod p, \quad \begin{cases} a = \displaystyle\prod_{(m_i'=1)\wedge(m_i=0)} p_i \\ b = \displaystyle\prod_{(m_i'=0)\wedge(m_i=1)} p_i \end{cases} \tag{10}$$

and since there are at most t errors, we must have :

$$a \cdot b \leq (p_k)^t \tag{11}$$

We define a finite sequence $\{A_i, B_i\}$ of integers such that $A_i = 2^{u \cdot i}$ and $B_i = \lfloor 2p/A_i \rfloor$. From Eqs. (9) and (11) there must be at least one index i such that $0 \leq a \leq A_i$ and $0 < b \leq B_i$. Then using Theorem 1, given A_i, B_i, p and s, the receiver can recover a and b, and eventually m.

The problem with that approach is that we lost the guarantee that $\{a, b\}$ is unique. Namely we may find another $\{a', b'\}$ satisfying Eq. (10) for some other index i'. We expect this to happen with negligible probability for large enough u, but this makes the modified code heuristic (while perfectly implementable for all practical purposes).

4.1   Performance

Lemma 2. *The bit-size of $c(m)$ is:*

$$\log_2 p \simeq u + t \log_2(k \ln k). \tag{12}$$

Proof. Using Eq. (9) and the Prime Number Theorem.   □

Thus, the smaller prime variant has a shorter $c(m)$.

As u is a small integer (*e.g.* $u = 50$), it follows immediately from Eq. (1) that, for large n and t, the size of the new prime p will be approximately half the size of the prime p generated in the preceding section.

This brings down the minimum message size k above which our construction provides an improvement over the bare underlying correcting code.

Note: In the case of Reed-Muller codes, this variant provides no improvement over the technique described in Sect. 3 for the following reasons: (1) by design, Reed-Muller codewords are powers of 2; and (2) Eq. (12) cannot yield a twofold reduction in p. Therefore we cannot hope to reduce p enough to get a smaller codeword.

That doesn't preclude other codes to show benefits, but the authors did not look for such codes.

5   Prime Packing Encoding

It is interesting to see whether the optimization technique of [2] yields more efficient ECCs. Recall that in [2], the p_is are distributed amongst κ packs. Information is encoded by picking one p_i per pack. This has an immediate impact on decoding: when an error occurs and a symbol σ is replaced by a symbol σ', both the numerator and the denominator of s are affected by *additional* prime factors.

Let $C = (\mu, \mu^{-1}, \mathcal{M}, \mathcal{C}, \mathcal{P})$ be a t-error capacity code, such that it is possible to efficiently recover c from $\mu(c) \oplus e$ for any c and any e, where $h(e) \le t$. Let $\gamma \ge 2$ be a positive integer.

Before we proceed, we define $\kappa := \lceil k / \log_2 \gamma \rceil$ and

$$f := f(\gamma, \kappa, t) = \prod_{i=k-t}^{k} p_{\gamma i}.$$

Parameter Generation: Let p be a prime number such that:

$$2 \cdot f^2 < p < 4 \cdot f^2 \tag{13}$$

Let $\hat{\mathcal{C}} = \mathcal{M} \times \mathbb{Z}_p$ and $\hat{\mathcal{P}} = (\mathcal{P} \cup \mathfrak{P}) \times \mathbb{N}$. We now construct a variant of the ECC presented in Sect. 3 from C and denote it

$$\hat{C} = \left(\nu, \nu^{-1}, \mathcal{M}, \hat{\mathcal{C}}, \hat{\mathcal{P}} \right).$$

Encoding: We define the "redundancy" of a k-bit message $m \in \mathcal{M}$ (represented as κ digits in base γ) by:

$$\hat{c}(m) := \prod_{i=0}^{\kappa-1} p_{i\gamma + m_i + 1} \bmod p$$

A message m is encoded as follows:

$$\nu(m) := m \| \mu \left(\hat{c}(m) \right)$$

Decoding: The received information α differs from $\nu(m)$ by a certain number of bits. Again, we assume that the number of these differing bits is at most t. Therefore $\alpha = \nu(m) \oplus e$, where $h(e) \leq t$. Write $e = e_m \| e_{\hat{c}}$ such that

$$\alpha = \nu(m) \oplus e = m \oplus e_m \| \mu(\hat{c}(m)) \oplus e_{\hat{c}} = m' \| \mu(\hat{c}(m)) \oplus e_{\hat{c}}.$$

Since $h(e) = h(e_m) + h(e_{\hat{c}}) \leq t$, the receiver can recover efficiently $\hat{c}(m)$ from α. It is then possible to compute

$$s := \frac{\hat{c}(m')}{\hat{c}(m)} \bmod p = \frac{\displaystyle\prod_{i=0}^{\kappa-1} p_{i\gamma+m'_i+1}}{\displaystyle\prod_{i=0}^{\kappa-1} p_{i\gamma+m_i+1}} \bmod p.$$

$$s = \frac{a}{b} \bmod p, \quad \begin{cases} a = \displaystyle\prod_{m'_i \neq m_i} p_{i\gamma+m'_i+1} \\ b = \displaystyle\prod_{m_i \neq m'_i} p_{i\gamma+m_i+1} \end{cases} \tag{14}$$

As $h(e) = h(e_m) + h(e_{\hat{c}}) \leq t$, we have that a and b are strictly smaller than $f(\gamma, \kappa)^{2t}$. As $A = B = f(\gamma, \kappa)^{2t} - 1$, we observe from Eq. (13) that $2AB < p$. We are now able to recover a, b, $\gcd(a, b) = 1$ such that $s = a/b \bmod p$ using lattice reduction [14].

Testing the divisibility of a and b by $p_1, \ldots, p_{\kappa\gamma}$ the receiver can recover $e_m = m' \oplus m$, and from that get $m = m' \oplus e_m$. Note that by construction only one prime amongst γ is used per "pack": the receiver can therefore skip on average $\gamma/2$ primes in the divisibility testing phase.

5.1   Performance

Rosser's theorem [3, 12] states that for $n \geq 6$,

$$\ln n + \ln \ln n - 1 < \frac{p_n}{n} < \ln n + \ln \ln n$$

i.e. $p_n < n(\ln n + \ln \ln n)$. Hence a crude upper bound of p is

$$p < 4f(\kappa, \gamma, t)^2$$

$$= 4 \left(\prod_{i=\kappa-t}^{\kappa} p_{\gamma i} \right)^2$$

$$\leq 4 \prod_{i=\kappa-t}^{\kappa} (i\gamma(\ln i\gamma + \ln \ln(i\gamma)))^2$$

$$\leq 4\gamma^{2t} \left(\frac{\kappa!}{(\kappa - t - 1)!} \right)^2 (\ln \kappa\gamma + \ln \ln \kappa\gamma)^{2t}$$

Again, the total output length of the new error-correcting code is $n' = k + |p|$.

Plugging $\gamma = 3$, $\kappa = 10^6$ and $t = 7$ into Eq. (13) we get a 410-bit p. This improves over Example 1 where p was 690 bits long.

A   Toy Example

Let m be the 10-bit message 1100100111. For $t = 2$, we let p be the smallest prime number greater than $2 \cdot 29^4$, $i.e.$ $p = 707293$. We generate the redundancy:

$$c(m) = 2^1 \cdot 3^1 \cdot 5^0 \cdot 7^0 \cdot 11^1 \cdot 13^0 \cdot 17^0 \cdot 19^1 \cdot 23^1 \cdot 29^1 \bmod 707293$$

$$\Rightarrow c(m) = 836418 \bmod 707293 = 129125.$$

As we focus on the new error-correcting code we simply omit the Reed-Muller component. The encoded message is

$$\nu(m) = 1100100111_2 \| 129125_{10}.$$

Let the received encoded message be $\alpha = 1100101011_2 \| 129125_{10}$. Thus,

$$c(m') = 2^1 \cdot 3^1 \cdot 5^0 \cdot 7^0 \cdot 11^1 \cdot 13^0 \cdot 17^1 \cdot 19^0 \cdot 23^1 \cdot 29^1 \bmod p$$

$$\Rightarrow c(m') = 748374 \bmod 707293 = 41081.$$

Dividing by $c(m)$ we get

$$s = \frac{c(m')}{c(m)} = \frac{41081}{129125} \bmod 707293 = 632842$$

Applying the rationalize and factor technique we obtain $s = \dfrac{17}{19} \bmod 707293$. It follows that $m' \oplus m = 0000001100$. Flipping the bits retrieved by this calculation, we recover m.

References

1. Berrou, C., Glavieux, A., Thitimajshima, P.: Near Shannon limit error-correcting coding and decoding: turbo-codes. In: IEEE International Conference on Communications - ICC 1993, vol. 2, pp. 1064–1070, May 1993
2. Chevallier-Mames, B., Naccache, D., Stern, J.: Linear bandwidth naccache-stern encryption. In: Ostrovsky, R., De Prisco, R., Visconti, I. (eds.) SCN 2008. LNCS, vol. 5229, pp. 327–339. Springer, Heidelberg (2008)
3. Dusart, P.: The kth prime is greater than $k(\ln k + \ln \ln k - 1)$ for $k \geq 2$. Math. Comput. **68**, 411–415 (1999)
4. Elias, P.: Coding for noisy channels. In: IRE Convention Record, pp. 37–46 (1955)
5. Fouque, P.-A., Stern, J., Wackers, G.-J.: CryptoComputing with rationals. In: Blaze, M. (ed.) FC 2002. LNCS, vol. 2357, pp. 136–146. Springer, Heidelberg (2003)
6. Goppa, V.D.: Codes on algebraic curves. Sov. Math. Dokl. **24**, 170–172 (1981)
7. Hamming, R.W.: Error detecting and error correcting codes. Bell Syst. Tech. J. **29**(2), 147–160 (1950)
8. Muller, D.E.: Application of boolean algebra to switching circuit design and to error detection. IRE Trans. Inf. Theory **3**, 6–12 (1954)

9. Naccache, D., Stern, J.: A new public-key cryptosystem. In: Fumy, W. (ed.) EURO-CRYPT 1997. LNCS, vol. 1233, pp. 27–36. Springer, Heidelberg (1997)
10. Reed, I.: A class of multiple-error-correcting codes and the decoding scheme. IRE Trans. Inf. Theory **4**, 38–49 (1954)
11. Reed, I.S., Solomon, G.: Polynomial codes over certain finite fields. J. Soc. Ind. Appl. Math. **8**(2), 300–304 (1960)
12. Rosser, J.B.: The n-th prime is greater than $n \ln n$. Proc. Lond. Math. Soc. **45**, 21–44 (1938)
13. Shannon, C.: A mathematical theory of communication. Bell Syst. Tech. J. **27**(379–423), 623–656 (1948)
14. Vallée, B.: Gauss' algorithm revisited. J. Algorithms **12**(4), 556–572 (1991)

Cryptographic Algorithms and Protocols

Full Duplex OTP Cryptosystem Based on DNA Key for Text Transmissions

Dumitru Balanici, Vlad Tomsa, Monica Borda$^{(\boxtimes)}$, and Raul Malutan

Communication Department, Technical University of Cluj-Napoca,
Cluj-Napoca, Romania
{dumitru.balanici,tomsavlad90}@gmail.com,
{Monica.Borda,Raul.Malutan}@com.utcluj.ro

Abstract. The present work aims at finding an alternative way to set up an OTP cryptosystem which generates secret keys based on DNA random sequences. The main advantage of the proposed procedure is that it generates a pure random secret key based on multiplexing genetic sequences randomly selected. Experimental results are given for text transmissions.

Keywords: Cryptography · DNA cryptography · DNA cryptographic key · Fullduplex OTP cryptosystem · Transmission protocol · Security parameters

1 Introduction

Cryptography manipulates the information in order to make it incompressible for adversaries, using an algorithm and a secret key [1–3].

Pure random sequences are widely used in cryptographic applications for cryptographic keys. The use of OTP (One Time Pad) is of great interest in cryptography, where a key is only used once in a confidential communication and the length of the key is at least as long as the message in plaintext. Such a system was proved to be unbreakable [1,4]. One of the most important problems which occur in OTP implementation of usable cryptographic systems is the number of very long keys required and their management.

The construction of an OTP cryptosystem that is capable of transmitting encrypted messages opens an entirely new field of analysis. The main reason for using DNA (Dezoxyribonucleic Acid) sequences for secret keys generation, is that these sequences were proved to be incompressible, thus such sequences can be considered random sequences [5].

Based on [6–8], we propose a full duplex OTP cryptosystem using DNA keys. The paper is structured in eight sections: 1. Introduction, 2. Access to the DNA Sequences, 3. Key generation method, 4. Full duplex OTP cryptosystem and protocol based on DNA sequences, 5. Efficiency analysis of the algorithm for text transmissions, 6. Conclusions, 7. Future implementations and 8. References.

© Springer International Publishing Switzerland 2015
I. Bica et al. (Eds.): SECITC 2015, LNCS 9522, pp. 39–48, 2015.
DOI: 10.1007/978-3-319-27179-8_3

2   Access to the DNA Sequences

DNA sequences can be accessed using provided biological databases that store genetic sequences, and can be used to generate as long desired sequences as needed. The structure of DNA sequences is random, so it cannot be compressed, or the compression ratio is very small. The genetic code has four bases: A Adenine, C Cytosine, G Guanine, and T Thymine [10, 11]. It is important to mention that these bases are converted in binary using the following relations: $A = 00$; $B = 01$; $C = 10$; $D = 11$ [11]. This substitution is used for a better interpretation of the genetic code in programming language. In order to obtain a random sequence for OTP cryptographic applications, the sequences should be at least equal to the length of the message in plaintext and need to be used only once. For this reason, the minimum length of the generated sequence should match the message length, which varies depending on its format and type [5, 7, 8]. For implementation of this application it was chosen a personal database, to store cryptographic keys, in order to not dependent on access to servers of other entities. In this way a server capable of storing a database of DNA structure of various organisms and their chromosomes was created. These sequences were imported from the databases of NCBI (The National Center for Biotechnology Information) and inserted into the local database [9]. Thus, this application is capable of transmitting messages, with size limitations set only by the server, fact which may result in low processing speeds of encryption. The structure of the local database is presented in Fig. 1. For testing, a number of 200 items (DNA structures) was introduced in the database. This number will be further increased for future development.

keyID	keyValue
1	AAGCTTCAGGCTTCCTTTTGCTGTTGGGAGTATTCAACTTTTTCCTTTCA...
2	GCCATCGTCACCGTTTTACATCTTTAACCCTCCAATTACTATATCTTAAT...
3	TGAAGTACAACTGGCATACTGGGCTCTGGTCCCGAGCCTGCCTTGGAGGT...
4	GCAGTAATGGTAGAGTTCCATGACACCAGGGACCTTCCTAAGAATTGGCA...
5	TTATAATGCCTTTTGGGAAGAAGTAGACTCATCACTATCGTCGTAGTAGA...
6	TTGCAAAGATGCGGTTTCAAACTAGGAAACGGAGTGAAGGATGCCCCACA...
7	ACAAAATATCCAGGATCGATCATAAGGCGGATAGACACCACCCTTATTAT...
8	TATCCAGGATCGATCATAAGGCGGATAGACACCACCCTTATTATCCTCTA...

Fig. 1. Structure of the local DNA sequence database

3   Key Generation Method

For obtaining a high number of random sequences based on the DNA structure, the key used in the encryption process is generated by multiplexing different sequences stored in the DNA server database [6–8]. In this database, each individual DNA sequence has its own associated identification (ID) number. The number of sequences used during the multiplexing process is selected arbitrary. After obtaining the number of sequences, each individual sequence is selected randomly by its associated identification number. Figure 2 presents the process of multiplexing 3 DNA sequences.

DNA sequence #1: TGCTCGTGACTATTGTGA...
DNA sequence #2: GACTATTGTAAAGTGAGA...
DNA sequence #3: ACTATTTGCGCATGGTGA...
MUX (DNA{#1, #2, #3}): TGAGACCCTTTACAT...

Fig. 2. Cryptographic key resulted from the multiplexing of 3 DNA sequences stored in the local database

The total number of sequences used in multiplexing and the identification number of each sequence are used for generation of the cryptosystems private key. Another field introduced in the private key is the sequence offset. The offset is referring to the possibility of selecting only segments of the chosen sequences from the database. Beside these fields, the total length of the plaintext message value is also introduced into the private key. This value will be used at the reception, within the decryption algorithm. The private key (seed) structure is presented in Fig. 3.

No. Seq (k)	Offset	$ID_0 ... ID_k$	Clear Message Length

Fig. 3. Cryptosystem private key (seed) structure

The main advantages of this method are:

- DNA sequences are random (cannot be compressed);
- The variety of DNA sequences is very large considering the multitude types of organisms;
- A wide range of keys resulted from sequences multiplexing due to the random selection and arbitrary number of used sequences;
- There is no need to send the entire key, only the private key (Fig. 3), which requires a high level of security in transmission.

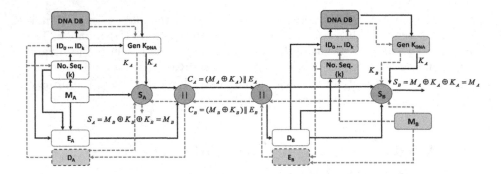

Fig. 4. DNA sequences based OTP cryptosystem block diagram

4 Full Duplex OTP Transmission Cryptosystem Based on DNA Keys and its Associated Protocol

Legend of the block diagram (Fig. 4):

- M_A - plaintext message from user A;
- M_B - plaintext message from user B;
- No. Seq - block that generates a random number (k) of sequences used for generating the private key;
- $ID_0 \ldots ID_k$ - identification number of each individual DNA sequence used in the generation of the private key;
- DNA DB - local database of DNA sequences, identical for both users. This database can be private or public;
- Gen K_{DNA} - key generation block. The resulted key (K_A,K_B) is obtained after multiplexing the DNA sequences received from the local database and converted into binary code according to the method mentioned in Sect. 2;
- S_A - modulo 2 adder used in the procedure of encryption and decryption by user A;
- S_B - modulo 2 adder used in the procedure of encryption and decryption by user A;
- $E_{A,B}$ - encryption block for users A and B, that generates the private key by encrypting the number of DNA sequences used, their identification numbers and the value of the plaintext length. This encryption procedure can be realized using a symmetric or public algorithm;
- $D_{A,B}$ - decryption block for users A and B. The output of this block consists of the number of DNA sequences used, their identification numbers and the value of the plaintext length. The algorithm used for decryption of the private key must be the same as the one chosen for encryption;
- || - concatenation block.

The following subsection defines the communication protocol between user A, the transmitter, and user B, the receiver. The structure of the cryptogram is illustrated in Fig. 5.

No. Seq (k)	Offset	ID₀ ... IDₖ	Clear Message Length	Encrypted Message

No. Seq (k)	Offset	$ID_0 \dots ID_k$	Clear Message Length	Encrypted Message

Encrypted seed

Fig. 5. Structure of the cryptogram transmitted from user A to user B

4.1   Encryption and Transmission of the Cryptogram

1. After the plaintext message is provided, a random number is generated, representing the number of sequences used for the generation of the OTP key;
2. Based on the arbitrary number generated, a list of sequence identification numbers is generated randomly. The range of these numbers corresponds to the total number of sequences stored in the local database;
3. For each identification number generated, the local database generates its corresponding DNA sequence;
4. The OTP key is created by the DNA key generator, from multiplexing all the sequences provided from the DNA database and converting the resulted sequence into binary code according to the method mentioned in Sect. 2;
5. The private key is created by the encryption block E_A, from encrypting the arbitrary number of sequences used in multiplexing, their associated identification numbers, and the plaintext length value, using a symmetric or public algorithm;
6. OTP encryption is deployed by applying the modulo 2 adder S_A, adding the plaintext and the OTP key provided from the DNA key generator. After all the characters of the plaintext are encrypted, the remaining characters of the OTP key are encrypted using a symmetric or public algorithm and added as padding;
7. The cryptogram is the result of concatenating the private key with the OTP encrypted message. This cryptogram is transmitted to the receiver.

4.2   Reception and Decryption of the Cryptogram

1. Providing the cryptogram, the receivers block separates the private key from the OTP encrypted message;
2. The private key is received by the decryption block D_A, which extracts the number of sequences used in generating the OTP key, their associated identification numbers, and the plaintext length value. The identification numbers extracted are transmitted to the local DNA database;
3. For each identification number extracted, the local database generates its corresponding DNA sequence and transmits it to the DNA key generator;
4. The OTP key is created by the receivers DNA key generator, after multiplexing all the sequences provided from the DNA database and converting the resulted sequence into binary code according to the method mentioned in Sect. 2. This key is the same as the one generated at the transmitting side;

5. OTP decryption is realized by means of modulo 2 adder S_B, adding the OTP encrypted message and the OTP key provided from the DNA key generator. This procedure is realized character wise, until the final character is decrypted. This final character is determined from the plain message length value extracted from the private key. The remaining characters from the cryptogram are considered padding, and will not be processed.

5   Security Analysis

In order to measure the security of the algorithm key space, known plaintext and chosen plaintext analysis were done, and statistical measurements were performed in order to measure the security of the algorithm, to illustrate the randomness and dissimilarity of the ciphertext from the plaintext.

Experimental results were realized using a plaintext of 6000 characters. The following statistical evaluations were made: histogram, correlation and measurement of the entropies. Matlab simulations were used [14].

5.1   Key Space

The key space represents the total number of possible keys used. This parameter reveals the capacity of the algorithm to resist possible brute force attack.

Our algorithm is proposing a key generation method using a number of DNA sequences chosen from a public database which contains millions of sequences. The number of chosen sequences is randomly variable. The selected sequences are then multiplexed using an appropriate offset, which can be variable as well. All these data (seed), necessary to generate the OTP key (as presented in Fig. 3) are encrypted using a secure algorithm (for example AES-128/ AES-256), meaning that the brute force to crack it is strong enough for most applications ($2^{128}/2^{256}$).

5.2   Known Plaintext and Chosen Plaintext Analysis

The database, being public, could be vulnerable to known plaintext or chosen plaintext attacks, but taking into account that in the key generation method, the number of used sequences is random, the offset is also variable and that the resulted key represents the outcome of multiplexing the selected sequences, the proposed method is able to avoid the known plaintext and chosen plaintext attack.

It should be noted that the genetic database is not compulsory public, it could be a private database, and it is not necessary that this database should store real genomic sequences.

5.3   Histogram Analysis

Histogram permits visualizing the distribution of the characters contained in a given plaintext [12]. The histograms of the plaintext and of the ciphertext are given in Fig. 6.

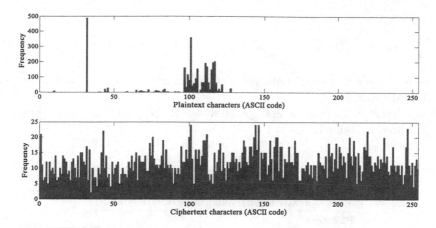

Fig. 6. Histograms of the plaintext (a) and the ciphertext (b)

From the plaintext histogram it can be observed that there is a small range of used characters, and their appearance frequency has a high value, while in the ciphertext histogram, the entire range of characters is applied, all of them having an approximately equal probability of occurring. The same behavior is observed if the plaintext is using only one character (Fig. 7).

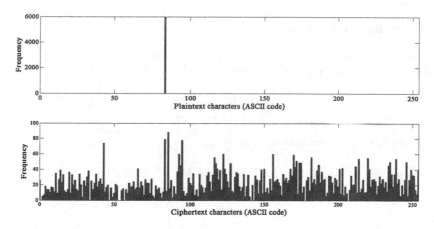

Fig. 7. Histograms of the plaintext (a) and the ciphertext (b) of a sequence that contain 6000 characters of the same symbol

5.4   Information Entropy Analysis

Under the assumption that the plaintext and the ciphertext are memoryless [1,11], the information entropy, which measures the randomness of a variable, is given by Shannons formula:

$$H(s) = -\sum_{i=1}^{M} p_i \cdot \log_2 p_i \qquad [bits/symbol] \tag{1}$$

p_i meaning the occurrence probability of the character i of the alphabet composed of M symbols.

Experimental information entropy analyses of the plaintext and cryptogram are presented in Table 1.

Table 1. Plaintext and ciphertext entropy analysis.

Type of text	Entropy value(bits/ASCII symbol)
Plaintext	4.5372
Ciphertext	7.9797

While both (the plaintext and the ciphertext) being assumed memoryless, it can be noticed that there is a great increase of the entropy in the cryptogram compared with the plaintext, reaching a value close to its maximum value (8 bits/symbol) for the ASCII code, which shows that the proposed algorithm is effective [1].

5.5   Correlation Analysis

In statistics, correlation measures the relationship between two sets of data. The correlation coefficient between the random variables X and Y is [13]:

$$\rho_{X,Y} = \frac{Cov\{X,Y\}}{\sqrt{\sigma_x^2 + \sigma_Y^2}} \tag{2}$$

where $CovX, Y$ is the covariance function:

$$Cov\{X,Y\} = E\{[X - E\{X\}] \cdot [Y - E\{Y\}]\} \tag{3}$$

E{} is the average(expectation) operator:

$$E\{X\} = \frac{1}{M} \sum_{i=1}^{M} x_i \cdot p_i \tag{4}$$

and $\sigma^2\{\}$ is the dispersion operator:

$$\sigma_x^2 = E\{[X - E\{X\}]^2\} = \frac{1}{M} \sum_{i=1}^{M} (x_i - E\{X\})^2 \tag{5}$$

The range of values the correlation coefficient takes is $\rho \in [-1; 1]$. If $\rho = 1$, the variables X and Y are linearly dependent, meaning that the knowledge of

Table 2. Autocorrelation and intercorrelation analysis.

Correlation analysis	Coeficient value
Plaintext autocorrelation	1
Intercorrelation between plaintext and ciphertext	0.0806

one variable reveals totally the behavior of the other variable. If $\rho = 0$, the two variables analyzed are uncorrelated.

In cryptography, the correlation between the plaintext and the ciphertext should be as small as possible ($\rho \to 0$), which means that there is no possible link between the two.

Table 2 presents the measured correlation coefficient values for the plaintext auto-correlation and for plaintext-ciphertext intercorrelation. The decreasing of ρ from its maximum value (1) in the case of plaintext autocorrelation to 0.0806 for the intercorrelation means that the proposed algorithm is effective from this point of view too.

6   Conclusions

In this article a new OTP cryptosystem based on DNA random sequences was presented. Starting from the DNA structure, an infinite number of OTP keys can be generated by multiplexing these sequences. This algorithm can be useful in full duplex communication applications.

There is no need to send the entire OTP key, only a private key (seed), which consists of the total number of DNA sequences used in the process of multiplexing and their associated identification number. Thus the key management becomes very easy. The transmission of the private key requires a high level of security (e.q. AES-128/256 or other).

An implementation for text transmission and security measurements that proves its effectiveness were done.

7   Future Work

Further implementation of this algorithm would consist in:

- Expanding the application for image transmission;
- Implementing a procedure that dynamically updates the sequences stored in the local database when the receiver decrypts the cryptogram. The new sequence will be the OTP key resulted from the multiplexing procedure;
- Improvement of the algorithm by introducing a permutation block to create confusion;
- Comparison with other algorithms (e.q. chaos based).

References

1. Shannon, C.E.: Communication theory of secrecy systems. Bell Syst. Tech. J. **28**(4), 656–715 (1949)
2. Schneier, B.: Applied Cryptography: Protocols, Algorithms, and Source Code. Wiley, New York (1996)
3. Stallings, W.: Cryptography and Network Security: Principles and Practice, 5th edn. Prentice Hall, Englewood Cliffs (2011)
4. Vernam, G.S.: Cipher printing telegraph systems. J. Am. Inst. Electr. Eng. **11**(5), 109–115 (1926)
5. Nevill-Manning, C.G., Witten, I.H.: Protein is incompressible. In: Proceedings of the Conference on Data Compression, p. 257 (1999)
6. Borda, M., Tornea, M., Terebes, R., Malutan, R.: New DNA based random sequence generation and OTP encryption systems for transmission and storage. In: Proceedings of SECITC (2013)
7. Borda, M., Tornea, M., Terebes, R., Malutan, R.: Method and Cryptographic OTP System Based on DNA Random Sequences. Best Patent Request at ProInvent 2013, No. of patent application A10003/14.02.2013 (2013)
8. Tornea, O.: Ph.D. thesis Contributions to DNA Cryptography: Applications to Text and Image Secure Transmission. UTCN (2013)
9. Besnon, D.A., Karsch-Mizrachi, I., Lipman, D.J., Ostell, J., Sayers, E.W.: National Center for Bio-technology Information. http://www.ncbi.nlm.nih.gov/pubmed/21071399
10. Calladine, C.R., Drew, H.R., Luisi, B.F., Travers, A.A.: Understanding DNA the Molecule & How it Works. Academic Press, Amsterdam (2004)
11. Borda, M.: Fundamentals in Information Theory and Coding. Springer, Heidelberg (2011)
12. Stark, H., Woods, J.W.: Probability and Random Processes with Application to Signal Processing, 3rd edn. Prentice Hall, Upper Saddle River (2002)
13. Kay, S.M.: Statistical Signal Processing. Prentice Hall, Englewood Cliffs (1993/1998)
14. Mathworks (2015): Global Optimization Toolbox: User's Guide (R2015a), The MathWorks (1994–2015), Inc. http://www.mathworks.com/help/matlab/index.html

Evaluation of Lightweight Block Ciphers
for Embedded Systems

Oana Barahtian[1], Mihai Cuciuc[2], Lucian Petcana[1], Cătălin Leordeanu[1](✉),
and Valentin Cristea[1]

[1] Faculty of Automatic Control and Computers,
University 'Politehnica' of Bucharest, Bucharest, Romania
{oana.barahtian,lucian.petcana}@cti.pub.ro,
{catalin.leordeanu,valentin.cristea}@cs.pub.ro
[2] Microchip Technology Inc., Bucharest, Romania
mihai.cuciuc@gmail.com

Abstract. Ubiquitous Computing and the Internet of Things are two
paradigms which have gained a lot of popularity lately. They are based
on a multitude of low power devices which usually communicate through
wireless connections. To avoid security and reliability problems, efficient
cryptographic algorithms must be used for authentication, key exchange
and message encryption. Due to the wide range of such algorithms and
their characteristics, some ciphers are more suitable for implementation
on certain platforms than others. In this paper we propose solutions
for the implementation and evaluation of block ciphers on 8-bit, 16-bit
and 32-bit microcontrollers. We focus on widely used algorithms such as
AES (the tinyAES implementation), as well as others which are suitable
for embedded platforms, such as the Simon and Speck family of block
ciphers. The conclusions of this paper are drawn based on the performance and energy efficiency of each algorithm.

Keywords: Block ciphers · Embedded systems · Cryptographic algorithms · Simon and Speck

1 Introduction

Computing systems have spread beyond the traditional desktop, leading to the
paradigm known as Ubiquitous Computing [2]. It refers to the fact that computation can take place at any time, on any device, on any platform, thus leading
to the emergence of smart environments. This shift of the computing paradigm
brings along a number of other challenges and issues which need to be resolved.
For example, as such devices are usually very small, driven by microcontrollers
and can communicate through wireless connections, power consumption becomes
a very important factor which influences their capabilities. Many algorithms
previously established for use on desktop systems were reevaluated in order to
efficiently run on such devices.

© Springer International Publishing Switzerland 2015
I. Bica et al. (Eds.): SECITC 2015, LNCS 9522, pp. 49–58, 2015.
DOI: 10.1007/978-3-319-27179-8_4

The need for security is also very important in this discussion [3]. Cryptographic algorithms are essential in order to provide authentication, protection against eavesdropping or to verify data integrity. The AES algorithm [4] is considered the reference block cipher and it is in use for a very large number of applications and communication protocols [5]. It is in use on a wide range of devices, from powerful servers to very lightweight devices, such as fitness bracelets and other wearables [1,6]. However, it may not be the most suitable block cipher, compared to others which are not as widespread.

This paper proposes an evaluation methodology for block ciphers on various embedded systems and argues that there are other existing algorithms more suitable than AES. Notable candidates include TEA [11] as well as the Simon and Speck family of block ciphers [9]. We propose a thorough evaluation on a wide range of hardware platforms, such as 8-bit, 16-bit and 32-bit microcontrollers. Our analysis focuses on the performance (and consequently, energy efficiency) of each algorithm and based on the test results we draw conclusions regarding their suitability.

The rest of the paper is structured as follows. In Sect. 2 we study similar evaluations present in the scientific literature. Section 3 describes the encryption algorithms which are used in this paper while Sect. 4 draws conclusions on their suitability for each platform and describes the hardware setup of the experiments, which are detailed in Sect. 5. Section 6 draws the conclusions of the paper and outlines the areas for further research.

2   Related Work

Testing and evaluation of cryptographic algorithms is not a new field. In an era when there are many research groups dedicated to cryptology, this is a very dynamic field. The interval between the publication of a new cipher and the time when attacks are developed for it is becoming shorter and shorter. Also, organizations such as the National Institute of Standards and Technology (NIST) are helping by publishing standards and official test suites for such algorithms [18,19].

A general characteristic of most block ciphers is the fact that most allow parallel execution with very little overhead. This lead to the search for different hardware platforms, in order to gain speed or energy efficiency. One such approach is COPACOBANA (Cost-Optimized Parallel COde Breaker) [20]. Their solution was based on a modular structure of FPGAs. Due to the fact that a cryptographic algorithm is usually based on the execution of multiple rounds, with little or no communication inside a single round, it can be mapped to a simple FPGA architecture, similar to a Spartan3.

The COPACOBANA architecture can be used for multiple applications for encryption or hash functions. It can be used for the evaluation of algorithms such as DES, AES or SHA-1 or the testing of different attacks on these algorithms [21]. However, this approach is oriented towards the use of their COPACOBANA FPGA-based architecture for different cryptographic tasks, not the evaluation and deployment of the algorithms on different hardware platforms.

Apart from this approach, there are other research papers oriented towards the use of cryptographic algorithms on different hardware platforms. AES has received a lot of attention, of course [5,16]. Other algorithms, such as TEA and xTEA have been initially developed for such embedded systems [7]. This paper however evaluates a wide range of systems from 8-bit to 32-bit microcontrollers, which provides a more comprehensive analysis than if it would have been focused on a single platform.

3 Block Ciphers

In block ciphers the plaintext is divided in blocks (usually 64-bits or 128-bits) of fixed-length, which are then encrypted into blocks of ciphertexts using the secret key. Techniques known as modes of operation have to be used when we encrypt messages longer than the block size. To be useful, a mode must be at least as secure and efficient as the underlying cipher.

A block cipher is called iterated cipher if the ciphertext is computed by iteratively applying an invertible transformation (round function) several times to the plaintext. All round transformations are key-dependend and transformations of the round i obtains its own subkey k_i obtained from the key scheduling algorithm applied to the cipher key, K.

There are many ways of building iterative ciphers, but the two most widespread approaches are: Balanced Feistel Networks (BFNs) and substitution-permutation networks (SPNs). A Feistel cipher with block size of $2n$ and r rounds could be defined as follows [17]. Let C_0^L and C_0^R be the left and the right halves of the plaintext, respectively, each of n bits. The round function G operates as follows:

$$C_i^L = C_{i-1}^R$$
$$C_i^R = F(K, C_{i-1}^R) \oplus C_i^L,$$

The ciphertext is the concatenation of C_r^L and C_r^R. Typically, the round F-functions are chosen to be highly nonlinear key-dependent transformation with good diffusion. A standard way to provide these properties is to use substitution-permutation structure consisting of three layers [15]: In the first layer the subkey k_i is added to x_i (the input of the round i), which provides key dependency. In the second layer, nonlinear functions ($S-boxes$) acting on parts are applied in parallel. In the third layer, these parts are diffused using a linear mapping (permutation).

Because in this paper we deal with lightweight cryptographic algorithms, we choose to present the AES and the rest of algorithms used in our test configuration. Compared with traditional block ciphers, lightweight ciphers have three main properties. Firstly, applications for constrained devices are unlikely to require the encryption of large amounts of data, and hence there is no requirement of high throughput. Secondly, in these environments due to lack of data for attackers the lightweight ciphers only need to achieve moderate security. Lastly, lightweight ciphers are usually implemented on hardware devices and a small part of them will be also implemented on software platforms, such as 8-bit controllers. Therefore, hardware performance will be the primary consideration for these ciphers.

3.1   AES

The block cipher Rijndael was designed by Daemen and Rijmen and standardized by NIST in 2000 as the Advanced Encryption Standard (AES) [4]. In 2005, Feldhofer et al. proposed a hardware implementation of the AES which is brought down to a size of only 3100 gate equivalents, optimized for low-resource requirements [16]. Most AES operations are byte oriented, executing efficiently on 8-bit processors. As 8-bits operations can be combined to form a 32-bit operations, AES can be implemented with success on 32-bit processors too. Several other implementations [12,13,16] show that AES-128 can also be used as a secure and lightweight block cipher in many constrained environments.

3.2   TEA and xTEA

The block cipher xTEA, designed by Needham and Wheeler, was published as a technical report in 1997. The cipher was a result of fixing some weaknesses in TEA (designed by the same authors) used in Microsoft's Xboxes. xTEA is a 64-round Feistel cipher with a block size of 64 bits and a key size of 128 bits. The best known hardware implementation of xTEA requires 3490 gate equivalents [11].

3.3   Simon and Speck

Simon and Speck are two families of ciphers proposed by the NSA in June 2013 [9], and were designed to provide high performance across a wide range of devices. Simon has been optimized for hardware implementations, while its sister algorithm, Speck, has been optimized for software implementations. They were both built on ARX (Add-Rotate-XOR) philosophy, using only basic arithmetic operations such as modular addition, XOR, bitwise AND and bit rotation on different block sizes (32, 48 and 64 bits) with key sizes (64, 72 or 96, 96 or 128 respectively).

Block cipher Simon has a Feistel structure and its round function under a fixed round key k is defined on inputs x and y as:

$$R_k(x,y) = ((y \oplus f(x) \oplus k), x), where$$
$$f_k(x,y) = ((x \lll 1) \ \& \ (x \lll 8)) \oplus (x \lll 2)$$

The Speck block cipher has a structure similar to that of Threefish. Its round function under a fixed round key k is defined on inputs x and y as:

$$R_k(x,y) = (f_k(x,y), f_k(x,y) \oplus (y \lll \beta)), where$$
$$f_k(x,y) = ((x \ggg \alpha) + y) \oplus k,$$
$$\alpha = 7, \beta = 2 \ for \ block \ size \ 32 \ and \ \alpha = 8, \beta = 3 \ otherwise.$$

Although Speck is not a Feistel cipher itself, it can be represented as a composition of two Feistel maps as described in [9].

Hardware efficiency can be measured in many different ways: latency, clock cycles, power consumption, throughput, area requirements and so on. Among them, area requirements (measured as GE - gate equivalents) is the most important parameter [14] because it minimize the cost and the power efficiency requirements.

4 Testing Environments

Contrary to a general purpose computer, embedded systems are designed to run a specific task while being constrained by very limited resources. However, they still can run a wide range of algorithms, usually incurring a penalty in performance. The industry has developed many architectures of varying complexities to address the growing need for embedded computing and as such testing the suitability of an algorithm for embedded platforms cannot be done on a single system. In order to evaluate the potential of security algorithms on embedded platforms this paper targets the following architectures, represented by specific microcontrollers (Table 1).

Table 1. The architectures used for evaluation.

Architecture	ALU width [bits]	Microcontroller
AVR32	32	AT32UC3A0128
AVR mega	8	ATmega328P
dsPIC	16	dsPIC30F5013
MSP430	16	MSP430FG4619
PIC16	8	PIC16F1947
PIC18	8	PIC18F46K22
PIC24	16	PIC24FJ128GA
PIC32	32	PIC32MX270F256D
PIC32	32	PIC32MZ2048ECH144

Ideally one could test the same implementation on each architecture in order to assess its performance, but since these are not instruction-set compatible this is impossible. In order to keep the implementation identical only algorithms developed in C have been employed, but in this case the effects of the compiler's optimizations can also be noticed in the results. As such, the architecture is considered only together with the compiler it was used with. Where multiple compilers have been tested, only the best results are being considered. The measure of an algorithm's performance on a particular implementation is considered the number of instruction cycles it takes to encode and decode particular sets of data. This, rather than the code size is considered more important on the basis of the fact that currently most architectures offer large internal program memories and all are limited by power used. Since the energy required to execute an instruction cycle can be obtained from the microcontroller's datasheet, the total impact on battery life can be derived for each algorithm and architecture. This test does not target the security of an algorithm, nor its susceptibility to side-channel attacks.

The algorithms chosen for this analysis are AES (the tinyAES implementation [8]), TEA and Speck. While other algorithms are also targeted at resource-constrained devices, these three cover a wide range of scenarios: AES is a standard reference point, TEA benefits from a very simple implementation while Speck is a comparatively new algorithm optimized for software implementations.

5   Experimental Results

In this section we provide details on the experiments we performed on using the previously mentioned architectures. We started with performance evaluation for each algorithm.

Table 2. Instruction cycles taken for one encryption and one decryption of a 64 byte block using the AES-128 implementation on the specific architecture, with compiler optimizations for execution speed enabled.

MCU	Compiler	Algorithm	Cycles
PIC24EP128GP202	XC16 v1.24	AES/64 Byte	50699
dsPIC30F5013	XC16 v1.24	AES/64 Byte	51751
AT32UC3A0128	AVR32 GCC 4.4.7	AES/64 Byte	58773
PIC32MX270F256D	XC32 v1.34	AES/64 Byte	63694
PIC32MZ2048ECH144	XC32 v1.34	AES/64 Byte	67266
ATmega328P	AVR8 GCC 4.8.1	AES/64 Byte	85106
MSP430FG4619	IAR 6.30	AES/64 Byte	259178
PIC18F46K22	XC8 v1.33	AES/64 Byte	606352
PIC16F1947	XC8 v1.33	AES/64 Byte	2518930

5.1   Performance Evaluation

The AES [8] implementation shows little performance improvements when being run on larger architectures, having comparable performances on both 8 bit and 32 bit AVR cores. This similarity can be traced back to the implementation of tinyAES which makes extensive use of single byte operations, thus leaving the larger possible data throughput for bigger architectures unused (Table 2).

Notable exceptions are the 8 bit PIC architectures that have a single accumulator and relatively small numbers of instructions. These particularities require these architectures to do a lot of extra moving of data for processing, but also provide the implementation advantages of simpler cores.

The single result that stands out for this implementation is the relatively low performance provided by the MSP430 MCU. However, given that this algorithm relies heavily on multiplications it incurs a penalty on this architecture that provides a hardware multiplier but it takes 8 CPU cycles to perform the operation. Although this is a separate peripheral, leaving the CPU free while it is performing the computation, the algorithm is not optimized for this setup, stalling the program to perform many multiplications in sequence. The AVR 8 bit core, having a 2 cycle multiplier can thus score better in this situation.

Table 3. Instruction cycles required to do one encryption and one decryption of an 8 byte block using the Speck algorithm with compiler optimizations for speed enabled.

MCU	Compiler	Algorithm	Cycles
PIC32MZ2048ECH144	XC32 v1.34	Speck/8 Byte	2374
PIC32MX270F256D	XC32 v1.34	Speck/8 Byte	2428
AT32UC3A0128	AVR32 GCC 4.4.7	Speck/8 Byte	2802
dsPIC30F5013	XC16 v1.24	Speck/8 Byte	4915
PIC24EP128GP202	XC16 v1.24	Speck/8 Byte	5221
MSP430FG4619	IAR 6.30	Speck/8 Byte	12338
ATmega328P	AVR8 GCC 4.8.1	Speck/8 Byte	28518
PIC16F1947	XC8 v1.33	Speck/8 Byte	87362
PIC18F46K22	XC8 v1.33	Speck/8 Byte	94941

Since the Speck implementation uses 32 bit data extensively, the performances are clearly clustered according to specific architecture sizes. Both PIC32 architectures score the lowest numbers of instructions, closely followed by the AVR32 core, the three 16 bit cores follow (the dsPIC30, the PIC24 and the MSP430) while the 8 bit machines require the most work additional work to process the large data (Table 3).

The results of the TEA implementation follow a similar trend to those for the Speck algorithm. This is expected as both implementations rely heavily on using 32 bit data (Table 4).

Ideally one would clearly determine which algorithms are faster regardless of architecture, but this cannot be established in this case. Naively considering encryption of a 64 byte block to take 4 times longer than an 8 byte block with the Speck algorithm (and 4 times longer than a 16 byte block using the TEA algorithm) the algorithm performances can be compared for a single architecture.

Tables 5 and 6 show that even for similar architectures the compiler optimizations can have a very large effect on the execution speeds, enough to change the

Table 4. Instruction cycles required to do one encryption and one decryption of a 16 byte block using the TEA algorithm with compiler optimizations for speed enabled.

MCU	Compiler	Algorithm	Cycles
PIC32MX270F256D	XC32 v1.34	TEA/16 Byte	1194
PIC32MZ2048ECH144	XC32 v1.34	TEA/16 Byte	1194
AT32UC3A0128	AVR32 GCC 4.4.7	TEA/16 Byte	1523
dsPIC30F5013	XC16 v1.24	TEA/16 Byte	3742
PIC24EP128GP202	XC16 v1.24	TEA/16 Byte	3942
MSP430FG4619	IAR 6.30	TEA/16 Byte	8960
ATmega328P	AVR8 GCC 4.8.1	TEA/16 Byte	13879
PIC16F1947	XC8 v1.33	TEA/16 Byte	21341
PIC18F46K22	XC8 v1.33	TEA/16 Byte	22381

Table 5. Algorithm execution cycles for a single architecture (PIC16F1947).

MCU	Compiler	Algorithm	Cycles
PIC16F1947	XC8 v1.33	TEA/64 Byte	85364
PIC16F1947	XC8 v1.33	Speck/64 Byte	698896
PIC16F1947	XC8 v1.33	AES/64 Byte	2518930

Table 6. Algorithm execution cycles for a single architecture (PIC18F46K22).

MCU	Compiler	Algorithm	Cycles
PIC18F46K22	XC8 v1.33	TEA/64 Byte	89524
PIC18F46K22	XC8 v1.33	AES/64 Byte	606352
PIC18F46K22	XC8 v1.33	Speck/64 Byte	759528

ranking of algorithms. While tinyAES performs faster than Speck on the PIC18, on the PIC16 it falls behind. Additionally, even the implementation choice of a particular algorithm can make it more suitable for a specific architecture, as is the case for AES which offers little improvement when migrating to large architectures.

6   Conclusions and Future Work

Our experiments show that the encryption algorithm needs to be considered closely with the whole system architecture both from a security standpoint as well as a performance one. As such, balancing security, low cost and performance requires embedded system designers to consider encryption a requirement of the product and take it into account when selecting microcontroller architecture.

However, it is to be noted that the simpler TEA algorithm outperforms the others on every architecture thus promising to offer security even to the tightest constrained devices. Another notable result is that the implementation details of the algorithm needs to be properly matched up with the targeted architecture, as using the AES implementation built around many 8-bit operations yields little improvement in performance when moving to more capable processors. The Speck algorithm's performance is situated in between the other two, with the exceptions of two 8-bit architectures (PIC18F46K22 and ATmega328P) where its running time is longer than that of AES.

As future work, we intend to perform an analysis of the algorithms using the NIST Statistical Tests. Although these tests are not specifically related to the algorithms themselves, this will offer insight into the security and possible attacks.

Acknowledgment. The work has been funded by the *"Sectoral Operational Programme Human Resources Development 2007–2013 of the Ministry of European Funds"* through the Financial Agreements POSDRU/159/1.5/S/134398 and POSDRU 187/1.5/S/155420.

This research presented is also supported by the project *clueFarm*: Information system based on cloud services accessible through mobile devices, to increase product quality and business development farms - PN-II-PT-PCCA-2013-4-0870.

References

1. Lee, H., Lee, K., Shin, Y.: AES implementation and performance evaluation on 8-bit microcontrollers, arXiv preprint (2009). arXiv:0911.0482
2. Abowd, G.D., Mynatt, E.D.: Charting past, present, and future research in ubiquitous computing. ACM Trans. Comput. Hum. Interact. (TOCHI) **7**(1), 29–58 (2000)
3. Buttyan, L., Hubaux, J.-P.: Security and cooperation in wireless networks. In: Thwarting Malicious and Selfish Behavior in the Age of Ubiquitous Computing. Cambridge University Press (2007)
4. Blumenthal, U., Maino, F., McCloghrie, K.: The advanced encryption standard (AES) cipher algorithm in the SNMP user-based security model. Internet proposed standard RFC 3826 (2004)
5. Hamalainen, P., Alho, T., Hannikainen, M., Hamalainen, T.D.: Design and implementation of low-area and low-power AES encryption hardware core. In: 9th EUROMICRO Conference on Digital System Design: Architectures, Methods and Tools, DSD 2006, pp. 577–583. IEEE (2006)
6. Passow, P., Stoll, N., Junginger, S., Thurow, K.: A wireless sensor node for long-term monitoring in life science applications. In: IEEE International Instrumentation and Measurement Technology Conference (I2MTC 2013), pp. 898–901. IEEE (2013)
7. Moon, D., Hwang, K., Lee, W.I., Lee, S.-J., Lim, J.-I.: Impossible differential cryptanalysis of reduced round XTEA and TEA. In: Daemen, J., Rijmen, V. (eds.) FSE 2002. LNCS, vol. 2365, pp. 49–60. Springer, Heidelberg (2002)
8. Dalmisli, K.V., Ors, B.: Design of new tiny circuits for AES encryption algorithm. In: 3rd International Conference on Signals, Circuits and Systems (SCS 2009), pp. 1–5. IEEE (2009)
9. Beaulieu, R., Shors, D., Smith, J., Treatman-Clark, S., Weeks, B., Wingers, L.: The SIMON and SPECK Families of Lightweight Block Ciphers. IACR Cryptology ePrint Archive 2013, p. 404 (2013)

10. Beaulieu, R., Douglas S., Smith, J., Treatman-Clark, S., Weeks, B., Wingers, L.: The SIMON and SPECK Block Ciphers on AVR 8-bit Microcontrollers (2015)
11. Kaps, J.-P.: Chai-tea, cryptographic hardware implementations of xTEA. In: Chowdhury, D.R., Rijmen, V., Das, A. (eds.) INDOCRYPT 2008. LNCS, vol. 5365, pp. 363–375. Springer, Heidelberg (2008)
12. Shirai, T., Shibutani, K., Akishita, T., Moriai, S., Iwata, T.: The 128-bit blockcipher CLEFIA (extended abstract). In: Biryukov, A. (ed.) FSE 2007. LNCS, vol. 4593, pp. 181–195. Springer, Heidelberg (2007)
13. Pramstaller, N., Mangard, S., Dominikus, S., Wolkerstorfer, J.: Efficient AES implementations on ASICs and FPGAs. In: Dobbertin, H., Rijmen, V., Sowa, A. (eds.) AES 2005. LNCS, vol. 3373, pp. 98–112. Springer, Heidelberg (2005)
14. Wu, W., Zhang, L.: LBlock: a lightweight block cipher. In: Lopez, J., Tsudik, G. (eds.) ACNS 2011. LNCS, vol. 6715, pp. 327–344. Springer, Heidelberg (2011)
15. Bogdanov, A.: Analysis and design of block cipher constructions. Europischer Univ.-Verlag (2010)
16. Feldhofer, M., Wolkerstorfer, J., Rijmen, V.: AES implementation on a grain of sand. IEEE Proc. Inf. Sec. 152(1), 13–20 (2005)
17. Knudsen, L.R.: Practically secure Feistel ciphers. In: Anderson, R. (ed.) FSE 1993. LNCS, vol. 809, pp. 211–221. Springer, Heidelberg (1994)
18. Murphy, S.: The power of NISTs statistical testing of AES candidates. Preprint, 17 January 2000
19. Soto, J.: Randomness testing of the AES candidate algorithms. In: NIST (1999). csrc.nist.gov
20. Kumar, S., Paar, C., Pelzl, J., Pfeiffer, G., Schimmler, M.: Breaking ciphers with COPACOBANA – a cost-optimized parallel code breaker. In: Goubin, L., Matsui, M. (eds.) CHES 2006. LNCS, vol. 4249, pp. 101–118. Springer, Heidelberg (2006)
21. Gneysu, T., Pfeiffer, G., Paar, C., Schimmler, M.: Three years of evolution: cryptanalysis with COPACOBANA. In: Workshop Record of SHARCS (2009)

CART Versus CHAID Behavioral Biometric Parameter Segmentation Analysis

Ionela Roxana Glăvan[1], Daniel Petcu[2]($\boxtimes$), and Emil Simion[3]

[1] Department of Statistics, The Bucharest University of Economic Studies,
Bucharest, Romania
roxana.glavan10@yahoo.com
[2] Doctoral School of Electronics, Telecommunications and Information Technology,
University Politehnica, Bucharest, Romania
danpetcu33@yahoo.com
[3] Department of Mathematical Models and Methods, Faculty of Applied Sciences,
University Politehnica, Bucharest, Romania
esimion@fmi.unibuc.ro

Abstract. With the large scale deployment of mobile telecommunication infrastructure offering fast access to mobile internet users, the data content on all internet web platforms will increase and thus, creates the necessity for the platform owners to effectively analyze the quality of internet traffic on their web pages. This implies in depth examination of user behavior based on the interaction with the web platform by further adapting non-intrusive techniques. Behavioral biometric techniques offer a positive solution in this regard and are implemented with success by different vendors. In this paper we propose an implementation analysis for CART and CHAID segmentation of behavioral biometric features. The two methods are compared in order to come forward with solution for the behavior categorization and segmentation of active users.

Keywords: Behavioral biometrics · Information security · Decision trees · Classification and regression tree (CART) · Chi-square automatic interaction detection (CHAID)

1 Introduction

Biometrics industry has the purpose of providing enhanced data security protection. Identity authentication and verification [1] is of great significance, as human behavior is gradually shifting from face to face to online interaction. This shift has become the primary driver in the implementation of networked society [4]. In scientific researches there are three major types of biometrics: behavioral, physiological, and token based. Physiological biometrics relies on biological traits such as face, iris, DNA, fingerprint and retina pattern. Token based biometrics requires the use of a security device that generates security keys and an ID card. Behavioral biometrics uses the way individuals interact with the authentication system. This measured level of behavioral interaction

© Springer International Publishing Switzerland 2015
I. Bica et al. (Eds.): SECITC 2015, LNCS 9522, pp. 59–68, 2015.
DOI: 10.1007/978-3-319-27179-8_5

can further be divided in two categories. The first category includes systems based on voice, dynamic signature, gait, eye motion and in the second category one may find systems that use keystroke dynamics, lexical and content specific behavior. The main reason that advocates for behavioral biometrics is that they offer increased convenience in data acquisition because they do not require any special or dedicated hardware. Another important aspect is that these systems use for input less invasive methods of acquiring biometric data, generally associated with machine based interaction. In terms of necessity, these traits need to be easy verifiable and identifiable. The user behavioral biometric traits depend on their permanence character and on the constructed distinctiveness metrics. Based on the user interaction perspective, physiological biometrics may be affected by skill of the individual as their use implies certain level of cooperation [3]. Furthermore, because behavioral biometrics technologies do not introduce delays in operation and are implemented silently, in most of the online platforms, one can state that their acceptance level in society is high [5]. This silent implementation is performed with no other cooperation requirements apart from the behavioral data storage user permission acknowledgment. By comparing the number of behavioral biometrics research papers with physiological ones we may see that techniques approaching online user interaction are fewer than traditional physiological approaches. Most of the traditional biometric systems approaches use extracted traits with specific predominance from fingerprint [2]. In current interconnected information based society, due to the mobility increase and the ease of access to internet connected devices, there is real challenge for extraction and segmentation of relevant behavioral traits [9]. The data that is extracted from human-device interaction offers less robustness for authentication purpose but nevertheless it can be used effectively for verification and user profile segmentation based on behavioral aspects. Furthermore the extraction was performed with notification of behavioral data storage and the permission of each user. This paper presents an indirect biometric based approach and establishes a segmentation parameter analysis of behavioral traits extracted from a developed online platform. In the following section two of this paper we present details for both CART and CHAID methodologies. In this section we also provide information on our related work implementation and further details. Finally the paper presents the delivered results and the obtained CART Tree and user behavior diagrams with IBM SPSS Statistics 20.

2   Methodology and Related Work Analysis

2.1   Methodology

CART and CHAID are decision algorithms that deliver solutions for data classification and segmentation offering output decision tree tables [8]. Classification and regression tree method, CART, represents a major milestone in the evolution of non-parametric statistics, machine learning, artificial intelligence and data mining. It is an algorithm, based on binary decision trees constructed by the re-cursive division of a parent node in two child nodes, capable of computing nominal and continuous attributes both as targets and predictors [10]. In order to construct the decision trees, CART methodology uses a set of historical data called learning samples with preassigned classes for all observations. The rule that is applied for split in CART algorithm follows the below:

If CONDITION is applied instance goes left, and goes right otherwise

for continuous attributes the CONDITION is treated as attribute Xi $<=$ C and for the nominal attributes the CONDITION is expressed as a member from an explicit list values [13].

The scope of this algorithm is to choose the division mechanism of each node in such a way that all child nodes become pure [8,13].

This is achieved based on the "Gini rule", similar to entropy or information-gain criterion. For a binary target, "Gini measure of impurity" of a node t is defined in Eq. 1

$$G(t) = 1 - p(t)^2 - (1 - p(t))^2 \qquad (1)$$

where $p(t)$ is defined as the relative frequency of class 1 in the node, and the improvement generated by a split into left (L) and right (R) children is defined in Eq. 2

$$I(P) = G(P) - qG(L) - (1 - q)G(R) \qquad (2)$$

where q is defined as the fraction of left going instances and P is defined as the parent node [13]. Further details regarding CART methodology may be found in [11,12].

Chi-square automatic interaction detection method, better known as CHAID relies on tree classification variance analysis in order to achieve segmentation and prediction of input data. All the values of potential predictor features are evaluated using a statistical significance test criterion. More specifically, it uses the p-value of the Chi-square.

In every point of the CHAID analysis, it is identified the best predictor from a subgroup of unities. The main aspect is to merge the nearest categories from the multitude of independent variables with many categories [8]. The outputs of our analysis are the computed trees from where decision and related information can be interpreted. The main difference between CART and CHAID resides in the tree construction process. In order to avoid overfitting the data, all methods try to limit the size of the resulting tree. CHAID algorithm achieves this by using a statistical end process rule that discontinuous the tree growth. In contrast, CART methodology firstly grows the full tree and then prunes it back. Another difference between these two methods is that CHAID algorithm uses a single dataset to construct the final tree, whereas CART uses a computed training set to build the tree and a holdout set to prune it. In terms of the splitting mechanism, CHAID methodology is more flexible as it allows multiple splits, compared with the binary split of the CART methodology. In addition to CART and CHAID methodology the unique behavior pattern for each user may further be accessed through the proposed user behavioral diagrams that are presented in the experimental results section.

2.2 Related Work Analysis

The structural functionality of the implemented web-platform can be described in three stages. Firstly the user has to access the web-platform. Second stage relates to the automatic run of the script implemented in the web platform. This implemented script is written in PHP (Hypertext Preprocessor), a programming language frequently used for online web applications development. In the last stage is performed the MySQL database storage of data parameters. The implemented web platform PHP script will verify if there is a new user or if the present user has previously visited the platform. This is performed with the use of the specified cookie in the PHP script. A new cookie of permanent persistence containing the unique "User Key" identifier will be created in the

Table 1. Behavioral and non-behavioral traits

Trait name	Definition	Unit of measure
User key	Unique generated user key allocated for each user that accesses the web platform	N/A
Session key	Defined as Unique generated session key by the web platform	N/A
IP	IP address of user	Standard IP v4 notation
Total number of unique user session keys	Defined as the number of distinct unique session keys per user	Decimal number
Total number of pages per all sessions per user	Defined as the number of pages per all sessions per user	Decimal number
Δweb-space	Defined web-space distance between source pace and next browsed page of the platform	a-dimensional
Δtime	Defined as difference between registered time of the incoming source page inside of platform and current accessed platform web page	Seconds
Search function used	Defined as the usage of search functionality by each user that access the web platform	Yes/No
Search function type speed	Defined as the time that user writes desired keyword in search functionality of the web platform	Seconds
Nr of usages of Backspace in Search function	Defined as the number of Backspace key usages for each session for unique user that accesses web platform	Decimal number

web browser, used for accessing the web-platform, for every new user. The "Session Key" parameter identifier is generated automatically with session lifetime duration of 30 min to differentiate different access sessions for same user. In all web pages of the developed online platform, a tracking function is called in order extract and to compute the behavioral biometric traits. The time spent on each web page is further given by the difference between the current web page access time and the previous web page access time. The number of backspaces and the insertion time in the search functionality extracted from the developed web page with a developed JavaScript. All these web platform functionalities run silently in real-time during the extraction of biometric and non-biometric parameters. The biometric traits are extracted and post-processed in order to obtain maximum relevant information. In our study, the behavioral traits that are used as measured parameters in the analysis are coded in Table 1. The first three traits defined in the Table 1 are non-behavioral and the rest of them are classified as behavioral traits. In order to find solution for the best decision tree with mini-

Table 2. Behavioral traits used in the CART and CHAID analysis

Trait name	SPSS label	Segmentation details
Total number of unique session keys per user	Unique_S	Very low −1 session
		Low −2 sessions
		Medium −3 to 7 sessions
		High −8 to 12 sessions
		Very High − more than 12
Total number of accessed web pages per all sessions per user	Total_pages_acc	1 − 1 web pages
		[2–10] − between 2 and 10
		[11–20] − between 11 and 20
		[21–50] − between 21 and 50
		>50 − more than 50
Δweb-space	Delta_web_sp	0
		[1–30]
		[31–60]
		[61–90]
		>90
Δtime	Delta_time	<15s
		[15 s 5 min]
		(5 min 15 min]
		(15 min 30 min]
		>30 min

mum standard deviation and to conclude the relevance of proposed behavioral traits we evaluate both CART and CHAID methodologies.

The web-space behavioral trait is constructed based on the Levenshtein distance [6, 7] between the accessed source web-page name and the incoming web-page name. It is measured per individual user key and session. In the developed web platform all web pages are named with desired associated keyword. Usually this distance between two keywords may be computed by the minimum number of single-character alterations. For these single-character alterations literature refers to deletions, insertions or substitutions necessary to change one word into the other [6, 7].

Therefore, because Levenshtein distance in information theory and computer science is a string metric used for measuring the difference between two sequences, in our proposed analysis we emphasized its use for the constructed behavioral biometric trait.

Furthermore in the proposed analysis for obtaining better results we included a filtering mechanism for discarding non-human behavior by removing all access inputs from different IP's in less than 30 s.

The implemented CART and CHAID methodology [8] uses following input nominal traits as in Table 2.

The implementation of both CART and CHAID analysis is performed using IBM SPSS 20 software [8]. In this data set, "Unique_S" is selected as the target variable while the other three variables remain independent variables. Further, the highest number of "levels" we want in the CART decision tree, is chosen to be three. The option of Pruning the tree is also selected in order to avoid overfitting.

In the proposed methodology the CHAID growing method uses the dependent variable "Unique_S" and the following independent variables "Total_pages_acc", "Delta_web_sp", "Delta_time". The maximum tree depth is set to three and minimum cases in parent node set to 2000 and minimum cases in child node set to 1000. All three independent variables specified are included in the model and there are no rejected variables.

3   Experimental Results

The data volume up to 28000 records extracted during one month of web-platform running is preprocessed according to described CART and CHAID analysis methodology.

Applying the CHAID methodology, the best predictor for "Unique_S" parameter is given by the "Total_pages_acc" behavioral trait parameter. The selected category "more than 50" of the "Total_pages_acc" is obtained as the only significant predictor of the total "Unique_S" variable. The "1 web pages" category related note is resulted as a terminal node in the output diagram. All the users in this category have "very low" total number of accessed web pages on all sessions per user. The next best predictor for the two computed categories, from the "Total_pages_acc" parameter, is Δweb-space metrics behavioral trait. Further, the best predictor for the "between 2 and 10" category from the "Total_pages_acc" is outputted as Δtime metrics parameter. With the same mentioned category that has Δtime in the [15 s 5 min] interval, the CHAID model includes one more predictor, Δweb-space.

Using the CART method the best predictor rating for the total number of unique session keys per user is also the level for the total number of accessed web pages on all sessions per user. The results of the implemented CART method with prune tree to avoid overfitting are presented below (such in Fig. 1).

It presents two subgroups of the biometric parameter "Total_pages_acc" that are considered an indication for "Unique_S" parameter.

Without pruning tree to avoid over fitting in the implemented CART method, "Total_pages_acc" is accepted as the primary factor in the prediction of "Unique_S" parameter. "Total_pages_acc" parameter classified as "more than 50" is considered an indication of a "Unique_S". This group of users is not further subdivided. The node of users with "Total_pages_acc" less than 50 is subdivided in two child nodes. These two nodes have their "Total_pages_acc" parameter "less than 10" and "between 11 and 50". The 4th node in the CART diagram, showed in Fig. 2, is further divided in 2 child nodes. For the "between 21 and 50" and "between 11 and 20" categories from the "Total_pages_acc" accessing web-platform, the CART model includes one more predictor, Δweb-space. Over 74 % of those users segmented in "[1–30]" or "[31–60]", Δweb-space classes have a "very low" rating of total number of unique session keys per user, while 63.6 % of these users segmented

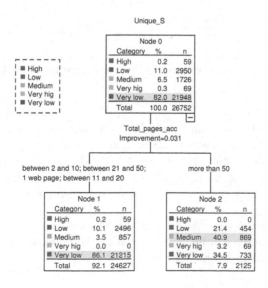

Fig. 1. CART Tree diagram with prune tree for behavioral traits model

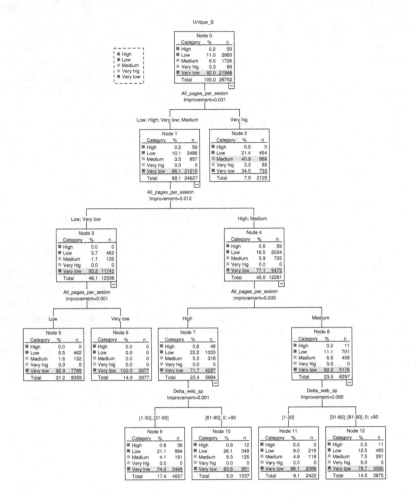

Fig. 2. CART Tree diagram without tree pruning for behavioral traits model

in "0", "[61–90]" and ">90" have "very low" unique session rating. In the second child node related to "between 11 and 20" category from the "Total_pages_acc", 86.1 % of users segmented in "[1–30]" or "0", ">31" have a "very low" rating of "Unique_S". Also approximately 80 % of users subdivided in "0" and ">31" category are categorized as "very low" total number of unique session keys per user rating.

After the conducted analysis, an important aspect that may further show the behavior pattern for each user may be seen in the constructed user behavioral diagrams such in above figure (Fig. 3).

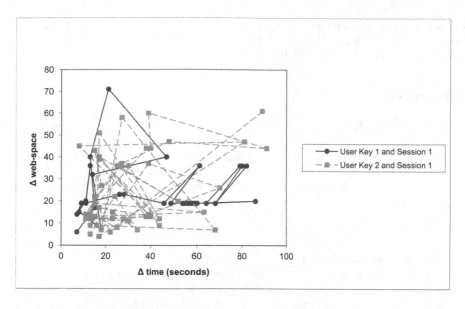

Fig. 3. User Behavior Diagram constructed per individual user key and session key

4 Conclusion

Based on the computed results, we conclude that the overall predictions for both implemented CHAID and CART show great resemblance. Both methods define the level for the total number of accessed web pages on all sessions per user as the best predictor of the rating for the total number of unique session keys per user. The defined "more than 50" category of the total number of accessed web pages on all sessions per user is the only significant predictor of total number of unique session keys per user in both methods. From all users accessing the web-platform in this category, 40.9 % have "medium" level for the total number of accessed web pages on all sessions per user. Thus, on the resulted diagram there are no child nodes below the above mentioned node, and this is considered a terminal node for CART and CHAID algorithm methods.

A significant difference between CART and CHAID is that the CART splitting rule allows only binary splits whereas CHAID allow multiple splits. Based on the obtained results we can say that CHAID methodology is most suitable to perform analysis and CART is better suited for prediction. For the studied behavioral based parameters, CHAID works best to describe the relationship between the set of explanatory variables and the response variable, while CART methodology may be used to create a model with high prediction for new cases.

Further studies are to be considered with the inclusion of emotion behavior parameters along with the studied behavior traits parameters.

Acknowledgments. The work has been funded by the Sectoral Operational Programme Human Resources Development 2007–2013 of the Ministry of European Funds through the Financial Agreement POSDRU/159/1.5/S/134398

References

1. Jain, A., Ross, A.A., Nandakumar, K.: Introduction to Biometrics. Springer, New York (2011)
2. Adler, A., Youmaran, R., Loyka, S.: Towards a measure of biometric feature information. Pattern Anal. Appl. **12**(3), 261–270 (2009). Springer
3. Ross, A.A., Nandakumar, K., Jain, A.: Handbook of Multibiometrics. Springer, New York (2006)
4. Wong, R., Poh, N., Kittler, J., Frohlich, D.: Towards inclusive design in mobile biometry. In: 3rd Conference on Human System Interactions (HSI). IEEE (2010)
5. Yampolskiy, R., Govindaraju, V.: Behavioral biometrics: a survey and classification. Int. J. Biomet. (IJBM) **1**(1), 81–113 (2008)
6. Jurafsky, D., Martin, J.H.: Speech and Language Processing, pp. 107–111. Pearson Education International, Upper Saddle River (2008)
7. Ukkonen, E.: On approximate string matching. In: Karpinski, M. (ed.) Foundations of Computation Theory. LNCS, vol. 158, pp. 487–495. Springer, Heidelberg (1983)
8. Rokach, L., Maimon, O.: Data Mining with Decision Trees: Theory and Applications. World Scientific Pub Co Inc., Singapore (2008)
9. Hogben, G.: Behavioural Biometrics Final Report, European Network and information Securty Agency (ENISA) (2010)
10. Breiman, L., Freidman, J., Olshen, R., Stone, C.J.: Classification and Regression Trees, 1st edn. Chapman and Hall, Boca Raton (1984)
11. Breiman, L., Friedman, J.H., Olshen, R.A., Stone, C.J.: Classification and regression trees. Wadsworth International Group, Belmont (1984)
12. Quinlan, J.R.: Induction of decision trees. Mach. Learn. **1**, 81–106 (1986)
13. Wu, X., Kumar, V., Quinlan, J.R., et al.: Top 10 algorithms in data mining. J. Knowl. Inf. Syst. **14**(1), 1–37 (2008)

SCA Resistance Analysis on FPGA Implementations of Sponge Based MAC – PHOTON

N. Nalla Anandakumar$^{(\boxtimes)}$

Hardware Security Research Group, Society for Electronic Transactions and Security,
Chennai, India
nallananth@gmail.com

Abstract. PHOTON is a lightweight hash function which was proposed by Guo et al. in CRYPTO 2011. This is used in low-resource ubiquitous computing devices such as RFID tags, wireless sensor nodes, smart cards and mobile devices. PHOTON is built using sponge construction and it provides a new MAC function called MAC – PHOTON. This paper deals with FPGA implementations of MAC – PHOTON and their side-channel attack (SCA) resistance. First, we describe three architectures of the MAC – PHOTON based on the concepts of iterative, folding and unrolling, and we provide their performance results on the Xilinx Virtex-5 FPGAs. Second, we analyse security of the MAC – PHOTON against side-channel attack using a SASEBO-GII development board. Finally, we present an analysis of its Threshold Implementation (TI) and discuss its resistance against first-order power analysis attacks.

Keywords: SCA · Lightweight cryptography · Sponge functions · MAC · PHOTON · Threshold implementation

1 Introduction

Hash functions are one of the most important and invaluable primitives in modern cryptography. Recently, Bertoni et al. [7] proposed a new way of building hash functions from a fixed permutation which is called sponge function. A sponge function H is a one-way function that converts arbitrary-length message M into variable-length hash code $H(M)$ (or digest). In practice, sponge based hash functions are very useful for constructing Message Authentication Codes (MACs) [6]. A MAC algorithm accepts as input a secret key K and a message M of arbitrary-length and produces a short-tag as output. The purpose of a MAC is to provide integrity and authenticity assurances on the message.

Recently, a sponge based hash function called PHOTON [15] has been proposed, especially for usage in lightweight security devices. The design structure of PHOTON has an AES like internal permutation. In this study, we present the iterative, folding and unrolling architectures of the MAC-PHOTON on FPGA (Field-Programmable Gate Array). The proposed constructions are suited for the lightweight cryptographic applications such as FPGA-based RFID tags [14],

© Springer International Publishing Switzerland 2015
I. Bica et al. (Eds.): SECITC 2015, LNCS 9522, pp. 69–86, 2015.
DOI: 10.1007/978-3-319-27179-8_6

FPGA-based wireless sensor nodes [13,25]. Moreover, the side-channel security resistance of these non-serialised implementations of MAC-PHOTON has not been evaluated quantitatively.

In 2013, Susana et al. [12] presented an analysis of side channel resistance of HMAC [4] based on fully serialized implementation of PHOTON [15] hash functions. They make strong assumptions on the target implementation to discover the state information, and they use same key variant for HMAC prefix-suffix construction. They also mention that their implementation is not suitable for high-speed resource constrained devices. Our goal in this work is to present implementations suitable for high-speed resource constrained devices.

Side-channel attacks on a non-serialised hardware implementation of MAC-PHOTON would be much more challenging to implement. Up until now, there has not been much prior work along this direction. In a side-channel attack, an adversary exploits the secret information which is leaking from a physical implementation of the algorithm. In MAC-PHOTON construction, obtaining the full secret information or even partial disclosure of secret information can lead to a forgery of the MAC for arbitrary messages. This work deals with security of three FPGA implementations against side-channel analysis such as correlation power analysis (CPA) [11]. We also provide Threshold Implementation (TI) of MAC-PHOTON and discuss its resistance against first-order power analysis attacks. To the best of our knowledge, this is the first security analysis of the unprotected and protected of MAC-PHOTON against first-order CPA attacks.

Our Contributions. The primary goal of this work is to provide an analysis of the SCA resistance of the sponge based MAC construction that uses either iterative or folding or unrolling based architecture of PHOTON hash function. We also analyse security of threshold implementation of the MAC-PHOTON against first-order CPA attacks. Our contributions are summarized as follows:

1. Our first contribution is to present the iterative, folding and unrolling architectures of the MAC-PHOTON, and to provide their performance results on the Xilinx Virtex-5 FPGAs. Our three implementations yield better throughput per area ratio when compared with existing FPGA implementation of PHOTON-80/20/16 [3,12] and HMAC-PHOTON-80/20/16 [12].
2. Our second contribution is to present the side channel security analysis of the iterative, folding and unrolling architectures of the MAC-PHOTON against first-order CPA attack. As a result, the iterative, folding and unrolling architectures have resistance against side channel attack up to 10000, 8000, 50000 messages, respectively. Moreover, our MAC-PHOTON implementations provide better security compared to Susana et al. [12].
3. Our third contribution is to present the iterative, folding based threshold implementations of MAC-PHOTON, and to analyse their security against first-order CPA attack. As a result, our implementations yield better throughput per area ratio when compared with existing FPGA implementations of PHOTON-80/20/16 [3,12] and HMAC-PHOTON-80/20/16 [12]. Moreover, our implementations are resistant against first-order CPA attacks even if an attacker is capable of measuring 100,000 power traces.

The rest of this paper is organised as follows. First we provide the several preliminaries on PHOTON, SCA and MAC calculation in Sect. 2. In Sect. 3 we present the hardware architecture of the MAC-PHOTON structure and implementation results for Xilinx FPGAs. In Sect. 4 we describe a CPA attack strategy to analyze its resistance against side-channel attacks. We then furnish its experimental results. In Sect. 5 we present the threshold implementation of the MAC-PHOTON-80/20/16 and to evaluate their security against first-order CPA attacks. The paper concludes in Sect. 6.

2   Technical Background

In this section, we give a brief description of the PHOTON hashing algorithm, followed by an overview of the MAC-PHOTON constructions and also give an overview of the side channel analysis.

2.1   PHOTON Description

PHOTON is a cryptographic hash function based on the sponge construction with arbitrary-length input and variable-length output. Each PHOTON hash function is denoted by PHOTON-$n/r/r'$, where its input bitrate r, its output bitrate r', and its hash output size n. There are five hash function in the PHOTON family: PHOTON-80/20/16, PHOTON-128/16/16, PHOTON-160/36/36, PHOTON-224/32/32, and PHOTON-256/32/32. The size of the internal state (t bits, $t = c + r$; r input bitrate and c capacity) depends on the hash output size.

PHOTON has three phases: (1) initialization, (2) absorbing and (3) squeezing. In the initialization phase, the input message is padded and cut blocks of r bits. During the absorption phase, the r-bit input message blocks are XORed into the first r bits of the state and then interleaved with the t-bit permutation function P. Once all message blocks have been handled the squeezing phase starts. During this phase, the extracting r' bits from the bitrate part of the internal state and then applying the permutation P on it. The squeezing process continues until the proper digest size n is reached.

The PHOTON internal permutation P is also AES-like permutations. It also consists of 12 rounds, each round is composed as the application of the following four operations:

- *AddConstants* (*AC*): first column of the internal state is bitwise XORed with round and internal constants;
- *SubCells* (*SC*): the PRESENT S-box [9] is applied to the internal state;
- *ShiftRows* (*SR*): cell row i of the internal state is cyclically shifted by i positions to the left;
- *MixColumnsSerial* (*MCS*): each cell column of the internal state is transformed by multiplying it once with MDS matrix $(A)^d$ (or d times with matrix A).

We focus on PHOTON-80/20/16 in our analysis, because it is the lightest and the simplest version of the family. It presents an internal state of (5×5) cells and each cell represents a 4-bit nibble. The PHOTON-80/20/16 MDS matrix $(A)^5$ is defined as follows:

$$A = \begin{pmatrix} 0\ 1\ 0\ 0\ 0 \\ 0\ 0\ 1\ 0\ 0 \\ 0\ 0\ 0\ 1\ 0 \\ 0\ 0\ 0\ 0\ 1 \\ 1\ 2\ 9\ 9\ 2 \end{pmatrix} ; \quad (A)^5 = \begin{pmatrix} 0\ 1\ 0\ 0\ 0 \\ 0\ 0\ 1\ 0\ 0 \\ 0\ 0\ 0\ 1\ 0 \\ 0\ 0\ 0\ 0\ 1 \\ 1\ 2\ 9\ 9\ 2 \end{pmatrix}^5 = \begin{pmatrix} 1 & 2 & 9 & 9 & 2 \\ 2 & 5 & 3 & 8 & 13 \\ 13 & 11 & 10 & 12 & 1 \\ 1 & 15 & 2 & 3 & 14 \\ 14 & 14 & 8 & 5 & 12 \end{pmatrix}$$

2.2 The MAC Construction

For sponge construction, the output is only a small part of the squeezing phase and hence it is protected from length extension weakness which is mentioned in [6,8,15]. Thus, the HMAC nested construction does not require for sponge based constructions [5,6,8,15,26]. Indeed, we simply prepend the key to the message and then we apply the sponge construction to generate a MAC as recommended by PHOTON [15] designers.

$$\text{MAC}(M, K) = H(K||M) \tag{1}$$

We will denote the MAC algorithm that uses PHOTON-80/20/16 to instantiate H by the term "MAC-PHOTON-80/20/16". We give in Fig. 1 the construction of the sponge based MAC-PHOTON-80/20/16. In the first step, the t-bit internal state A_i is initialized to initial vector $A_0 = IV$. Then, the secret key and the input message is split into blocks of r-bits each, which are denoted by key $K = (k_0, k_1, ..., k_{n-1})$ and message $M = (m_0, m_1, ..., m_{n-1})$ respectively. The absorbing phase, the r-bit input blocks are XORed with r leftmost bits of the state, then interleaved with the permutation function P. During this phase, the key blocks are processed first and then the message blocks are processed. Once all key and message blocks have been absorbed, the squeezing phase begins.

In the squeezing phase, the first r'-bits of the state are returned as output blocks z_i from the internal state, and then interleaved with the permutation function P. The squeezing process continues until the proper MAC $(z_0||...||z_{n-1})$ size is reached. In the above MAC construction, obtaining the actual secret key (K), or recovering the internal state A_i would be enough to forge the MAC for arbitrary messages.

2.3 Side Channel Analysis

Side channel attacks have become an important field of cryptographic research. It is a class of attack that exploits information leaking from physical implementation of cryptosystems. Differential Power Analysis (DPA) [20] and Correlation Power Analysis (CPA) [11] are most common forms of the side channel analysis. DPA exploits the relationship between power consumptions and data generated

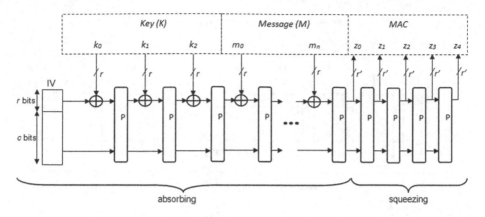

Fig. 1. The block diagram of the sponge based MAC-PHOTON-80/20/16 construction

during execution. In a CPA attack, the secret key can be derived by using the Pearson's correlation coefficient to correlate the recorded power consumption (so often power trace) with the hypothetical power consumption model. The hypothetical power consumption model is computed by using a Hamming Distance (HD) model [11]. The HD represents the number of bit-flips between two clock cycles. Side channel attack on MAC based on several hash functions was studied in [10,24,27]. In this paper, we demonstrate CPA attack on MAC-PHOTON-80/20/16.

3   FPGA Implementation of the MAC-PHOTON-80/20/16

In this section, we present three FPGA implementations of the MAC-PHOTON based on the concepts of iterative, folding and unrolling, and to provide their performance results on the Xilinx Virtex-5 FPGAs.

In order to demonstrate the security of the MAC-PHOTON-80/20/16 construction against CPA attacks, we implemented the MAC-PHOTON-80/20/16 in VerilogHDL and targeted Xilinx Virtex-5 FPGA (XC5VLX50-1FFG324). We used Mentor Graphics ModelSimPE for simulation purposes and Xilinx ISE v13.4 for synthesizing and implementation purposes. For MAC-PHOTON-80/20/16 analysis, we have selected 256 bits (260 bits with required padding) message length and 60 bits key length. A 60-bit key provides security for up to 30,000 messages per key [15]. For higher key length, the higher versions of the PHOTON hash core must be replaced as recommended by PHOTON [15]. We give in Table 1 the detailed synthesis results of the iterative, folding and unrolling based implementations of the MAC-PHOTON. The iterative architecture computes one round per clock cycle, while the folding architecture computes one round per 2 clock cycles. In the unrolling architecture computes 12 rounds per clock cycle.

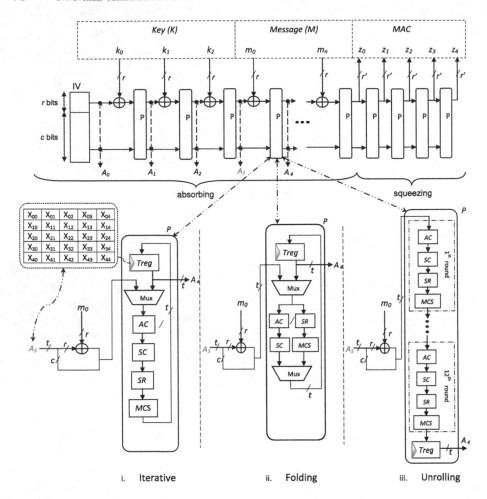

Fig. 2. The block diagram of the iterative, folding, unrolling implementations of the MAC-PHOTON-80/20/16

Iterative: The main goal of the design is moderate throughput and area requirements. We give in Fig. 2 the block diagram of the basic iterative (denoted (i) in Fig. 2) FPGA implementation of MAC-PHOTON-80/20/16. Initially, the key value and input message value split into blocks of r-bits (20-bit). In absorbing phase, first 3 key blocks are processed, after that 13 message blocks are processed, where each block consists of 12 rounds. The data register $Treg$ is updated every round after processing AC, SC, SR, and MCS operations in one clock cycle. Hence, it requires 192 clock cycles to process 16 blocks (where, 36 clock cycles for 3 key blocks and 156 clock cycles for 13 message blocks). In squeezing phase, r'-bit (16-bit) of 5 output blocks are extracted from the internal state which requires 48 clock cycles (i.e. only 4 permutations are executed). Therefore, 240 clock cycles are required in order to complete both phases. We obtain 302 slices, while the throughput reaches 287.83 Mbps. As can be seen from the Table 1, our work seems to require much less area than most ciphers [16–19] and also yields a better throughput per area ratio compared to MD5 [18], SHA-1 [17], SHA-256 [19], PHOTON-80/20/16 [3,12] and HMAC-PHOTON-80/20/16 [12].

Folding: The main goal of the design is reasonable throughput and better area requirements. In Fig. 2, horizontal folding by a factor of two is demonstrated (denoted (ii) in Fig. 2). In this architecture, a half of a round is implemented as combinational logic, and the entire round is executed using 2 clock cycles. The data register *Treg* is updated every half of a round (either after processing AC, and SC operations or after processing SR, and MCS operations in one clock cycle). The datapath width and state size are stays the same as in the basic iterative architecture. Hence, 384 clock cycles are required to process 16 blocks in absorbing phase and 96 clock cycles (i.e. only 4 permutations are executed) are required to process 5 output blocks in squeezing phase. Therefore, 480 clock cycles are required in order to complete both the phases. We obtain 251 slices, while the throughput reaches 171.42 Mbps. As seen from the Table 1, our folding based MAC-PHOTON implementation seems to require much less area than most ciphers [16–19] and also yields a better throughput per area ratio compared to MD5 [18], SHA-1 [17], SHA-256 [19], PHOTON-80/20/16 [3,12] and HMAC-PHOTON-80/20/16 [12].

Unrolling: The main goal of the design is on high throughput and not on low area requirements. We give in Fig. 2 the block diagram of the unrolling (denoted (iii) in Fig. 2) FPGA implementation of MAC-PHOTON-80/20/16. The combinational logic of a round is replicated, so now 12 rounds of internal permutation P are executed in one clock cycle. Thus, the data register *Treg* is updated after every permutation P. Hence, it requires 16 clock cycles to process 16 blocks in absorbing phase and 4 clock cycles (i.e. only 4 permutations are executed) are required to process 5 output blocks in squeezing phase. Therefore, 20 clock cycles are required in order to complete both the phases. We obtain 1066 slices, while the throughput reaches 508.6 Mbps. As seen from the Table 1, our unrolling based MAC-PHOTON implementation seems to require much less area than KECCAK-256 [16,19] and also yields a better throughput per area ratio compared to MD5 [18], SHA-1 [17], SHA-256 [19], PHOTON-80/20/16 [3,12] and HMAC-PHOTON-80/20/16 [12].

4   Side Channel Attack Resistance of MAC-PHOTON-80/20/16

In this section, we present a CPA attack strategy to analyze the security of MAC-PHOTON against side-channel attack using our communication interface (see Appendix A) on a SASEBO-GII development board, especially CPA with Hamming Distance model and we furnish experimental results of it.

Table 1. Performance Results of the MAC-PHOTON-80/20/16 and TI implementation of MAC-PHOTON-80/20/16 on Virtex-5-xc5vlx50.

Design	Area (slices)	LUTs	FFs	Max. freq (MHz)	Total Number of Clock Cycles (cycles)		T.put (Mbps)	T.put/Area (Mbps/slices)
					Internal permutation P	Whole hash function H		
Iterative	302	508	415	172.7	12	240	287.83	0.95
Folding	251	515	414	205.7	24	480	171.42	0.68
Unrolling	1066	3065	411	25.43	1	20	508.6	0.48
PHOTON-80 [3]	82	188	135	302.68	54	648	9.34	0.11
PHOTON-80 [3]	69	159	89	285.2	30	360	15.84	0.22
PHOTON-80 [12]	149	—	—	250	59	—	7	0.05
HMAC-PHOTON-80 [12]	199	—	—	114	59	17,700	38.64	0.19
MD5 [18]	613	—	—	96	—	—	77.4	0.12
SHA-1 [17]	518	—	—	82	—	—	51.8	0.10
SHA-256 [19]	609	—	—	260	—	—	198	0.32
KECCAK-256 [19]	1433	—	—	205	—	—	8397	5.86
KECCAK-256 [16]	1395	—	—	—	—	—	12777	9.16
KECCAK-256 [16]	1980	—	—	—	—	—	15362	7.76
KECCAK-256 [16]	3849	—	—	—	—	—	12652	3.29
TI implementation of MAC-PHOTON-80/20/16								
TI-iterative	739	1626	819	172.7	12	240	238.3	0.32
TI-folding	687	1738	814	194.3	24	480	162	0.24

4.1   Attacking MAC-PHOTON-80/20/16

The attacker needs either to recover the actual secret key K (see Table 2) or the internal state A_i ($t = 100$ bits; $r = 20$ bits and $c = 80$ bits) to forge MAC for arbitrary messages. In the MAC-PHOTON-80/20/16 construction (see Fig. 2), K only affects the internal state values A_1, A_2, A_3 before the message is inserted and also these internal state values are fixed and unknown. In order to perform a CPA attack, we require fixed unknown data to be combined with variable known data. This criterion is fulfilled, when the known and variable m is combined with the secret internal state A_3 (combined nibbles are represented in gray cells in Fig. 3). This internal state value A_3 (see Table 2) does not change if K is fixed for any message m. In summary, the goal of our attack is to recover the secret internal state A_3 (marked in red in Fig. 2) before the message digesting phase.

One can see that the incoming message block M is processed through the P permutation. First, the permutation P takes r-bit leftmost of the incoming internal state A_3 is XORed with r-bit known incoming first message block and storing the result in the first row (denoted m_{0i} in Fig. 3) of the matrix representing the internal state, while the four other rows (denoted x_{ij} in Fig. 3) are filled

Table 2. Secret values

Secret Key (K)	FA4B7 5A4BC 9AB8C
Secret internal state value (A_3)	8F4D6 0112A ABADC D0FF7 14971

with the remaining c-bits of the incoming internal state A_3. Second, *AddConstants* (denoted c_i in Fig. 3) are XORed to the first column of the internal state, then the *SC* and *SR* operations are performed (denoted s_{ij} in Fig. 3). Finally, the *MCS* operation is performed (denoted z_{ij} in Fig. 3).

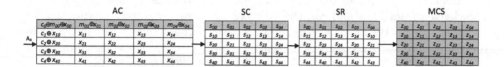

Fig. 3. One round of the internal permutation P of MAC-PHOTON-80/20/16.

Iterative: In the iterative architecture, we recover the incoming internal secret data (A_3) by correlating the power traces with a hypothetical model at a point of first round *MCS* state output during the A_4 permutation. In Fig. 3, we can see that known and internal secret data (2–5 rows) are mixed after *MCS* operation is performed, where each column will depend on one known value and five unknown secret values. Overall, at the end of the first round, the first column (z_{i0}) on the output can be written as in the following matrix

$$\begin{pmatrix} z_{00} \\ z_{10} \\ z_{20} \\ z_{30} \\ z_{40} \end{pmatrix} = \begin{pmatrix} 1 & 2 & 9 & 9 & 2 \\ 2 & 5 & 3 & 8 & 13 \\ 13 & 11 & 10 & 12 & 1 \\ 1 & 15 & 2 & 3 & 14 \\ 14 & 14 & 8 & 5 & 12 \end{pmatrix} \begin{pmatrix} s_{00} \\ s_{11} \\ s_{22} \\ s_{33} \\ s_{44} \end{pmatrix}$$

If we look at the first output nibble z_{00}, it is given by

$$z_{00} = 01 \cdot s_{00} \oplus 02 \cdot s_{11} \oplus 09 \cdot s_{22} \oplus 09 \cdot s_{33} \oplus 02 \cdot s_{44}$$

If we focus on the first round, we can substitute s_{00}, s_{11}, s_{22}, s_{33} and s_{44} with SC($x_{00} \oplus m_{00} \oplus c_0$), SC($x_{11}$), SC($x_{22}$), SC($x_{33}$) and SC($x_{44}$). The output nibble z_{00} can then be written as

$$z_{00} = 01 \cdot SC(x_{00} \oplus m_{00} \oplus c_0) + q_{00}; q_{00} \in [0, ..., 15] \tag{2}$$

where, known constant c_0 is 1; unknown constant q_{00} can write as follows:
$$q_{00} = 02 \cdot SC(x_{11}) + 09 \cdot SC(x_{22}) + 09 \cdot SC(x_{33}) + 02 \cdot SC(x_{44})$$

From Eq. 2, we observe that m_{00} is variable and known, whereas x_{00} is fixed and unknown secret. q_{00} is also fixed and unknown constant. Therefore, a CPA attack can be launched by making hypotheses about x_{00} and q_{00}, and computing the corresponding values of z_{00}. First, we recover the value of x_{00}, whereas hypotheses for q_{00} is initially ignored because it is not related to m_{00}. Hence, 2^4 hypotheses for x_{00} are required. Using the Hamming Distance (HD) model, the 2^4 possibilities for the previous state x_{00} (A_3), must also be taken into account. In our case same 2^4 hypotheses for the x_{00} are used in both the states. Therefore, the attacker correlates the power traces with the 2^4 hypotheses for HD(x_{00}, z_{00}). This allows the attacker to recover the secret value of x_{00}. Once recovering the secret value of x_{00}, the attacker can now make the 2^4 hypotheses on the q_{00} for HD(x_{00}, z_{00}). Hence, the fixed value of q_{00} is revealed. Furthermore, with knowledge of both x_{00} and q_{00}, the attacker can now accurately predict z_{00} for any message m. By following the above strategy, the attacker can recover the remaining internal state secrets. This attack model can decrease the complexity of internal state (A_3) from 2^{100} to 25×2^8 for MAC-PHOTON-80/20/16.

Folding: For folding architecture, we divide the attack in two phases. In the first one, we recover the bitrates part (first row in Fig. 3) of the incoming internal secret data (A_3) by correlating the power traces with a hypothetical model at a point of first round SC state output during the A_4 permutation. Once recovering the bitrates part, we recover the left part of the incoming internal secret data by correlating the power traces with a hypothetical model at a point in output of the second round SC state operation during the A_4 permutation. The SC state is denoted by s_{ij} for first round and by $s_{ij}^{\cdot\cdot}$ for second round, respectively.

$$s_{ij} = SC(x_{ij} \oplus m_{ij} \oplus 1) \tag{3}$$

$$s_{ij}^{\cdot\cdot} = SC(z_{ij} \oplus 3) \tag{4}$$

where z_{ij} value is obtained from Eq. 2

Focusing on Eq. 3, the attacker correlates the power traces with the 2^4 hypotheses HD(x_{ij}, s_{ij}) for each nibble to recover the bitrates part. Using Eq. 4, the attacker can launch a CPA attack on $s_{ij}^{\cdot\cdot}$ by forming hypotheses HD(z_{ij}, $s_{ij}^{\cdot\cdot}$) to recover the remaining state values of A_3. This attack model can efficiently decrease the complexity of internal state (A_3) from 2^{100} to 25×2^4 for MAC-PHOTON-80/20/16.

Unrolling: In the unrolling architecture, the data register *Treg* is updated only after processing every internal permutation P. Thus, the attacker can launch a CPA attack at a point of last round MCS state output during the A_4 permutation by forming hypotheses HD(A_3, A_4) to recover the state values of A_3. In this way, hypothesis test involves too many hypothesis for A_4 state which is derived from A_3 state. Therefore, we correlating the power traces with the following two hypothetical model approaches to recovers the internal state values of A_3.

First one is computed similar to iterative architecture, while second is computed similar to folding architecture.

4.2 Experimental Results

The SASEBO-GII hosts two FPGAs, i.e., one control FPGA (Xilinx XC3S400A-4FTG256, Spartan-3A series) and one cryptographic FPGA (Xilinx XC5VLX50-1FFG324, Virtex-5 series). In order to obtain CPA power traces from the design, the cryptographic FPGA was configured with the MAC-PHOTON-80/20/16 circuit through Parallel JTAG Cable. A USB cable to supply power to the SASEBO-GII board and to act as an interface between the board and the host PC. In all the experiments the clock signal is provided by a 24 MHz oscillator which is divided by 3 using a frequency divider, i.e., the cryptographic FPGA is clocked at a frequency of 8MHz. Measurements are performed using an Agilent MSO7104B 1GHz oscilloscope at a sampling rate of 4GS/s and by means of a SMA-BNC cable which captures the voltage drop over an 1Ω shunt resistor inserted into the 1V VCORE (J2) line of the targeted FPGA. Therefore, the traces recorded on the oscilloscope were proportional to the power consumption of the FPGA during the execution of MAC-PHOTON-80/20/16 algorithm.

Iterative: In the iterative architecture, using the previously defined set-up and hypothetical model approaches, a total of 10,000 input random messages and 10,000 points per trace were required to obtain a successful CPA attack, which recovers that conform the secret internal state A_3 of the MAC-PHOTON. Figure 4 shows the result of iterative MAC-PHOTON-80/20/16 against CPA analysis. The correct first nibble of intermediate state A_3 value is 8 (Matlab array index value minus one) shows up clearly after around 10,000 traces.

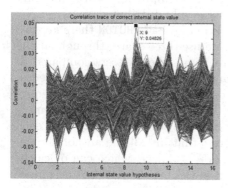 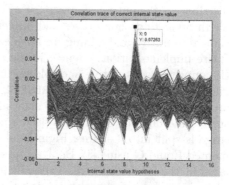

Fig. 4. Correlation Co-efficient plot for Side-channel attack (number of measurements = 10,000) on iterative based MAC-PHOTON implementation

Fig. 5. Correlation Co-efficient plot for Side-channel attack (number of measurements = 8,000) on folding based MAC-PHOTON implementation

Folding: In the folding architecture, using the previously defined set-up and hypothetical model approaches, a total of 8,000 input random messages and 10,000 points per trace were required to obtain a successful CPA attack, which recovers that conform the secret internal state A_3 of the MAC-PHOTON. Figure 5 shows the result of folding based MAC-PHOTON-80/20/16 against CPA analysis. The correct first nibble of intermediate state A_3 value is 8 (Matlab array index value minus one) shows up clearly after around 8,000 traces.

Unrolling: Usig the previously defined set-up and hypothetical model approaches, we performed CPA attacks on the unrolling implementation of MAC-PHOTON with 50,000 power traces. In the unrolling MAC-PHOTON-80/20/16 analysis, without any surprise, we could not reveal correct value of the intermediate state A_3 for our two hypothetical approaches. Hence, our unrolling MAC-PHOTON-80/20/16 design resist against correlation power analysis on Hamming distance model.

5   Threshold Implementation of the MAC-PHOTON-80/20/16

The preceding sections have analysed security of the MAC-PHOTON algorithm against first-order CPA attacks. We now examine security of threshold implementation (TI) of MAC-PHOTON against first-order CPA attacks. In 2006, Nikova et al. [22] introduced the concept of a threshold implementation scheme that is based on secret sharing techniques and is provable resistant against first order DPA even in the presence of glitches. The sharing can have three properties: *Correctness*, *Non-completeness* and *Uniformity*. *Correctness* means that combining the output of the different shares retrieves the original output in a correct way. *Non-completeness* means that each output share of a function is independent of at least one input share. *Uniformity* means that if the input shares are uniformly distributed, the output shares must also be uniformly distributed.

In order to design a threshold implementation for MAC-PHOTON there are two choices, iterative and folding. In both cases, we use three shares throughout the entire implementations. Hence, we need three times the registers compared to the unprotected iterative and folding implementations. Since the S-box used in PHOTON is same as that used in PRESENT, the decomposing and sharing techniques are borrowed from [23]. Figure 6 shows how to apply the threshold countermeasure to a 4-bit S-box: first it is decomposed into two stages G and F, then each stage is split into 3 shares. Figure 6 also shows that in [23] the authors implemented F and G using six Boolean functions $F_1, F_2, ..., G_3$ which can be calculated by the formulas in [23, Appendix A], but in this article the S-box decomposition is implemented without using a Y register [23] in between the G-function and the F-function. In our proposed two architectures where 25 instances of the TI S-box are implemented. We use the above analysis and provide a complete threshold implementation of MAC-PHOTON.

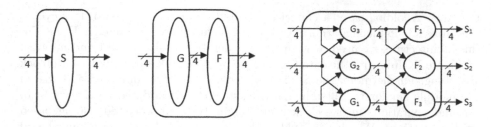

Fig. 6. Decomposition of an S-box

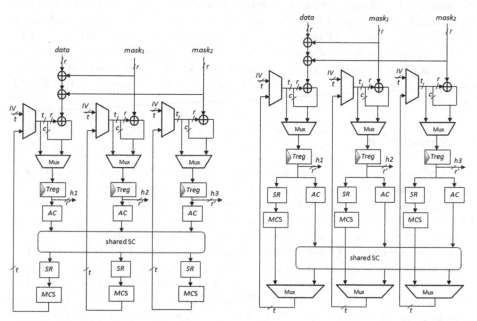

Fig. 7. Architecture of the round-based TI of MAC-PHOTON

Fig. 8. Architecture of the folding based TI of MAC-PHOTON

Iterative: A iterative based architecture computes one round per clock cycle. This architecture is depicted in Fig. 7. For this architecture, we need two randomly generated masks ($mask1$ and $mask2$), which are XORed with the data ($= key\|message$) chunk during input data block absorbing. The unmasking step is performed by simply XORing all three shares ($h1$, $h2$, $h3$) yielding the output MAC. Furthermore, the SC is now replaced by a decomposed and shared SC module similar to [23]. The data register $Treg$ is updated every round after processing AC, shared SC, SR, and MCS operations in one clock cycle. We give in Table 1 the detailed results of the iterative based TI implementation of the MAC-PHOTON. As seen from the Table 1, our threshold implementation of the iterative architecture seems to require much less area than KECCAK-256 [16,19] and also yields a better throughput per area ratio compared to MD5 [18], SHA-1 [17], SHA-256 [19], PHOTON-80/20/16 [3,12] and HMAC-PHOTON-80/20/16 [12].

Folding: A folding based architecture computes one round per two clock cycles. The threshold implementation of the folding architecture is depicted in Fig. 8. For this architecture, we need two randomly generated masks ($mask1$ and $mask2$), which are XORed with the data ($= key||message$) chunk during input data block absorbing. Furthermore, the SC is now replaced by a decomposed and shared SC module similar to [23]. The data register $Treg$ is updated on every half of a round operations in one clock cycle (similarly as unprotected folding based implementation). We give in Table 1 the detailed results of the folding based TI implementation of the MAC-PHOTON. As seen from the Table 1, our threshold implementation of the folding architecture seems to require much less area than KECCAK-256 [16,19] and also yields a better throughput per area ratio compared to MD5 [18], SHA-1 [17], PHOTON-80/20/16 [3,12] and HMAC-PHOTON-80/20/16 [12].

We repeat the experiments described in Sect. 4.1 on our threshold implementations of the iterative and folding architectures. We verify that our implementations are resistant against first order CPA attacks even if collects up to 100,000 power traces.

6   Conclusion

In this paper, we have presented an analysis of SCA resistance of implementation of PHOTON hash algorithm in MAC construction. The implemented MAC − PHOTON-80/20/16 features are more efficient for processing short messages when compared to HMAC construction. Without compromising the system security, our results show that without any protection and key refreshment, it is possible to interchange up to 10000, 8000, 50000 messages for iterative, folding and unrolling implementations, respectively. Resistance of TI implementations of MAC−PHOTON against first order CPA attacks has been tested. As we noted, our implementations are resistant against first order CPA attacks even if an attacker is capable of measuring 100,000 power traces. Our results showed that both protected and unprotected MAC − PHOTON constructions seems to be very well suited for lightweight applications (even high-speed) when compared to construction of HMAC design based protocols.

Acknowledgments. This research work has been funded by Department of Atomic Energy (DAE), Govt. of India under the grand number 12-R&D-IMS-5.01.0204. The author would like to thank Suganya Annadurai, M. Prem Laxman Das, Lakshmi Kuppusamy and Ravikumar Selvam for helpful discussions, and also thank the anonymous reviewers for their critical suggestions that greatly improved the quality of this paper.

A   Our Communication Interface for SASEBO-GII

Our communication interface for SASEBO-GII [2] is derived from the work proposed in [19] with slight modifications which is suitable and customisable for cryptographic primitives. Our entire interface control logic was implemented based on a finite-state machine and also provides the MATLAB solutions instead of SASEBO-Checker [19] to work with the FTDI chip. This choice is made for accessibility and ease of maintenance. Figure 9 shows the overview of the SASEBO-GII communication interface. This interface is used to communicate with the PC and two FPGAs of SASEBO-GII board. They are a cryptographic FPGA (Virtex-5) and control FPGA (Spartan-3A), a cryptographic FPGA usually implements the cryptographic algorithm and a control FPGA which communicates the data between the PC and the cryptographic FPGA. In our case, the MAC-PHOTON-80/20/16 module was ported into the cryptographic FPGA whereas the control FPGA acted as a bridge between the PC and the MAC-PHOTON-80/20/16 module.

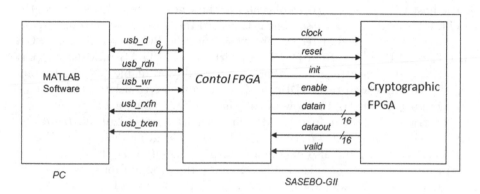

Fig. 9. SASEBO-GII communication Interface

A.1 The Interface Between the Control and Cryptographic FPGAs

The control FPGA module consists of the following 5 states: *initial, receiveusb, ControlFPGAsend, ControlFPGAreceive* and *sendusb*. During *initial* state, the USB module in the control FPGA is initialized through the FT2232D USB chip [1]. In *receiveusb* state, the input data is received 8-bits at a time from the PC (MATLAB) through the USB chip and then the values are stored in the data registers. During *ControlFPGAsend* state, a MAC-PHOTON-80/20/16 module in the cryptographic FPGA via *init* signal is initialized first. Then, the control FPGA sends the input data 16-bits wide via *datain* signal from the input data registers to the cryptographic FPGA. Once the data is processed the *ControlFPGAreceive* state receives the output data 16-bits-wide via *dataout* signal from the cryptographic FPGA and stores the data into the output data registers. During *sendusb* state, the output data (MAC) is sent back (8-bits wide) to the PC (MATLAB) from output data registers through the FT2232D USB chip. Hence, it requires 30 clock cycles to process the interface between the Control and Cryptographic FPGAs.

The cryptographic FPGA module consists of the following 3 states: *process, CryptoFPGAreceive* and *CryptoFPGAsend*. In *CryptoFPGAreceive* state, the cryptographic FPGA start to receives the input data from the control FPGA when the init signal is reached and then the values are stored in the data registers. The *process* state, is to execute the MAC-PHOTON-80/20/16 module. The *CryptoFPGAsend* state, once the MAC-PHOTON-80/20/16 module is processed, sends the output data (MAC) 16-bits wide via dataout signal to the control FPGA.

A.2   The Interface Between the PC and Control FPGA

The FT2232D USB chip was permanently mounted with the contol FPGA of the SASEBO-GII board. This chip acts as the communication interface between the MATLAB software and the control FPGA. This MATLAB software is run on the host PC and it is the control center of the whole system. In this work, the MATLAB is used for 2 purposes: one is to record the traces from the oscilloscope and the other is to send or receive the data from the PC to the control FPGA via FT2232D USB chip from FTDI inc. Although MATLAB provides support to call shared library functions, there is no readily available MATLAB solutions [21] to work with the FTDI chip. In this work, we translate from working .Net wrapper [21] to MATLAB with call shared library functions.

The translation program is divided into 4 parts: *initialization, transfer, receive* and *closing*. During *initialization*, the data length is defined, the library functions are loaded and also handle is defined to specify that the device (USB port) is opened. Once initialization is complete, the program tells the user that it is ready to receive data and asks the user to trigger the FPGA. During the *transfer* stage, the program continuously write the input data to the control FPGA until the expected number of data length. During the *receive* stage, the program read the output data from the control FPGA. Once *receive* stage is complete, handle device (USB port) is closed. Hence, it requires 216 clock cycles to process the interface between the PC and Control FPGA.

References

1. FT2232D DUAL USB TO SERIAL UART/FIFO IC Datasheet, 2nd edn. Future Technology Devices International Ltd. (2010)
2. Advanced Industrial Science Technology (AIST), N.I.: Side-channel Attack Standard Evaluation Board SASEBO-GII specification (2009). http://www.rcis.aist.go.jp/special/SASEBO/SASEBO-GII-ja.html
3. Anandakumar, N.N., Peyrin, T., Poschmann, A.: A very compact FPGA implementation of LED and PHOTON, Proceedings. In: Meier, W., Mukhopadhyay, D. (eds.) Progress in Cryptology – INDOCRYPT 2014. Lecture Notes in Computer Science, vol. 8885, pp. 304–321. Springer, Cham (2014). http://dx.doi.org/10.1007/978-3-319-13039-2_18
4. Bellare, M., Canetti, R., Krawczyk, H.: Keying hash functions for message authentication. In: Koblitz, N. (ed.) CRYPTO 1996. LNCS, vol. 1109, pp. 1–15. Springer, Heidelberg (1996)
5. Bertoni, G., Daemen, J., Peeters, M., Van Assche, G.: Duplexing the sponge: single-pass authenticated encryption and other applications. In: Miri, A., Vaudenay, S. (eds.) SAC 2011. LNCS, vol. 7118, pp. 320–337. Springer, Heidelberg (2012)

6. Bertoni, G., Daemen, J., Peeters, M., Van Assche, G.: On the security of the keyed sponge construction. In: Leander, G., Thomsen, S.S. (eds.) SKEW (2011)
7. Bertoni, G., Daemen, J., Peeters, M., Van Assche, G.: Cryptographic sponge functions (2011). http://sponge.noekeon.org/CSF-0.1.pdf
8. Bertoni, G., Daemen, J., Peeters, M., Van Assche, G.: The Keccak sponge function family (2011). http://keccak.noekeon.org/
9. Bogdanov, A.A., Knudsen, L.R., Leander, G., Paar, C., Poschmann, A., Robshaw, M., Seurin, Y., Vikkelsoe, C.: PRESENT: an ultra-lightweight block cipher. In: Paillier, P., Verbauwhede, I. (eds.) CHES 2007. LNCS, vol. 4727, pp. 450–466. Springer, Heidelberg (2007)
10. Boura, C., Lévêque, S., Vigilant, D.: Side-channel analysis of Grøstl and Skein. In: IEEE Symposium on Security and Privacy Workshops, pp. 16–26. IEEE Computer Society (2012)
11. Brier, E., Clavier, C., Olivier, F.: Correlation power analysis with a leakage model. In: Joye, M., Quisquater, J.-J. (eds.) CHES 2004. LNCS, vol. 3156, pp. 16–29. Springer, Heidelberg (2004)
12. Eiroa, S., Baturone, I.: FPGA implementation and DPA resistance analysis of a lightweight HMAC construction based on photon hash family. In: FPL, pp. 1–4. IEEE (2013)
13. Engel, A., Liebig, B., Koch, A.: Feasibility analysis of reconfigurable computing in low-power wireless sensor applications. In: Koch, A., Krishnamurthy, R., McAllister, J., Woods, R., El-Ghazawi, T. (eds.) ARC 2011. LNCS, vol. 6578, pp. 261–268. Springer, Heidelberg (2011)
14. Feldhofer, M., Aigner, M.J., Baier, T., Hutter, M., Plos, T., Wenger, E.: Semipassive RFID development platform for implementing and attacking security tags. In: ICITST. pp. 1–6. IEEE (2010)
15. Guo, J., Peyrin, T., Poschmann, A.: The PHOTON family of lightweight hash Functions. In: Rogaway, P. (ed.) CRYPTO 2011. LNCS, vol. 6841, pp. 222–239. Springer, Heidelberg (2011)
16. Homsirikamol, E., Rogawski, M., Gaj, K.: Throughput vs. area trade-offs in high-speed architectures of five round 3 SHA-3 candidates implemented using Xilinx and altera FPGAs. In: Preneel, B., Takagi, T. (eds.) CHES 2011. LNCS, vol. 6917, pp. 491–506. Springer, Heidelberg (2011)
17. Järvinen, K.: Design and implementation of a SHA-1 hash module on FPGAs. Helsinki University of Technology Signal Processing Laboratory (2004)
18. Järvinen, K.U., Tommiska, M., Skyttä, J.: Hardware implementation analysis of the MD5 hash algorithm. In: 38th Hawaii International Conference on System Sciences (HICSS-38 2005), CD-ROM/Abstracts Proceedings, 3–6 January 2005, Big Island, HI, USA. IEEE Computer Society (2005). http://dx.doi.org/10.1109/HICSS.2005.291
19. Kobayashi, K., Ikegami, J., Sakiyama, K., Ohta, K., Knezevic, M., Kocabas, Ü., Fan, J., Verbauwhede, I., Guo, E.X., Matsuo, S., Huang, S., Nazhandali, L., Satoh, A.: Prototyping platform for performance evaluation of SHA-3 candidates. In: Plusquellic, J., Mai, K. (eds.) HOST, pp. 60–63. IEEE Computer Society (2010)
20. Kocher, P.C., Jaffe, J., Jun, B.: Differential power analysis. In: Wiener, M. (ed.) CRYPTO 1999. LNCS, vol. 1666, p. 388. Springer, Heidelberg (1999)
21. Ltd, F.T.D.I.: CodeExamples. http://www.ftdichip.com/Support/Software Examples/CodeExamples/CSharp.htm
22. Nikova, S., Rechberger, C., Rijmen, V.: Threshold implementations against side-channel attacks and glitches. In: Ning, P., Qing, S., Li, N. (eds.) ICICS 2006. LNCS, vol. 4307, pp. 529–545. Springer, Heidelberg (2006)

23. Poschmann, A., Moradi, A., Khoo, K., Lim, C.W., Wang, H., Ling, S.: Side-channel resistant crypto for less than 2,300 GE. J. Crypt. **24**(2), 322–345 (2011)
24. Taha, M.M.I., Schaumont, P.: Side-channel analysis of MAC-Keccak. In: HOST, pp. 125–130. IEEE (2013)
25. Tuan, T., Rahman, A., Das, S., Trimberger, S., Kao, S.: A 90-nm low-power FPGA for battery-powered applications. IEEE Trans. CAD Integr. Circ. Syst. **26**(2), 296–300 (2007)
26. Yalçın, T., Kavun, E.B.: On the implementation aspects of sponge-based authenticated encryption for pervasive devices. In: Mangard, S. (ed.) CARDIS 2012. LNCS, vol. 7771, pp. 141–157. Springer, Heidelberg (2013)
27. Zohner, M., Kasper, M., Stöttinger, M., Huss, S.A.: Side channel analysis of the SHA-3 finalists. In: Rosenstiel, W., Thiele, L. (eds.) DATE, pp. 1012–1017. IEEE (2012)

A Novel Fast and Secure Chaos-Based Algorithm for Image Encryption

Jean De Dieu Nkapkop[1]([✉]), Joseph Yves Effa[1], Monica Borda[2], and Romulus Terebes[2]

[1] Department of Physics, Faculty of Science, The University of Ngaoundéré, P.O. Box 454, Ngaoundéré, Cameroon
{jdd.nkapkop,yveseffa}@gmail.com
[2] Department of Communications, Faculty of Electronics, Telecommunications and Information Technology, Technical University of Cluj-Napoca, 26-28 Baritiu Street, 400027 Cluj-Napoca, Romania
{monica.borda,romulus.terebes}@com.utcluj.ro

Abstract. Now in cryptography, the key challenge is to consider the trade-offs between the security level and speed performance. In this paper, a fast and secure algorithm for image encryption scheme based on chaotic generators is proposed. In the proposed method, permutation-diffusion design is used to create computationally secure encryption primitives and the integer sequences obtained by the sorting of chaotic Logistic map generator by descending order is used as the permutation key to shuffle the whole image. The iteration of the chaotic Skew Tent map is applied after, with an exclusive-or scheme to change the value of the entire pixel, in order to increase the entropy of encrypted image. Moreover, to further enhance the security of the cryptosystem, the keystream used in diffusion process is updated for each pixel and the computed encrypted pixel values depends on both the previously encrypted pixels and the random keystream. The proposed algorithm can resist the statistical and differential attacks. It also passed the information entropy and key sensitivity test. Experimental results indicate that the proposed algorithm has satisfactory speed and high security which makes it a very good candidate for real-time of multimedia data encryption applications.

Keywords: Secure encryption · Sorting of chaotic sequences · Permutation · Diffusion schemes

1 Introduction

In today's world, the extension of multimedia technology in which image covers the highest percentage, has promoted digital images to play a more significant role than the traditional texts. The Internet banking, e-business, e-commerce, etc., are the major fields where security is most important. So it is necessary to encrypt image data before transmission over the network to preserve its security and prevent unauthorized access. For this end, most of the conventional

© Springer International Publishing Switzerland 2015
I. Bica et al. (Eds.): SECITC 2015, LNCS 9522, pp. 87–101, 2015.
DOI: 10.1007/978-3-319-27179-8_7

encryption algorithms such as Advanced Encryption Standard (AES) [1] are designed with good properties [2,3]. However, due to bulk volume of data, high correlation among adjacent pixels, high redundancy and real time requirement [4], these ciphers may not be the most desired candidates for image encryption, particularly for fast and real-time communication applications [5]. To meet this challenge, the chaos-based encryption has suggested a new and efficient way to deal with the intractable problem of fast and highly secure image encryption [6]. The properties of chaos such as high sensitive dependence on initial conditions and control parameter, quasi-randomness, ergodicity, unpredictability, mixing, etc. [7], which are analogous to the confusion and diffusion properties of Shannon [8], have granted chaotic dynamics as a promising alternative for the traditional cryptographic algorithms, and also for generating keystream.

Depending on the type of key used in the encryption algorithms, chaos-based cryptosystems are either symmetric or asymmetric. Symmetric encryption, in which the decryption key is identical to the encryption key, is the oldest method in cryptology and is still used today. By contrast, asymmetric cryptosystems use different keys for decryption and encryption. We consider here typical (symmetric encryption) chaos-based image encryption techniques which rely on two processes: pixel permutation and pixel substitution [9,10]. The first one, also call pixel confusion is needed to scramble the pixels. But, due to the strong correlation between adjacent pixels of the images, this stage does not guarantee a good level of security [11]. The diffusion stage is thus used to modify the pixel values in order to increase the entropy of the entire image.

Several image encryption algorithms based on this structure are already available in the literature [10,12–14]. Each of them has its own strength and limitations more or less in terms of security level and computational speed. Accordingly, some of them have been cryptanalyzed successfully [15–19]. The common characteristic of these algorithms are: their chaotic generators need to be discretized to the finite sets of integers and that is time consuming and destroyed also their chaotic behaviors. Also, the keystream in the diffusion stage of these algorithms depends on the key only and that is less secured because an attacker can obtain that keystream by known/chosen plaintext attack [16]. So, to enhance the security, in [20], the keystream in the diffusion step depend on both the key and original image. Another method to obtain a high immunity to resist the differential cryptanalysis is to design strong substitution Boxes (S-Boxes) based on chaotic map or strong diffusion properties based on the combination of chaotic function and other techniques [21–23].

To improve the computational performance and to resist statistical, differential, brute-force attacks, this paper continues the same pursuit with further improvement, in which a one round chaos-based image encryption scheme based on the fast generation of large permutation key with a good level of randomness and a very high sensitivity on the keys is proposed. We use the integer sequences obtained by the descending sorting of the Logistic map as a secret key in the permutation stage. This technique avoids the excess digitization of chaotic values. As consequence, the sensitivity to small changes of the initial condition or control parameters is increased, as the true accuracy of the computer is exploited.

In diffusion process, at first, a random code is generated to get integer numbers from real numbers generated by Skew Tent map. Then, with that numbers, the exclusive-or is performed on the permuted image to computed the cipher image. The proposed approach can be easily implemented and is computationally simple.

The remaining of the paper is organized as follows. The chaotic maps are described in Sect. 2. In Sect. 3, the proposed encryption scheme is discussed in detail. Simulation results and security analysis are presented in Sect. 4 to show the efficacy and validity of the algorithm. Finally, conclusions are drawn in the last Section.

2   Chaotic Maps

Chaotic maps are nonlinear maps that exhibit chaotic behavior. The chaotic maps generate pseudo-random sequences, which are used during encryption process [24]. Many fundamental concepts in chaos theory, such as mixing and sensitivity to initial conditions and parameters, actually coincide with those in cryptography [25]. The only difference in this concern is that encryption operations are defined on finite sets of integers while chaos is defined on real numbers. The main advantage using chaos lies in the observation that a chaotic signal looks like noise for the unauthorized users. Moreover, generating chaotic values is often of low cost with simple iterations, which makes it suitable for the construction of stream ciphers. Therefore, cryptosystem can provide a secure and fast means for data encryption, which is crucial for data transmission in many applications. The proposed scheme uses Logistic and Skew Tent maps and they are both discussed hereafter.

2.1   Logistic Map

The Logistic map is a very simple non-linear dynamical and polynomial equation of degree two with x output and input variable, one initial condition x_0 and one control parameter λ and can be described as follows:

$$x_{n+1} = \lambda x_n(1 - x_n) \tag{1}$$

where $x_n \in (0, 1)$ is the state of the system, for $n = 0, 1, 2, ...$, and $\lambda \in (0, 4)$ is the control parameter. For different values of parameter λ, the Logistic sequence shows different characteristics [26]. For $3, 58 \leq \lambda \leq 4$, the Logistic map Eq. (1) has a positive Lyapunov exponent and thus is always chaotic. So all the (x_0, λ) where $x_0 \in (0, 1)$ and $3, 58 \leq \lambda \leq 4$ can be used as secret keys.

2.2   Skew Tent Map

The Skew Tent chaotic map [27] can be described as follows:

$$y_{n+1} = \begin{cases} y_n/\alpha, & \text{if } y_n \in [0, \alpha] \\ (1 - y_n)/(1 - \alpha), & \text{if } y_n \in [\alpha, 1] \end{cases} \tag{2}$$

Plain Image (I)

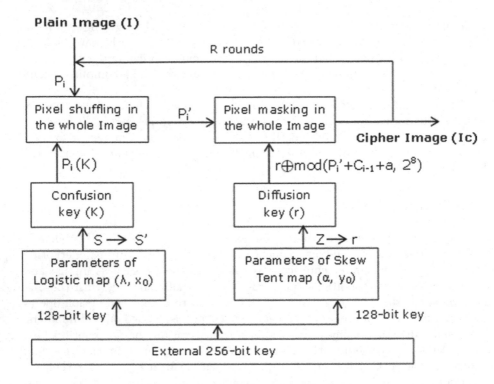

Fig. 1. Synoptic of the proposed scheme.

where α is controllable parameter for chaotic maps, y_i and y_{i+1} are the i-th and the $i+1$-th state of chaotic maps. For $\alpha \prec 1$ the system converges to 0 for all initial conditions. If $\alpha = 1$, then all initial conditions less than or equal to 0.5 are fixed points of the system, otherwise for initial conditions $y_0 \succ 0.5$ they converge to the fixed point $1 - y_0$. So all the y_0, $\alpha \in (0,1)$, can be used as secret keys.

3   Proposed Encryption Scheme

The encryption algorithm consists of two stages: permutation and diffusion of pixels of the entire image as shown in Fig. 1.

In the proposed algorithm, we use one round ($R = 1$) of confusion and diffusion for encryption.

3.1   Confusion

In this stage, the position of the pixels is scrambled over the entire image without change their values and the image becomes unrecognizable. The purpose of confusion is to reduce the high correlation between adjacent pixels in the plain image. To enhance the degree of randomness and the level of security, the Logistic map described in Subsect. 2.1 is used in order to generate pseudorandom key stream $S = \{x_1, x_2, \ldots, x_{M \times N}\}$ as the same size of the plain-image. Let I be a gray original image of size $M \times N$, containing M rows and N columns, and the gray values ranges from 0 to 255. Transform I to a one dimensional vector $P = \{P_1, P_2, \ldots, P_{M \times N}\}$, where P_i is the i-th pixel value. Then sort S by descending order, and note $S' = \{x_j, \ldots, x_8, \ldots, x_1\}$ with $x_1 \prec \ldots \prec x_8 \prec \ldots \prec x_j$, the sorted chaotic values. The positions of sorted chaotic values in the original chaotic sequence are found and stored in $K = \{j, \ldots, 8, \ldots, 1\}$. Now, the next step is to scramble the total one dimensional vector with by using the following formula:

$$P' = P(K) \tag{3}$$

where P' is the permuted image and K the permutation key. The reconstruction of P cannot be made unless the distribution of K is determined. The inverse transform for deciphering is given by:

$$P'(K) = P \tag{4}$$

This technique avoids the excess digitization of chaotic values. As consequence, the sensitivity to small changes of the initial condition or control parameters is increased, as the true accuracy of the computer is exploited and the computational time necessary for the generation of large permutation is reduced.

After obtaining the shuffled image, the correlation among the adjacent pixels is completely disturbed and the image is completely unrecognizable. Unfortunately, the histogram of the shuffled image is the same as that of the plain-image. Therefore, the shuffled image is weak against statistical attack and known plaintext attack. As a remedy, we design diffusion next to improve the security.

3.2   Diffusion

The total image is again encrypted with different chaotic numbers. Skew Tent map system shown in Sect. 2.2 is applied here to produce that numbers: $Z = \{y_1, y_2, \ldots, y_{M \times N}\}$. The masking process is employed to modify the gray values of the image pixels, to confuse the relationship between the plain image and the encrypted image in order to increase the entropy of the plain image by making its histogram uniform. The diffusion function is also used to ensure the plain image sensitivity so that, a very little change in any one pixel of plain image should spread out to almost all pixels in the whole image. Diffusion is performed by using following equation:

$$C_i = r \oplus mod(P_i' + C_{i-1} + a, 2^8) \tag{5}$$

where C_i and C_{i-1} are the value of the currently and previously masking pixel respectively; C_0 can be set as a constant; P_i' is the permuted pixels; $\oplus$ is bitwise XOR operation; a is a positive integer and r is a random code obtained according to the following formula:

$$r = mod(floor(y_n \times 2^{20}), 256) \tag{6}$$

where, mod (x, y) returns the remainder after division and y_n is the state value corresponding to the n-th iteration of the skew tent map from initial state value y_0 and α.

A random code r is computed to get integer numbers from real numbers generated by Skew Tent map.

The key formula in decryption procedure is as follows:

$$P_i' = mod(r \oplus C_i - C_{i-1} - a, 2^8) \tag{7}$$

To compute the first encrypted pixel, Eq. 8 is used.

$$C_1 = r \oplus mod(P_1' + C_0 + a, 2^8) \tag{8}$$

where r is evaluated by using Skew Tent map parameters below for $i = 1$ to generate y.

$$\begin{cases} y_0 = (C_{i-1} + a)/(255 + a + b) \\ \alpha = (P_i' + a)/(M \times N + a + b) \end{cases} \tag{9}$$

With $a, b, C_0 \succ 0$.

For the security to be strengthened, the keystream r is updated for each pixel and the computed encrypted pixel values C_i depends on the previously encrypted pixels and the keystream, hence algorithm shows resistance to the differential attacks such as known plain-text attack and known cipher-text attack.

3.3   Encryption Scheme

Encryption Algorithm. The encryption algorithm is composed of thirteen steps.

Step 1: Reshape the plaintext image I into 1-D signal P and choose x_0 and λ in (0, 1) and (3.58, 4) respectively;

Step 2: Iterate the Logistic map given in Eq. 1 for T times to get rid of transient effect, where T is a constant;

Step 3: Continue to iterate the Logistic map for $M \times N$ times, and take out the state values $S = \{x_{1+T}, x_{2+T}, ..., x_{M \times N+T}\}$;

Step 4: Sort S and get S' then, generate the permutation keys K as explained in Subsect. 3.1;

Step 5: Shuffle the pixels of the whole 1-D signal P with K using Eq. 3 and get P';

Step 6: Give C_0, choose a, b and evaluate y_0 and α in (0, 1) respectively as shown in Eq. 9;

Step 7: Iterate the Skew Tent map T times by using Eq. 2 and get the random code r;

Step 8: Compute the first cipher-pixel C_1 using Eq. 8 for $i = 1$;

Step 9: Set $i = i + 1$ and update y_0 and α in (0, 1) and get a new chaotic sequence y_t;

Step 10: Evaluate the new random code r by using Eq. 6;

Step 11: Compute cipher-pixel C_i according to the formula 5;

Step 12: Repeat step 9 to 11 until i reaches $M \times N$, the length of the whole 1-D signal;

Step 13: Reshape the 1-D signal into the 2-D image and get ciphered image.

The decryption involves reconstructing gray levels of the original image from the encrypted image. It is a simple inverse process of the proposed encryption algorithm.

Key Schedule. A key of 128 bits or 256 bits is required for symmetric-key cryptosystems for more security [29]. We used an external 256-bit key ($E_1 E_2 \cdots E_i \cdots E_{32}$, where E_i are ASCII symbols) to derive initial conditions and control parameters of the chaotic systems. The key is divided into two blocks of 16 ASCII symbols for the determination of the system control parameter and the initial condition respectively. For each block of 128 bits (corresponding to 16 ASCII symbols), we defined

$$W = \sum_{i=0}^{15} 2^{\frac{i}{i+1}} P_i \qquad (10)$$

where P_i are values (0–255) of ASCII symbols E_i and W is the value from which the control parameters and initial conditions are deduced, depending on the chaotic system. By considering the possible maximum value of ASCII symbols equal to 255 and the upper limit of the weight coefficient $2^{\frac{i}{i+1}}$ equal to 2, the value of W presents an upper limit $W_r = 8160$, which is used for its normalization.

The flowchart of the proposed encryption algorithm is then described in Fig. 2.

4 Experiments and Security Analysis

In this section, the proposed image cryptosystem is analyzed using different security measures. These measures consist of statistical analysis, sensibility analysis, information entropy analysis and differential attack analysis. Each of these measures which are widely used in the literature in the field of chaos-based cryptography [10,22,23] is described in detail in the following subsections.

4.1 Visual Test

In this subsection, we perform visual test using Lena and Black images of size 512×512 encrypted using parameters $x_0 = 0.75$, $\lambda = 3.393695629843$, for the permutation and $a = 7$, $b = 4$ and $C_0 = 23$ for the diffusion. As shown in Fig. 3(b) and (b'), the encrypted image is non-recognizable in appearance, unintelligible, incomprehensible, random and noise-like image without any leakage of the original information. This demonstrates that the proposed algorithm can be used to protect various images for diverse protections. The decrypted images are exactly same as the original images (Fig. 3(c) and (c')).

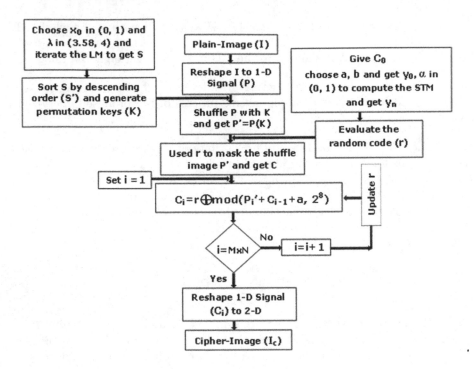

Fig. 2. Flowchart of the encryption algorithm.

4.2 Histogram Analysis

The histogram of the plain-image and cipher image is in Fig. 3(e) and (f) respectively. We found that the histogram of the ciphered image has approximately a uniform distribution. For instance, the histogram in Fig. 3(f') which corresponds to the ciphered Black image highlights the effectiveness of the algorithm, as all the 256 gray-levels present the same probability. To confirm this result, we measured the entropy for the ciphered image and we found that it has the value 7.9996 which is close to the ideal value 8.

4.3 Key Space Analysis

The key space is the total number of different keys that can be used in the encryption/decryption procedure. For an effective cryptosystem, the key space should be sufficiently large enough to resist brute-force attacks. In the proposed algorithm a 256-bit key corresponding to 32 ASCII symbols is considered and the key consists of the initial value x_0, a, b and the parameter λ, where $x_0 \in (0,1)$, $\lambda \in (3.58,4)$ et $a,b \succ 0$. In hexadecimal representation, the number of different combinations of secret keys is equal to 2^{256}. Accordingly, the theoretical key space is not less than 2^{256}, which is large enough to resist brute-force attack [10].

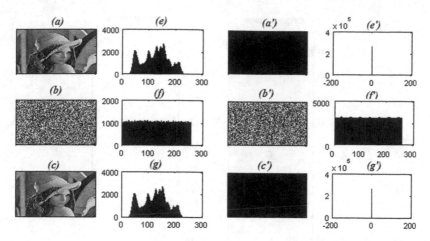

Fig. 3. Histogram: $(a), (a')$ *original image*; $(b), (b')$ *ciphered image* of $(a), (a'); (c), (c')$ *decrypted image* of $(b), (b'); (e), (e'), (f), (f'), (g), (g')$ histogram of $(a), (a'), (b), (b'), (c), (c')$ respectively.

4.4 Correlation Analysis

The proposed chaotic encryption system should be resistant to statistical attacks. Correlation coefficients of adjacent pixels in the encrypted image should be as low as possible [28] A thousand pairs of two adjacent pixels are selected randomly in vertical, horizontal, and diagonal direction from the original and encrypted images. And then, the correlation coefficient was computed using the formulas below and the results are shown in Table 1 and the visual testing of the correlation distribution of two horizontally adjacent pixels of the plain image and the cipher image produced by the proposed scheme is shown in Fig. 4. It is clear from Table 1 and Fig. 4 that the proposed approach is resistant to statistical attacks. We can also find in Table 1 that the proposed encryption algorithm has a much better statistic properties than those in [10] and [22] using respectively the same standard gray scale image Barbara and Lena with size 512×512.

$$r_{xy} = \frac{\frac{1}{N} \sum_{i=1}^{N} (x_i - \bar{x})(y_i - \bar{y})}{\sqrt{\left(\frac{1}{N} \sum_{i=1}^{N} (x_i - \bar{x})^2\right)\left(\frac{1}{N} \sum_{i=1}^{N} (x_i - \bar{y})^2\right)}} \tag{11}$$

$$\bar{x} = \frac{1}{N} \sum_{i=1}^{N} x_i \tag{12}$$

$$\bar{y} = \frac{1}{N} \sum_{i=1}^{N} y_i \tag{13}$$

where x_i and y_i are greyscale values of i-th pair of adjacent pixels, and N denotes the total numbers of samples.

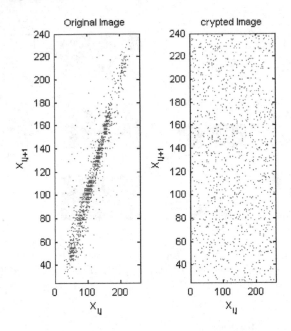

Fig. 4. Correlation of horizontally adjacent pixels of the image Lena.

4.5 Differential Attack Analysis

In general, a desirable property for an encrypted image must be sensitive to the small changes in plain-image. An opponent may make a slight change, usually one pixel, in the plain image and compare the cipher images (corresponding to very similar plain images and obtained by the same key) to find out some meaningful relationship between plain image and cipher image, which further facilitates in determining the secret key. If one minor change in the plain image can be effectively diffused to the whole ciphered image, then such differential analysis may become inefficient and practically useless. The diffusion performance is commonly measured by means of two criteria, namely, the Number of Pixel Change Rate (NPCR) and the Unified Average Changing Intensity (UACI). NPCR is used to measure the percentage of different pixel numbers between two images. The NPCR between two ciphered images A and B of size $M \times N$ is [28]:

$$NPCR_{AB} = \frac{\sum\limits_{i=1}^{M} \sum\limits_{j}^{N} D(i,j)}{M \times N} \times 100 \qquad (14)$$

where

$$D(i,j) = \begin{cases} 1, & A(i,j) \neq B(i,j) \\ 0, & otherwise \end{cases} \qquad (15)$$

The expected NPCR for two random images with 256 gray levels is 99.609 %. The second criterion, UACI is used to measure the average intensity of differences between the two images. It is defined as [27]:

Table 1. Correlation coefficients of two adjacent pixels for two plain and cipher images.

Name	Plain image of Lena			Cipher image of Lena		
	Horizontal	*Vertical*	*Diagonal*	*Horizontal*	*Vertical*	*Diagonal*
Proposed Algorithm	0.9395	0.9789	0.9286	0.0002	0.0030	0.0008
[22]				0.0097	0.0136	0.0178
Name	Plain image of Barbara			Cipher image of Barbara		
	Horizontal	*Vertical*	*Diagonal*	*Horizontal*	*Vertical*	*Diagonal*
Proposed Algorithm	0.9792	0.9809	0.9551	−0.0031	−0.0175	0.0010
[10]				0.0217	0.0086	0.0118

$$UACI_{AB} = \frac{100}{M \times N} \sum_{1}^{M} \sum_{1}^{N} \frac{|A(i,j) - B(i,j)|}{255} \tag{16}$$

For a 256 gray levels image, the expected UACI value is 33.464 %.

The NPCR and UACI test results are shown in Table 2. The proposed cryptosystem achieves high performance by having $NPCR \succ 0.99609$ and $UACI \succ 0.33464$ and can well resist the known-plaintext and the chosen-plaintext attacks. Also, the results in Table 3 show that the proposed scheme requires fewer permutation and diffusion rounds than the other algorithms. Indeed, the proposed scheme requires few chaotic numbers for the generation of complex permutation and diffusion keys, which contributes to the raise of the speed performance as compared to the other algorithms.

4.6 Information Entropy

The information entropy can be calculated by:

$$H = -\sum_{i=1}^{2^M} p(m_i) log_2(p(m_i)) \tag{17}$$

where M is the number of bits to represent a symbol; $p(m_i)$ represents the probability of occurrence of symbol m_i and *log* denotes the base 2 logarithm so that the entropy is expressed in bits. It is known that if the information entropy is close to 8, the encryption algorithm is secure upon the entropy attack. The results in Table 4 show that, our scheme is better in the aspect of the information entropy than the other encryption schemes.

4.7 Key Sensitivity Analysis

An ideal image encryption procedure should have not only a large key space but also a high key sensitivity. Key sensitivity implies that the small change in the secret key should produce entirely different encrypted image. It means

Table 2. NPCR and UACI of image Lena by proposed method

NPCR	UACI
0.99693	0.33621

Table 3. Comparison of round number of scanning-image Lena, confusion and diffusion to achieve $NPCR > 99.6\%$ and $UACI > 33.4\%$

Algorithm	NPCR %	UACI %	Round number of scanning-image	Round number of confusion	Round number of diffusion
Proposed	>99.6	>33.4	1	1	1
Ref. [22]	>99.6	>33.4	2	-	2
Ref. [28]	>99.6	>33.4	2	2	2
Ref. [29]	>99.6	>33.4	1	5	1

that a slight change in the key should cause some large changes in the ciphered image [28]. This property makes the cryptosystem of high security against statistical or differential attacks. Figure 5 shows key sensitivity test result. Where the plain Lena image is firstly encrypted using the test key ($x_0 = 0.75, \lambda = 3.93695629843, a = 9, b = 2$). Then the ciphered image is tried to be decrypted using five decryption keys:
(i) $x_0 = 0.75, \lambda = 3.93695629843, a = 9, b = 2$; (ii) $x_0 = 0.74, \lambda = 3.93695629843, a = 9, b = 2$; (iii) $x_0 = 0.75, \lambda = 3.93695629842, a = 9, b = 2$; (iv) $x_0 = 0.75, \lambda = 3.93695629843, a = 8, b = 2$; (v) $x_0 = 0.75, \lambda = 3.93695629843, a = 9, b = 3$.

It can be observed that the decryption with a slightly different key fails completely. Therefore, the proposed image encryption scheme is highly key sensitive.

4.8 Efficiency Analysis

Running speed of the algorithm is an important aspect for a good encryption algorithm, particularly for the real-time internet applications. In general, encryption speed is highly dependent on the CPU/MPU structure, RAM size, Operating System platform, the programming language and also on the compiler options. So, it is senseless to compare the encryption speeds of two ciphers image. We evaluated the performance of encryption scheme by using Matlab 7.10.0. Although the algorithm was not optimized, performances measured on a 2.0 GHz Pentium Dual-Core with 3GB RAM running Windows XP are satisfactory.

The average running speed depends on the precision used for the quantization of chaotic values.

For $p = 8$, the average computational time required for 256 gray-scale images of size 512×512 is shorter than 100 ms. By comparing this result with those presented in Ref. [28], the scheme can be said high-speed as we only used a 2.0 GHz processor and the Matlab 7.10.0 software. Indeed, the modulus and the XOR

Table 4. Information Entropy of Lena cipher image

Algorithm	Entropy
Proposed	7.9996
Ref. [22]	7.9971
Ref. [23]	7.9993
Ref. [29]	7.9902

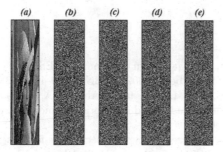

Fig. 5. Key sensitivity test: (a) Deciphered image using key (i); (b) Deciphered image using key (ii); (c) Deciphered image using key (iii); (d) Deciphered image using key (iv); (e) Deciphered image using key (v).

functions are the most used basic operations in our algorithm. Also, the comparison between the simulations times required at the permutation stage shows that the computational time required in our experiment is three times less than that of Chong Fu et al's. [29]. This means that the actual computational times of our scheme could be at least smaller if implemented in the same conditions than the Chong Fu et al's. algorithm. So, referring to actual fast ciphers [22,23], our proposed algorithm has a fast running speed. Such a speed is promising for real time applications of multimedia data encryption.

5   Conclusion

In this paper, we proposed a new fast and secure chaos-based algorithm for image encryption. In the proposed scheme, the permutation-diffusion design based on the fast generation of large permutation and diffusion key with a good level of randomness and a very high sensitivity has been investigated. In order to shuffle entire image, we have proposed to sort chaotic sequences of the logistic map. This procedure allows avoiding the cyclic digitization of chaotic numbers in the generation of permutation key. In the diffusion stage, in order to avoid the known/chosen plaintext attack, we have proposed to link keystream with both the key and original image to mask the whole image. By using these techniques, the spreading process is significantly accelerated contrary to that of Chong Fu et al. [29]. Also, we proved the very good cryptographic performances of the proposed image scheme through an extensive analysis, performed with respect to the latest methodology from this field. As a result, one round of encryption with the proposed algorithm is safe enough to resist exhaustive attack, chosen plaintext attack and statistical attack. The new scheme has higher security and faster enciphering/deciphering speeds. This makes it a very good candidate for real-time image encryption applications.

Acknowledgement. J.D.D Nkapkop gratefully acknowledges the AUF for their financial support.

References

1. Daemen, J., Rijmen, V.: The Design of Rijndael: AES - The Advanced Encryption Standard. Springer, Heidelberg (2002). ISBN 3-540-42580-2
2. Riaz, F., Hameed, S., Shafi, I., Kausar, R., Ahmed, A.: Enhanced image encryption techniques using modified advanced encryption standard. Commun. Comput. Inf. Sci. **281**, 385–396 (2012)
3. Dey, S.: SD-AEI: an advanced encryption technique for images. In: Proceedings of the Second International Conference on Digital Information Processing and Communications (ICDIPC), Klaipeda, Lithuania, pp. 68–73 (2012)
4. Mohammed, A.: A novel encryption method for image security. Int. J. Secur. Its App. **6**, 1–8 (2012)
5. Li, S., Chen, G., Cheung, A., Bhargava, B., Lo, K.T.: On the design of perceptual MPEG-video encryption algorithms. In: IEEE Transactions on Circuits and Systems for Video Technology, pp. 214–223 (2007)
6. Mohammad, S., Mirzakuchaki, S.: A fast color image encryption algorithm based on coupled two-dimensional piecewise chaotic map. Sig. Process. **92**, 1202–1215 (2012)
7. Lin, C-F., Chung, C-H.: A fast chaos-based visual encryption mecanism for integrated ECG/EEG medical signals with transmission error. In: 12th WSEAS International Conference on SYSTEMS, pp. 355–360, Heraklion, Greece (2008)
8. Shannon, C.: Communication theory of secrecy systems. Bell Syst. Tech. J. **28**, 656–715 (1949)
9. Srivastava, A.: A survey report on Different Techniques of Image Encryption. Int. J. Emerg. Technol. Adv. Eng. **2**, 163–167 (2012)
10. Wang, J-Y., Chen, G.: Design of a chaos-based digital image encryption algorithm in time domain. In: IEEE International Conference on Computational Intelligence & Communication Technology (CICT), pp. 26–28 (2015)
11. Li, S., Li, C., Chen, G., Bourbakis, N.G., Lo, K.T.: A general quantitative cryptanalysis of permutation-only multimedia ciphers against plaintext attacks. Sig. Process. Image Commun. **23**, 212–223 (2008)
12. Sivakumar, T., Venkatesan, R.: A novel approach for image encryption using dynamic SCAN patter. IAENG Int. J. Comput. Sci. **4**, 91–101 (2014)
13. Boriga, R., Dsclescu, A.C., Diaconu, A.V.: A new image cryptosystem based on some chaotic maps. IAENG Int. J. Comput. Sci. **41**, 41–51 (2014)
14. Ghebleh, M., Kanso, A., Noura, H.: An image encryption scheme based on irregularly decimated chaotic maps. Sig. Process. Image Commun. **29**, 618–627 (2014)
15. Alvarez, G., Li, S.: Cryptanalyzing a nonlinear chaotic algorithm (NCA) for image encryption. Commun. Nonlinear Sci. Numer. Simul. **4**, 3743–3749 (2009)

16. Rhouma, R., Solak, E., Belghith, S.: Cryptanalysis of a new substitution-difusion based image cipher. Commun Nonlinear. Sci. Numer. Simul. **15**, 1887–1892 (2010)
17. Li, C., Arroyo, D., Lo, K.: Breaking a chaotic cryptographic scheme based on composition maps. In. J. Bifurcat. Chaos **20**, 2561–2568 (2010)
18. Rhouma, R., Belghith, S.: Cryptanalysis of a new image encryption algorithm based on hyper-chaos. Phys. Lett. A. **372**, 5973–5978 (2008)
19. Solak, E., Çokal, C., Yildiz, O.T., Biyikoglu, T.: Cryptanalysis of Fridrichs chaotic image encryption. Int. J. Bifurcat. Chaos. **20**, 1405–14013 (2010)
20. Zhu, C., Liao, C., Deng, X.: Breaking and improving an image encryption scheme based on total shuffling scheme. Nonlinear Dyn. **71**, 25–34 (2013)
21. Guesmi, R., Farah, B., Kachouri, A., Samet, M.: A novel design of Chaos based S-Boxes using genetic algorithm techniques. In: IEEE 11th International Conference on Computer Systems and Applications (AICCSA), pp. 678–684 (2014)
22. Wang, X., Wang, Q.: A Novel image encryption algorithm based on dynamic S-boxes construted by chaos. Nonlinear Dyn. **75**, 567–576 (2014). doi:10.1007/s11071-013-1086-2
23. Wang, Y., Zhang, X., Zheng, Z., Qiu, W.: A colour image encryption algorithm using 4-pixel Feistel structure and multiple chaotic systems. Nonlinear Dyn. **81**, 1–18 (2015). doi:10.1007/s11071-015-1979-3
24. Şerbănescu, A., Rîncu, C.I.: Systemes et signaux face au chaos: applications aux communications. Editura Academiei Tehnice Militare, Bucureşti (2008)
25. Gonzalo, A., Shujun, L.: Some basic cryptographic requirements for chaos-based cryptosystems. Int. J. Bifurcat. Chaos **16**, 2129 (2006). doi:10.1142/S0218127406015970
26. Zhang, Q., Guo, L., Wei, X.: Image encryption using DNA addition combining with chaotic maps. Math. Comput. Model. **52**, 2028–2035 (2010)
27. Billings, L., Bollt, E.: Probability density functions of some skew tent maps. Chaos Solitons Fractals **12**, 365–376 (2001)
28. Wang, Y., Wong, K.-W., Liao, X., Chen, G.: A new chaos-based fast image encryption algorithm. Appl. Soft Comput. **11**, 514–522 (2011)
29. Chong, F., Chen, J.-J., Zou, H., Meng, W.-H., Zhan, Y.-F.: A chaos-based digital image encryption with an improved permutation strategy. Optic. Express. **20**, 2363–2378 (2012)

A Novel Key Management for Virtually Limitless Key Size

Damir Omerasevic[1]([✉]), Narcis Behlilovic[2], and Sasa Mrdovic[2]

[1] PBH Technologies, PrinTec Group of Companies,
Sarajevo, Bosnia and Herzegovina
d.omerasevic@printec.ba
[2] Faculty of Electrical Engineering, University of Sarajevo,
Sarajevo, Bosnia and Herzegovina
{narcis.behlilovic,sasa.mrdovic}@etf.unsa.ba

Abstract. The paper proposes key management between two parties, based on set of multimedia files shared by sender and recipient. The method is simple, fast, secure and robust. Possible key sizes are virtually limitless. One implementation, which uses YouTube website as a source of multimedia files, is presented.

Keywords: Entropy · Key creation · Key exchange · Key management · Randomness

1 Introduction

The goal of this paper is to propose simple, fast, secure and robust key management between two parties. We separated key management problem into three parts:

1. Creation of session-based type of keys, based on set of images, shared by sender and recipient,
2. Finding types of images with entropy suitable for session-based type of keys, and
3. Implementation with robust and secure key exchange properties, for creating key encryption key (KEK), for session-based type of keys.

1.1 Creation of Session-Based Type of Keys

All modern ciphers, like AES [1] or RSA [2], implement Kerckhoffs' principle [3] and Shannon's Maxim [4] that security of system is in security of secret key. Therefore, secret keys needs to be safe.

There are two possible ways to attack cipher secret key. One is to try all possible values of the key until the correct key is guessed, brute force attack. To prevent this kind of attack key needs to be as long as possible. The other way of attack is to try to get hold of the secret key.

© Springer International Publishing Switzerland 2015
I. Bica et al. (Eds.): SECITC 2015, LNCS 9522, pp. 102–118, 2015.
DOI: 10.1007/978-3-319-27179-8_8

To protect secret key various key establishment protocols have been developed. They all address the problem of how to securely make secret key available to all pairs that need to use it to encrypt messages.

In this paper we use multimedia files to establish secret key for encryption, between two parties. There is no need to exchange keys. Keys are generated from multimedia files that both sides have. This is similar to session-based or one-time keys. Exchange parties have to exchange information on which set of files they use, from time to time, which is similar to KEK.

It is not good enough to use any set of multimedia files for session-based type of keys. Therefore, we had to discover adequate types of multimedia files for that purpose.

1.2 Discovering Types of Multimedia Files Suitable for Session-Based Type of Keys

Using entropy to measure randomness on series of data values is a well-accepted statistical practice in information theory [4].

In information theory, entropy is a measure of uncertainty. Under this term is commonly understood Shannon's entropy (although her origin comes from Pauli's [5] and von Neumann's quantum statistical mechanics [6]), which quantifies the expected value of the information contained in the message, usually in units such as bits.

According to Shannon, entropy H of any message or state is the following:

$$H = -K \sum_{i=1}^{n} p_i \log p_i \qquad (1)$$

where p_i is probability of the state i from n possible states, and K is an optional constant.

By measuring entropy of different sets of multimedia files, we could also measure randomness on the sets, and therefore we could discover adequate types of multimedia files for session-based type of keys.

1.3 Implementation with Secure and Robust Key Exchange Properties

GNU Privacy Guard (GnuPG or GPG) is a General Public Licence (GPL) alternative to the Pretty Good Privacy (PGP) suite of cryptographic software. The GNU General Public License (GNU GPL or GPL) is the most common used free software license today. GPL allows freedom to use, study, share (copy), charge and modify the software [7,8]. GPG is a part of the Free Software Foundation's GNU software project, and has received major funding from the German government.

The implementation with secure and robust exchange properties, described in this paper, proposes that the data set (i.e. sets and ordering of files) is first signed and encrypted by GNU Privacy Guard (GnuPG or GPG), which is compliant with RFC 4880 [9], which is the current IETF standards track specification of OpenPGP. After that, secure message is converter into Quick Response (QR) code.

GPG now supports RSA signing and encryption keys (in addition to the older DSA for signing and ElGamal for encryption methods). DSA signing keys are limited to 1024 bit lengths, while RSA signing keys can be much longer (512 to 4096 bits are commonly used). In GnuPG version 2, the default is to create two RSA keys for the account now, one for encryption and one for signing.

We use QR codes error correction levels (L up to 7 % of damage, M up to 15 % of damage, Q up to 25 % of damage and H up to 30 % of damage) for including robustness in our proposition.

1.4   Our Contributions

Idea of this paper is to use a set of multimedia files, in order to establish secret key for encryption, between two parties. With proposed approach, key space and therefore key length, is virtually limitless.

In addition, there is no need to exchange keys. Keys are generated from multimedia files that both sides have. Our idea is to use image bits directly from files. Exchange parties have to exchange information on which set of files they use, from time to time. This information can be updated dynamically, by using encrypted channel that has been established.

The main question here is how securely exchange information on which set of files parties use. The implementation of proposed key management, described in this paper, proposes that the data set of files parties use, is first signed and encrypted by GPG, and after that converted to QR code. GPG use RSA keys for signing and encryption. Robustness of presented implementation is due to QR code features, which are resistant to a certain level on errors.

1.5   Paper Organization

The paper is organized as follows. Related work is addressed in Sect. 2. Section 3 explains how to measure entropy in different video and audio media files. Section 4 explains our idea on how to establish encryption keys. Conclusion and discussion, as well as directions for future research work are in Sect. 5.

2   Related Work

We separated related work into two parts:

1. Creation of keys, and
2. QR codes, as a base for robustness.

2.1 Related Work on Creation of Keys

Basic issues of key establishment with various key transport and key agreement protocols are well covered in books [11,12].

We use some concepts and ideas from both steganography and cryptography, when we use multimedia files to establish secret key for encryption, between two parties.

Steganography deals with ways of embedding secret messages on carrier media [13]. The characteristics of the carrier medium depend on the amount of secret information that can be hidden, on the perceptibility of carrier media and its robustness [14–18].

Different ideas on combining cryptography with steganography have appeared [19–24]. One idea is to hide ciphertext within an image using steganography, like it was proposed in [25]. To further complicate things [26] proposes encrypting plaintext twice before hiding it in an image. Paper [27] proposes doing encryption and hiding in one step, and saving time and resources.

According to authors' best knowledge and available data, the focus of the most of ideas is mainly on steganography, where cover medium is used as a carrier.

Idea to use different kind of media files to generate cryptographic keys is not new. Most of proposed solutions were to generate personalized keys based on biometric features like fingerprint [28], voice [29] or face [30]. Good recent overview of biometric key generation methods and issues can be found in [31]. However, all of ideas mentioned here requiring certain processing time, which prolongs total encryption time. Again, our method borrows some ideas from this area of research, but does not propose permanent personal keys, rather one time session keys.

The most similar idea to the one we propose is expressed in [32]. Their method uses image features for key generation. Process of key generation is rather complicated, and requires time. They also use their own encryption algorithm.

Our idea is to use image bits directly.

2.2 Related Work on QR Codes

We use error correction levels embedded into QR code for improving robustness of our secure information (on data set).

In the last few years we experienced a very large application of QR codes in steganography, authentication and video watermarking. In [33], QR code and image processing techniques are used to construct a nested steganography scheme. A lossless data is embedded into a cover image. The data does not have any distortion, when comparing with the extracted data and original data. Since the extracted text is lossless, the error correction rate of QR encoding must be carefully designed. Authors of [33] found out that 25 % error correction rate is suitable for the goal. This scheme is also robust to Joint Photographic Experts Group (JPEG) attacks.

In [34] authors proposed a geo-location based QR-code authentication scheme using mobile phone, to defeat against man-in-the-middle phishing attacks. The proposed scheme provides convenience, mobility, and security for the user.

Paper [35], proposes a video watermarking with text data (verification message) by using QR code. QR code is prepared to be watermarked by SVD (singular value decomposition) and DWT (Discrete Wavelet Transform). In addition to that, logo/watermark gives the authorized ownership of video document.

3 How to Measure Randomness in Different Video and Audio Media Files

By using existing sets of already existing sources of media file types, which are good enough from randomness perspective to be used in everyday practice, we are shortening time for encryption/decryption, and therefore making the whole encryption/decryption process faster.

3.1 Randomness Tests

In order to test which media file types are good enough from randomness perspective to be used in everyday practice, we were using different statistical tests [10, 36], namely the following:

1. Entropy Test
   Entropy originally was introduced in thermodynamics and Shannon applied it on digital communications [4]. Entropy is a measure of the uncertainty in a random variable in information theory, so we could interpret entropy as the measurement of randomness. Shannon was interested in determining what was theoretical maximum amount for file compression, i.e. more entropy means less compression (and better quality of randomness) and vice versa. We tested entropy as percentage, which means that results which are the closest to 100 % are the best.
2. Arithmetic Mean Test
   Arithmetic Mean Test is simply the result of summing all of bits in tested file and divide with the length of the file. If bits in tested file are close to random, the result should be close to 0.5.
3. Serial Correlation Test
   Serial Correlation Test measures coefficient or extent to which each byte in tested file depends on the previous byte [36]. If the coefficient in tested file are close to random, the result should be close to 0.
4. Lempel-Ziv Compression Test [37]
   The purpose of the test is to determine if and how much of testing sequence can be compressed. The sequence is considered to be random if it can not be significantly compressed. If the sequence in tested file is close to random, the result should be close to 0.

3.2 Testing Environment for Randomness Tests

Testing environment for randomness tests was set on laptop, with the following hardware: CPU Intel Core i7-3610QM, CPU working frequency 2.30 GHz, and RAM memory 12 GB. The laptop had the following software installed: operating system Windows 7 Professional Edition with SP1, and compiler Borland C++ version 5.02.

As a source for our testing sets of file types, we used the following sets: JPG, WAV, FLV WEBM and MP3 set of files.

3.3 Testing Procedure

We used compiler Borland C++ and adopted source code from [36] and we created additional scripts for faster processing. Scripts are done in that way that we use [36] not only for one file, but for the whole folder, so we made efficiency and performance improvement for overall measurement process.

The measurement is done by running scripts, one time for each tested file type, and after that we collected results. We extracted all tables and comparisons, which are presented in next subsections of this paper, from collected results.

We used file indexes instead of real file names, due to space reduction and better table data clarity. File size is given in bits, for calculating purposes.

3.4 Test Results

Test results are presented for two best suited types of files:

- FLV set of files, and
- WEBM set of files.

FLV Testing. Test results for FLV file types are given in Table 1. As we could see from the results, FLV files have very good test results, for the purpose of this work, for all of four tests, as the following:

- File entropy expressed as a percentage varies from 99.9531 to 100.0000, which is very close to 100.0000,
- Arithmetic mean varies from 0.4939 to 0.50004, which is very close to 0.5,
- Serial correlation varies from 0.001153 to 0.019413, which is very close to 0, and
- Reduction of compression is expressed as a percentage and is not varying, which means that is exactly equal to 0.

WEBM Testing. Test results for WEBM file types are given in Table 2. As we could see from the results, WEBM files have very good test results, very close to FLV results, for the purpose of this work, for all of four tests, as the following:

Table 1. Results of comparison for FLV files

File index	File size	Entropy (%)	Arithmetic mean	Serial correlation	Compression (%)
FLV1	149177272	99.9531	0.4872	0.019413	0
FLV2	59895888	99.9994	0.4985	0.005974	0
FLV3	158340880	99.9984	0.4977	0.00546	0
FLV4	700971952	100.0000	0.5004	0.001153	0
FLV5	33027968	99.9891	0.4939	0.012764	0
FLV6	361880112	99.9993	0.4985	0.003405	0
FLV7	460491968	99.9983	0.4975	0.00545	0
FLV8	309196744	100.0000	0.4999	0.002019	0
FLV9	58047696	99.9982	0.4975	0.005092	0
FLV10	156009472	99.9983	0.4975	0.00545	0

Table 2. Results of Comparison for WEBM files

File Index	File size	Entropy (%)	Arithmetic mean	Serial correlation	Compression (%)
WEBM1	113135048	99.9295	0.4844	0.020691	0
WEBM2	1244183048	99.9998	0.4993	0.003173	0
WEBM3	311626752	99.9834	0.4924	0.005272	0
WEBM4	101210448	99.9960	0.4963	0.014056	0
WEBM5	365222584	99.9995	0.4986	0.011864	0
WEBM6	320629952	99.9969	0.4967	0.009266	0
WEBM7	228198976	99.9995	0.4987	0.006817	0
WEBM8	219042400	99.9909	0.4944	0.012517	0
WEBM9	314455432	99.9862	0.4931	0.006153	0
WEBM10	601979712	99.9976	0.4971	0.009781	0

- File entropy expressed as a percentage varies from 99.9295 to 99.9998, which is very close to 100.0000,
- Arithmetic mean varies from 0.4844 to 0.4993, which is very close to 0.5,
- Serial correlation varies from 0.003173 to 0.014056, which is very close to 0, and
- Reduction of compression is expressed as a percentage and is not varying, which means that is exactly equal to 0.

4   Proposed Implementation for Key Exchange

Parties in secret communication need to agree on a set of files (some kind of keys) they are going to use for encryption. Therefore, it is a very important issue of distribution of this "master" key. We address that problem in the following subsection.

4.1 Distribution of the "Master" Key

We proposed a solution to the issue, of distribution of "master" key.

We show by experiment that the best source for "master" key are FLV/WEBM files. Very good source of FLV files is YouTube website. All YouTube video files could be accessed by the following Uniform Resource Locator (URL) syntax:

https://www.youtube.com/watch?v=key

where *key* is 11-alphanumeric YouTube video identification (ID), like, for example, *"voLNA8LdcCw"* (without quotes).

Our initial message (and the size of the set) has 256 *key*, i.e. 256 file set is described with 256 lines of 11-alphanumeric YouTube IDs.

By using YouTube IDs, we could access all format of video files from one place and, depending of device and appropriate web browser, automatically show the best fitted video format for device which is currently used.

In order to get specific video format from specific YouTube IDs, we need to parse HyperText Markup Language (HTML) code for each of 256 YouTube IDs, and identify exact URL locations for FLV/WEBM files.

Considering the fact that we have all information about complete file set in one initial message, there is no need in this implementation to have separate messages for file sets and orders. We show processes from both sender and receiver side.

4.2 Distribution of the "Master" Key - Sender Side

In Fig. 1 we described secure exchange process, initiated from sender side.

The process from sender side consists of eight steps:

1. Prepare initial message by sender,
2. Sign and encrypt initial message with GPG,
3. Prepare/encode QR code,
4. Send QR code to recipient,
5. Receive QR code by recipient,
6. Decode QR code,
7. Decrypt and verify signature with GPG, and
8. Prepare/calculate identical copy of initial message.

The most important parts from sender side are located in the first and the fourth step. We describe all steps in more details. After the last step is executed, we have to let sender know, that recipient received initial message.

Prepare Initial Message by Sender. Initial message file consist of 256 lines. In each line is 11-alphanumeric YouTube video identification (ID), plus additional end of line characters, like line feed (LF) and carriage return (CR). The total of 3,328 bytes is used.

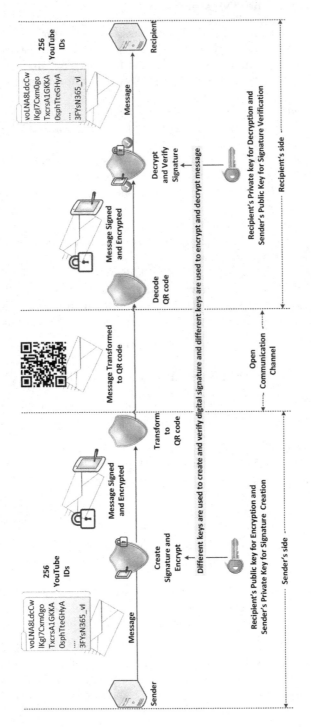

Fig. 1. Secure key exchange with QR code (sender side)

We could manually type into initial message file all of 256 lines (YouTube IDs), but it not convenient. Although YouTube has a huge set of video files, it is not correct that we just randomly generate 256 of 11-alphanumeric IDs, because some of IDs generated on that way will no exist. We have to be sure that all of 11-alphanumeric IDs really exist on YouTube site.

Therefore, we suggest the following steps for creation of non-manual initial message file.

1. Randomly create 256 three-character (al least) strings,
2. Fetch from YouTube site pseudo-random chosen video, for each of three-character (al least) string, by using YouTube application programming interface (API),
3. Extract YouTube ID, for all of fetched YouTube videos.

Sign and Encrypt Initial Message with GPG. We used GPG4Win command-line utility *gpg.exe*, together with appropriate parameters, for signing and encrypting of initial message.

The syntax for signing and encrypting is the following:

gpg –armor –recipient Damir –encrypt –sign keys.txt

where *Damir* is recipient name, and *keys.txt* contains the initial message file.

Prepare/Encode QR Code. For QR codes, we used compiler Microsoft Studio 2005, Visual C# part of the Studio, and adopted source code from [38], by making command-line applications. We were making additional batch scripts for easier usage. Scripts are done in that way that we write in advance parameters needed for command-line application, so we made efficiency and performance improvement for overall measurement process.

The syntax for creating QR code is the following:

QRCodeConsoleApp.exe keys.txt.asc jpg keys.jpg

where *QRCodeConsoleApp.exe* is name for QR code console application, *keys.txt.asc* contains GPG-signed and encrypted initial message file, *jpg* is type of graphical format used for QR code and *keys.jpg* if file name for created QR code.

Send QR Code to Recipient. While sender is sending QR code to the recipient, an adversary could only listen (passive adversary), in order to try to learn more about messages exchanged. Adversary could try to put some noise into communication channel, or deliberately change some bits in the message, in order to prevent communication (active adversary).

Robustness of proposed key exchange is in the fact that we still can decode original (ciphertext) message, although QR code is damaged. Damage recovery is dependent on error level correction which we use during QR code encoding.

Receive QR Code by Recipient. Recipient receives QR code and he does not know if QR code is sent by sender or not. In order to check it, recipient first has to decode QR code.

Decode QR Code. Result of decoding QR code should be (identical copy of) the initial message file. However, recipient still does not know if initial message is send by sender or not. In order to check it, recipient has to decrypts and verify signature with GPG.

Decrypt and Verify Signature with GPG. The syntax for decrypting and verifying initial message is the following:

gpg –output decrypt-keys.txt –decrypt keys.txt.asc

where *keys.txt.asc* is GPG-signed and encrypted message, and *decrypt-keys.txt* contains (identical copy of) the initial message file, if sender signature is verified.

Prepare/Calculate Identical Copy of Initial Message. After confirming authenticity of (identical copy of) the initial message file, the result of previous step is creating *decrypt-keys.txt* file, which contains decrypted (identical copy of) the initial message file.

4.3   Distribution of the "Master" Key - Recipient Side

The process from recipient side consists of six steps:

1. Sign and encrypt (identical copy of) initial message with GPG,
2. Prepare/encode QR code,
3. Send QR code to sender,
4. Receive QR code by sender,
5. Decode QR code, and
6. Decrypt and verify signature with GPG.

It is important to stress here that it is not enough just to sign (identical copy of) initial message with GPG, but the message must be signed and encrypted, in order to preserve secrecy of the message.

As soon as sender decrypt and verify signature with GPG, which is send from recipient side as an acknowledgment of receiving ordered set of files, secret message communication could begin.

4.4   Secret Message Communication

As soon as sender and a recipient securely exchange an information of ordered set of files that are, individually, much bigger then messages being exchanged, secret message communication could start.

For each message to be encrypted the sender picks a file from the set and a position within that file. The bits of a plaintext message are XOR-ed with the bits of the selected file from the selected position to generate a ciphertext. The ciphertext with an index of the selected file and the position within the file is sent to the recipient. Using the index and the position, recipient can transform the ciphertext back to plaintext by XOR-ing it with the bits of the same file from the same position.

We describe formal model in the following subsection.

Formal Model. Formal model of secret message has the following notation:

- k - key space (FLV files),
- P_k - ordered set of files P from key space k,
- i - file index i,
- P_i - selected file i from ordered set of files P,
- p - starting position p in bits in file P_i,
- $bP_i(j)$ - bit j in file P_i,
- m - plaintext message only,
- L_{UH} - length of unencrypted header,
- L_{EH} - length of encrypted header,
- L_m - length of the plaintext message,
- L_{EF} - length of encrypted footer,
- C - ciphertext message,
- bM_j - bit j of to-be-encrypted header, plaintext message and to-be-encrypted footer,
- bC_j - bit j of encrypted header, ciphertext message and encrypted footer.

Using above notation, encryption for part of secret message which is to-be-encrypted can be expressed with:

Algorithm 1. Encryption for part of secret message which is to-be-encrypted

---
1: **for** j = 1 to $(L_{EH} + L_m + L_{EF})$ **do**
2:     $bC_j = bM_j \oplus bP_i(p + j - 1)$
3: **end for**

Similarly, decryption for part of secret message which is encrypted can be expressed with:

Algorithm 2. Decryption for part of secret message which is encrypted

---
1: **for** j = 1 to $(L_{EH} + L_m + L_{EF})$ **do**
2:     $bM_j = bC_j \oplus bP_i(p + j - 1)$
3: **end for**

Table 3. The structure of unencrypted part of the header of the message

Header field description	Length
File index i	1 byte
Position p in file P_i	4 bytes

Table 4. The structure of encrypted part of the header of the message

Header field description	Length
Datetime stamp sender	8 bytes
Datetime stamp recipient	8 bytes

Table 5. The structure of encrypted footer of the message

Footer field description	Length
Secure Hash Algorithm-1 (SHA-1) of the whole message	20 bytes
Secure Hash Algorithm-1 (SHA-1) of the file used for encryption	20 bytes

Message Format. Since messages with a ciphertext need to include file index i and starting position p, within unencrypted part of the message, we defined message format, for implementation we created.

The structure of unencrypted part of the header of the message is given in Table 3.

The structure of encrypted part of the header of the message is in Table 4.

The structure of encrypted footer of the message is given in Table 5.

The structure of the message is given in Table 6.

4.5 Security Analysis

It is obvious that security of proposed key exchange method is in secrecy of a set of files. The set of files might be considered as a master key or some sort of key encryption key, while the bits of files used to encrypt messages have a role of session keys. Key size of this master key is practically limitless since the number of possible file sets is practically limitless. There are implementation issues regarding the size of the set and the size of the files that might limit the possible size of this "master" key for a particular implementation.

A third party that monitors the communication channel can capture the ciphertext, the index and the position. The index and the position are of no value without knowledge of the file set. The ciphertext is the result of XOR-ing plaintext message with the key, the bits form the selected file, that is the same length as the message. Since each message is encrypted with a different key, that has the same length as the message, our method resembles one-time pads.

Message format described assumes that there are maximum of 256 files in set (File index is 1 byte long), meaning 256! of permutations for selected file

Table 6. The structure of the message

Field description	Length
Unencrypted header	5 bytes
Encrypted header	16 bytes
Bits of ciphertext	L - length of plaintext/ciphertext in bits
Encrypted footer	40 bytes

set. Position is defined with four bytes that allows for 2^{32}, over 4 billion, positions. Encrypted header contains encrypted time stamps for sender and recipient. Encrypted footer is SHA-1 hash for the complete message. The session key is selected from key space of randomly selected FLV files.

The attacker could only find out unencrypted part of the header of the message, i.e. file number and position in the file. The attacker can not decrypt the message, since he has no knowledge about KEK. However, the attacker/adversary could change unencrypted part of the header of the message, and therefore prevent communication between two parties.

Therefore, we use encrypted footer. Within encrypted footer we have two SHA-1 hash values. The first SHA-1 hash protects the whole message, including timestamps from sender and recipient, which could prevent replay attack. By calculating SHA-1 hash of received message on recipient side, we could also know if any other attempt was made, in order to change the message, by comparing calculated SHA-1 hash value with the first SHA-1 hash value in encrypted footer of the message received.

The second SHA-1 hash is calculated from the file which is used for encryption/decryption. The file is downloaded from YouTube site, at different time, on sender and recipient sides. In order to be sure that sender and recipient have the same file for encryption/decryption, we calculate SHA-1 hash and use it during secure communication.

We describe in Sect. 3 how to measure entropy in different video and audio media files. In a case that the set of files used to encrypt the message is revealed in future, it is possible to decrypt the message for anyone with an access to the set and the encrypted message with the index and the position. However, considering the fact that we are using GPG with RSA keys for signing and encrypting, we consider our proposition safe and secure.

5   Conclusion

Key management presented in this paper is simple and fast. Presented solution resembles One-Time-Pads (OTP). Each message is encrypted with a different key. A length of the key is the same as the length of the message. Parties in secret communication need only to have an ordered set of files that are, individually, much bigger than messages being exchanged.

Easily available sets of already existing sources of media file types were tested on entropy. Files with content that is random could be the source for short lived cryptographic keys. Otherwise, key generation could take time. Using such files could make the whole encryption/decryption process faster.

Entropy/randomness measuring was performed using different statistical tests. Testing showed that FLV set of files, compared with all other above mentioned audio and video files, have the best results for all given statistical tests.

Each user is distributed with a unique and secret RSA key pair. Using RSA key pairs is reasonable, because of its general acceptance and safety checked during long time. However, it is only used in a minimum volume, not in full capacity, like in transport of symmetric keys, where we have to have keys longer than 2048 bits. In this paper is not an essence of RSA keys to protect keys, because, if that protection is broken, an adversary does not get key (which resembles OTP). In this paper, RSA has, except protective function, an important aspect in the phase of creating non-repudiation.

Key exchange implemented is not only secure, but also more robust. The most of well-known and widely-used cryptographic techniques are out of order, if we change a single bit of secret message. Therefore, we use QR code to add robustness/self-healing feature, up to a certain level, to our solution.

Robustness of presented implementation is due to QR code features, based on Reed-Solomon error correction codes, which are resistant to a certain level on errors. In our case we showed that we could use up to 25 percent error level correction, due to the length of the message (information on ordered set of files).

Our future work is oriented mostly towards transformation of the implementation to other platforms/operating systems, like Android, Windows Mobile platform or IOS, and compare performances from smartphone platform(s) to laptop/desktop platform based on Windows operating system.

References

1. Daemen, J., Rijmen, V.: The Design of Rijndael: AES - The Advanced Encryption Standard. Springer, Heidelberg (2002)
2. Rivest, R.L., Shamir, A., Adleman, L.: A method for obtaining digital signatures and public-key cryptosystems. Commun. ACM **21**(2), 120–126 (1978)
3. Kerckhoffs, A.: La cryptographie militaire - partie I. J. Sci. Mil. **9**, 5–83 (1883)
4. Shannon, C.E., Weaver, W.: A Mathematical Theory of Communication. University of Illinois Press, Champaign (1963)
5. Pauli, W.: Über das H-theorem vom anwachsen der entropie vom standpunkt der neuen quantenmechanik (On the H-theorem of entropy increase from the standpoint of the new quantum mechanics). In: Probleme der Modernen Physik, Arnold Sommerfeld zum 60. Geburtstage, gewidmet von seinen Schülern (Problems of Modern Physics, Arnold Sommerfeld's 60th Birthday, dedicated by his students), pp. 30–45 (1928). (In German)
6. Petz, D.: Entropy, von Neumann and the von Neumann entropy. In: ArXiv Mathematical Physics e-prints, pp. 83–96 (2001)
7. GNU: GNU General Public License, version 3. https://www.gnu.org/copyleft/gpl.html (2007)

8. Wikipedia: GNU General Public License (2007). http://en.wikipedia.org/wiki/GNU_General_Public_License
9. Callas, J., Donnerhacke, L., Finney, H., Shaw, D., Thayer, F.: RFC 4880 - OpenPGP Message Format. http://tools.ietf.org/html/rfc4880 (2007)
10. Rukhin, A., Soto, J., Nechvatal, J., Smid, M., Barker, E., Leigh, S., Levenson, M., Vangel, M., Banks, D., Heckert, A., Dray, J., Vo, S.: A statistical test suite for random and pseudorandom number generators for cryptographic application. National Institute of Standards and Technology, pp. 2–3 (2010)
11. Menezes, A.J., Vanstone, S.A., Oorschot, P.C.V.: Handbook of Applied Cryptography. CRC Press, Boca Raton (1996)
12. Schneier, B.: Applied cryptography: Protocols, Algorithms, and Source Code in C, 2nd edn. Wiley, New York (1996)
13. Anderson, R., Petitcolas, F.: On the limits of steganography. IEEE J. Sel. Areas Commun. 16, 474–481 (1998)
14. Amin, M.M., Salleh, M., Ibrahim, S., Katmin, M.R., Shamsuddin, M.Z.I.: Information hiding using steganography. In: 4th National Conference on Telecommunication Technology (NCTT), pp. 21–25 (2003)
15. Johnson, N.F., Jajodia, S.: Exploring steganography: seeing the unseen. Computer 31(2), 26–34 (1998)
16. Sahoo, G., Tiwari, R.K.: Some new methodologies for secured data coding and transmission. Int. J. Electron. Secur. Digit. Forensics 3(2), 120–137 (2010)
17. Marvel, L.M., Retter, C.T., Boncelet, C.G.Jr.: A methodology for data hiding using images. In: IEEE Military Communications Conference, MILCOM 1998, vol. 3, pp. 1044–1047 (1998)
18. Cachin, C.: An information-theoretic model for steganography. In: Aucsmith, D. (ed.) IH 1998. LNCS, vol. 1525, pp. 306–318. Springer, Heidelberg (1998)
19. Provos, N., Honeyman, P.: Hide and seek: an introduction to steganography. IEEE Secur. Priv. 1(3), 32–44 (2003). International Conference on Computational Intelligence and Communication Networks
20. Krishna B, Anindya J.P., Geetam S.T., Sarkar P.P.: Audio Steganography Using GA. In: IEEE Security & Privacy, pp. 449–453. IEEE Computer Society, Los Alamitos (2010)
21. Sharp, T.: An implementation of key-based digital signal steganography. In: Moskowitz, I.S. (ed.) IH 2001. LNCS, vol. 2137, pp. 13–26. Springer, Heidelberg (2001)
22. Chan, C.K., Cheng, L.M.: Hiding data in images by simple LSB substitution. In: Pattern Recognition, pp. 469–474 (2004)
23. Lin, I.C., Lin, Y.B., Wang, C.M.: Hiding data in spatial domain images with distortion tolerance. Comput. Stand. Interfaces 31(2), 458–464 (2009)
24. Wang, R.Z., Lin, C.F., Lin, J.C.: Image hiding by optimal LSB substitution and genetic algorithm. In: Pattern Recognition, pp. 671–683 (2001)
25. Marwaha, P., Marwaha, P.: Visual cryptographic steganography in images. In: 2010 International Conference on Computing Communication and Networking Technologies (ICCCNT), pp. 1–6 (2010)
26. Usha, S., Kumar, G.A.S., Boopathybagan, K.: A secure triple level encryption method using cryptography and steganography. In: 2011 International Conference on Computer Science and Network Technology (ICCSNT), vol 2, pp. 1017–1020 (2011)
27. Song, S., Zhang, J., Liao, X., Du, J., Wen, Q.: A novel secure communication protocol combining steganography and cryptography. Procedia Eng. 15, 2767–2772 (2011)

28. Soutar, C., Tomko, G.J.: Secure private key generation using a fingerprint. In: Cardtech/Securetech Conference Proceedings, vol. 1, pp. 245–252 (1996)
29. Monrose, F., Reiter, M.K., Li, Q., Wetzel, S.: Cryptographic key generation from voice. In: IEEE Symposium on Security and Privacy, pp. 202–213 (2001)
30. Teoh, A.B.J., Ngo, D.C.L., Goh, A.: Personalised cryptographic key generation based on FaceHashing. Comput. Secur. **23**(7), 606–614 (2004)
31. Ballard, L., Kamara, S., Reiter, M.K.: The practical subtleties of biometric key generation. In: 17th USENIX Security Symposium, pp. 61–74 (2008)
32. Santhi, B., Ravichandran, K.S., Arun, A.P., Chakkarapani, L.: A novel cryptographic key generation method using image features. Res. J. Inf. Technol. **4**(2), 88–92 (2012)
33. Chung, C.H., Chen, W.Y., Tu, C.M.: Image hidden technique using QR-barcode. In: Fifth International Conference on Intelligent Information Hiding and Multimedia Signal Processing (IIH-MSP), pp. 522–525 (2009)
34. Liao, K.C., Lee, W.H.: A novel user authentication scheme based on QR-code. J. Netw. **5**(8), 937–941 (2010)
35. Prabakaran, G., Bhavani, R., Ramesh, M.: A robust QR-Code video watermarking scheme based on SVD and DWT composite domain. In: 2013 International Conference on Pattern Recognition, Informatics and Mobile Engineering (PRIME), pp. 251–257 (2013)
36. Walker, J.: ENT - A Pseudorandom Number Sequence Test Program (2008). http://www.fourmilab.ch/random/
37. Ziv, J., Lempel, A.: A universal algorithm for sequential data compression. IEEE Trans. Inf. Theor. **23**(3), 337–343 (1977)
38. Codeproject: Open Source QRCode Library (2007). http://www.codeproject.com/Articles/20574/Open-Source-QRCode-Library

Efficient Montgomery Multiplication on GPUs

Nicolae Roşia[1,2(✉)], Virgil Cervicescu[2], and Mihai Togan[3]

[1] Advanced Technology Institute, Bucharest, Romania
[2] Military Technical Academy, Bucharest, Romania
{nicolae.rosia,virgil.cervicescu}@gmail.com
[3] certSIGN, Bucharest, Romania
mihai.togan@certsign.ro

Abstract. Public-key cryptosystems and algorithms, including RSA [20], EC and Diffie-Hellman key exchange [5], require efficient large integer arithmetic in finite fields. Contemporary processors are not designed to support such operations in a productive manner, since most of them natively work on 8 to 64 bit word sizes. Thus, an expensive cryptographic accelerator is frequently required to offload the computational burden. In this paper, we focus on a highly parallel architecture which is commonly found in commodity computers, *i.e.* the Graphical Processing Unit (GPU). Recently, GPUs have known an exponential growth in terms of computing power, becoming a cost-effective option for offloading computationally intensive tasks. This paper describes a parallel implementation of the Montgomery Multiplication, as well as optimizations that enable efficient exploitation of the CUDA GPU architecture.

Keywords: Mongtomery multiplication · Modular exponentiation · CUDA · GPGPU

1 Introduction

Asymmetric cryptographic algorithms and protocols, including RSA, EC-based and Diffie-Hellman key exchange, require efficient large integer arithmetic. This implies performing exponentiations and modular reductions, therefore a chain of repetitive operations upon different data. Typically, the sizes of the operands are between 1024 and 4096-bit. Given two operands, A and B, of S_A and S_B bits, the result of $A \times B$ will have a maximum of $S_A + S_B + 1$ bits. Considering the operands sizes and the fact that most processors have a word length between 8 and 64-bits, multiple precision arithmetic is implemented in software, in the detriment of computational performance.

N. Roşia—Author partially supported by the Romanian National Authority for Scientific Research (CNCS-UEFISCDI) under the project PN-II-PT-PCCA-2013-4-1651.

M. Togan—Author partially supported by the Romanian National Authority for Scientific Research (CNCS-UEFISCDI) under the project PN-II-IN-DPST-2012-1-0087 (ctr. 10DPST/2013). All the authors contributed equally to this work.

© Springer International Publishing Switzerland 2015
I. Bica et al. (Eds.): SECITC 2015, LNCS 9522, pp. 119–129, 2015.
DOI: 10.1007/978-3-319-27179-8_9

Large numbers are usually represented in polynomial form as an array of native word size integers:

$$a = \overline{a_{n-1}a_{n-2}\cdots a_0}_{(\beta)} = \sum_{i=0}^{n-1} a_i \beta^i \tag{1}$$

General Purpose GPU Programming became easier with the introduction of programming frameworks like OpenCL and CUDA which enable the use of a GPU as a coprocessor. Current GPUs exhibit good Floating-point Operations Per Second (FLOPS) per dollar ratio and represent an attractive way to offload computationally intensive tasks.

1.1   Related Work

One of the first usages of the graphical processing units within the cryptography field was focused on accelerating of symmetric ciphers. The first known implementation of this kind was made by Cook et al. [4]. Further on, researchers have developed various solutions for this purpose using parallel architecture of the GPUs. These implementations have been proven to be more useful than the usual CPU-based implementations. The [13] presents a CUDA-based implementation for AES algorithm which was tested on the NVidia GeForce 8700 and 8800 GTX graphical cards. At the time of writing, the developed solution ran up to 20 times faster than the OpenSSL [1] CPU-based solution. A new block based conventional implementation of AES having a 4-10x speed improvements over CPU solutions is pointed out in [9]. They outlined a general purpose data model for encapsulating cryptographic functions (client requests) which is suitable for an execution on a GPU. They used this general model to investigate how the data input can be mapped to the threading model of the GPUs for several of the AES operation modes.

Currently, there are a number of publications presenting mathematical results and optimizations for the modular multiplication (and exponentiation) algorithms. Various techniques were proposed in addition to practical implementations of these algorithms. These techniques are mainly based on parallelization which is a mechanism perfectly applicable on hardware processing technologies like FPGAs or GPUs.

The integration of multiple-precision multiplication with modular reduction as stated by Montgomery's method [14] along with improvements regarding the interleaving of multiplication and reduction are described in [6]. Five Montgomery Multiplication algorithm flavours along with their space, time requirements and actual performance results are discussed in [10]. The *Coarsely Integrated Operand Scanning (CIOS)* method proved to be the most efficient of all. Given two operands of sizes s, *CIOS* requires $2s^2 + s$ multiplications, $4s^2 + 4s + 2$ additions, $6s^2 + 7s + 2$ reads, and $2s^2 + 5s + 1$ writes and needs $s + 3$ words of memory space.

Many papers present GPU implementations of public key and elliptic curve cryptography needed primitives. All of these were focused on speeding up operations like modular multiplication, exponentiation or elliptic curve scalar multiplication. One of the first was performed in [21], where by using an NVIDIA 7800 GTX GPU, they reported, at the paper time, a speedup factor of 3 relative to the reference CPU. Other works in this way are referenced by [2,3,7,8,15,21]. A more recent GPU implementation of the Montgomery multiplication algorithm for a field size of 112 to 521 bits is discussed in [12]. Their work, which is an improvement of a previous approach [11], regards the GPU-based NIST prime field multiplication and employs Montgomery algorithm to allow any field prime to be used in this case. They also bring some new implementation techniques which led to eliminating the need for GPU cache accesses and to gaining this way a bigger throughput that could to accelerate EC cryptography. Experiments and measurements have been conducted on an NVIDIA GTX 480 GPU with reported speeds significantly higher than other published CPU and GPU-based implementations. In [22] are proposed several optimizations on modular multiplication algorithms. The implementation uses the OpenCL framework and the tests have been conducted on an AMD Radeon HD5870 graphic card. After applying the optimizations, they could deliver up to 11 % more arithmetical throughput.

Structure of the Paper. The rest of this paper is organized as follows:

Section 2 reviews the basic concepts and introduces the notions used throughout the paper. Namely, summary elements about *Montgomery Reduction, Binary exponentiation* and *Montgomery's ladder technique* are presented in Subsects. 2.1, 2.2, and respectively 2.3, while an overview of the GPU architecture used is presented in Subsect. 2.4. Section 3 describes our implementation details regarding the *CIOS Method* on CUDA, along with the results obtained and their interpretation (Sect. 3.1). Finally, conclusions are outlined in Sect. 4.

2   Preliminaries

2.1   Montgomery Multiplication

Commonly used public key cryptographic algorithms imply large integer arithmetic operations, *e.g.* modular multiplication and exponentiation [20]. A straightforward approach when computing a modular product consists of operands' multiplication followed by the reduction of the partial result. Considering the magnitude of the numbers (thousands of bits), multiprecision multiplications and repeated subtractions are necessary steps. From a computational perspective, both of the previously mentioned operations are costly. Modular exponentiation, *i.e.* $a^b \bmod n$, can be computed by multiplying a by itself b times and then reducing the result modulo n. After each multiplication, the memory requirements increase by a number of bits equivalent to the size of a. In practice, this is clearly not a feasible way of tackling the problem. Applying the modulus reduction at each step reduces the required memory. However, by doing so the number of operations greatly increases.

In 1985, Peter Montgomery introduced the *Montgomery Reduction* algorithm [14], which enables the modular multiplication ($c \equiv a \times b \bmod N$) to be computed using a different modulo. This method requires using a *residue* form of the operands, $\bar{a}$ and $\bar{b}$.

The first step of the *Montgomery Reduction* algorithm consists of choosing a number R s.t. $R > N$ and $\gcd(R, N) = 1$. Moreover, R is often conveniently chosen to be a power of base β in which the processor operates. In our case, the basis is $\beta = 2$. Assuming that N is an odd prime number of w bits, choosing $R = 2^w$ satisfies the requirements. With such an R, division and remainder operations become bitwise mask and shifting operations.

The next step involves transforming the operands a and b into their reduced forms, as illustrated in (2), and finding R's inverse, *i.e.* $RR^{-1} \equiv 1 \bmod N$.

$$\bar{a} \equiv aR \bmod N$$
$$\bar{b} \equiv bR \bmod N \tag{2}$$

Having $\bar{a}$ and $\bar{b}$, we can further compute $\bar{c}$:

$$\bar{c} \equiv cR \equiv (a \times b)R \equiv (aR \times bR)R^{-1} \equiv (\bar{a} \times \bar{b})R^{-1} \bmod N \tag{3}$$

The initial c, can be calculated by applying the inverse Montgomery transformation:

$$c \equiv \bar{c}R^{-1} \bmod N \tag{4}$$

The above presented steps, represent the conversion to and from the Montgomery reduced form, and do not serve in the speed up of the commencing computation. Moreover, converting operands of a single multiplication to their *residue* form, in order to apply *Montgomery Reduction* is disadvantageous compared to the straightforward method, but a substantial gain is obtained in exponentiation operations. Algorithm 1 illustrates the computation of $\bar{c}$. It can be observed that all arithmetic operations are performed modulo R, task which can be easily solved by means of the processor. A performance analysis of the algorithm (together with its multiple implementations) can be found in [10]. The *Coarsely Integrated Operand Scanning (CIOS)* method proved to be the most efficient of all five algorithms analyzed.

The Coarsely Integrated Operand Scanning (CIOS) Method. The Montgomery reduction is intrinsically a right-to-left procedure. This allows us to compute one word at a time of t since $m[i]$ depends only on $t[i]$, [6]. The *CIOS* method (Algorithm 2) takes advantage of this property and integrates the multiplication and reduction steps by alternating between the iterations of the outer loops. Assuming that both $\bar{a}$ and $\bar{b}$ have s words, the *CIOS* variant requires:

- $2s^2 + s$ multiplications
- $4s^2 + 4s + 2$ additions
- $6s^2 + 7s + 2$ reads
- $2s^2 + 5s + 1$ writes
- $s + 3$ words of memory space

Algorithm 1. Montgomery multiplication

Input: $\overline{a}, \overline{b}, N, R$
Output: $(\overline{a} \times \overline{b})R^{-1} \bmod N$
1: $n' \equiv -N^{-1} \bmod R$
2: $t \leftarrow (\overline{a} \times \overline{b})$
3: $m \leftarrow t \times n' \bmod R$
4: $t \leftarrow (t + m \times N)/R$
5: **if** $t \geq N$ **then**
6:     **return** $t - N$
7: **else**
8:     **return** t
9: **end if**

2.2 Binary Exponentiation

Given a large integer exponent, e, with its binary representation $e = \overline{e_{n-1}e_{n-2}\cdots e_0}_{(2)}$, the computation of a^e resumes to a series of square and multiply operations, as we can see within the Algorithm 3. The computational complexity of the algorithm is $\mathcal{O}(\log_2 n)$ since there are $log_2 n$ squarings and a maximum of $log_2 n$ multiplications. In asymmetric cryptosystems, the encryption often involves the use of an exponent which must be kept secret. In this the method, the number of multiplications depend on the value of exponent which makes it vulnerable to side-channel attacks.

2.3 Montgomery's Ladder Technique

The technique presented in Algorithm 4 addresses the side-channel vulnerability of Algorithm 3 by performing a fixed sequence of operations regardless of the bit's value in exponent.

2.4 Compute Unified Device Architecture (CUDA)

The GPU and CPU architectures are very different. CPUs have few cores (*e.g.* 1 to 32) running at high clock rates and put a great emphasis on big memory caches, complex control logic including branch prediction, speculative execution but have expensive context switching between threads. In contrast, GPUs have many cores (*e.g.* 128 to 2048) running at lower clock rates and are designed to execute hundreds of threads at the same time [17,18]. These cores have small memory caches and simple control logic. The downside is that GPUs are only efficient in processing tasks which are highly data parallel. In *CUDA*, the basic working unit is the *thread* and is executed by a *CUDA Core*. A *Streaming Multiprocessor (SM)* creates and executes groups of 32 threads called *warps*. The threads are characterized by having their own stack and set of registers including program counter and by being free to branch and execute independently. On the other hand, a *warp* executes a single common instruction at a time, so full

---

Algorithm 2. CIOS method for Montgomery multiplication

Input: $\bar{a}$, $\bar{b}$, N, $R = 2^{s \cdot w}$, w being the processor word size and s the number of words.
Output: $(\bar{a} \times \bar{b})R^{-1} \bmod N$
1: $n' \equiv -N[0]^{-1} \bmod R$
2: $t \leftarrow 0$
3: **for** $i = 0 \rightarrow s - 1$ **do**
4:     $C \leftarrow 0$
5:     **for** $j = 0 \rightarrow s - 1$ **do**
6:         $(C, S) \leftarrow t[j] + \bar{a}[j] \cdot \bar{b}[i] + C$
7:         $t[j] \leftarrow S$
8:     **end for**
9:     $t[s] \leftarrow S$
10:    $t[s + 1] \leftarrow C$
11:    $C \leftarrow 0$
12:    $m \leftarrow t[0] \cdot n' \bmod 2^w$
13:    $(C, S) \leftarrow t[0] + m \cdot N[0]$
14:    **for** $j = 1 \rightarrow s - 1$ **do**
15:       $(C, S) \leftarrow t[j] + m \cdot N[j] + C$
16:       $t[j - 1] \leftarrow S$
17:    **end for**
18:    $(C, S) \leftarrow t[s] + C$
19:    $t[s - 1] \leftarrow S$
20:    $t[s] \leftarrow t[s + 1] + C$
21: **end for**
22: **if** $t \geq N$ **then**
23:    **return** $t - N$
24: **else**
25:    **return** t
26: **end if**

Algorithm 3. Binary Exponentiation

Input: a, $e = \overline{e_{n-1}e_{n-2} \ldots e_0}_{(2)}$
Output: a^e
1: $x \leftarrow 1$
2: **for** $i = n - 1 \rightarrow 0$ **do**
3:    $x \leftarrow x \cdot x$
4:    **if** $e_i = 1$ **then**
5:       $x \leftarrow x \cdot a$
6:    **end if**
7: **end for**
8: **return** x

---

efficiency is achieved when all threads of a *warp* follow a common path. Multiple *warps* compose into *thread blocks (TB)* which in turn reside on a *SM*. The *SMs* have limited resources and developers using *CUDA* must take in account these hardware limitations in order to maximize the occupancy and to exploit the hardware-based task switching designed to hide memory access latency.

Algorithm 4. Montgomery's ladder technique

Input: $a, e = \overline{e_{n-1}e_{n-2}\ldots e_0}_{(2)}$
Output: a^e
1: $x_1 \leftarrow a$
2: $x_2 \leftarrow a^2$
3: **for** $i = n - 2 \rightarrow 0$ **do**
4:      **if** $e_i = 0$ **then**
5:          $x_2 \leftarrow x_1 \cdot x_2$
6:          $x_1 \leftarrow x_1^2$
7:      **else**
8:          $x_1 \leftarrow x_1 \cdot x_2$
9:          $x_2 \leftarrow x_2^2$
10:     **end if**
11: **end for**
12: **return** x_1

The level of occupancy depends on the amount of registers and shared memory used by the *kernel* and the generation of the *CUDA Architecture* being used. The current *GPUs* tend to have multiple *SMs*. Communication between *SMs* is not recommended since it is done through the *global memory* which is slower than the *shared memory* available per *thread block*. Unique IDs are given to *threads* and *blocks*, which are accessible through built-in variables, *threadIdx* and *blockIdx*, thus allowing the *threads* to uniquely identify the data which is going to operate on. Threads within a *thread block* can communicate efficiently through shared memory and synchronize through hardware barriers invoked by calling the intrinsic function, __syncthreads().

CUDA C [18] allows developers to use the C programming language to create C functions called *kernels* which are executed in parallel by *CUDA Cores* on the device. A *CUDA Program* consists of a device kernel and a host program. Since the CPU and GPU have their own separate memory, the host program is responsible for transferring the required data necessary for execution. A typical workflow consists of the following steps achieved by calling the relevant *CUDA Application Programming Interface (API)*:

1. Allocate memory on the device;
2. Transfer data from host to device;
3. Start the execution of the kernel;
4. When the kernel is done executing, transfer the result from the device.

3   Implementation and Results

Our implementation leverages the Montgomery Reduction and Montgomery Ladder technique to efficiently compute the exponentiation required by the RSA encryption. The GPU used in our work, *Gefore GTX 750* [16], has a *CUDA Compute Capability 5.0* architecture, with 512 *CUDA Cores* running at a base clock of $1.14\,\text{GHz}$ and a memory bandwidth of $80\,\text{GB/s}$. These cores are partitioned over 4 *Streaming Multiprocessors*, each having its own resources. To obtain the maximum device utilization and to ensure that the memory latency doesn't affect performance, 8 blocks per *Streaming Multiprocessor* were allocated and the number of registers per thread was limited to 32. Each thread operates on word level and calculates a word of the output. The CUDA Architecture has a 32 bit word size, hence the number of threads needed to operate on a number can be calculated by diving the number's bit size to 32.

Memory coalescing of GPU RAM operations is mandatory to obtain peak memory transfer bandwidth. This is guaranteed by having consecutive threads accessing consecutive memory locations, *i.e.* thread 0 reads and writes to word index 0. This is illustrated in Fig. 1, where a block of $n \cdot s$ threads are processing operands of s words.

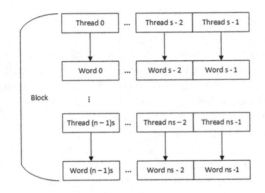

Fig. 1. Threads organization inside a thread block.

Square and multiply are handled differently, exploiting the fact that when computing, $\bar{a} \cdot \bar{a}$, the processor needs a single memory access.

In the scenario where batch operations are performed, *e.g.* RSA encryptions with the same private key, we can precompute the value of N and $n'[0]$ used in Algorithm 2 and embed the results in the code. The compiler is then able to reduce the number of required registers and memory accesses, resulting in a relevant performance gain.

Loop unrolling eliminates the overhead implied by loop counters and loop arithmetic and facilitates additional compiler optimizations.

Shared memory at block level was used for its low latency access times. The 64KB shared memory [19] is big enough to cache the input operands and store the intermediate results accessed by all worker threads.

3.1 Results

The Table 1 presents the speedups obtained, relative to a CPU-based implementation (Intel i7-4790K at 4.0 GHz). The variable factors taken into account were the *Loop Unroll depth*, whether the precomputed n' is embedded in the code, and the operands bit-size.

It is worth noting that these results were obtained at 100 % GPU utilization. In order to obtain this degree of utilization, it is necessary to queue multiple requests which can lead to increased latency in processing. Depending on the actual setup, it might not always be beneficial to offload the computations if low latency is required.

Firstly, it can be observed that increasing the operands bit-size, degrades performance. This can be explained by the increased number of threads required to compute the result which need to synchronize. The biggest speedup is obtained with 1024 bit operands because 32 threads are needed to compute the result, resembling a *warp*, which is inherently synchronized.

Secondly, (as expected) precomputing n', yields a significant boost in speedup since we eliminate the memory access penalty associated with reading the n' variable.

Finally, loop unrolling depth affects performance in a not so obvious way. The best results for 1024 bit operands, were obtained at a depth of value 8. This is not the case for 2048/4096 bit operands since the best speedup was obtained when performing full loop unrolling.

Table 1. Results for 1024/2048/4096 exponentiation

Unroll depth	n' constant	Speedup		
		1024	2048	4096
1	false	5.83	5.10	4.70
1	true	5.86	5.35	4.73
2	false	5.98	5.39	4.88
2	true	6.18	5.56	4.91
4	false	6.17	5.48	4.98
4	true	6.25	5.68	5.02
8	false	6.25	5.57	5.03
8	true	6.55	5.63	5.26
16	false	6.20	5.61	5.07
16	true	6.52	5.66	5.28
32	false	6.29	5.59	5.06
32	true	6.44	5.67	5.29

4   Conclusions

This paper has presented a high throughput GPU implementation of modular exponentiation, as well as optimization suitable for the SIMT (*Single Instruction Multiple Threads*) architecture. This design could be used in the context of a cryptographic accelerator. As shown in this article, parallel architecture has proven to be a feasible approach to overcome operating frequency limitations imposed by the current state of technology in CPUs. Despite the increased latency that they may cause, considering the encouraging results obtained, we are confident that further research, coupled with the increase of core count in GPUs, will only increase performance of many-core architectures. As further steps, we plan to embed this work within an open cryptographic API (e.g. OpenSSL) in order to evaluate the real acceleration gained at the high level protocols and applications like SSL and web servers.

References

1. OpenSSL: The Open Source toolkit for SSL/TLS. http://www.openssl.org
2. Antao, S., Bajard, J.C., Sousa, L.: Elliptic curve point multiplication on GPUs. In: Charot, F., Hannig, F., Teich, J., Wolinski, C., (Eds.) ASAP, pp. 192–199. IEEE (2010)
3. Cohen, A.E., Parhi, K.K.: GPU accelerated elliptic curve cryptography in $GF(2^m)$. In: Proceedings of the 2010 IEEE International Midwest Symposium on Circuits and Systems (MWSCAS), Seattle, WA, pp. 57–60 (2010)
4. Cook, D.L., Ioannidis, J., Keromytis, A.D., Luck, J.: CryptoGraphics: secret key cryptography using graphics cards. In: Menezes, A. (ed.) CT-RSA 2005. LNCS, vol. 3376, pp. 334–350. Springer, Heidelberg (2005)
5. Diffie, W., Hellman, M.: New directions in cryptography. IEEE Trans. Inf. Theor. **22**(6), 644–654 (2006). http://dx.doi.org/10.1109/TIT.1976.1055638
6. Dussé, S.R., Kaliski, Jr., B.S.: A cryptographic library for the Motorola DSP 56000. In: Damgård, I.B. (ed.) EUROCRYPT 1990. LNCS, vol. 473, pp. 230–244. Springer, Heidelberg (1991)
7. Fleissner, S.: GPU-accelerated Montgomery exponentiation. In: Shi, Y., van Albada, G.D., Dongarra, J., Sloot, P.M.A. (eds.) ICCS 2007, Part I. LNCS, vol. 4487, pp. 213–220. Springer, Heidelberg (2007)
8. Giorgi, P., Izard, T., Tisserand, A.: Comparison of modular arithmetic algorithms on GPUs. In: Proceedings of International Conference on Parallel Computing ParCo, Lyon, France (2009)
9. Harrison, O., Waldron, J.: Practical symmetric key cryptography on modern graphics hardware. In: 17th USENIX Security Symposium, pp. 195–209 (2008)
10. Koç, C., Acar, T., Kaliski, B.J.: Analyzing and comparing Montgomery multiplication algorithms. IEEE Micro **16**(3), 26–33 (1996)
11. Leboeuf, K., Muscedere, R., Ahmadi, M.: High performance prime field multiplication for GPU. In: 2012 IEEE International Symposium on Circuits and Systems (ISCAS), pp. 93–96, May 2012
12. Leboeuf, K., Muscedere, R., Ahmadi, M.: A GPU implementation of the Montgomery multiplication algorithm for elliptic curve cryptography. In: IEEE International Symposium on Circuits and Systems (ISCAS 2013), pp. 2593–2596, May 2013
13. Manavski, S.A.: CUDA compatible GPU as an efficient hardware accelerator for AES cryptography. In: IEEE International Conference on Signal Processing and Communications (ICSPC 2007), 24–27 November 2007, Dubai, United Arab Emirates, pp. 65–68 (2007)

14. Montgomery, P.L.: Modular multiplication without trial division. Math. Comput. **44**(170), 519–521 (1985)
15. Moss, A., Page, D., Smart, N.P.: Toward acceleration of RSA using 3D graphics hardware. In: Galbraith, S.D. (ed.) Cryptography and Coding 2007. LNCS, vol. 4887, pp. 364–383. Springer, Heidelberg (2007)
16. NVIDIA Corporation: GeForce GTX 750 Specifications
17. NVIDIA Corporation: CUDA C Best Practices Guide, 7.0 edn. (2015)
18. NVIDIA Corporation: CUDA C Programming Guide, 7.0 edn. (2015)
19. NVIDIA Corporation: Tuning CUDA Applications for Maxwell, 7.0 edn. (2015)
20. Rivest, R., Shamir, A., Adleman, L.: A method for obtaining digital signatures and public-key cryptosystems. Commun. ACM **21**, 120–126 (1978)
21. Szerwinski, R., Güneysu, T.: Exploiting the power of GPUs for asymmetric cryptography. In: Oswald, E., Rohatgi, P. (eds.) CHES 2008. LNCS, vol. 5154, pp. 79–99. Springer, Heidelberg (2008)
22. Trei, W.: Efficient Modular Arithmetic for SIMD Devices. In: IACR Cryptology ePrint Archive 2013, 652 (2013)

Stateful Certificateless Public Key Encryption with Application in Public Cloud

S. Sree Vivek$^{(\boxtimes)}$

Samsung Research Institute, Bangalore, India
sreevivek.s@samsung.com

Abstract. Certificateless cryptography eliminates the key escrow problem inherent in identity based cryptosystem. Certificatateless systems are preferred in public cloud to offer security because it solves two different problems simultaneously, namely, the key escrow problem and the cumbersome certificate management. A stateful public key encryption scheme is a cryptographic primitive, in which the sender maintains state information to perform encryption. The encryption algorithm takes the intended message, receiver's public key and the current state information to produce the ciphertext, and possibly updates the state information. Decryption is straightforward and depends only on the ciphertext and secret key of the receiver. In this paper, we propose the first stateful certificateless public key encryption scheme and prove the security of the scheme in the random oracle model. This scheme finds very interesting application for sharing data in an encrypted cloud storage system.

Keywords: Certificateless encryption · Stateful cryptography · Random oracle model · Provable security · Cloud data security · Sharing cloud data

1 Introduction

Certificateless Cryptography (CLC) introduced by Al-Riyami et al. [2] is a variant of Identity Based Cryptography (IBC), which intends to prevent the key escrow problem. Usually, in IBC the private key of a user is generated by the Private Key Generator (PKG), who has to be trusted by all users of the system. In the case of a PKG compromise, a total-break of the system is possible. This is called the key escrow problem. In order to prevent this, the key generation process is split between the KGC (Key Generation Center - The central authority in CLC) and the user. The KGC first generates the private key for a user, which is called as the partial private key of the user. The remaining part of the private key is a random secret value generated by the user, and is never revealed to anyone, not even to the KGC. This key is called as the user secret value and the user generates the public key corresponding to this key. All cryptographic operations by the user are performed by using the full private key which involves both the partial private key and the user secret value.

© Springer International Publishing Switzerland 2015
I. Bica et al. (Eds.): SECITC 2015, LNCS 9522, pp. 130–149, 2015.
DOI: 10.1007/978-3-319-27179-8_10

Having introduced CLC, we now move on to stateful public key encryption (PKE) schemes. PKE schemes make use of compute intensive exponentiation computations to perform encryption as well as decryption. The order of complexity is roughly considered to be one thousand times that of a block cipher or hash function evaluation. This results in slowdown of the system as well as hinders the use of public key cryptography in systems with limited computing power. Public key cryptography operations are very expensive that they drain the battery of devices easily. This seems to be a very important and severe limitation on cell phones, personal digital assistants, tablets, wearables, RFID chips and sensors. Hence, researchers are very much interested in reducing the cost of exponentiation, which is a very crucial operation for PKE schemes. It was stated by Bellare et al. [5] that "a 10% improvement would be very welcome and a 50% improvement would be dramatic". However, lot of intellectual energy is pumped in to improve the schemes by proposing time-space trade-off mechanisms like pre-computation of exponentiation and faster implementations for exponentiations.

In a stateful encryption scheme, the sender maintains a state information that can be reused across various encryptions during a session. A session may be marked by the communication between a sender and a fixed receiver. Thus if the communication has to occur between two fixed entities, the sender has to use a symmetric key (the key used for encryption and decryption in any symmetric key encryption scheme) which is derived using the public key of the receiver. A stateful encryption algorithm is deterministic with respect to the state and public key. Thus, this key has to be computed only for the first time the sender communicates with the receiver. After which the key can be reused through out the state, which reduces the cost of further public key encryptions to that receiver.

Moreover, it should be noticed that reusing randomness is not straightforward in any cryptographic operation. In the history, we have learned hard lessons due to reuse of randomness. One of the well known examples is the attack on Sony's PlayStation 3 in 2010. A group of attackers recovered the private key of Elliptic Curve Digital Signature Algorithm (ECDSA) used by Sony to sign software for the PlayStation 3 game console. This attack was possible because ECDSA has a randomized signature generation algorithm and Sony reused the randomness used to generate the signature [6]. One more well known example is in the case of RSA. The entropy of the output distribution of standardized RSA key generation is always almost maximal. The outputs are hard to factor if factoring in general is hard where the primes were chosen at random but it was identified in [12] that the random primes did not satisfy this requirement on the distribution of the RSA keys. This exposed a considerable number of RSA private keys used in PGP system. Hence we emphasize that reuse of randomness should be done with utmost care and the resulting scheme should be proven secure, taking the reuse into account.

Motivation: Recent advancements in technology has made huge data storage available for users in the name of Cloud Storage. Cloud platforms such as

Dropbox, Skybox, Oracle, Amazon provide users with huge space for them to store their data. However reputed the cloud storage provider is, other organizations who want to make use of the cloud storage do no trust them to store sensitive data. Hence a need for secure cloud storage arose. In secure cloud storage, each user has a public/private key pair created by the user. The public key is used to encrypt a symmetric key which in turn is used to encrypt the data. The encrypted data (ciphertext) is then stored in the cloud. The corresponding private key is used to decrypt and obtain the symmetric key which is used to decrypt the ciphertext and obtain the actual message. However, this approach requires a certified public key in order to withstand man-in-the-middle attacks and public key replacement attacks, and requires the presence of a Certification Authority (CA).

To make the system more convenient, the identity of the user could be used to generate the public keys and the corresponding private key could be obtained from the trusted authority (PKG). In this case the PKG (the cloud service provider) is a fully trusted entity and knows the private key of all users in the system. Certificateless Encryption (CLE) schemes find great application in this scenario. In a CLE, the identity of a user along with a user defined public key acts as the full public key of the user. Unlike Public Key Infrastructure (PKI), these public keys need not be certified by centralized authorities, because changing the public key in the public repository will be useful only to the trusted KGC in the CLE and hence the KGC will be accountable for any replacement of the public keys in the repository.

Consider a scenario wherein a user has n different files (may be photos, documents etc.). In order to maintain privacy, the user has to encrypt each file with different symmetric keys. This is because, if all the files were encrypted with the same key and if the user shares the key of one file, he is loosing the keys of all other files too. In order to avoid this each file should be encrypted with different symmetric keys. Thus all the n files are encrypted with n different symmetric keys and stored in the cloud storage. In case, if the user (owner of the files) wants to share a subset of k files to another user (the receiver), the naive way is to use a PKE scheme and encrypt the symmetric keys to the receiver. The receiver on receiving the encrypted keys can decrypt them using his private key and use the symmetric keys to decrypt the actual file from the downloaded ciphertext. If k is large and if the owner uses a stateless encryption scheme, he has to perform $\mathcal{O}(k)$ exponentiations. The advantage of using a stateful PKE scheme is that it requires only $\mathcal{O}(1)$ exponentiation when the receiver is fixed.

Figure 1 shows how a user registers with the KGC to avail secure cloud storage and how his data is encrypted and stored in the cloud. User A sends his identity, ID_A and requests for the partial private key to the KGC. The KGC has a master private key msk and a set of public system parameters $params$, which are used to generate the partial private key SK_A of the user A. SK_A is sent to A through a secure channel. After receiving the partial private key user A chooses his own user defined private key sk_A and computes the corresponding public key pk_A. The user defined public key pk_A is sent to the KGC and is stored in the user

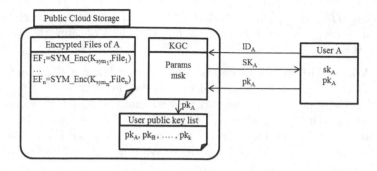

Fig. 1. User registration and encryption on cloud

public key list maintained by the KGC. Hence the private key of A is $\langle sk_A, SK_A \rangle$ and the corresponding public key is $\langle pk_A, ID_A \rangle$. To encrypt a message to A, the sender has to use ID_A and pk_A along with *params*. When user A wants to upload a file $File_i$ to the cloud, he has to encrypt the file using a symmetric key encryption scheme with a symmetric key K_{sym_i} to obtain the encrypted file $EF_i = SYM\_Enc(K_{sym_i}, File_i)$. (Note that we assume that each symmetric key is unique and there is an efficient way for the owner of the file to uniquely obtain the key using a private Pseudo Random Number Generator and other attributes such as file name, modified and created date etc., in a secure way. We do not explain it here since it is out of the scope of the problem addressed here) The encrypted file EF_i is then stored in the cloud.

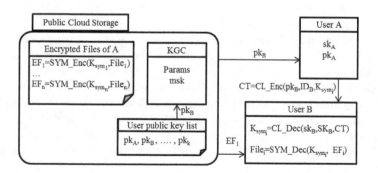

Fig. 2. Sharing encrypted contents using CLE

Figure 2 shows how user A shares an encrypted file to another user. Let us consider that user A wants to share his contents to user B, whose public key is $\langle pk_B, ID_B \rangle$. The owner A shares the encrypted file to user B first. Then he obtains the user public key pk_B of B from the user public key list maintained by the KGC. Using pk_B and ID_B with a CLE scheme he encrypts the symmetric key K_{sym_i} corresponding to the file $File_i$ to user B as $CT =$

$CL\_Enc(pk_B, ID_B, K_{sym_i})$ and sends CT to B. User B upon receiving CT, decrypts it as: $K_{sym_i} = CL\_Dec(sk_B, SK_B, CT)$ and obtains the symmetric key. Now, B uses K_{sym_i} to decrypt EF_i as $File_i = SYM\_Dec(K_{sym_i}, EF_i)$.

Related Work: Al-Riyami and Paterson in [2] have shown realization for CLE, signature (CLS) and key exchange (CLK) schemes in their work. Huang et al. [10] and Castro et al. [7] independently showed that the signature scheme in [2] is not secure against Type-I adversary (explained in later sections). In fact they showed that it is possible for a Type-I adversary to replace the public key of the user and attack the scheme. They also gave a new certificateless signature scheme. A lot of CLE schemes were proposed, whose security were proved both in the random oracle model [4,8,17,18] and standard model [13,15]. Recently, Dent [9] gave a survey on the various security models for CLE schemes, mentioning the subtle difference in the level of security offered by each model. Dent also gave a generic construction and an efficient construction for CLE. The initial constructs for certificateless cryptosystem were all based on bilinear pairing [8,13,15,17]. Baek et al. [4] were the first to propose a CLE scheme without bilinear pairing. Certificateless cryptosystem are prone to key replacement attack because the public keys are not certified and anyone can replace the public key of any legitimate user in the system. The challenging task in the design of certificateless cryptosystem is to come up with schemes which resists key replacement attacks. The CLE in [4] did not withstand key replacement attack, which was pointed out by Sun et al. in [18]. Sun et al. fixed the problem by changing the partial key extract and setting public key procedures. Both the aforementioned schemes, namely [4,18] were based on multiplicative groups. Lai et al. in [11] proposed the first RSA-based CLE scheme. They have proved their scheme secure against chosen plaintext attack (CPA). Later, in [19] Vivek et al. proposed a CCA secure scheme based on the RSA assumption.

There are several PKE schemes, which make use of transformations to achieve CCA security and some of them are customized design. There is no known straightforward ways to make these schemes stateful. Even though some efforts were made in this direction, the ciphertext size will be large due to the usage of CCA secure symmetric key encryption schemes. However, there are PKE schemes that are designed to be stateful, namely [3,5,20] and few stateful IBE schemes were also found in the literature [3,16]. There are no known stateful certificateless PKE schemes present in the literature, which motivated us to look forward in this direction.

Our Contribution: In this paper we propose the first stateful certificateless encryption scheme. Our scheme finds straightforward application in sharing encrypted contents in the cloud efficiently when the cloud data is accessed through resource constrained devices. This efficiency comes in due to the fact that when different files are encrypted with different keys as shown in Fig. 1, sharing huge number of encrypted files will involve transportation of huge number of symmetric keys. Since in a stateful encryption scheme, the randomness used to encrypt the data is reused across a session for communication with a fixed receiver, we are able to reduce the cost of encryption required to share the keys. In the example stated above if there are k files to be shared with a receiver, the owner has to perform only $\mathcal{O}(1)$ exponentiation operations, where as in the naive way, the owner has to perform $\mathcal{O}(k)$ exponentiations. Our scheme offers compact ciphertext with ciphertext verifiability.

2   Preliminaries

In this section, we give the definition of hardness assumptions, framework and the security model used in our paper.

2.1   Review of Computational Assumptions

Definition 1 *Computational Diffie-Hellman Problem (CDHP). Given* $\langle g, g^a, g^b \rangle \in \mathbb{G}^3$ *for unknown* $a, b \in \mathbb{Z}_q^*$, *where* $\mathbb{G}$ *is a cyclic prime order multiplicative group with* g *as a generator and* q *the order of the group, the CDH problem in* $\mathbb{G}$ *is to compute* g^{ab}.

The advantage of any probabilistic polynomial time algorithm $\mathcal{A}$ *in solving the CDH problem in* $\mathbb{G}$ *is defined as*

$$Adv_{\mathcal{A}}^{CDH} = Pr\left[\mathcal{A}(g, g^a, g^b) = g^{ab} \mid a, b \in \mathbb{Z}_q^*\right]$$

The CDH Assumption is that, for any probabilistic polynomial time algorithm $\mathcal{A}$, *the advantage* $Adv_{\mathcal{A}}^{CDH}$ *is negligibly small.*

Definition 2 *(Strong Diffie Hellman (SDH) Problem as given in [1]). Let* κ *be the security parameter and* $\mathbb{G}$ *be a multiplicative group of order* q, *where* $|q| = \kappa$. *Given* $\langle g, g^a, g^b \rangle \in_R \mathbb{G}^3$ *and access to a Decision Diffie Hellman (DDH) oracle* $\mathcal{DDH}_{g,a}(.,.)$ *which on input* g^b *and* g^c *outputs* **true** *if and only if* $g^{ab} = g^c$, *the strong Diffie Hellman problem is to compute* $g^{ab} \in \mathbb{G}$.

The advantage of an adversary $\mathcal{A}$ in solving the strong Diffie Hellman problem is defined as the probability with which $\mathcal{A}$ solves the above strong Diffie Hellman problem.

$$Adv_{\mathcal{A}}^{SDH} = Pr[\mathcal{A}(g, g^a, g^b) = g^{ab}|\mathcal{DDH}_{g,a}(.,.)]$$

The strong Diffie Hellman assumption holds in $\mathbb{G}$ if for all polynomial time adversaries $\mathcal{A}$, the advantage $Adv_{\mathcal{A}}^{SDH}$ is negligible.

Note: In pairing groups (also known as gap groups), the DDH oracle can be efficiently instantiated and hence the strong Diffie Hellman problem is equivalent to the Gap Diffie Hellman problem [14].

2.2   Framework for Stateful CLE

In this section, we discuss the general framework for stateful CLE. We adopt the definition of certificateless public key encryption, given by Baek et al. [4]. Their definition of CLE is weaker than the original definition by Al-Riyami and Paterson [2] because the user has to obtain a partial public key from the KGC before he can create his public key (While in Al-Riyami and Paterson's original CLE this is not the case). A stateful certificateless public-key encryption scheme is defined by seven probabilistic, polynomial-time algorithms which are defined below:

Setup: This algorithm takes as input a security parameter κ and returns the master private key msk and the system public parameters $params$. This algorithm is run by the KGC in order to initialize a certificateless system.

Partial Private Key Extract: This algorithm takes as input the public parameters $params$, the master private key msk and an identity $ID_A \in \{0,1\}^*$ of a user A. It outputs the partial private key d_A and a partial public key y_A of user A. This algorithm is run by the KGC once for each user and the corresponding partial private key and partial public key is given to A through a secure and authenticated channel.

Set Full Private Key: This algorithm is run once by each user. It takes the public parameters $params$, the user identity ID_A and A's partial private key d_A as input. The algorithm generates a secret value $sk_A \in \mathcal{S}$, where $\mathcal{S}$ is the secret value space. Now, the full private key D_A of A, is a combination of the secret value sk_A and the partial private key d_A.

Set Full Public Key: This algorithm run by the user, takes as input the public parameters $params$, a user, say A's partial public key y_A and the full private key D_A. It outputs the full public key PK_A for A. This algorithm is run once by each user and the resulting full public key is widely and freely distributed. The full public key of user A consists of PK_A and ID_A.

New State Generation: This algorithm is used to generate a set of state information used for encryption. The sender executes this algorithm and keeps the information confidential. The sender's state information is not known to any entity. The state information st is generated by taking $params$ as input.

Encryption: This algorithm takes as input the public parameters $params$, a receiver identity, say ID_A, the corresponding full public key PK_A, the state information st_i (corresponding to the ith state) and a message $m \in \mathcal{M}$. The output of this algorithm is the ciphertext $CT \in \mathcal{CS}$. Note that $\mathcal{M}$ is the message space and $\mathcal{CS}$ is the ciphertext space.

Decryption: This algorithm takes as input the public parameters $params$, a user, say A's private key D_A and a ciphertext $CT \in \mathcal{CS}$. It returns either a message $m \in \mathcal{M}$ - if the ciphertext is valid, or $'Invalid'$ - otherwise.

2.3   Security Model for CLE

We review the notion of Type-I and Type-II adversaries and provide the security model for stateful CLE. The confidentiality of a stateful CLE scheme is proved by means of an interactive game between a challenger C and an adversary. In the confidentiality game for stateful certificateless encryption (IND-stCLE-CCA2), the adversary is given access to the following six oracles. These oracles are simulated by C:

Partial Key Extract for ID_A: C responds by returning the partial private key SK_A and the partial public key PPK_A of the user A.

Extract Secret Value for ID_A: If A's public key has not been replaced then C responds with the secret value sk_A for user A. If the adversary has already replaced A's public key, then C does not provide the corresponding private key to the adversary.

Request Public Key for ID_A: C responds by returning the full public key PK_A for user A. (First by choosing a secret value if necessary).

Replace Public Key for ID_A: The adversary can repeatedly replace the public key PK_A for a user A with any valid public key PK'_A of its choice. The adversary generates the new valid public key and sends it to C. The current value of the user's public key is used by C in any computations or responses.

Encryption(ID_i, st_j, m_k): Encryption queries for any number of messages ($k = 1$ to $\hat{m}$) for a given state st_j ($j = 1$ to $\hat{n}$), where $\hat{m}$ and $\hat{n}$ are the upper bounds for the number of messages that can be encrypted in a state and total number of states respectively, for whose combination A can query this oracle.

Decryption(CT, ID_A): The adversary can issue a decryption query for ciphertext CT and identity ID_A of its choice, C decrypts CT and returns the corresponding message to the adversary. C should be able to properly decrypt ciphertexts, even for those users whose public key has been replaced, i.e. this oracle provides the decryption of a ciphertext, which is generated with the current valid public key. The strong decryption oracle returns *Invalid*, if the ciphertext corresponding to any of the previous public keys were queried. This is a strong property of the security model (Note that, C may not know the private key corresponding to the current public key of the user. This is true if public key is replaced by the adversary). However, this property ensures that the model captures the fact that changing a user's public key to a value of the adversary's choice may give the adversary an advantage in breaking the scheme. This is called as strong decryption in [9]. Our scheme provides strong decryption for Type-I adversary.

There are two types of adversaries (namely Type-I and Type-II) to be considered for stateful certificateless encryption scheme. The Type-I adversary models the attack by a third party attacker, (i.e. anyone except the legitimate receiver or the KGC) who is trying to gain some information about a message from the encryption. The Type-II adversary models the honest-but-curious KGC who tries to break the confidentiality of the scheme. Here, the attacker is allowed to have access to master private key msk. This means that we do not have to give the attacker explicit access to partial key extraction, as the adversary is able to compute these value on its own. The most important point about Type-II security is that the adversary modeling the KGC should not have replaced the public key for the target identity before the challenge is issued.

Constraints for Type-I and Type-II Adversaries: The IND-stCLE-CCA2 security model distinguishes the two types of adversary Type-I and Type-II with the following constraints.

- Type-I adversary $\mathcal{A}_I$ is allowed to change the public keys of users at will but does not have access to the master private key msk.
- Type-II adversary $\mathcal{A}_{II}$ is equipped with the master private key msk but is not allowed to replace public keys corresponding to the target identity.

IND-stCLE-CCA2 Game for Type-I Adversary: The game is named as IND-stCLE-CCA2-I. This game, played between the challenger $\mathcal{C}$ and the Type-I adversary $\mathcal{A}_I$, is defined below:

Setup: Challenger $\mathcal{C}$ runs the setup algorithm to generate master private key msk and public parameters $params$. $\mathcal{C}$ gives $params$ to $\mathcal{A}_I$ while keeping msk secret. After receiving $params$, $\mathcal{A}_I$ interacts with $\mathcal{C}$ in two phases:

Phase I: $\mathcal{A}_I$ is given access to all the six oracles. $\mathcal{A}_I$ adaptively queries the oracles consistent with the constraint that the type-I adversary $\mathcal{A}_I$ is allowed to change the public keys of users at will but does not have access to the master private key msk.

Challenge: At the end of **Phase I**, $\mathcal{A}_I$ gives two messages m_0 and m_1 of equal length to $\mathcal{C}$ on which it wishes to be challenged. $\mathcal{C}$ randomly chooses a bit $\delta \in_R \{0,1\}$ and encrypts m_δ with the target identity ID^*'s public key for the state st^* to form the challenge ciphertext CT^* and sends it to $\mathcal{A}_I$ as the challenge. (Note that the partial Private Key corresponding to ID^* should not be queried by $\mathcal{A}_I$ but the secret value corresponding to ID^* may be queried. This makes our security model stronger when compared to the security models of [11,18].)

Phase II: $\mathcal{A}_I$ adaptively queries the oracles consistent with the constraints for Type-I adversary described above. Besides this $\mathcal{A}_I$ cannot query *Decryption* on (CT^*, ID^*) and the partial private key of the receiver should not have been queried to the *Extract Partial Private Key* oracle. $\mathcal{A}_I$ gets oracle access to all ciphertexts for any message including m_0 and m_1 for the state information st^* through the encryption oracle $Encryption(params, st^*, m_j)$, where $j \leq \hat{m}$.

Guess: $\mathcal{A}_I$ outputs a bit δ' at the end of the game. $\mathcal{A}_I$ wins the IND-stCLE-CCA2-I game if $\delta' = \delta$. The advantage of $\mathcal{A}_I$ is defined as -

$$Adv_{\mathcal{A}_I}^{IND-stCLE-CCA2-I} = |2Pr\left[\delta = \delta'\right] - 1|$$

IND-stCLE-CCA2 Game for Type-II Adversary: The game is named as IND-stCLE-CCA2-II. This game, played between the challenger $\mathcal{C}$ and the Type-II adversary $\mathcal{A}_{II}$, is defined below:

Setup: Challenger $\mathcal{C}$ runs the setup algorithm to generate master private key msk and public parameters $params$. $\mathcal{C}$ gives $params$ and the master private key msk to $\mathcal{A}_{II}$. After receiving $params$, $\mathcal{A}_{II}$ interacts with $\mathcal{C}$ in two phases:

Phase I: $\mathcal{A}_{II}$ is not given access to the *Extract partial Private Key* oracle because $\mathcal{A}_{II}$ knows msk, it can generate the partial private key of any user in the system. All other oracles are accessible by $\mathcal{A}_{II}$. $\mathcal{A}_{II}$ adaptively queries the oracles consistent with the constraint that the type-II adversary $\mathcal{A}_{II}$ is equipped with the master private key msk but is not allowed to replace public keys corresponding to the target identity.

Challenge: At the end of *Phase I*, $\mathcal{A}_{II}$ gives two messages m_0 and m_1 of equal length to $\mathcal{C}$ on which it wishes to be challenged. $\mathcal{C}$ randomly chooses a bit $\delta \in_R \{0,1\}$ and encrypts m_δ with the target identity ID^*'s public key using the state information st^* to form the challenge ciphertext CT^* and sends it to $\mathcal{A}_{II}$ as the challenge. (Note that the Secret Value Corresponding to ID^* should not be queried by $\mathcal{A}_{II}$ and the public key corresponding to ID^* should not be replaced during *Phase I*.)

Phase II: $\mathcal{A}_{II}$ adaptively queries the oracles consistent with the constraints for Type-II adversary described above. Besides this $\mathcal{A}_{II}$ cannot query *Decryption* on (CT^*, ID^*) and the Secret Value corresponding to the receiver should not be queried to the *Extract Secret Value* oracle and the public key corresponding to ID^* should not be replaced during *Phase I*. $\mathcal{A}_{II}$ gets oracle access to all ciphertexts for any message including m_0 and m_1 for the state information st^* through the encryption oracle $Encryption(params, st^*, m_j)$, where $j \leq \hat{m}$.

Guess: $\mathcal{A}_{II}$ outputs a bit δ' at the end of the game. $\mathcal{A}_{II}$ wins the IND-stCLE-CCA2-II game if $\delta' = \delta$. The advantage of $\mathcal{A}_{II}$ is defined as -

$$Adv_{\mathcal{A}_{II}}^{IND-stCLE-CCA2-II} = |2Pr\left[\delta = \delta'\right] - 1|$$

3   Our Scheme - StCLE

In this section, we propose our stateful certificateless encryption scheme. The scheme has the following algorithms. Unless stated otherwise, all computations are done *mod p*.

Setup: The KGC does the following to initialize the system and to setup the public parameters. Let κ be the security parameter.

– Choose two large primes p and q such that $q|(p-1)$ and $|q| \geq \kappa$. Choose $g \in_R \mathbb{Z}_p^*$ with order q, $z \in_R \mathbb{Z}_q^*$ and compute $y = g^z$. Choose five cryptographic hash functions $F : \mathbb{Z}_p^* \to \mathbb{Z}_q^*$, $G : \{0,1\}^* \to \mathbb{Z}_q^*$, $H : \{0,1\}^* \to \{0,1\}^{l_m}$, $H_1 : \{0,1\}^* \to \mathbb{Z}_q^*$ and $H_2 : \{0,1\}^* \to \mathbb{Z}_q^*$, where l_m is the size of the message.

- The KGC publicizes the system parameters, $params = \langle p, q, g, y, F, G, H, H_1, H_2 \rangle$ and keeps z as the master private key.

Partial Key Extract: This algorithm is executed by the KGC and upon receiving the identity ID_A of a user A the KGC performs the following to generate the corresponding partial private key d_A.

- Choose $s_{i0}, s_{i1} \in_R \mathbb{Z}_q^*$, compute $y_{A0} = g^{s_{i0}}$ and $y_{A1} = g^{s_{i1}}$.
- Compute $d_{A0} = s_{i0} + z H_1(ID_A, y_{A0}) \mod q$ and $d_{A1} = s_{i1} + z H_2(ID_A, y_{A0}, y_{A1}) \mod q$.
- Output $d_A = \langle d_{A0}, d_{A1} \rangle$ and $y_A = \langle y_{A0}, y, A1 \rangle$.

The validity of the partial private key can be verified by user A by performing the following check:

$$g^{d_{A0}} g^{d_{A1}} \stackrel{?}{=} y_{A0} y^{H_1(ID_A, y_{A0})} y_{A1} y^{H_2(ID_A, y_{A0}, y_{A1})} \tag{1}$$

Set Full Private Key: On receiving the partial private key the user with identity ID_A does the following to generate his full private key.

- Choose $x_A \in_R \mathbb{Z}_q^*$ as his secret value.
- Set the private key as $D_A = \langle D_A^{(1)}, D_A^{(2)} \rangle = \langle d_{A0}, x_A \rangle$. (Note that both the KGC and the corresponding user knows $D_A^{(1)}$ and the user with identity ID_A alone knows $D_A^{(2)}$).

Set Full Public Key: The user with identity ID_A computes the public key corresponding to his private key as described below:

- Compute $g_A = g^{D_A^{(2)}}$.
- Make $PK_A = \langle PK_A^{(1)}, PK_A^{(2)}, PK_A^{(3)}, PK_A^{(4)} \rangle = \langle y_{A0}, y_{A1}, d_{A1}, g_A \rangle$ public.

Now, any one can verify the public key by checking:

$$g^{PK_A^{(3)}} \stackrel{?}{=} PK_A^{(2)} y^{H_2(ID_A, PK_A^{(1)}, PK_A^{(2)})} \tag{2}$$

It should be noted that there is no verification for $PK_A^{(4)}$.

New State Generation: Recall that the sender's state information is not known to any entity other than the sender himself. Let i represent the index of the current state and hence the current state will be referred as st_i. The sender generates the state information as follows:

- Choose $r_i \in_R \mathbb{Z}_q^*$. Compute $u_i = F(g^{r_i}) \in \mathbb{Z}_q^*$, $s_i = r_i u_i \mod q$, $v_i = g^{s_i}$, $w_{i1} = (PK_A^{(1)} y^{H_1(ID_A, y_{A0})})^{s_i}$ and $w_{i2} = (PK_A^{(4)})^{s_i}$.

The state information $st_i = \langle u_i, v_i, s_i, w_{i1}, w_{i2}, \text{index} \rangle$.

Encryption: To encrypt a message m to a user with identity ID_A, one has to perform the following steps:

- Compute $c_1 = g^{si}$, $c_2 = u_i \oplus G(ID_A, c_1, m, w_{i1}, w_{i2}, \texttt{index})$ and $c_3 = m \oplus H(ID_A, c_1, c_2, w_{i1}, w_{i2}, \texttt{index})$

Now, $CT = \langle c_1, c_2, c_3, \texttt{index} \rangle$ is send as the ciphertext to the user A. To reuse the state information st_i, the sender has to just increment $\texttt{index}$ and use st_i, It is not required to send the component c_1 throughout the session and hence from the second encryption onwards the ciphertext size will be $|q| + |m| + |\texttt{index}|$ which is much less than $|q| + |m| + |p|$ in the most efficient CLE [4] with ciphertext verifiability.

It should be noted that the maximum number of encryptions to be performed in a session will be determined by the sender. Thus, $\texttt{index}$ is a user determined integer value and to perform one million encryptions in a session, the value of index may be utmost 2^{20}. Hence, $\texttt{index}$ may typically be a value from $1 \leq \texttt{index} \leq 2^{20}$ and thus of size less than 20-bits.

Decryption: The receiver with identity ID_A does the following to decrypt a ciphertext $CT = (c_1, c_2, c_3, \texttt{index})$:

- Compute $w'_{i1} = c_1^{D_A^{(1)}}$ and $w'_{i2} = c_1^{D_A^{(2)}}$, $m' = c_3 \oplus H(ID_A, c_1, c_2, w'_{i1}, w'_{i2}, \texttt{index})$ and $u' = c_2 \oplus G(ID_A, c_1, m, w'_{i1}, w'_{i2}, \texttt{index})$
- Check whether $u' \stackrel{?}{=} F(c_1^{(u')^{-1}})$. If the check holds output m', otherwise output $\bot$. This check helps in identifying whether a ciphertext is well formed or not.

Correctness: We have to show that the u' computed by the decryption algorithm passes the verification test $u' \stackrel{?}{=} F(c_1^{(u')^{-1}})$, if $u' = u_i = F(g^{r_i})$.

$$RHS = F(c_1^{(u')^{-1}}) = F(v_i^{(u')^{-1}}) = F(g^{s_i(u')^{-1}}) = F(g^{r_i u_i (u')^{-1}})$$
$$= F(g^{r_i}) \text{ (If } u' = u_i = F(g^{r_i})\text{)}$$
$$= u' = LHS$$

Thus, the decryption will hold if $u' = u_i = F(g^{r_i})$.

3.1 Security Proof

To prove the confidentiality of a certificateless encryption scheme, it is required to consider the attacks by Type-I and Type-II adversaries. In the two existing secure schemes [11,18], the Type-I adversary is not allowed to extract the secret value corresponding to the target identity. To capture the ability of the adversary who can access the user secret keys of the target identity, we give access to the user secret value of the target identity to the Type-I adversary. We also state that, allowing the extract secret value query corresponding to the target identity makes the security model for Type-I adversary more stronger. For a stateful certificateless encryption scheme, the adversary may be interested in analyzing the ciphertexts of different messages of his choice, encrypted during a particular session. Since the adversary does not know the state information, the challenger has to provide the encryption oracle to the adversary.

Confidentiality Against Type-I Adversary

Theorem 1. *The stateful certificateless encryption scheme* stCLE *is IND-stCLE-CCA2-I secure in the random oracle model, if the SDH problem is intractable.*

Proof. The challenger $\mathcal{C}$ is challenged with an instance of the SDH problem, say $\langle g, g^a, g^b \rangle \in_R \mathbb{G}^3$ and is given access to a Decision Diffie Hellman (DDH) oracle $\mathcal{DDH}_{g,a}(.,.)$ which on input g^b and g^c outputs True if and only if $g^{ab} = g^c$. The challenger's aim is to solve the SDH problem, which is to compute $g^{ab} \in \mathbb{G}$. In our scheme $\mathbb{Z}_p^*$ forms a group which can be represented as $\mathbb{G}$. Let us consider that there exists an adversary $\mathcal{A}_I$ who is capable of breaking the IND-stCLE-CCA2-I security of the stCLE scheme. $\mathcal{C}$ can make use of $\mathcal{A}_I$ to compute g^{ab} by playing the following interactive game with $\mathcal{A}_I$.

Setup: $\mathcal{C}$ begins the game by setting up the system parameters as in the stCLE scheme. $\mathcal{C}$ takes g and g^a from the instance of the SDH problem sets $y = g^a$ and sends $params = \langle p, q, g, y \rangle$ to $\mathcal{A}_I$. This makes an implicit assignment to the master private key as $z = a$, where $\mathcal{C}$ doenot know z. $\mathcal{C}$ also designs the five hash functions F, G, H, H_1 and H_2 as random oracles $\mathcal{O}_F, \mathcal{O}_G, \mathcal{O}_H, \mathcal{O}_{H_1}$ and $\mathcal{O}_{H_2}$. $\mathcal{C}$ maintains five lists L_F, L_G, L_H, L_{H_1} and L_{H_2} in order to consistently respond to the queries to the random oracles $\mathcal{O}_F, \mathcal{O}_G, \mathcal{O}_H, \mathcal{O}_{H_1}$ and $\mathcal{O}_{H_2}$ respectively. To maintain the consistency of the private key request and public key request oracle queries, $\mathcal{C}$ maintains lists L_S and L_P respectively. A typical entity in list L_i for $i = \{F, G, H, H_1, H_2\}$ will have the input parameters of the oracles, followed by the corresponding hash value returned as the response to the hash oracle query. The list L_S consists of the tuples of the form $\langle ID_i, D_i^{(1)}, D_i^{(2)} \rangle$ and that of L_P consists of the tuples of the form $\langle ID_i, PK_i^{(1)}, PK_i^{(2)}, PK_i^{(3)}, PK_i^{(4)} \rangle \rangle$. In order to generate stateful encryptions, $\mathcal{C}$ generates $\hat{n}$ tuples of state informations and stores them in a state list L_{st}. Each tuple in the list corresponds to a state information. This is done as follows.

For each identity ID_i created by $\mathcal{A}_I$ and $j = 1$ to $\hat{n}$, $\mathcal{C}$ performs the following:

- Choose $r_j \in_R \mathbb{Z}_q^*$, compute $k_j = g^{r_j}$, choose $u_j \in_R \mathbb{Z}_q^*$ and add the tuple $\langle k_j, u_j \rangle$ in the list L_F.
- Compute $s_j = r_j u_j$ and $v_j = g^{s_j}$.
- The state information $st_j = \langle ID_i, u_j, v_j, s_j, \text{index}_j \rangle$.
- Store the tuple st_j in list L_{st}.

The game proceeds as described in the security model for Type-I adversary in Sect. 2.3.

Phase I: $\mathcal{A}_I$ performs a series of queries to the oracles provided by $\mathcal{C}$. The descriptions of the oracles and the responses given by $\mathcal{C}$ to the corresponding oracle queries by $\mathcal{A}_I$ are described below:

$\mathcal{O}_F(g^{r_i})$: For answering the $\mathcal{O}_F$ query, $\mathcal{C}$ performs the following:

- If a tuple of the form $\langle g^{r_i}, u_i \rangle$ exists in the list L_F then $\mathcal{C}$ retrieves the corresponding u_i and sends it to $\mathcal{A}_I$.

- Else, $\mathcal{C}$ chooses $u_i \in_R \mathbb{Z}_q^*$, stores the tuple $\langle g^{r_i}, u_i \rangle$ in the list L_F and sends u_i to $\mathcal{A}_I$

$\mathcal{O}_G(ID_j, c_1, m, w_{i1}, w_{i2}, \textbf{index})$: For answering the $\mathcal{O}_G$ query, $\mathcal{C}$ performs the following:

- If a tuple of the form $\langle ID_j, c_1, m, w_{i1}, w_{i2}, \textbf{index}, \mathcal{G} \rangle$ exists in the list L_G then $\mathcal{C}$ retrieves the corresponding $\mathcal{G}$ and sends it to $\mathcal{A}_I$.
- Else, $\mathcal{C}$ chooses $\mathcal{G} \in_R \mathbb{Z}_q^*$, stores the tuple $\langle ID_j, c_1, m, w_{i1}, w_{i2}, \textbf{index}, \mathcal{G} \rangle$ in the list L_G and sends $\mathcal{G}$ to $\mathcal{A}_I$

$\mathcal{O}_H(ID_j, c_1, c_2, w_{i1}, w_{i2}, \textbf{index})$: For answering the $\mathcal{O}_H$ query, $\mathcal{C}$ performs the following:

- If a tuple of the form $\langle ID_j, c_1, c_2, w_{i1}, w_{i2}, \textbf{index}, \mathcal{H} \rangle$ exists in the list L_H then $\mathcal{C}$ retrieves the corresponding $\mathcal{H}$ and sends it to $\mathcal{A}_I$.
- Else, $\mathcal{C}$ chooses $\mathcal{H} \in_R \{0,1\}^{l_m}$, stores the tuple $\langle ID_j, c_1, m, w_{i1}, w_{i2}, \textbf{index}, \mathcal{H} \rangle$ in the list L_H and sends $\mathcal{H}$ to $\mathcal{A}_I$

$\mathcal{O}_{H_1}(ID_i, y_{i0})$: To respond to this query, $\mathcal{C}$ checks whether a tuple of the form $\langle ID_i, y_{i0}, h_{i1} \rangle$ exists in the list L_{H_1}. If a tuple of this form exists, $\mathcal{C}$ returns the corresponding h_{i1}, else chooses $h_{i1} \in_R \mathbb{Z}_q^*$ and adds the tuple $\langle ID_i, y_{i0}, h_{i1} \rangle$ to the list L_{H_1} and returns h_{i1} to $\mathcal{A}_I$.

$\mathcal{O}_{H_2}(ID_i, y_{i0}, y_{i1})$: To respond to this query, $\mathcal{C}$ checks whether a tuple of the form $\langle ID_i, y_{i0}, y_{i1}, h_{i2} \rangle$ exists in the list L_{H_2}. If a tuple of this form exists, $\mathcal{C}$ returns the corresponding h_{i2}, else chooses $h_{i2} \in_R \mathbb{Z}_q^*$, adds the tuple $\langle ID_i, y_{i0}, y_{i1}, h_{i2} \rangle$ to the list L_{H_2} and returns h_{i2} to $\mathcal{A}_I$.

$\mathcal{O}_{RequestPublicKey}(ID_i)$: $\mathcal{C}$ selects a random index γ, where $1 \leq \gamma \leq q_{PK}$ and $\mathcal{C}$ does not reveal γ to $\mathcal{A}_I$. Here q_{PK} is the maximum number of Request Public Key oracle queries. When $\mathcal{A}_I$ makes the γth query on ID_γ, $\mathcal{C}$ fixes ID_γ as target identity for the challenge phase.

If a tuple of the form $\langle ID_i, PK_i^{(1)}, PK_i^{(2)}, PK_i^{(3)}, PK_i^{(4)} \rangle$ exists in the list L_P, return the items corresponding to the identity ID_i in the list as the public key. If a tuple does not exist, check whether $i \neq \gamma$. In this case, $\mathcal{C}$ queries $\mathcal{O}_{PartialKeyExtract}(ID_i)$ and then retrieves the tuple of the form $\langle ID_i, PK_i^{(1)}, PK_i^{(2)}, PK_i^{(3)}, PK_i^{(4)} \rangle$ from the list L_P and returns it as the public key corresponding to the identity ID_i. If $i = \gamma$, then perform the following:

- Choose $s_{i0}, d_{i1}, h_{i1}, h_{i2}, x_i \in_R \mathbb{Z}_q^*$.
- Compute $y_{i0} = g^{s_{i0}}$, $y_{i1} = g^{d_{i1}} (g^a)^{-h_{i2}}$ and $g_i = g^{x_i}$.
- Add the tuple $\langle ID_i, D_i^{(1)}, D_i^{(2)} \rangle = \langle ID_i, -, x_i \rangle$ in the list L_S and add the tuple $\langle ID_i, PK_i^{(1)}, PK_i^{(2)}, PK_i^{(3)}, PK_i^{(4)} \rangle = \langle ID_i, y_{i0}, y_{i1}, d_{i1}, g_i \rangle$ to the list L_P.
- Add the tuple $\langle ID_i, y_{i0}, h_{i1} \rangle$ to list L_{H_1} and the tuple $\langle ID_i, y_{i0}, y_{i1}, h_{i2} \rangle$ to list L_{H_2}
- Return $\langle ID_i, PK_i^{(1)}, PK_i^{(2)}, PK_i^{(3)}, PK_i^{(4)} \rangle$ to $\mathcal{A}_I$.

$\mathcal{O}_{PartialKeyExtract}(ID_i)$: In order to answer a query to the oracle, $\mathcal{C}$ checks whether a tuple of the form $\langle ID_i, D_i^{(1)}, D_i^{(2)} \rangle$ exists in the list L_S and if a tuple of this form exists, $\mathcal{C}$ returns the corresponding $D_i^{(1)}$. If it does not exist, $\mathcal{C}$ checks whether $i \stackrel{?}{=} \gamma$. If $i = \gamma$, $\mathcal{C}$ *Aborts* the game. If $i \neq \gamma$, $\mathcal{C}$ performs the following:

- Choose $d_{i0}, d_{i1}, h_{i1}, h_{i2}, x_i \in_R \mathbb{Z}_q^*$.
- Compute $y_{i0} = g^{d_{i0}}(g^a)^{-h_{i1}}$, $y_{i1} = g^{d_{i1}} (g^a)^{-h_{i2}}$ and $g_i = g^{x_i}$.
- Add the tuple $\langle ID_i, D_i^{(1)}, D_i^{(2)} \rangle = \langle ID_i, d_{i0}, x_i \rangle$ in the list L_S and add the tuple $\langle ID_i, PK_i^{(1)}, PK_i^{(2)}, PK_i^{(3)}, PK_i^{(4)} \rangle = \langle ID_i, y_{i0}, y_{i1}, d_{i1}, g_i \rangle$ to the list L_P.
- Add the tuple $\langle ID_i, y_{i0}, h_{i1} \rangle$ to list L_{H_1} and the tuple $\langle ID_i, y_{i0}, y_{i1}, h_{i2} \rangle$ to list L_{H_2}
- Return $D_i^{(1)}$ to $\mathcal{A}_I$.

$\mathcal{O}_{ExtractSecretValue}(ID_i)$: $\mathcal{C}$ retrieves the tuple of the form $\langle ID_i, d_{i0}, x_i \rangle$ from the list L_S and returns the corresponding x_i as the secret value corresponding to the identity ID_i. If the entry corresponding to x_i in the tuple is "$-$" then it indicates the fact that $\mathcal{A}_I$ has replaced the public key corresponding to ID_i. By the definition of the model, such queries by $\mathcal{A}_I$ are not allowed and hence $\mathcal{C}$ can ignore such queries.

$\mathcal{O}_{ReplacePublicKey}(ID_i, PK_i')$: To replace the public key of ID_i with a new public key $PK_i' = \langle ID_i, PK_i^{(1)'}, PK_i^{(2)'}, PK_i^{(3)'}, PK_i^{(4)'} \rangle$, sent by $\mathcal{A}_I$, $\mathcal{C}$ updates the corresponding tuples in the list L_P, only if PK_i' satisfies equation (2). If the equation is not satisfied return *Invalid*.

$\mathcal{O}_{Encryption}(ID_i, st_j, m_k)$: $\mathcal{A}_I$ may perform encryption with respect to any state information st_j, chosen by $\mathcal{C}$. $\mathcal{C}$ performs the following to encrypt the message m_k with respect to the state information st_j, where $j = 1$ to $\hat{n}$, where $\hat{n}$ is the upper bound for the total number of states and $k = 1$ to $\hat{m}$ is bound by the maximum number of messages that can be encrypted in one session:

- Retrieves the tuple st_j of the form $\langle ID_i, u_j, v_j, s_j, \text{index}_j \rangle$ from L_{st}, sets $c_1 = v_j$, compute $w_{j1} = (PK_i^{(1)} y^{h_{i1}})^{s_j}$ and $w_{j2} = (PK_i^{(4)})^{s_j}$
- Choose $\mathcal{G} \in_R \mathbb{Z}_q^*$, store the tuple $\langle ID_i, c_1, m_k, w_{j1}, w_{j2}, \text{index}_j, \mathcal{G} \rangle$ in the list $L_{\mathcal{G}}$ and computes $c_2 = u_j \oplus \mathcal{G}$.
- Choose $\mathcal{H} \in_R \{0,1\}^{l_m}$, store the tuple $\langle ID_i, c_1, c_2, w_{j1}, w_{j2}, \text{index}_j, \mathcal{H} \rangle$ in the list L_H and computes $c_3 = m_k \oplus \mathcal{H}$.
- Returns $c = \langle c_1, c_2, c_3 \rangle$ as the ciphertext, increments index_j and updates the state information st_j.

$\mathcal{O}_{Decryption}(CT = (c_1, c_2, c_3, \text{index}), ID_i, PK_i)$: If $i \neq \gamma$, $\mathcal{C}$ performs decryption in the normal way since $\mathcal{C}$ knows the private key corresponding to ID_i. If $i = \gamma$, $\mathcal{C}$ performs the following to decrypt the ciphertext $CT = \langle c_1, c_2, c_3, \text{index} \rangle$:

- Check the validity of PK_i and reject the ciphertext CT if this check fails; else, proceed.

- Retrieve the tuples of the form $\langle ID_i, c_1, m, w_{i1}, w_{i2}, \mathsf{index}, \mathcal{G} \rangle$ and $\langle ID_i, c_1, c_2, w_{i1}, w_{i2}, \mathsf{index}, \mathcal{H} \rangle$ from the lists L_G and L_H respectively. Retrieve the tuple $\langle ID_i, y_{i0}, h_{i1} \rangle$ from the list L_{H_1}.
- Compute $\alpha = (w_{i1} c_1^{-s_{i0}})^{h_{i1}^{-1}}$ by taking the corresponding values from the tuples retrieved in the above step.
- Check whether $\langle g, c_1, g^a, \alpha \rangle$ is a valid DDH tuple using the $\mathcal{DDH}_{g,a}(.,.)$ oracle. If the oracle outputs true, proceed else reject the ciphertext CT.
- Compute $m' = c_3 \oplus \mathcal{H}$ and check whether $m' = m$, where $\mathcal{H}$ and m are retrieved from the lists L_H and L_G respectively. If $m' \neq m$ reject the ciphertext CT.
- If the check holds, compute $u' = c_2 \oplus \mathcal{G}$. Retrieve the tuple of the form $\langle g^{r_i}, u' \rangle$ from the list L_F and check whether $c_1^{u'^{-1}} \stackrel{?}{=} g^{r_i}$. If the check does not hold reject the ciphertext CT.

If any of the fetched tuple is not available in any of the lists or any of the tests fails, returns *Invalid* else return m as the message.

Challenge: At the end of **Phase I**, $\mathcal{A}_I$ produces two messages m_0 and m_1 of equal length and an identity ID^*. $\mathcal{C}$ *Aborts* the game if $ID^* \neq ID_\gamma$, else randomly chooses a bit $\delta \in_R \{0,1\}$ and computes a ciphertext CT^* with ID_γ as the receiver by performing the following steps:

- Choose $u \in_R \mathbb{Z}_q^*$ and add the tuple $\langle g^b, u \rangle$ to the list L_F.
- Set $\mathsf{index}^* = 1$ and compute $c_1^* = g^{bu}$
- Retrieve the tuple of the form $\langle ID^*, d_0^*, x^* \rangle$ from the list L_S and compute $w_2^* = (c_1^*)^{x^*}$.
- Choose $\mathcal{G} \in_R \mathbb{Z}_q^*$, store the tuple $\langle ID^*, c_1^*, m_\delta, -, w_2^*, \mathsf{index}^*, \mathcal{G} \rangle$ in list L_G and compute $c_2^* = u \oplus \mathcal{G}$.
- Choose $\mathcal{H} \in_R \{0,1\}^{l_m}$, store the tuple $\langle ID^*, c_1^*, m_\delta, -, w_2^*, \mathsf{index}^*, \mathcal{H} \rangle$ in list L_H and compute $c_3^* = m_\delta \oplus \mathcal{H}$.
- Here the state information $st^* = \langle ID^*, u^*, v^*, s^*, \mathsf{index}^* \rangle = \langle ID^*, u, g^{bu}, -, \mathsf{index}^* \rangle$

Now, $CT^* = \langle c_1^*, c_2^*, c_3^*, \mathsf{index}^* \rangle$ is sent to $\mathcal{A}_I$ as the challenge ciphertext.

Phase II: $\mathcal{A}_I$ performs the second phase of interaction, where it makes polynomial number of queries to the oracles provided by $\mathcal{C}$ with the following conditions:

- $\mathcal{A}_I$ should not have queried the *Strong Decryption* oracle with $(CT^*, PK_\gamma, ID_\gamma)$ as input. (It is to be noted that PK_γ is the public key corresponding to ID_γ during the challenge phase. $\mathcal{A}_I$ can query the decryption oracle with (CT^*, PK^*, ID_γ) as input, $\forall PK^* \neq PK_\gamma$)
- $\mathcal{A}_I$ should not query the partial private key of ID_γ.
- $\mathcal{A}_I$ can query the secret value and PK_γ of ID_γ.

Encryption oracle has to be provided to $\mathcal{A}_I$ with respect to the state information st^*. This is because, $\mathcal{A}_I$ should have access to any number of ciphertexts generated during this state. Moreover, the decryption oracle has to respond to decryption queries corresponding to any ciphertext generated during the state st^*. These two oracles are described here and all other oracles are same as in Phase I.

$\mathcal{O}_{Encryption}(ID_i, st_j, m_k)$: For any state $st_j \neq st^*$, $\mathcal{C}$ performs the encryption as in Phase I. If $st_j = st^*$, $\mathcal{C}$ performs the following to encrypt the message m_k with respect to the state information st^*.

- Retrieve the tuple st^* of the form $\langle ID^*, u, g^{bu}, -, \text{index}^* \rangle$ from the list L_{st}, set $c_1 = g^{bu}$.
- Choose $\mathcal{G} \in_R \mathbb{Z}_q^*$, store the tuple $\langle ID^*, c_1, m_k, -, -, \text{index}^*, \mathcal{G} \rangle$ in the list L_G and computes $c_2 = u \oplus \mathcal{G}$.
- Choose $\mathcal{H} \in_R \{0,1\}^{l_m}$, store the tuple $\langle ID^*, c_1, c_2, -, -, \text{index}^*, \mathcal{H} \rangle$ in the list L_H and computes $c_3 = m_k \oplus \mathcal{H}$.
- Returns $c = \langle c_1, c_2, c_3 \rangle$ as the ciphertext, increments index_j and updates the state information st_j.

$\mathcal{O}_{Decryption}(CT = (c_1, c_2, c_3, \text{index}), ID_i, PK_i)$: If $i \neq \gamma$ and $c_1 \neq c_1^*$, $\mathcal{C}$ performs decryption in the normal way since $\mathcal{C}$ knows the private key corresponding to ID_i. If $i = \gamma$ and $c_1 \neq c_1^*$, $\mathcal{C}$ performs the decryption as in Phase I. If $i = \gamma$ and $c_1 = c_1^*$ then $\mathcal{C}$ performs the following. It should be noted that the state information st^* is with respect to the identity ID^* and hence for all other identities, decryption oracle proceeds as in Phase I.

- Check the validity of PK_i and reject the ciphertext CT if this check fails; else, proceed.
- Retrieve the tuples of the form $\langle ID^*, c_1^*, m, -, -, \text{index}^*, \mathcal{G} \rangle$ and $\langle ID^*, c_1^*, c_2, -, -, \text{index}, \mathcal{H} \rangle$ from the lists L_G and L_H respectively. Retrieve the tuple $\langle ID_i, y_{i0}, h_{i1} \rangle$ from the list L_{H_1}.
- Compute $m' = c_3 \oplus \mathcal{H}$ and check whether $m' = m$, where $\mathcal{H}$ and m are retrieved from the lists L_H and L_G respectively. If $m' \neq m$ reject the ciphertext CT. Note that $\mathcal{C}$ can even work consistently with the tuples of this form. In this case, $\mathcal{C}$ takes the values $\mathcal{G}$ and $\mathcal{H}$ without consulting the DDH oracle because these tuples were generated by $\mathcal{C}$ without knowing the values of w_1^* and w_2^*.
- Compute $u' = c_2 \oplus \mathcal{G}$. Retrieve the tuple of the form $\langle g^{r_i}, u' \rangle$ from the list L_F and check whether $c_1^{* u'^{-1}} = g^{r_i}$. If the check does not hold reject the ciphertext CT.
- If in the process of finding out the tuples of the form $\langle ID^*, c_1^*, m, w_1^*, w_2^*, \text{index}^*, \mathcal{G} \rangle$ and $\langle ID^*, c_1^*, c_2^*, w_1^*, w_2^*, \text{index}^*, \mathcal{H} \rangle$ appeared in the lists L_G and L_H respectively then retrieve the tuple $\langle ID^*, y_0^*, h_1^* \rangle$ from the list L_{H_1}, compute $\alpha = (w_1^* c_1^{* -s_0^*})^{h_1^{* -1}}$ by taking the corresponding values from the tuples retrieved in the above step and check whether $\langle g, c_1^*, g^a, \alpha \rangle$ is a valid DDH tuple using the $\mathcal{DDH}_{g,a}(.,.)$ oracle. If the oracle outputs true, output α as the solution to the SDH problem instance.

If any tuple is not available in any of the lists or any of the tests fails, returns *Invalid*.

Guess: At the end of **Phase II**, $\mathcal{A}_I$ produces a bit δ' to $\mathcal{C}$, $\mathcal{C}$ performs the following to output the solution for the SDH problem instance.

- Retrieve the tuple $\langle ID^*, y_0^*, h_1^* \rangle$ from the list L_{H_1}.
- For each tuple of the form $\langle ID^*, c_1^*, m, w_1^*, w_2^*, \text{index}^*, \mathcal{G} \rangle$ and $\langle ID^*, c_1^*, c_2^*, w_1^*, w_2^*, \text{index}^*, \mathcal{H} \rangle$ in the lists L_G and L_H, compute $\alpha = (w_1^* c_1^{*-s_0^*})^{h_1^{*-1}}$ by taking the corresponding values from the tuples.
- Check whether $\langle g, c_1^*, g^a, \alpha \rangle$ is a valid DDH tuple using the $\mathcal{DDH}_{g,a}(.,.)$ oracle. If the oracle outputs $\texttt{true}$, output α as the solution to the SDH problem instance.

Thus, $\mathcal{C}$ obtains the solution to the SDH problem with almost the same advantage of $\mathcal{A}_I$ in the IND-stCLE-CCA2-I game. $\qquad\square$

Analysis: We now derive the advantage of $\mathcal{C}$ in solving the SDH problem using the adversary $\mathcal{A}_I$. The simulations of F, G, H, H_1 and H_2 clearly shows that the hash oracles are perfectly random. Let ϵ be the non-negligible advantage of $\mathcal{A}_I$ in winning the IND-stCLE-CCA2-I game.
The events in which $\mathcal{C}$ aborts the game and the respective probabilities are given below:

1. $\mathcal{E}_1$ - The event in which $\mathcal{A}_I$ queries the partial private key of ID_γ.
2. $\mathcal{E}_2$ - The event in which ID_γ is not chosen as the target identity by $\mathcal{A}_I$ for the challenge.

Suppose, $\mathcal{A}_I$ has asked q_{PK} queries to the $\mathcal{O}_{RequestPublicKey}$ oracle and q_P queries to the $\mathcal{O}_{PartialKeyExtract}$ oracle. Let us consider that there are a total of q_I individual identities, where $q_I \leq q_{PK} + q_P$ queried by $\mathcal{A}_I$ to these oracles, then:

$\Pr[\mathcal{E}_1] = \frac{q_P}{q_I}$ and $\Pr[\mathcal{E}_2] = 1 - \frac{1}{q_I - q_P}$.
Therefore,
$\Pr[\neg abort] = [\neg\mathcal{E}_1 \wedge \neg\mathcal{E}_2] = \left[1 - \frac{q_P}{q_I}\right] \cdot \left[1 - 1 - \frac{1}{q_I - q_P}\right] = \frac{1}{q_I}$.

Therefore, the advantage of $\mathcal{C}$ solving the SDH problem is $\epsilon' \geq \left(\epsilon \cdot \frac{1}{q_I}\right)$. Since ϵ is assumed to be non-negligible and $frac1q_I$ is also non-negligible, ϵ' will be non-negligible. This contradicts the assumption that there is no polynomial time algorithm to solve the SDH problem. Thus, we conclude that there does not exist a polynomial time adversary that can break the IND-stCLE-CCA2-I security of the $\texttt{stCLE}$ scheme.

Confidentiality Against Type-II Adversary

Theorem 2. *Our certificateless public key encryption scheme* $\texttt{stCLE}$ *is IND-stCLE-CCA2-II secure in the random oracle model, if the SDH problem is intractable.*

The proof of this theorem is omitted here due to page limitation and will appear in the full version of the paper.

4   Conclusion

In this paper, we have proposed the first stateful certificateless PKE scheme. We have formally proved the scheme in the random oracle model assuming the strongest adversary. Our scheme finds straightforward application in secure sharing of encrypted cloud data with a very minimum cost. Assuming the security aspects, all the files of a user stored in the cloud are encrypted with unique symmetric keys. The existing method is to use a PKE scheme and encrypt the symmetric keys to the receiver. The receiver on receiving the encrypted keys can decrypt them using his private key and use them to decrypt the actual file from the downloaded ciphertext. Our approach reduces the cost of performing this encryption of symmetric keys from $\mathcal{O}(k)$ to $\mathcal{O}(1)$ exponentiations. This efficiency come because our scheme is stateful, which suits for resource constrained devices such as cell phones, personal digital assistants, tablets, wearables and sensors, where each exponentiation costs on the battery life of the device.

References

1. Abe, M., Kiltz, E., Okamoto, T.: Compact CCA-secure encryption for messages of arbitrary length. In: Jarecki, S., Tsudik, G. (eds.) PKC 2009. LNCS, vol. 5443, pp. 377–392. Springer, Heidelberg (2009)
2. Al-Riyami, S.S., Paterson, K.G.: Certificateless public key cryptography. In: Laih, C.-S. (ed.) ASIACRYPT 2003. LNCS, vol. 2894, pp. 452–473. Springer, Heidelberg (2003)
3. Baek, J., Chu, C.-K., Zhou, J.: On shortening ciphertexts: new constructions for compact public key and stateful encryption schemes. In: Kiayias, A. (ed.) CT-RSA 2011. LNCS, vol. 6558, pp. 302–318. Springer, Heidelberg (2011)
4. Baek, J., Safavi-Naini, R., Susilo, W.: Certificateless public key encryption without pairing. In: Zhou, J., López, J., Deng, R.H., Bao, F. (eds.) ISC 2005. LNCS, vol. 3650, pp. 134–148. Springer, Heidelberg (2005)
5. Bellare, M., Kohno, T., Shoup, V.: Stateful public-key cryptosystems: how to encrypt with one 160-bit exponentiation. In: ACM Conference on Computer and Communications Security - ACM-CCS 2006, pp. 380–389. ACM (2006)
6. Bendel, M.: Hackers describe ps3 security as epic fail, gain unrestricted access (2010). http://www.exophase.com/20540/hackers-describe-ps3-security-as-epic-fail-gain-unrestricted-access/
7. Castro, R., Dahab, R.: Two notes on the security of certificateless signatures. In: Susilo, W., Liu, J.K., Mu, Y. (eds.) ProvSec 2007. LNCS, vol. 4784, pp. 85–102. Springer, Heidelberg (2007)
8. Cheng, Z., Comley, R.: Efficient certificateless public key encryption. Cryptology ePrint Archive, Report 2005/012 (2005). http://eprint.iacr.org/
9. Dent, A.W.: A survey of certificateless encryption schemes and security models. Int. J. Inf. Secur. 7(5), 349–377 (2008)
10. Huang, X., Susilo, W., Mu, Y., Zhang, F.T.: On the security of certificateless signature schemes from Asiacrypt 2003. In: Desmedt, Y.G., Wang, H., Mu, Y., Li, Y. (eds.) CANS 2005. LNCS, vol. 3810, pp. 13–25. Springer, Heidelberg (2005)
11. Lai, J., Deng, R.H., Liu, S., Kou, W.: RSA-Based Certificateless Public Key Encryption. In: Bao, F., Li, H., Wang, G. (eds.) ISPEC 2009. LNCS, vol. 5451, pp. 24–34. Springer, Heidelberg (2009)

12. Lenstra, A.K., Hughes, J.P., Augier, M., Bos, J.W., Kleinjung, T., Wachter, C.: Ron was wrong, whit is right. IACR Cryptology ePrint Archive (2012)
13. Liu, J.K., Au, M.H., Susilo, W.: Self-generated-certificate public key cryptography and certificateless signature/encryption scheme in the standard model: extended abstract. In: Proceedings of the ACM Symposium on Information, Computer and Communications Security - ASIA-CCS 2007, pp. 273–283. ACM (2007)
14. Okamoto, T., Pointcheval, D.: The gap-problems: a new class of problems for the security of cryptographic schemes. In: Kim, K. (ed.) PKC 2001. LNCS, vol. 1992, pp. 104–118. Springer, Heidelberg (2001)
15. Park, J.-H., Choi, K.Y., Hwang, J.Y., Lee, D.-H.: Certificateless public key encryption in the selective-ID security model (without random oracles). In: Takagi, T., Okamoto, E., Okamoto, T., Okamoto, T. (eds.) Pairing 2007. LNCS, vol. 4575, pp. 60–82. Springer, Heidelberg (2007)
16. Phong, L.T., Matsuoka, H., Ogata, W.: Stateful identity-based encryption scheme: faster encryption and decryption. In: Proceedings of the 2008 ACM Symposium on Information, Computer and Communications Security - ASIACCS 2008, pp. 381–388. ACM (2008)
17. Shi, Y., Li, J.: Provable efficient certificateless public key encryption. Cryptology ePrint Archive, Report 2005/287 (2005). http://eprint.iacr.org/
18. Sun, Y., Zhang, F.T., Baek, J.: Strongly secure certificateless public key encryption without pairing. In: Bao, F., Ling, S., Okamoto, T., Wang, H., Xing, C. (eds.) CANS 2007. LNCS, vol. 4856, pp. 194–208. Springer, Heidelberg (2007)
19. Sree Vivek, S., Selvi, S., Rangan, C.P.: CCA secure certificateless encryption schemes based on RSA. In: SECRYPT 2011 - Proceedings of the International Conference on Security and Cryptography, pp. 208–217. SciTePress (2011)
20. Vivek, S.S., Selvi, S.S.D., Rangan, C.P.: Compact stateful encryption schemes with ciphertext verifiability. In: Hanaoka, G., Yamauchi, T. (eds.) IWSEC 2012. LNCS, vol. 7631, pp. 87–104. Springer, Heidelberg (2012)

Applying Cryptographic Acceleration Techniques to Error Correction

Rémi Géraud[2,4], Diana-Ştefania Maimuţ[2(✉)], David Naccache[1,2],
Rodrigo Portella do Canto[1], and Emil Simion[3]

[1] Sorbonne Universités, Université Paris II,
12 Place du Panthéon, 75231 Paris, France
rodrigo.portella-do-canto@etudiants.u-paris2.fr
[2] Département d'Informatique, École Normale Supérieure,
45, Rue d'Ulm, 75230 Paris Cedex 05, France
{remi.geraud,diana-stefania.maimut,david.naccache}@ens.fr
[3] University Politehnica of Bucharest,
313 Splaiul Independenţei, Bucharest, Romania
esimion@fmi.unibuc.ro
[4] Ingenico Group, 28–32 Boulevard de Grenelle, 75015 Paris, France
remi.geraud@ingenico.com

Abstract. Modular reduction is the basic building block of many public-key cryptosystems. BCH codes require repeated polynomial reductions modulo the same constant polynomial. This is conceptually very similar to the implementation of public-key cryptography where repeated modular reduction in $\mathbb{Z}_n$ or $\mathbb{Z}_p$ are required for some fixed n or p. It is hence natural to try and transfer the modular reduction expertise developed by cryptographers during the past decades to obtain new BCH speed-up strategies. Error correction codes (ECCs) are deployed in digital communication systems to enforce transmission accuracy. BCH codes are a particularly popular ECC family. This paper generalizes Barrett's modular reduction to polynomials to speed-up BCH ECCs. A BCH(15, 7, 2) encoder was implemented in Verilog and synthesized. Results show substantial improvements when compared to traditional polynomial reduction implementations. We present two BCH code implementations (regular and pipelined) using Barrett polynomial reduction. These implementations, are respectively 4.3 and 6.7 faster than an improved BCH LFSR design. The regular Barrett design consumes around 53 % less power than the BCH LFSR design, while the faster pipelined version consumes 2.3 times more power than the BCH LFSR design.

1 Introduction

Modular reduction (*e.g.* [3,4,8,10]) is the basic building block of many public-key cryptosystems. We refer the reader to [3] for a detailed comparison of various modular reduction strategies.

BCH codes are widely used for error correction in digital systems, memory devices and computer networks. For example, the shortened BCH(48,36,5) was

© Springer International Publishing Switzerland 2015
I. Bica et al. (Eds.): SECITC 2015, LNCS 9522, pp. 150–168, 2015.
DOI: 10.1007/978-3-319-27179-8_11

accepted by the U.S. Telecommunications Industry Association as a standard for the cellular Time Division Multiple Access protocol (TDMA) [11]. Another example is BCH(511, 493) which was adopted by International Telecommunication Union as a standard for video conferencing and video phone codecs (Rec. H.26) [5]. BCH codes require repeated polynomial reductions modulo the same constant polynomial. This is conceptually very similar to the implementation of public-key cryptography where repeated modular reduction in $\mathbb{Z}_n$ or $\mathbb{Z}_p$ are required for some fixed n or p [1].

It is hence natural to try and transfer the modular reduction expertise developed by cryptographers during the past decades to obtain new BCH speed-up strategies. This work focuses on the "polynomialization" of Barrett's modular reduction algorithm [1]. Barrett's method creates the operation $a \bmod b$ from bit shifts, multiplications and additions in $\mathbb{Z}$. This allows to build modular reduction at very marginal code or silicon costs by leveraging existing hardware or software multipliers.

Reduction modulo fixed multivariate polynomials is also very useful in other fields such as robotics and computer algebra (*e.g.* for computing Gröbner bases).

Structure of the Paper: Section 2 recalls Barrett's algorithm. Section 3 presents our main theoretical results, *i.e.* a polynomial variant of [1]. Section 4 recalls the basics of BCH error correcting codes (ECC). Section 4.2 describes the integration of the Barrett polynomial variant in a BCH circuit and provides benchmark results.

2   Barrett's Reduction Algorithm

Notations. $\|x\|$ will denote the bit-length of x throughout this paper. $y \gg z$ will denote binary shift-to-the-right of y by z bits *i.e.*:

$$y \gg z = \left\lfloor \frac{y}{2^z} \right\rfloor .$$

Barrett's algorithm (Algorithm 1) approximates the result $c = d \bmod n$ by a quasi-reduced integer $c + \epsilon n$, where $0 \le \epsilon \le 2$. Let $N = \|n\|, D = \|d\|$ and fix a maximal bit-length reduction capacity L such that $N \le D \le L$. The algorithm will work if $D \le L$. In most implementations, $D = L = 2N$. The algorithm uses the pre-computed constant $\kappa = \lfloor 2^L/n \rfloor$ that depends only on n and L. The reader is referred to [1] for a proof and an analysis of Algorithm 1.

Example 1. Reduce $8619 \bmod 93 = 63$.

$n = 93 \ \Rightarrow \ N = 7$

$\kappa = \left\lfloor \frac{2^{32}}{n} \right\rfloor$ =10110000001011000000101100

$d = 8619$ =10000110101011

c_1 =10000110~~101011~~   = 10000110

c_2 =10111000011011100001101110001000

c_3 =1011100 ~~001101110000110111000011000~~ =1011100

nc_3 =10000101101100

c_4 = 63

Algorithm 1. Barrett's Algorithm

Input: $n < 2^N, d < 2^D, \kappa = \left\lfloor \frac{2^L}{n} \right\rfloor$ where $N \leq D \leq L$
Output: $c = d \mod n$

1 $c_1 \leftarrow d \gg (N-1)$

2 $c_2 \leftarrow c_1 \kappa$

3 $c_3 \leftarrow c_2 \gg (L - N + 1)$

4 $c_4 \leftarrow d - n c_3$

5 **while** $c_4 \geq n$ **do**

6 $\quad\big|\quad c_4 \leftarrow c_4 - n$

7 **end**

8 **return** c_4

Work Factor: $\|c_1\| = D - N + 1 \simeq D - N$ and $\|\kappa\| = L - N$ hence their product requires $w = (D - N)(L - N)$ elementary operations. $\|c_3\| = (D - N) + (L - N) - (L - N + 1) = D - N - 1 \simeq D - N$. The product $n c_3$ will therefore claim $w' = (D - N)N$ elementary operations. All in all, work amounts to $w + w' = (D - N)(L - N) + (D - N)N = (D - N)L$.

2.1 Dynamic Constant Scaling

The constant κ can be adjusted on the fly thanks to Lemma 1.

Lemma 1. *If* $U \leq L$, *then* $\bar{\kappa} = \kappa \gg U = \left\lfloor \frac{2^{L-U}}{n} \right\rfloor$.

Proof. $\exists\ \alpha < 2^U$ and $\beta < n$ (integers) verifying:

$$\bar{\kappa} = \frac{\kappa}{2^U} - \frac{\alpha}{2^U} \text{ and } \kappa = \frac{2^L}{n} - \frac{\beta}{n}.$$

Therefore,

$$\min_{\alpha\beta} \left(\frac{2^{L-U}}{n} - \frac{\beta + \alpha n}{2^U n} \right) \leq \bar{\kappa} = \frac{2^{L-U}}{n} - \frac{\beta + \alpha n}{2^U n} \leq \max_{\alpha,\beta} \left(\frac{2^{L-U}}{n} - \frac{\beta + \alpha n}{2^U n} \right)$$

and finally,

$$\frac{2^{L-U}}{n} - 1 < \frac{2^{L-U}}{n} - 1 + \frac{1}{2^U n} \leq \bar{\kappa} \leq \frac{2^{L-U}}{n}.$$

□

Work factor: We know that $\bar{\kappa} = \kappa \gg L - D$. Let $c_5 = D - N + 1$. Replacing step 4 of Algorithm 1 with

$$c_6 \leftarrow d - n(\bar{\kappa} c_1 \gg c_5),$$

the multiplication of c_1 by $\bar{\kappa}$ (κ adjusted to $D - N$ bits, shifting by $L - D$ bits to the right), will be done in $O((D - N)^2)$.

Hence, the new work factor decreases to $(D - N)^2 + N(D - N) = (D - N)D$.

Example 2. Reconsidering Example 1, *i.e.* computing 8619 mod 93 using the above technique, we obtain:

$$D = \lceil \log_2 8619 \rceil = 14$$

$\bar{\kappa}$	=10110000 ~~001011000000101100~~	
c_1	=10000110 ~~101011~~	=10000110
$\bar{\kappa}c_1$	=101110000100000	
$\bar{\kappa}c_1 \gg c_5$	=1011100 ~~00100000~~	
$n(\bar{\kappa}c_1 \gg c_5)$	=10000101101100	
c_6	= 63	

3 Barrett's Algorithm for Polynomials

3.1 Orders

Definition 1 (Monomial Order). *Let P, Q and R be three monomials in ν variables. $\triangleright$ is a monomial order if the following conditions are fulfilled:*

- $P \triangleright 1$
- $P \triangleright Q \Rightarrow \forall R, \ PR \ \triangleright \ QR$

Example 3. The lexicographic order on exponent vectors defined by

$$\prod_{i=1}^{\nu} x^{a_i} \succ \prod_{i=1}^{\nu} x^{b_i} \Leftrightarrow \exists i, a_j = b_j \text{ for } i < j \text{ and } a_i > b_i$$

is a monomial order. We denote the lexicographic order by $\succ$.

3.2 Terminology

In the following, capital letters will next denote polynomials and $\nu \in \mathbb{N}$.

Let $P = \sum_{i=0}^{\alpha} p_i \prod_{j=1}^{\nu} x_j^{y_{j,i}} \in \mathbb{Q}[\boldsymbol{x}] = \mathbb{Q}[x_1, x_2, ..., x_\nu]$.

The leading term of P according to $\triangleright$, will be denoted by $\mathrm{lt}(P) = p_0 \prod_{j=1}^{\nu} x_j^{y_{j,0}}$.

The leading coefficient of P according to $\triangleright$ will be denoted by $\mathrm{lc}(P) = p_0 \in \mathbb{Q}$.

The quotient $\mathrm{lm}(P) = \dfrac{\mathrm{lt}(P)}{\mathrm{lc}(P)} = \prod_{j=1}^{\nu} x_j^{y_{j,0}}$ is the leading monomial of P according to $\triangleright$.

The above notations generalize the notion of degree to exponent vectors:

$$\deg(P) = \deg(\mathrm{lm}(P)) = \boldsymbol{y_0} = \langle y_{0,0}, \ldots, y_{\nu,0} \rangle.$$

Example 4. For $\succ$ and $P(x, y) = 2x_1^2 x_2^2 + 11x_1 + 15$, we have:

$$\mathrm{lt}(P) = 2x_1^2 x_2^2, \; \mathrm{lm}(P) = x_1^2 x_2^2, \deg(P) = \langle 2, 2 \rangle \text{ and } \mathrm{lc}(P) = 2.$$

Definition 2 (Reduction Step). *Let* $P, Q \in \mathbb{Q}[\boldsymbol{x}]$. *We denote by* $Q \underset{P}{\rightarrow} Q_1$ *the* **reduction step** *of* Q *(with respect to* P *and according to* $\rhd$*) defined as the result given by the following operations:*

1. *Find a term* t *of* Q *such that monomial(t)=*lm*(P)m*
2. *If such a* t *exists, return* $Q_1 = Q - \dfrac{Pm}{\mathrm{lc}(P)}$. *Else return* $Q_1 = Q$.

Example 5. Let $Q(x_1, x_2) = 3x_1^2 x_2^2$ and $P(x_1, x_2) = 2x_1^2 x_2 - 1$. The reduction step of Q (with respect to P) is $Q \underset{P}{\rightarrow} Q_1 = \dfrac{3x_2}{2}$.

Lemma 2. *Let* $P, Q \in \mathbb{Q}[\boldsymbol{x}]$ *and* $\{Q_i\}$ *such that* $Q \underset{P}{\rightarrow} Q_1 \underset{P}{\rightarrow} Q_2 \underset{P}{\rightarrow} \cdots$

1. $\exists i \in \mathbb{N}$ *such that* $j \geq i \Rightarrow Q_j = Q_i$
2. Q_i *is unique*

We denote $Q \underset{P}{\overset{*}{\rightarrow}} Q_i = Q \bmod P$ *and* $\left\lfloor \dfrac{Q}{P} \right\rfloor = \dfrac{Q - Q \bmod P}{P} \in \mathbb{Q}[\boldsymbol{x}]$ *and call* Q_i *the "residue of* Q *(with respect to* P *and according to* $\rhd$*)".*

Example 6. Euclidean division is a reduction in which $i = 1$.

3.3 Barrett's Algorithm for Multivariate Polynomials

We will now adapt Barrett's algorithm to $\mathbb{Q}[\boldsymbol{x}]$.

Barrett's algorithm and Lemma 1 can be generalised to $\mathbb{Q}[\boldsymbol{x}]$, by shifting polynomials instead of shifting integers.

Definition 3 (Polynomial Right Shift). *Let* $P = \sum_{i=0}^{\alpha} p_i \prod_{j=1}^{\nu} x_j^{y_{j,i}} \in \mathbb{Q}[\boldsymbol{x}]$ *and* $\boldsymbol{a} = \langle a_1, a_2, ..., a_\nu \rangle \in \mathbb{N}^\nu$. *We denote*

$$P \gg \boldsymbol{a} = \sum_{\varphi(\boldsymbol{a})} p_i \prod_{j=1}^{\nu} x_j^{y_{j,i} - a_i} \in \mathbb{Q}[\boldsymbol{x}], \text{ where } \varphi(\boldsymbol{a}) = \{i, \; \forall j, \; y_{i,j} \geq a_i\}.$$

Example 7.

If $P(x) = 17x^7 + 26x^6 + 37x^4 + 48x^3 + 11$, then $P \gg \langle 5 \rangle = 17x^2 + 26x$.

Theorem 1 (Barrett's Algorithm for Polynomials). *Let:*

$$- P = \sum_{i=0}^{\alpha} p_i \prod_{j=1}^{\nu} x_j^{y_{j,0}} \in \mathbb{Q}[\boldsymbol{x}] \text{ and } Q = \sum_{i=0}^{\beta} q_i \prod_{j=1}^{\nu} x_j^{w_{j,i}} \in \mathbb{Q}[\boldsymbol{x}] \; s.t. \; \mathrm{lm}(Q) \rhd \mathrm{lm}(P)$$

- $L \geq \max(w_{i,j}) \in \mathbb{N}, h(L) = \prod_{j=1}^{\nu} x_j^L$ and $K = \left\lfloor \dfrac{h(L)}{P} \right\rfloor$
- $\boldsymbol{y_0} = \langle y_{1,0}, y_{2,0}, ..., y_{\nu,0} \rangle \in \mathbb{N}^{\nu}$

Given the above notations, $(K(Q \gg \boldsymbol{y_0})) \gg (\langle L^{\nu} \rangle - \boldsymbol{y_0}) = \left\lfloor \dfrac{Q}{P} \right\rfloor$.

Proof. Let $G = h(L) \mod P$ and $B = (K(Q \gg \boldsymbol{y_0})) = \dfrac{h(L) - G}{P} \left\lfloor \dfrac{Q}{\mathrm{lm}(P)} \right\rfloor$.

$$\Downarrow$$

$$B = \dfrac{\sum_{\varphi(\boldsymbol{y_0})} q_i \prod_{j=1}^{\nu} x_j^{L+w_{j,i}-y_{j,0}} - G \sum_{\varphi(\boldsymbol{y_0})} q_i \prod_{j=1}^{\nu} x_j^{w_{j,i}-y_{j,0}}}{P}$$

Applying the definition of "$\gg$", we obtain

$$B \gg (\langle L \rangle^{\nu} - \boldsymbol{y_0}) = \deg_{\geq 0} \dfrac{Q_{\varphi(\boldsymbol{y_0})} - G \sum_{\varphi(\boldsymbol{y_0})} q_i \prod_{j=1}^{\nu} x^{w_{j,i}-L}}{P}, \text{ where } \boldsymbol{0} = \langle 0 \rangle^{\nu}.$$

Thus,

$$B \gg (\langle L^{\nu} \rangle - \boldsymbol{y_0}) = \left\lfloor \dfrac{Q_{\varphi(\boldsymbol{y_0})}}{P} \right\rfloor - \deg_{\geq 0} \dfrac{G}{P} \sum_{\varphi(\boldsymbol{y_0})} q_i \prod_{j=1}^{\nu} x^{w_{j,i}-L} = \left\lfloor \dfrac{Q_{\varphi(\boldsymbol{y_0})}}{P} \right\rfloor.$$

We know that

$$P \triangleright G \text{ and } L \geq \max(w_{i,j}), \text{ therefore } \deg_{\geq 0} \dfrac{G}{P} \sum_{\varphi(\boldsymbol{y_0})} q_i \prod_{j=1}^{\nu} x^{w_{j,i}-L} = 0.$$

Let $\bar{Q}$ be the irreducible polynomial with respect to P, obtained by removing from Q the terms that exceed $\mathrm{lm}(P)$.

$$\left\lfloor \dfrac{Q_{\varphi(y)}}{P} \right\rfloor = \dfrac{Q_{\varphi(y)} - (Q_{\varphi(y)} \mod P)}{P} = \dfrac{(Q - \bar{Q})((Q - \bar{Q}) \mod P)}{P}.$$

Hence,

$$B \gg (\langle L \rangle^{\nu} - \boldsymbol{y_0}) = \dfrac{(Q - \bar{Q})((Q - \bar{Q}) \mod P)}{P}$$

$$\Downarrow$$

$$B \gg (\langle L \rangle^{\nu} - \boldsymbol{y_0}) = \left\lfloor \dfrac{Q}{P} \right\rfloor - \dfrac{\bar{Q} - \bar{Q} \mod P}{P} = \left\lfloor \dfrac{Q}{P} \right\rfloor.$$

$$\square$$

Algorithm 2. Polynomial Barrett Algorithm

Input: $P, Q \in \mathbb{Q}[x]$ s.t. $P \triangleright Q$

$h(L) = x^L$, $y_0 = \deg P$ and $K = h(L) \mod P$, where $\deg Q \leq \langle L, \ldots, L \rangle$

Output: $R = Q \mod P$

1 $B \leftarrow (K(Q \gg y_0)) \gg (L - y_0)$

2 $R \leftarrow Q - BP$

3 **return** R

Remark. Let $Q = \sum_{i=0}^{\alpha} q_{i,j} \prod_{j=1}^{\nu} x_j^{w_{j,i}}$, $K = \sum_{i=0}^{\beta} k_{i,j} \prod_{j=1}^{\nu} x_j^{t_{j,i}}$, $\boldsymbol{y} = \langle y_1, \ldots, y_\nu \rangle$ and $\boldsymbol{z} = \langle z_1, \ldots, z_\nu \rangle$.

Let us have a closer look at the expression $B = (K(Q \gg \boldsymbol{y})) \gg \boldsymbol{z}$.

Given the final shifting by $\boldsymbol{z}$, the multiplication of K by $Q \gg \boldsymbol{y}$ can be optimised by being only partially accomplished. Indeed, during multiplication, we only have to form monomials whose exponent vectors $\boldsymbol{b} = \boldsymbol{w}_i + \boldsymbol{t}_{i'} - \boldsymbol{y} - \boldsymbol{z} = \langle b_1, \ldots, b_\nu \rangle$ are such that $b_j \geq 0$ for $1 \leq j \leq \nu$.

We implicitly apply the above in the following example.

Example 8. Let

$$\triangleright = \succ$$

$$P = x_1^2 x_2^2 + x_1^2 + 2x_1 x_2^2 + 2x_1 x_2 + x_1 + 1$$

$$Q = x_1^3 x_2^3 - 2x_1^3 + x_2^2 x_2^2 + 3.$$

We let $L = 6$ and we observe that $\nu = 2$. We pre-compute K:

$K = x_1^4 x_2^4 - x_1^4 x_2^2 + x_1^4 - 2x_1^3 x_2^4 - 2x_1^3 x_2^3 + 3x_1^3 x_2^2 + 4x_1^3 x_2 - 4x_1^3$

$$+4x_1^2 x_2^4 + 8x_1^2 x_2^3 - 5x_1^2 x_2^2 - 20x_1^2 x_2 + 3x_1^2 - 8x_1 x_2^4 - 24x_1 x_2^3$$

$$+68x_1 x_2 + 36x_1 + 16x_2^4 + 64x_2^3 + 36x_2^2 - 184x_2 - 239.$$

We first shift Q by $\boldsymbol{y_0} = \langle 2, 2 \rangle$, which is the vector of exponents for $\mathrm{lm}(P)$.

$$Q \gg \boldsymbol{y_0} = (x_1^3 x_2^3 - 2x_1^3 + x_2^2 x_2^2 + 3) \gg \langle 2, 2 \rangle = (x_1 x_2 + 1)$$

Then, we compute $K(x_1 x_2 + 1) = x_1^5 x_2^5 - 2x_1^4 x_2^5 - x_1^4 y^4 + \{\text{terms} \prec x_1^4 x_2^4\}$. This result shifted by $\langle L \rangle^\nu - \boldsymbol{y_0} = \langle 6, 6 \rangle - \langle 2, 2 \rangle = \langle 4, 4 \rangle$ to the right gives:

$$A = x_1^5 x_2^5 - 2x_1^4 x_2^5 - x_1^4 y^4 + \{\text{terms} \succ x_1^4 x_2^4\} \gg \langle 4, 4 \rangle = x_1 x_2 - 2x_2 - 1.$$

It is easy to verify that:

$$Q - PA =$$

$$= (x_1^3 x_2^3 - 2x_1^3 + x_1^2 x_2^2 + 3) - (x_1^2 x_2^2 + x_1^2 + 2x_1 x_2^2 + 2x_1 x_2 + x_1 + 1)(x_1 x_2 - 2x_2 - 1)$$

$$\Downarrow$$

$$Q - PA = 4x_1 x_2^3 + 6x_1 x_2^2 - x_1^3 x_2 + x_1^2 x_2 + 3x_1 x_2 + 2x_2 - 2x_1^3 + x_1^2 + x_1 + 4 \prec P.$$

Complexity: We refer the reader to Appendix A for a detailed computation of the complexity of Algorithm 2.

3.4   Dynamic Constant Scaling in $\mathbb{Q}[x]$

Lemma 3. *If* $0 \leq u \leq L$, *then* $\bar{K} = K \gg \langle u \rangle^{\nu} = \left\lfloor \frac{h(L-u)}{P} \right\rfloor$.

Proof. $K = \left\lfloor \frac{h(L)}{P} \right\rfloor \Rightarrow K = \frac{h(L) - h(L) \bmod P}{P}.$

Let $G = h(L) \bmod P \Rightarrow K = \dfrac{\displaystyle\prod_{j=1}^{\nu} x_j{}^{L} - G}{P}.$

Since

$$\langle u \rangle^{\nu} \in \mathbb{N}^{\nu} \Rightarrow K \gg \langle u \rangle^{\nu} = \deg_{\geq 0} \frac{\displaystyle\prod_{j=1}^{\nu} x_j{}^{L-u} - G_{\varphi(\langle u \rangle^{\nu})}}{P}$$

$$\Downarrow$$

$$K \gg \langle u \rangle^{\nu} = \deg_{\geq 0} \frac{\displaystyle\prod_{j=1}^{\nu} x_j{}^{L-u}}{P} - \deg_{\geq 0} \frac{G_{\varphi(\langle u \rangle^{\nu})}}{P}.$$

We know that $P \rhd G$, thus $P \rhd G_{\varphi(\langle u \rangle^{\nu})}$, thus $\deg_{\geq 0} \dfrac{G_{\varphi(\langle u \rangle^{\nu})}}{P} = 0.$
Finally,

$$K \gg \langle u \rangle^{\nu} = \left\lfloor \frac{\prod_{j=1}^{\nu} x_j{}^{L-u}}{P} \right\rfloor = \left\lfloor \frac{h(L-u)}{P} \right\rfloor.$$

$\square$

Example 9. Let

$\rhd \ = \ \succ$

$P = x_1^2 x_2^2 + x_1^2 + 2x_1 x_2^2 + 2x_1 x_2 + x_1 + 1$

$Q = x_1^3 x_2^3 - 2x_1^3 + x_2^2 x_2^2 + 3.$

We let $u = 4$ and we observe that $\nu = 2$. We pre-compute $\bar{K}$:

$$\bar{K} = x_1^2 x_2^2 - x_1^2 - 2x_1 x_2^2 - 2x_1 x_2 + 3x_1 + 4x_2^2 + 8x_2 - 5.$$

We first shift Q by $\boldsymbol{y_0} = \langle 2, 2 \rangle$, which is the vector of exponents for $\mathrm{lm}(P)$.

$$Q \gg \boldsymbol{y_0} = (x_1^3 x_2^3 - 2x_1^3 + x_2^2 x_2^2 + 3) \gg \langle 2, 2 \rangle = (x_1 x_2 + 1)$$

Then, we compute $\bar{K}(x_1 x_2 + 1) = x_1^3 x_2^3 - 2x_1^2 x_2^3 - x_1^2 x_2^2 + \{\text{terms} \prec x_1^2 x_2^2\}$.
This result shifted by $\langle u \rangle^\nu - \boldsymbol{y_0} = \langle 4, 4 \rangle - \langle 2, 2 \rangle = \langle 2, 2 \rangle$ to the right gives:

$$A = x_1^3 x_2^3 - 2x_1^2 x_2^3 - x_1^2 x_2^2 + \{\text{terms} \succ x_1^2 x_2^2\} \gg \langle 2, 2 \rangle = x_1 x_2 - 2x_2 - 1.$$

It is easy to verify that:

$$Q - PA =$$
$$= (x_1^3 x_2^3 - 2x_1^3 + x_1^2 x_2^2 + 3) - (x_1^2 x_2^2 + x_1^2 + 2x_1 x_2^2 + 2x_1 x_2 + x_1 + 1)(x_1 x_2 - 2x_2 - 1)$$

$$\Downarrow$$

$$Q - PA = 4x_1 x_2^3 + 6x_1 x_2^2 - x_1^3 x_2 + x_1^2 x_2 + 3x_1 x_2 + 2x_2 - 2x_1^3 + x_1^2 + x_1 + 4 \prec P.$$

4   Application to BCH Codes

4.1   General Remarks

BCH codes are cyclic codes that form a large class of multiple random error-correcting codes. Originally discovered as binary codes of length $2^m - 1$, BCH codes were subsequently extended to non-binary settings. Binary BCH codes are a generalization of Hamming codes, discovered by Hocquenghem, Bose and Chaudhuri [2,4] featuring a better error correction capability. Gorestein and Ziersler [6] generalised BCH codes to p^m symbols, for p prime. Two important BCH code sub-classes exist. Typical representatives of these sub-classes are Hamming codes (binary BCH) and Reed Solomon codes (non-binary BCH).

Terminology: We further refer to the vectors of an error correction code as *codewords*. The codewords' size is called the *length* of the code. The *distance* between two codewords is the number of coordinates at which they differ. The *minimum distance* of a code is the minimum distance between two codewords.

Recall that a *primitive element* of a finite field is a generator of the multiplicative group of the field.

4.1.1   BCH Preliminaries

Definition 4. *Let $m \geq 3$. For a length $n = 2^m - 1$, a distance d and a primitive element $\alpha \in \mathbb{F}_{2^m}^*$, we define the binary BCH code:*

$$\mathrm{BCH}(n,d) = \{(c_0, c_1, ..., c_{n-1}) \in \mathbb{F}_2^n \mid c(x) = \sum_{i=0}^{n-1} c_i x^i \text{ satisfies}$$

$$c(\alpha) = c(\alpha^2) = ... = c(\alpha^{d-1})\}$$

Let $m \geq 3$ and $0 < t < 2^{m-1}$ be two integers. There exists a binary BCH code (called a t−error correcting BCH code) with parameters $n = 2^m - 1$ (the block length), $n - k \leq mt$ (the number of parity-check digits) and $d \geq 2t + 1$ (the minimum distance).

Definition 5. *Let α be a primitive element in $\mathbb{F}_{2^m}$. The generator polynomial $g(x) \in \mathbb{F}_2[x]$ of the t−error-correcting BCH code of length 2^{m-1} is the lowest-degree polynomial in $\mathbb{F}_2[x]$ having roots $\alpha, \alpha^2, ..., \alpha^{2t}$.*

Definition 6. *Let $\phi_i(x)$ be the minimal polynomial of α^i. Then,*

$$g(x) = \mathrm{lcm}\{\phi_1(x), \phi_2(x), ..., \phi_{2t}(x)\}.$$

The degree of $g(x)$, which is the number of parity-check digits $n - k$, is at most mt.

Let $i \in \mathbb{N}$ and denote $i = 2^r j$ for odd j and $r \geq 1$. Then $\alpha^i = (\alpha^j)^{2^r}$ is a conjugate of α^j which implies that α^i and α^j have the same minimal polynomial, and therefore $\phi_i(x) = \phi_j(x)$. Consequently, the generator polynomial $g(x)$ of the t-error correcting BCH code can be written as follow:

$$g(x) = \mathrm{lcm}\{\phi_1(x), \phi_3(x), \phi_3(x), ..., \phi_{2t-1}(x)\}.$$

Definition 7 (Codeword). *An n−tuple $c = (c_0, c_1, ..., c_{n-1}) \in \mathbb{F}_{2^n}$ is a codeword if the polynomial $c(x) = \sum c_i x^i$ has $\alpha, \alpha^2, ..., \alpha^{2t}$ as its roots.*

Definition 8 (Dual Code). *Given a linear code $C \subset \mathbb{F}_q^n$ of length n, the dual code of C (denoted by $C^{\perp}$) is defined to be the set of those vectors in $\mathbb{F}_q^n$ which are orthogonal[1] to every codeword of C, i.e.:*

$$C^{\perp} = \{v \in \mathbb{F}_q^n | v \cdot c = 0, \forall c \in C\}.$$

As α^i is a root of $c(x)$ for $1 \leq i \leq 2t$, then $c(\alpha^i) = \sum c_i \alpha^{ij}$. This equality can be written as a matrix product and results in the next property:

---

[1] The scalar product of the two vectors is equal to 0.

Property 1. If $c = (c_0, c_1, ..., c_{n-1})$ is a codeword, then the parity-check matrix H of this code satisfies $c \cdot H^T = 0$, where:

$$H = \begin{pmatrix} 1 & \alpha & \alpha^2 & \cdots & \alpha^{n-1} \\ 1 & \alpha^2 & (\alpha^2)^2 & \cdots & (\alpha^2)^{n-1} \\ 1 & \alpha^3 & (\alpha^3)^2 & \cdots & (\alpha^3)^{n-1} \\ \vdots & \vdots & \vdots & & \vdots \\ 1 & \alpha^{2t} & (\alpha^{2t})^2 & \cdots & (\alpha^{2t})^{n-1} \end{pmatrix}.$$

If $c \cdot H^T = 0$, then $c(\alpha^i) = 0$.

Remark 1. A parity check matrix of a linear block code is a generator matrix of the dual code. Therefore, c must be a codeword of the $t-$error correcting BCH code. If each entry of H is replaced by its corresponding $m-$tuple over $\mathbb{F}_2$ arranged in column form, we obtain a binary *parity-check matrix* for the code.

Definition 9 (Systematic Encoding). *In systematic encoding, information and check bits are concatenated to form the message transmitted over the noisy channel.*

The speed-up described in this paper applies to systematic BCH coding only.

Consider an (n, k) BCH code. Let $m(x)$ be the information polynomial to be coded and $m' x^{n-k} = m(x)$.

We can write $m'(x)$ as $m(x)g(x) + b(x)$.

The message $m(x)$ is coded as $c(x) = m'(x) - b(x)^2$.

BCH Decoding. *Syndrome decoding* is a decoding process for linear codes using the parity-check matrix.

Definition 10 (Syndrome). *Let c be the emitted word and r the received one. We call the quantity $S(r) = r \cdot H^T$ the syndrome of r .*

If $r \cdot H^T = 0$ then no errors occurred, with overwhelming probability. If $r \cdot H^T \neq 0$, at least one error occurred and $r = c + e$, where e is an error vector. Note that $S(r) = S(e)$. The syndrome circuit consists of $2t$ components in $\mathbb{F}_{2^m}$. To correct t errors, the syndrome has to be a $2t$-tuple of the form $S = (S_1, S_2, \cdots, S_{2t})$.

Syndrome. In the polynomial setting, S_i is obtained by evaluating r at the roots of $g(x)$.

Indeed, letting $r(x) = c(x) + e(x)$, we have

$$S_i = r(\alpha^j) = c(\alpha^j) + e(\alpha^j) = e(\alpha^j) = \sum_{k=0}^{\nu-1} e_k \alpha^{ik}, \text{ for } i \leq 1 \leq 2t.$$

Suppose that r has ν errors denoted e_{j_i}. Then

$$S_i = \sum_{j=1}^{\nu} e_{j_i} (\alpha^i)^{j_\ell} = \sum_{j=1}^{\nu} e_{j_i} (\alpha^{j_\ell})^i.$$

---

[2] where $b(x)$ is the remainder of the division of $c(x)$ by $g(x)$.

Algorithm 3. Peterson's Algorithm

---

1 Initialization $\nu \leftarrow t$

2 Compute the determinant of S

$$\det(S) \leftarrow \det \begin{pmatrix} S_1 & S_2 & \cdots & S_t \\ S_2 & S_3 & \cdots & S_{t+1} \\ \vdots & \vdots & \ddots & \vdots \\ S_t & S_{t+1} & \cdots & S_{2t-1} \end{pmatrix}$$

3 Find the correct value of ν

$$\begin{cases} \det(S) \neq 0 & \longrightarrow & \text{go to step 4} \\ \\ \det(S) = 0 & \longrightarrow & \begin{cases} \textbf{if } \nu = 0 \textbf{ then} \\ \quad \text{The error locator polynomial is empty} \\ \quad \text{stop} \\ \textbf{else} \\ \quad \nu \longleftarrow \nu - 1, \text{ and then repeat step 2} \\ \textbf{end if} \end{cases} \end{cases}$$

4 Invert S and compute $\Lambda(x)$

$$\begin{bmatrix} \sigma_\nu \\ \sigma_{\nu-1} \\ \vdots \\ \sigma_1 \end{bmatrix} = S^{-1} \times \begin{bmatrix} -S_{\nu+1} \\ -S_{\nu+2} \\ \vdots \\ -S_{2\nu} \end{bmatrix}$$

Error Location. Let $X_\ell = \alpha^{j_\ell}$. Then, for binary BCH codes, we have $S_i = \sum_{j=1}^{\nu} X_\ell^i$. The X_ℓs are called *error locators* and the *error locator polynomial* is defined as:

$$\Lambda(x) = \prod_{\ell=1}^{\nu} (1 - X_\ell) = 1 + \Lambda_1 x + \ldots + \Lambda_\nu x^\nu.$$

Note that the roots of $\Lambda(x)$ point out errors' places and the number of errors ν is unknown.

There are several ways to compute $\Lambda(x)$, *e.g.* Peterson's algorithm [7] or Berlekamp-Massey algorithm [8]. Chien's search method [9] is applied to determine the roots of $\Lambda(x)$.

Peterson's Algorithm. Peterson's Algorithm 3 solves a set of linear equations to find the value of the coefficients $\sigma_1, \sigma_2, \ldots \sigma_t$.

$$\Lambda(x) = \prod_{\ell=1}^{\nu} (1 + \alpha^{j_l}) = 1 + \sigma_1 x + \sigma_2 x^2 + \cdots + \sigma_t x^t$$

At the beginning of Algorithm 3, the number of errors is undefined. Hence the maximum number of errors to resolve the linear equations generated by the matrix S is assumed. Let this number be $i = \nu = t$.

Chien's Error Search. Chien search finds the roots of $\Lambda(x)$ by brute force [4,9]. The algorithm evaluates $\Lambda(\alpha^i)$ for $i = 1, 2, \ldots, 2^m - 1$. Whenever the result is zero, the algorithm assumes that an error occurred, thus the position of that

162   R. Géraud et al.

error is located. A way to reduce the complexity of Chien search circuits stems from Eq. 1 for $\Lambda(\alpha^{i+1})$.

$$\Lambda(\alpha^i) = 1 + \sigma_1\,\alpha^i + \sigma_2\,(\alpha^i)^2 + \cdots + \sigma_t\,(\alpha^i)^t$$
$$= 1 + \sigma_1\,\alpha^i + \sigma_2\,\alpha^{2i} + \cdots + \sigma_t\,\alpha^{it}$$
$$\Lambda(\alpha^{i+1}) = 1 + \sigma_1\,\alpha^{i+1} + \sigma_2\,(\alpha^{i+1})^2 + \cdots + \sigma_t\,(\alpha^{i+1})^t$$
$$= 1 + \alpha\,(\sigma_1\,\alpha^i) + \alpha^2\,(\sigma_2\,\alpha^{2i}) + \cdots + \alpha^t\,(\sigma_t\,\alpha^{it}) \tag{1}$$

4.2 Implementation and Results

To evaluate the efficiency of Barrett's modular division in hardware, the BCH$(15, 7, 2)$ was chosen as a case study code. Five BCH encoder versions were designed and synthesized. Results are presented in detail in the coming sections.

4.2.1 Standard Architecture

The BCH-standard architecture consists of applying the modular division using shifts and XORs. Initially, to determine the degree of the input polynomials, each bit[3] of the dividend and of the divisor are checked until the first bit one is found. Then, the two polynomials are left-aligned (*i.e.*, the two most significant ones are aligned) and XORed. The resulting polynomial is right shifted and again left-aligned with the dividend and XORed. This process is repeated until the dividend and the resulting polynomial are right-aligned. The final resulting polynomial represents the remainder of the division. Algorithm 4 provides the pseudocode for the standard architecture.

Algorithm 4. Standard modular division (BCH-standard)

Input: P, Q
Output: remainder $= Q \mod P$

1 diff_degree $\leftarrow \deg(Q) - \deg(P)$

2 shift_counter $\leftarrow$ diff_degree $+ 1$

3 shift_divisor $\leftarrow P \ll$ diff_degree

4 remainder $\leftarrow Q$

5 while shift_counter $\neq 0$ do

6   if remainder[p_degree + shift_counter $- 1] = 1$ then

7   shift_counter $\leftarrow$ shift_counter $- 1$
      shift_divisor $\leftarrow$ shift_divisor $\gg 1$

8   end

9 end

10 return remainder

---

[3] Considered in big endian order.

4.2.2   LFSR and Improved LFSR Architectures

The BCH–LFSR design is composed of a control unit and a Linear-Feedback Shift Register (LFSR) submodule. The LFSR submodule receives the input data serially and shifts it to the internal registers, controlled by the enable signal. The LFSR's size (the number of parallel flip-flops) is defined by the BCH parameters n and k, i.e., size(LFSR) $= n - k$, and the LFSR registers are called d_i, enumerated from 0 to $n - k - 1$. The feedback value is defined by the XOR of the last LFSR register (d_{nk-1}) and the input data. The feedback connections are defined by the generator polynomial $g(x)$. In the case of BCH$(15, 7, 2)$, $g(x) = x^8 + x^7 + x^6 + x^4 + 1$, therefore the input of registers d_0, d_4, d_6 and d_7 are XORed with the feedback value. As shown in Fig. 1, the multiplexer that selects the bits to compose the final codeword is controlled by the counter. The LFSR is shifted k times with the feedback connections enabled. After that, the LFSR state contains the result of the modular division, therefore the bits can be serially shifted out from the LFSR register.

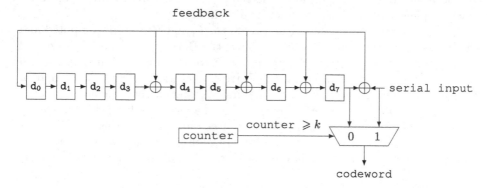

Fig. 1. Standard LFSR architecture block diagram. (Design BCH–LFSR)

To calculate the correct codeword, the LFSR must shift the input data during k clock cycles. After that, the output is serially composed by $n - k$ extra shifts. This means that the LFSR implementation's total latency is n clock cycles. Nevertheless, it is possible to save $n - k - 1$ clock cycles by outputting the LFSR in parallel from the sub-module to the control unit after k iterations, while during the k first cycles the input data is shifted to the output register, as we perform systematic BCH encoding. This decreases the total latency to $k + 1$ clock cycles. This method was applied to the BCH–LFSR-improved design depicted in Fig. 2.

4.2.3   Barrett Architecture (Regular and Pipelined)

The LFSR submodule can be replaced by the Barrett submodule to evaluate its performance. Two Barrett implementations were designed: the first computes all the Barrett steps in one clock cycle, while the second approach, a pipelined block, works with the idea that Barrett operations can be broken down into up to $k + 1$

feedback

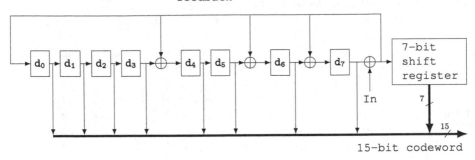

15-bit codeword

Fig. 2. Improved LFSR architecture block diagram. In denotes the module's serial input. (Design BCH-LFSR-improved)

pipeline stages, to match the LFSR's latency. The fact that Barrett operations can be easily pipelined drastically increases the final throughput, while both LFSR implementations do not allow for pipelining.

In the Barrett submodule, the constants y_0, L, and K are pre-computed and are defined as parameters of the block. Since the Barrett parameter P is defined as the generator polynomial, P does not need to be defined as an input, which saves registers. As previously stated, Barrett operations were cut down to k iterations (in our example, $k = 7$). The first register in the pipeline stores the result of $Q \gg y_0$. The multiplication by K is the most costly operation, taking 5 clock cycles to complete. Each cycle operates on 3 bits, shifting and XORing at each one bit of K, according to the rules of multiplication. The last operation simply computes the intermediate result from the multiplication left-shifted by $L - y_0$.

4.2.4 Performance

The gate equivalent (GE) metric is the ratio between the total cell area of a design and the size of the smallest NAND-2 cell of the digital library. This metric allows comparing circuit areas while abstracting away technology node sizes. *FreePDK45* (an open source 45 nm Process Design Kit [12]) was used as a digital library to map the design into logic cells. Synthesis results were generated by Cadence Encounter RTL Compiler RC13.12 (v13.10-s021_1). BCH-Barrett presented an area comparable to the smallest design (BCH-LFSR). Although BCH-Barrett does not reach the maximum clock frequency, Table 1 shows that it actually reaches the best throughput among the non-pipelined designs, around 2.08 Gbps. The BCH-Barrett-pipelined achieves the best throughput, but it reresents the biggest area and the more power consuming core. This is mainly due to the parallelizable nature of Barrett's operations, allowing the design to be easily pipelined and therefore further speed-up. The extra register barriers introduced in BCH-Barrett-pipelined forces the design to present bigger area and a higher switching activity, which increases power consumption.

Table 1. Synthesis results of the four BCH designs.

Design	Gate instances	Gate equivalent	Max frequency (MHz)	Throughput (Mbps)	Power (μW)
BCH–Standard	310	447	741	690	978
BCH–LFSR	155	223	1043	972	920
BCH–LFSR–improved	160	236	1043	2080	952
BCH–Barrett	194	260	655	9150	512
BCH–Barrett–pipelined	426	591	995	13900	2208

A   Polynomial Barrett Complexity

We decompose the algorithm's analysis into steps and determine at each step the *cost* and the *size* of the result. Size is measured in the number of terms. In all the following we assume that polynomial multiplication is performed using traditional cross product. Faster (*e.g.* ν-dimensional FFT [13]) polynomial multiplication strategies may grandly improve the following complexities for asymptotically increasing L and ν.

Given our focus on on-line operations we do not count the effort required to compute K (that we assume given). We also do not account for the partial multiplication trick for the sake of clarity and conciseness.

Let $\boldsymbol{\omega} \in \mathbb{Z}^\nu$, in this appendix we denote by $\|\boldsymbol{\omega}\|$ the quantity

$$\|\boldsymbol{\omega}\| = \prod_{j=1}^{\nu} \omega_j \in \mathbb{Z}.$$

1. $Q \gg \boldsymbol{y_0}$

  1.1. **Cost:** $\text{lm}(Q)$ is at most $\langle L, ..., L \rangle$ hence Q has at most L^ν monomials. Shifting discards all monomials having exponent vectors $\boldsymbol{\omega}$ for which $\exists j$ such that $\omega_j < y_{j,0}$. The number of such discarded monomials is $\text{O}(\|\boldsymbol{y_0}\|)$, hence the overall complexity of this step is:

$$\text{cost}_1 = \text{O}((L^\nu - \|\boldsymbol{y_0}\|)\nu) = \text{O}((L^\nu - \prod_{j=1}^{\nu} y_{j,0})\nu).$$

  1.2. **Size:** The number of monomials remaining after the shift is

$$\text{size}_1 = \text{O}(L^\nu - \|\boldsymbol{y_0}\|) = \text{O}(L^\nu - \prod_{j=1}^{\nu} y_{j,0}).$$

2. $K(Q \gg \boldsymbol{y_0})$

Because K is the result of the division of $h(L) = \prod_{j=1}^{\nu} x_j^L$ by P, the leading term of K has an exponent vector equal to $\boldsymbol{L} - \boldsymbol{y_0}$. This means that K's second biggest term can be $x_1^{L-y_{1,0}} \prod_{j=2}^{\nu} x_j^L$. Hence, the size of K is

$$\text{size}_K = \mathrm{O}((L - y_{1,0})L^{\nu-1}).$$

2.1. **Cost:** The cost of computing $K(Q \gg \boldsymbol{y_0})$ is

$$\text{cost}_2 = \mathrm{O}(\nu \times \text{size}_1 \times \text{size}_K).$$

2.2. **Size:** The size of $K(Q \gg \boldsymbol{y_0})$ is determined by $\mathrm{lm}(K(Q \gg \boldsymbol{y_0})) = \mathrm{lm}(K) \times \mathrm{lm}(Q \gg \boldsymbol{y_0})$ which has the exponent vector $\boldsymbol{u} = (\boldsymbol{L} - \boldsymbol{y_0}) + \langle L - y_{1,0}, L, ..., L \rangle$.

$$\text{size}_2 = \mathrm{O}(||\boldsymbol{u}||) = \mathrm{O}(2(L - y_{1,0}) \prod_{j=2}^{\nu} (2L - y_{j,0}))$$

$$= \mathrm{O}((L - y_{1,0}) \prod_{j=2}^{\nu} (2L - y_{j,0})).$$

3. $B = (K(Q \gg \boldsymbol{y_0})) \gg (\boldsymbol{L} - \boldsymbol{y_0})$

3.1. **Cost:** The number of discarded monomials is $\mathrm{O}(||\boldsymbol{L} - \boldsymbol{y_0}||)$, hence the cost of this step is

$$\text{cost}_3 = \mathrm{O}((2(L - y_{1,0}) \prod_{j=2}^{\nu} (2L - y_{j,0}) - \prod_{j=1}^{\nu} (L - y_{j,0}))\nu).$$

3.2. **Size:** The leading monomial of B has the exponent vector $\boldsymbol{u} - \boldsymbol{L} - \boldsymbol{y_0}$ which is equal to $\langle L - y_{1,0}, L, ..., L \rangle$. We thus have $\text{size}_B = \text{size}_K$.

4. BP

The cost of this step is

$$\text{cost}_4 = \mathrm{O}(\nu \times \text{size}_B \times \text{size}_P) = \mathrm{O}(\nu \times \text{size}_B \times ||\boldsymbol{y_0}||).$$

5. Final subtraction $Q - BP$

The cost of polynomial subtraction is negligible with respect to cost_4.

6. **Overall complexity**

The algorithm's overall complexity is hence

$$\max(\text{cost}_1, \text{cost}_2, \text{cost}_3, \text{cost}_4) = \text{cost}_2.$$

B Polynomial Barrett: Scheme Code

$p_1(x) = \sum_{i=0}^{7}(10+i)x^i$ and $p_2(x) = x^3 + x^2 + 110$

```scheme
(define p1 '((7 17) (6 16) (5 15) (4 14) (3 13) (2 12) (1 11) (0 10)))
```

```scheme
(define p2 '((3 1) (2 1) (0 110)))
```

;shifting a polynomial to the right

```scheme
(define shift (lambda (l q)
```

```scheme
if (or (null?  l) (<   (caar l) q)) '() (cons (cons (- (caar l) q)
(cdar  l))
```

```scheme
(shift (cdr l) q)))))
```

;adding polynomials

```scheme
(define add (lambda (p q)
```

```scheme
(degre (if (>= (caar p) (caar q)) (cons p (list q)) (add q p)))))
```

;multiplying a term by a polynomial, without monomials $\prec x^{\mathrm{lim}}$

```scheme
(define txp (lambda (terme p lim)
```

```scheme
(if (or (null?p) (>   lim (+ (car terme) (caar p)))) '() (cons (cons
(+ (car terme)
```

```scheme
(caar p)) (list (* (cadr terme) (cadar p)))) (txp terme (cdr p)
lim)))))
```

;multiplying a polynomial by a polynomial, without monomials $\prec x^{\mathrm{lim}}$

```scheme
(define mul (lambda (p1 p2 lim)
```

```scheme
(if p1 (cons (txp (car p1) p2 lim) (mul (cdr p1) p2 lim)) '()))))
```

;management of the exponents

```scheme
(define sort (lambda (p n)
```

```scheme
(if p (+ ((lambda(x) (if x (cadr x) 0)) (assoc n (car p))) (sort (cdr p)
n)) 0)))
```

```scheme
(define order (lambda (p n)
```

```scheme
(if(> 0 n) '() (let ((factor (sort p n))) (if (not (zero?factor))
(cons (cons n (list factor)) (order p (-n 1))) (order p (-n
1)))))))
```

```scheme
(define degre (lambda(p) (order p ((lambda(x)(if x x -1)) (caaar
p)))))
```

;Euclidean division

```scheme
(define divide (lambda (q p r)
```

```scheme
(if (and p (<= (caar p) (caar q))) (let ((tampon (cons (- (caar
q)(caar p))
```

```scheme
(list (/ (cadar q) (cadar p)))))) (divide (add (map (lambda(x)
(cons (car x)
```

```
(list (-cadr x)))))(txp tampon p -1)) q) p (cons tampon r)))
(reverse r)))

(define division (lambda (q p) (divide q p '()))))
```

;*Barrett(k, L, last_P and Y representing K, L, P and y)*

```
(define k)

(define y)

(define L 8)

(define last)

(define barrett (lambda (q p)

(if (eq ? last p) (letrec ((g (caar q)) (h (- (+ g 1) y))) (shift (degre
(mul

(shift k (-L g 1)) (shift q y) h)) h)) (begin (set! k (division (list
(cons L '(1) )) p)) (set! y (caar (set! last p))) (barrett q p)))))
```

References

1. Barrett, P.: Implementing the Rivest Shamir and Adleman public key encryption algorithm on a standard digital signal processor. In: Odlyzko, A.M. (ed.) CRYPTO 1986. LNCS, vol. 263, pp. 311–323. Springer, Heidelberg (1987)
2. Bose, R.C., Ray-Chaudhuri, D.K.: On a class of error correcting binary group codes. Inf. Control **3**(1), 68–79 (1960)
3. Bosselaers, A., Govaerts, R., Vandewalle, J.: Comparison of three modular reduction functions. In: Stinson, D.R. (ed.) CRYPTO 1993. LNCS, vol. 773, pp. 175–186. Springer, Heidelberg (1994)
4. Chien, R.: Cyclic decoding procedures for Bose-Chaudhuri-Hocquenghem codes. IEEE Trans. Inf. Theor. **10**(4), 357–363 (2006)
5. Côté, G., Erol, B., Gallant, M., Kossentini, F.: H.263+. IEEE Trans. Circuits Syst. Video Technol. **8**, 849–866 (1998)
6. Gorenstein, D., Zierler, N.: A class of cyclic linear error-correcting codes in p^m symbols. J. Soc. Ind. Appl. Math. **9**, 207–214 (1961)
7. Greuel, G.-M., Pfister, G.: A Singular Introduction to Commutative Algebra, 2nd edn. Springer, Heidelberg (2007)
8. Hocquenghem, A.: Codes correcteurs d'erreurs. Chiffres **2**, 147–158 (1959)
9. MacWilliams, F.J., Sloane, N.J.A.: The Theory of Error-Correcting Codes, 2nd edn. North-holland Publishing Company, Amsterdam (1978)
10. Naccache, D., Msilti, H.: A new modulo computation algorithm. Recherche Operationnelle - Operations Research (RAIRO-OR) **24**(3), 307–313 (1990)
11. Steele, R.: Mobile Radio Communications. IEEE Press, Piscataway (1994)
12. Stine, J.E., Castellanos, I.D., Wood, M., Henson, J., Love, F., Davis, W.R., Franzon, P. D., Bucher, M., Basavarajaiah, S., Oh, J., Jenkal, R.: FreePDK: an open-source variation-aware design kit. In: IEEE International Conference on Microelectronic Systems Education, MSE 2007, pp. 173–174 (2007)
13. Tolimieri, R., An, M., Lu, C.: Mathematics of Multidimensional Fourier Transform Algorithms. Springer, New York (1993)

Security Technologies for ITC

A Cooperative Black Hole Node Detection and Mitigation Approach for MANETs

Vimal Kumar$^{(\boxtimes)}$ and Rakesh Kumar

Department of Computer Science and Engineering, Madan Mohan Malaviya
University of Technology, Gorakhpur 273010, UP, India
{vimaliitr10,rkiitr}@gmail.com

Abstract. Mobile ad hoc networks (MANETs) do not depend on any
fixed infrastructure, but communicate in a self-unified way. In order to
provide secure communication, researchers are working specifically on the
security issues in MANETs, and many secure routing protocols/measures
within the networks have been proposed. Our proposed work presents a
more efficient approach for detecting the cooperative black hole attack
in a MANET, which is particularly vulnerable compared to traditional
wired networks due to its mobility and broadcast nature. An opponent
can easily deploy black hole attack in the MANETs, therefore, to detect
cooperative black hole attack, our mechanism modifies the Ad hoc On
Demand Distance Vector (AODV) routing protocol by introducing two
special packets, (i) query packet and (ii) further route request (FRREQ)
packet. Our simulation results show that attack is detected successfully
and it outperforms existing attack detection methods.

Keywords: Mobile ad hoc networks · Black hole attack · Secure AODV ·
Query packet · Malicious node

1 Introduction

Nowadays, mobile ad hoc networks are one of the fastest growing areas of
research. It is a collection of mobile nodes that is connected through a wireless network interfaces, forming dynamic topology. In a MANET, each node
acts either as a source, destination or as a router. The main characteristics of
MANET are lack of any type of infrastructure or central authority. They can be
easily deployed in places where it is difficult to set up any wired infrastructure. It
also avoids single point of failure due to its nature of decentralized architecture.
Routing protocols in MANETs can be divided into three main categories, namely,
table driven, which is proactive, on-demand, which is reactive, and hybrid one,
depending on how the source finds a route to the destination node for transmitting a message [1–5]. Designing a security protocol for ad hoc network is a very
difficult task due to certain unique characteristics of ad hoc wireless network,
namely, shared broadcast medium, insecure operational environment, lack of
central control, lack of association among nodes, limited availability of resource
and physical vulnerability [6, 7].

© Springer International Publishing Switzerland 2015
I. Bica et al. (Eds.): SECITC 2015, LNCS 9522, pp. 171–183, 2015.
DOI: 10.1007/978-3-319-27179-8_12

1.1 Taxonomy of Security Attacks

A taxonomy of security attacks over a mobile ad hoc network is given in Fig. 1. It can be divided into two main categories, namely active and passive attacks. A passive attacker does not modify the transmitted message while an active attacker attempts to modify or destroy the message being exchanged between two nodes [8,9]. Active attackers can also insert false information and send to another node. Active attacks are more harmful than passive attacks [10–13].

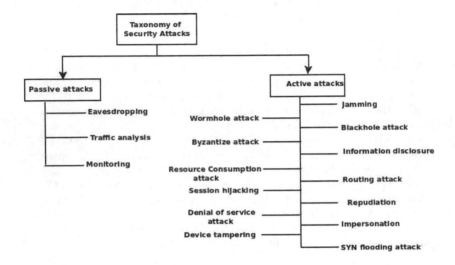

Fig. 1. Taxonomy of Security Attacks

Ad hoc On-Demand Distance Vector (AODV) is a well-known reactive routing protocol for mobile ad hoc network that maintains routes only when it is required by the source node for communication. When a node wants to send a data packet to the other nodes, it initiates a route discovery process by sending a route request (RREQ) packet. Neighbouring nodes after receiving a RREQ packet check routes for the destination node. In case a route to the destination node is not available, they further forward RREQ packet to its neighbor node. In case a fresh route to the destination node is available on an intermediate node, then intermediate node sends route reply (RREP) packet to source node. If a route request packet reaches to the destination node, then destination node sends a RREP packet to source node with the help of intermediate nodes [12,13]. AODV routing protocol is vulnerable to several security attacks such as black hole (malicious node) [14]. A black hole node could advertise that it has fresh and shortest path to a destination node, thereby discarding all packets without forwarding to a destination node. Cooperative black hole attack means black hole nodes act in a group. A black hole node does not compare destination sequence number in RREQ packet to its destination sequence number entry currently in its routing table for a path.

The rest of the paper is organized as follows: Sect. 2 presents related work. Proposed scheme/algorithm for detection of cooperative black hole attack is presented in Sect. 3 while its performance evaluation & result analysis has been presented in Sect. 4. Finally, conclusion and future work are given in Sect. 5.

2   Related Work

Sen et al. [15] gave a novel mechanism to detect coordinated black hole attack in a MANET. This mechanism modifies the standard AODV routing protocol by introducing two special parameters, (i) data routing information (DRI) and (ii) Cross checking. Tamilselvan et al. [16] proposed a technique to combat a black hole attack by fidelity table where all participating nodes will be assigned a new parameter fidelity level that is used to measure reliability of the participating node. In case the fidelity level of any node drops to 0, it is considered to be a black hole node.

Banerjee et al. [17] proposed a technique for protecting the mobile ad-hoc network from gray/black hole attack. It also provides a technique to discover cooperating black hole nodes. Sharma et al. [18] tried to investigate the effects of a black hole attack over the performance of a mobile ad hoc network. Experimental results show that network performance, reduced up to 26 % in the presence of black hole attack. Konate et al. [19] gave an analytical model to model some of these attacks like cooperative black hole, blackmail, overflow, selfish and a simulation study of these attacks by using a network simulator tool.

Munjal et al. [20] proposed a scheme to detect cooperative black hole attack and examination has been done by considering three different cases. In the first case there is no malicious node in the network, there are cooperative black hole nodes and node is reliable. Bindra et al. [21] proposed a technique to detect and remove the gray/black hole attacks. Extended data routing information (EDRI) table is used for detection/removal of cooperative black hole/gray hole attacks. It also maintains all malicious activities of a particular node. Gupta et al. [22] tried to avoid black hole attack without use of special hardware and dependency on any physical medium of wireless network.

3   Proposed Detection Scheme

In this section, we present a technique to identify cooperative black hole attack and a safe route in a mobile ad hoc network. In Fig. 2, source node S initiates route discovery process by flooding a RREQ packet in the entire network. When nodes 1, 2 and 3 receive RREQ packet, they check availability of routes to the destination node. If it is not available then simply they forward a RREQ packet to neighbor node. In case route is available to the destination then an intermediate node (having fresh information for the route to a destination) simply sends a RREP packet to source node. When black hole node B enters into MANET then it exploits the inherent routing behaviour of MANET and pretends to have an optimal path to a destination node. Figure 2 shows a black hole node B, which

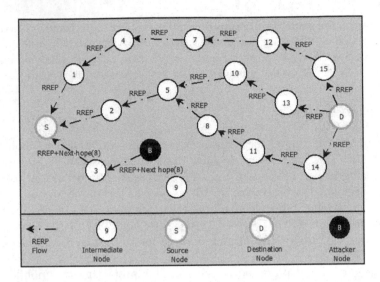

Fig. 2. Sending false route by attacker

receives a RREQ packet then it simply generates a route reply to a source node S, which carry a large value of destination sequence number in order to pretend freshest routing information of a destination. Once the source node broadcasts a RREQ packet, either intermediate nodes or destination node itself generates one or more RREP packet (containing the information of next hop node). Unlike AODV protocol, we store all these replies into the coming route reply table (CRRT) at source node, it stores all route replies coming from the destination or an intermediate node. As soon as a source node receives the very first RREP packet, it assumes that RREP comes from a black hole node and make a confirmation about node behaviour. Collection of route reply performs until the time to live (TTL) expires. In our proposed work, an extra field get included in RREP packet, which is used to store an additional information of next hop of originator of RREP. We use this information in the future for detecting black hole behaviour of a node. We introduced two new special packets, viz. Query Packet (QP) and Further Route Request Packet (FRREQ), which is used for detection of cooperative black hole attack.

3.1 Query Packet

A query packet contains two basic queries:

- Query 1: Is node (next hop of the originator of RREP) has a route to the destination?
- Query 2: Is node lies in the neighborhood proximity of the originator of RREP?

Structure of query packet (QP) is shown in Fig. 3. This query packet contains a field dubbed check results which might be filled by next hop of the originator of RREP.

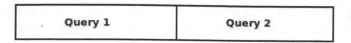

Query 1	Query 2

Fig. 3. Query Packet

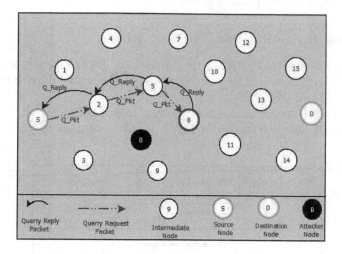

Fig. 4. Request/Reply Process for Query Packet

We discovered a route to next hop of the originator of RREP node for sending a query packet via another path. When the node receives query packet, it sets a flag for query packet. Four possible conditions arise which are (0, 0) (0, 1) (1, 0) (1, 1). Here, 1 stands for 'YES' and 0 for 'NO'. In Fig. 4, source node S unicast a query packet (QP) to node 8 (next hop of originator of RREP) via another path. Upon receiving QP, node 8 sends answer of query to the source node S. When source node S receives outcome of query by node 8. If outcome of any query is 'NO', then it is sure that originator of RREP node B is a black hole node but if both outcome is 'YES' then there might be a possibility of cooperative black

Table 1. Decision table for query packet

S.N.	Case	Query 1 outcomes	Query 2 outcomes	Conclusion
1.	I	YES	YES	Legitimate node/Cooperative black hole attack
2.	II	NO	NO	Only originator of RREP node is black hole attack
3.	III	YES	NO	Only originator of RREP node is black hole attack
4.	IV	NO	YES	Only originator of RREP node is black hole attack

hole attack (black hole attack performed by originator of RREP and its next hop). These answers are given in the decision Table 1. To detect a cooperative black hole attack, we use another control packet i.e. further route request packet (FRREQ). Based on query outcomes, we reach on a conclusion that whether we use further route request packets or not.

3.2 Further Route Request (FRREQ) Packet

Source node S unicasts a FRREQ (packet having similar packet format as in basic AODV, but the source node placed a fake destination address) to the next hop of originator of RREP.

Further route request is slightly different from RREQ packet of standard AODV protocol, which is shown in Fig. 5. In place of destination address, we

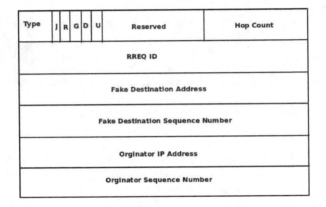

Fig. 5. FRREQ Packet Format

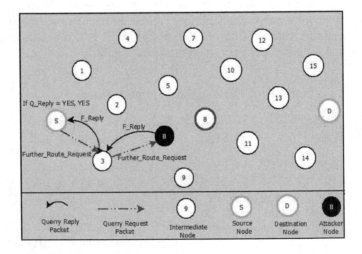

Fig. 6. Request/Reply Process for FRREQ Packet

Table 2. Decision table for FRREQ Packet

S.N.	Case	Query 1 outcomes	Query 2 outcomes	FRREQ reply arrived	Conclusion
1.	I	YES	YES	NO	Legitimate node
2.	II	YES	YES	YES	Cooperative black hole attack

place an address of a hypothetical node, which does not exist in the network. FRREQ packet also contains a random number instead of destination sequence number field during the route discovery phase. Upon receiving a FRREQ packet, a suspect node sends a route reply or simply forward the packet to its next hop as per basic AODV mechanism. If a RREP is generated and arrived at the source S, then originator of RREP node is surely a black hole node just because it reply to claim that it has a short and fresh enough route for a destination D, which is not exist in the network, otherwise originator of RREP node is a legitimate.

When the node receives a FRREQ Packet, it sets a flag for FRREQ Packet. Two possible conditions arise which are (1, 1, 0) (1, 1, 1). Here, 1 stands for 'YES' and 0 for 'NO'. If both answer is YES then source node S broadcasts FRREQ packet to the black hole node B, which is shown in Fig. 6. Upon receiving FRREQ packet, if a RREP packet generation by black node B then source node S simply detects cooperative black hole attack, otherwise node is legitimate. These outcomes are better explained in the decision Table 2.

3.3 Detection Algorithm

The various notations used in the proposed algorithm are given in Table 3 while Algorithm 1 presents detection of cooperative black hole attack.

Table 3. Notations

I	Intermediate node
DSRREQ	Destination Sequence Number of Route Request
DSRREP	Destination Sequence Number of Route Reply
t	Time of Arrival

4   Performance Evaluation

In this section, we apply proposed algorithm for detection of cooperative black hole attack, which is implemented using network simulator (ns-2.34) and it is compared with standard AODV protocol under black hole node.

Algorithm 1. Detection of Cooperative Black hole attack

$D/I \xrightarrow{RREP} S$

for each route reply[i] **do**

  if DSRREP[i] >DSRREQ[i] **then**

    Insert.RREP[i] into CRRT

    t_i= t.RREP[i]

    $S \xrightarrow{QP}$ next_hop of the originator of RREP

    Next_hop of the originator of RREP $\xrightarrow{outcomes} S$

    if First_query_outcome==1 **then**

      if Second_query_outcome==1 **then**

        $S \xrightarrow{unicasts\,FRREQ}$ Next_hop of the originator of RREP

        if FRREP is arrived from Next_hop of the originator of RREP **then**

          Cooperative black hole node

        else

          It is legitimate node

        end if

      else

        Only originator of RREP is black hole node

      end if

      if *second_query_outcome* == 1 **then**

        Only originator of RREP is black hole node

      else

        Only originator of RREP is black hole node

      end if

    end if

  end if

end for

4.1 Simulation Environment and Scenarios

The network topology is a rectangular area with 800 m height and 501 m width. All the fix links have chosen speed from 10 m/s to 90 m/s. We use the IEEE 802.11 algorithms at physical and data link layer. We use AODV as the routing algorithm at network layer. Finally, user datagram protocol (UDP) is used in transport layer. The simulation parameters are given in Table 4.

4.2 Movement Model

The propagation model uses two ray ground in simulation. The Random Waypoint Model is used for mobility in mobile ad hoc network. Mobility model is generated using setdest utility.

4.3 Communication Model

CBR (continuous bit rate) and size of each packet is 512 bytes. A Packet transmission rate in scenario considered is 0.20 Mbps. The connection pattern is generated using cbrgen.

Table 4. Simulation parameters

Parameter	Value
Simulator	ns-2.34
Simulation time	21 s
Number of nodes	10 to 90
Routing protocol	AODV
Traffic agent	TCP
Pause time	2 s
Node speed	10–90 m/s
Terrain area	850 m × 501 m
Transmission range	250 m
Number of malicious node	2

4.4 Performance Metrics

The metrics used to evaluate the performance of these contexts are given below:

- Packet Delivery Ratio (PDR): It is the ratio between total number of packets transmitted by a traffic source and total number of packets received by a traffic sinks.
- Throughput: Throughput is the ratio of total number of packets (data bits) successfully delivered to a destination node in given simulation time.

4.5 Results and Analysis

We examine the performance of AODV routing protocol in terms of two metrics: packet delivery ratio and throughput. Simulation is done with source node transmitting maximum 410 packets to a destination node. To analyze performance with our solution, various contexts are created by varying mobility and number of nodes. We used these performance metrics to validate proposed approach against cooperative black hole attack and result obtained is shown in Figs. 7, 8, 9 and 10.

Figure 7 shows a comparison graph of % PDR v/s node speed. Here, we compare our proposed algorithm % PDR outcomes with two others (AODV without black hole node and AODV with black hole node). AODV is a basic algorithm, which is supposed to free from black hole attack. Another one is simulated under presence of one black hole node nearer to a source node S. Here, proposed approach gets an unprecedented rise in the % PDR as compared to AODV with the black hole node.

It can be seen that % PDR of AODV dropped by 96 % in presence of cooperative black hole node with varying node mobility. The same increased by 98 % when our proposed approach is used under cooperative black hole attack. Figure 8 represents the comparison graph of throughput v/s node speed. Hence,

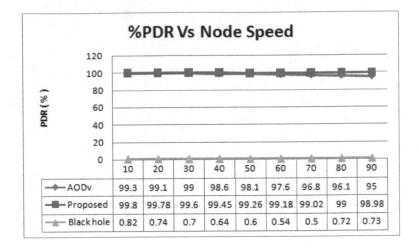

Fig. 7. PDR vs Node Speed

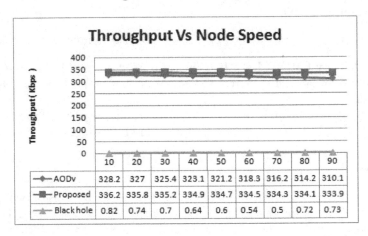

Fig. 8. Throughput vs Node Speed

proposed approach gives better performance with respect to throughput outcomes to two others.

In Fig. 9, we find that when the number of nodes is minimum, standard AODV achieved good % PDR. Now as the number of nodes is increased then the % PDR decrease. Hence, our proposed algorithm shows better performance with respect to % PDR when increasing the number of nodes.

In Fig. 10, it is observed that standard AODV gives better throughput. When number of nodes are minimum. As the number of node increases, throughput of standard AODV decreases while throughput of our propose approach is higher than two others. Hence, our proposed algorithm showing better performance with respect to throughput.

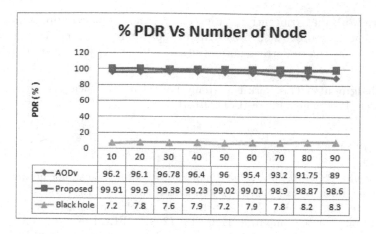

Fig. 9. PDR vs No. of nodes

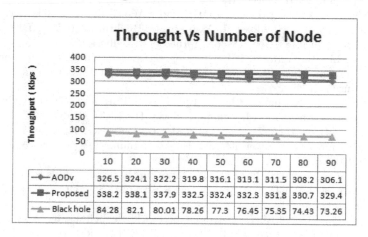

Fig. 10. Throughput vs No. of nodes

5 Conclusion and Future Work

Standard AODV routing protocol is vulnerable to black hole attack. Due to this attack, packet delivery ratio (PDR) and throughput of AODV routing protocol decreases drastically. Existing solutions have been evaluated. Having justified a need for further improvements, we proposed a Query Packet with FRREQ approach to counter the cooperative black hole attack in AODV routing protocol in MANETs. From the experimental results, we conclude that proposed solution achieves a very good rise in PDR and throughput as node mobility in the network increases. Moreover, the proposed approach does not involve much hidden overhead on their intermediate/destination node.

Future work may concentrate on extending the proposed approach to other reactive routing protocols such as dynamic source routing (DSR). An another future work may be to detract false positive (FP) in the proposed approach.

Acknowledgments. This work is partially funded by Technical Education Quality Improvement Programme Phase-II (TEQIP-II)

References

1. Argyroudis, P.G., Mahony, D.O.: Secure routing for mobile ad hoc networks. IEEE Commun. Surv. Tutor. **7**, 2–21 (2005). Third Quarter, IEEE Press
2. Burmeste, M., Medeiros, B.D.: On the security of route discovery in MANETs. IEEE Trans. Mob. Comput. **8**, 1180–1187 (2009). IEEE Press
3. Hu, Y.-C., Perrig, A.: A survey of secure wireless ad hoc routing. IEEE Secur. Priv. **2**, 28–39 (2004). IEEE Press
4. Abdelshafy, M.A., King, P.J.B.: AODV and SAODV under attack: performance comparison. In: Guo, S., Lloret, J., Manzoni, P., Ruehrup, S. (eds.) ADHOC-NOW 2014. LNCS, vol. 8487, pp. 318–331. Springer, Heidelberg (2014)
5. Deng, H., Li, W., Agrawal, D.P.: Routing security in wireless ad hoc networks. IEEE Commun. Mag. **40**, 70–75 (2002). Proceedings of Telecommunications Network Security. IEEE Press
6. Marimuthu, M., Krishnamurthi, I.: Enhanced OLSR for defence against DOS attack in ad hoc networks. J. Commun. Netw. **15**, 31–37 (2013). IEEE Press
7. Nadeem, A., Howarth, M.P.: A survey of MANET intrusion detection & prevention approaches for network layer attacks. IEEE Commun. Surv. Tutor. **15**, 2027–2045 (2013). IEEE Press
8. Tripathi, M., Gaur, M.S., Laxmi, V.: Comparing the impact of black hole and gray hole attack on LEACH in WSN. Procedia Comput. Sci. **19**, 1101–1107 (2013). Elsevier
9. Nabarun, C., Mandal, J.K.: Detection of blackhole behaviour using triangular encryption. Procedia Technol. **10**, 524–529 (2013). Elsevier
10. Bar, R.K., Mandal, J.K., Singh, M.M.: QoS of MANET through trust based AODV routing protocol by exclusion of blak hole attack. Procedia Technol. **10**, 530–537 (2013). Elsevier
11. Manoranjini, J., Chandrasekar, A., Rajinigirinath, D.: Hybrid detector for detection of black holes in MANETs. IERI Procedia **4**, 376–382 (2013). Elsevier
12. Sharma, S., Pandey, R.P., Shukla, V.: Bluff-Probe based black hole node detection and prevention. In: Proceedings of IEEE International Advance Computing Conference (IACC), pp. 458–461. IEEE Press (2009)
13. Djahel, S., Nait-Abdesselam, F., Khokhar, A.: An acknowledgment-based scheme to defend against cooperative black hole attacks in optimized link state routing protocol. In: Proceedings of IEEE Communications Society Subject Matter Experts for Publication in the ICC Proceedings, pp. 2780–2785. IEEE Press (2008)
14. Jhaveri, R.H., Patel, S.J., Jinwala, D.C.: A novel approach for grayhole and black hole attacks in mobile ad-hoc networks. In: Proceedings of International Conference on Advanced Computing and Communication Technologies, pp. 556–570. IEEE Press (2012)

15. Sen, J., Koilakonda, S., Ukil, A.: A mechanism for detection of cooperative black hole attack in mobile ad hoc networks. In: Proceedings of IEEE International Conference on Intelligent Systems, Modeling and Simulation, pp. 338–343. IEEE Press (2011)
16. Tamilselvan, L., Sankaranarayanan, V.: Prevention of co-operative black hole attack in MANET. J. Netw. **3**, 13–20 (2008). Academy Publisher
17. Banerjee, S.: Detection/removal of cooperative black and gray hole attack in mobile ad-hoc networks. In: Proceedings of the World Congress on Engineering and Computer Science, San Francisco (2008)
18. Sharma, S., Gupta, R.: Simulation study of blackhole attack in the mobile ad hoc networks. J. Eng. Sci. Technol. JEST **4**, 243–250 (2009)
19. Konate, K., Abdourahime, G.: Attacks analysis in mobile ad hoc networks: modeling and simulation. In: Proceedings of IEEE International Conference on Intelligent Systems, Modeling and Simulation, pp. 367–372. IEEE Press (2011)
20. Munjal, K., Verma, S., Bakshi, A.: Cooperative black hole node detection by modifying AODV. Int. J. Manag. IT Eng. (IJMIE) **2**, 484–501 (2012). IJMRA
21. Bindra, G.S., Kapoor, A., Narang, A., Agrawal, A.: Detection and removal of cooperative blackhole and grayhole attacks in MANETs. In: Proceedings of IEEE International Conference on System Engineering and Technology, pp. 1–5, IEEE Press, Bandung (2012)
22. Gupta, S., Kar, S., Dharmaraja, S.: BAAP: blackhole attack avoidance protocol for ad hoc network. In: Proceedings of IEEE International Conference on Computer and Communication Technology (ICCCT 2011), pp. 468–473. IEEE Press (2011)

Up-High to Down-Low: Applying Machine Learning to an Exploit Database

Yisroel Mirsky$^{(\boxtimes)}$, Noam Cohen, and Asaf Shabtai

Department of Information Systems Engineering,
Ben-Gurion University, Beersheba, Israel
{yisroel,grossno,shabtaia}@post.bgu.ac.il

Abstract. Today machine learning is primarily applied to low level features such as machine code and measurable behaviors. However, a great asset for exploit type classifications is public exploit databases. Unfortunately, these databases contain only meta-data (high level or abstract data) of these exploits. Considering that classification depends on the raw measurements found in the field, these databases have been overlooked. In this study, we offer two usages for these high level datasets and evaluate their performance. The first usage is classification by using meta-data as a bridge (supervised), and the second usage is the study of exploits' relations using clustering and Self Organizing Maps (unsupervised). Both offer insights into exploit detection and can be used as a means to better define exploit classes.

Keywords: Exploit database · Machine learning · Supervised · Unsupervised · Pattern abstraction · Data mining

1 Introduction

Machine learning offers a multitude of applications from automated predictions, classification and other data mining tools. Today it is becoming more and more popular to apply machine learning to the domain of cyberspace security [3,8]. The reason for this is because machine learning is very good at dealing with abstract situations and problems [8]. However, aside from anomaly detection, these algorithms tend to be supervised machine learning problems which require a large labelled datasets. Acquiring these datasets can take many man hours or in some cases be impossible. For this reason it is desirable to use existing databases to build preliminary models for testing and evaluation before investing the man hours to build the final product. For instance, should one wish to train a model to classify exploit code, he would need a dataset or database filled with examples of exploit code. Although these databases exist, they have been largely overlooked by machine learning applications. The main reason for this is that they only contain meta-information about the threats and not the threats themselves. For example, an instance in such a database would contain information on the type of threat, platform or steps taken to perform it and not the

I. Bica et al. (Eds.): SECITC 2015, LNCS 9522, pp. 184–200, 2015.
DOI: 10.1007/978-3-319-27179-8_13

exploit code itself or its concrete behaviors. This makes it difficult to use them as a basis for training a model on existing threats. Furthermore, machine learning is commonly applied to low level features such as machine code [5,11] and measurable behaviors [1,14]. The point that is overlooked is that a lot can be learned and obtained from meta-information on exploits. When an exploit is discovered and submitted to a database its high level description, in a way, paints an image of its behavior or intents. For example, take an instance of exploit code written in C. In the code the variables have a particular significance to the author. Furthermore, the imported library names also have a correlation to the intended exploit [12]. Once all the instances have been refined, correlated and grouped, it is possible to build a model which can identify the type of exploit based on these high level indicators. Although this alone provides no benefit to detecting true malware, it is possible to build a reverse model that can connect machine code (OP Codes) to this higher level abstraction (or source-code). In other words, using the meta-data as a target, it is possible to identify the malware's intents straight from the OP codes (using a supervised machine learning algorithm). Furthermore, most malicious programs found in the wild are variants of some previous one [13]. There is another useful application of machine learning to a dataset of exploit metadata. This is when it is applied to a unsupervised machine learning algorithm. Doing so allows us to find meaningful patterns and possibly new classes/behaviors of malware. One such algorithm is the Self Organizing Map (SOM) [9]. After training a SOM on the metadata, queries can be input to find their correction among similar or close clusters [7]. For instance, if we look for where all denial of service (DoS) exploit instances are within the SOM topology and compare that to where all remote exploits are. In such a case we may find that they have an overlap "in interests" or that they are disjoint but close in proximity (similarity) or very far apart. These can be used as clues in exploit behaviors that can be used in training and labeling future classes. In this article we investigate some applications of meta-exploit databases to supervised and un-supervised machine learning algorithms. In the case of supervised learning, we evaluate the performance of a direct and indirect high level (metadata) classifier. The indirect classifier is a two stage learning model. It first predicts the metadata from N-grams of OP Codes, and then submits these results as features to a meta-classifier. The meta-classifier's job is to determine the machine code's type of exploit. The indirect classifier builds a single model that predicts the exploit type directly from the N-grams of OP Codes. In our evaluation, we contrast the performance of both methods. It is important to note that these OP codes were compiled from the meta-data supplied (which includes the source code). In the domain of unsupervised machine learning algorithms, we apply a SOM to the dataset and offer explanations of the results. The rest of the article is divided into section as follows. In Sect. 2, the database used for our models is presented. In Sect. 3, the supervised machine learning algorithm's application to a parsed version of the database is evaluated. In Sect. 4, the unsupervised machine learning algorithm's application to a different parsed version of the database is evaluated. Lastly, in Sect. 5, a conclusion with future work is proposed.

2   The Exploit Database

There are many repositories of existing exploits available to the public. However, very few actually provide the high level code used to carry them out. For instance, the National Vulnerability Database (NVD) is an extensive and current database which details known vulnerabilities and their details. What NVD does not provide are concrete examples of performing these exploits. One database that does offer the meta-information along with the exploit code is Exploit DB. Exploit DB is a community based database filled with labelled code submissions in many different coding languages (C/C++, python, JavaScript, ASM etc.)[1]. The database is constantly updated including instances submitted from 1994 until today. The downloaded database contains a compressed directories of all the exploit's source-code files and a spreadsheet labeling each exploit's meta-information. We decide to use Exploit DB for our evaluation due to its simple organization and readily available source-code. Furthermore, although the database contained thousands of exploit written in different languages, be focused only on those written in C. Due to time constraints, we could not parse (or compile) and extract features from all the available languages. However, we believe that our feature extraction process can also be applied other languages as well. Therefore, our work should serve as a sample of what is possible as well as what can be extendible to the other source-codes (written in other programming languages). In terms of final labels, we used the provide "exploit type". The offered exploit types were: local, remote, DoS and Shell-code. We needed to remove the "Web apps" exploit type instances due to heavy class skewage. As seen from the WEKA data visualizations below, afterwards, dataset did not suffer from class skewage. Figure. 1 shows the distribution of instances in the data set by submission year, and Figs. 2 and 3 shows the instances division between exploit type and target platform respectively. Although Fig. 2 shows that there were fewer Shell-code type exploits than others, they are not too small in comparison. Furthermore, on a yearly basis, the distribution between the exploit types persists. This is important when we attempt to find the correlations between the two using the SOM in Sect. 4. It is interesting to point out that number of C code submissions per year has a very obvious "prime" and then becomes less frequent. This may have a negative impact in terms of how relevant the models trained on this data will be for present day applications. However, this issue does not affect out evaluation since our goal is the effective use of applying machine learning to meta-data. Should the reader desire to apply our research, he should use a database with a stronger relevance (population) to modern exploits. Lastly, note the target-platform distribution in Fig. 3 This distribution is based on the original labels pulled from the database. In order to fix the problem of scarcity between groupings we applied a filter which grouped all similar platforms together to form a new platform label. For instance, bsd, bsd_ppc, bsd_x86, bsdi_x86, freebsd_x86 and freebsd_x86-64 were all grouped under one label "bsd". In the end there were 6 parent labels: Windows, Linux, Solaris, BSD, Unix, and Other. These

---

[1] The Exploit DataBase – http://www.exploit-db.com/.

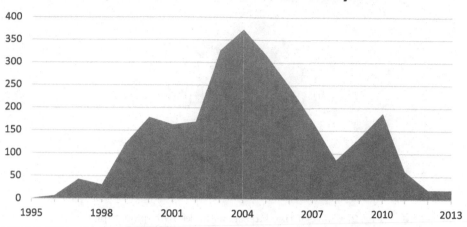

Fig. 1. Plot of the dataset instances by year of submission: 1994 to 2013

groupings were exceptionally important for the SOM. This way we were able to find more meaningful relations between the platforms. In total the database contains 2486 instances of exploits. For each case in this article, we generated a dataset using a subset of these instances. The details of these datasets are described later on.

3   Applying Supervised Learning

In this section we apply supervised machine learning algorithms to the meta-information database (exploit DB). The intent here is to determine whether this type of data can be used for classifying exploit types based on their machine code. Throughout this article, we used MATLAB as the choice machine learning environment, due to its familiarity, extensive libraries and SOM features.

3.1   Creation of the Datasets

Two datasets built around the same instances were needed to accomplish our objectives. Both datasets' features were generated from the source code (provided by the database) while their labels were taken from the meta-data that accompanied them. We considered both the source code and informational meta-data to be the "metadata" referred to in section I. The first dataset was a dataset of high level features (HLF) such as the number of libraries imported and the existence of similar variable names in the source code. The second dataset was of low level features (LLF) specifically the 2-grams document frequency (df) on the OP-codes of the compiled exploits.

Exploit DB Dataset: Instances by Exploit Type

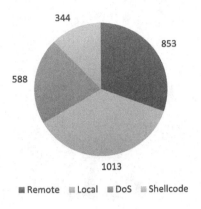

Fig. 2. Chart of the dataset instances by exploit type.

Exploit DB Dataset: Instances by Target Platform

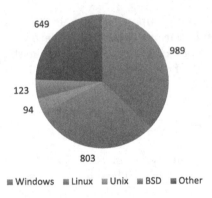

Fig. 3. Chart of the dataset instances by target platform.

The HLF Dataset. Because Exploit DB is a collection of non-standardized community submissions, extensive parsing and filtering was required in order to obtain the HLF dataset. Therefore all of the processing was done through a series of well-planned automated Python scripts. The reason we chose Python, is because of its versatility and well supported community of libraries. The first step was to decide on what features to extract. We decided that since the source code holds linguistic significance we should extract this content as a feature. Furthermore, we felt that the number of different variable and function types hold a subtle significance as well; so these too were taken into account. Unfortunately, the source code was filled with comments and debugging code (printf, cout, etc.). Therefore before any feature extraction, we used regular expressions and the CTAGS programming tool[2] to remove and collect all relevant information. Once the source code was clear of irrelevant "words", we began collecting a list of the names of all imported libraries, library functions, user functions, and variables. In addition, we also collected their frequency amongst on a per file basis as well as a global sum (for feature selection purposes). After this process we obtained 16,384 features. It was obvious that a dataset with only 2486 instances would suffer from the "curse of dimensionality" [2]. Therefore it was required that we perform feature selection to find the most useful subset. In the end we decided to create new compound features by grouping them by similarity in names. These groupings were done with respect to each category (libraries, user functions, etc.). Using a Python library, we used a similarity threshold of 0.7 to group names which yielded the results in Table 1. Afterwards, we performed feature selection by taking the top 10 most popular results from each category (across the entire dataset) seen in Table 2. It is clear that each of the groups in Table 2 represent a common theme and therefore a particular behavior of the exploit. The way each of these groupings where converted into a feature was: if the any of the names in the group were present in an instance then it would receive the value "1". If none of the names in that grouping were present then it would receive the value "0". Altogether, the 4 categories with 10 groups each created a 40 element binary feature vector. To complete the feature set, we also took the number (frequency) of imported libraries, library functions, user functions and variables as features. The final HLF dataset contained 2486 instances with 44 features, and 4 target classes (the exploit types).

Table 1. Feature selection statistics

	Before grouping	After grouping	Taken as features
# Library Names	405	190	10
# Lib. Function Names	2399	1405	10
# User Function Names	3502	1790	10
# Variable Names	7460	2947	10

The LLF Dataset. The second dataset represented the instances found in reality. This dataset contains features strictly obtained from the machine code (Opcodes) of the exploits themselves. Unfortunately, Exploit DB does not provide the assembled exploits rather only their source code. Due to the sheer amount of instances, compiling the code manually was not an option. Therefore an automated process was programmed. This was a difficult task since the source codes were full of typos, uncommon libraries and had platform dependencies which caused the compilations to fail.

---

[2] CTAGS by Darren Hiebert – http://ctags.sourceforge.net/.

Table 2. Final name groupings taken as a binary feature vector

Imported Libraries	1	lib stdio.h, stdlib.h, cstdio, 'stdio.h, stdio.h, stdint.h, stdbool.h
	2	lib, 'strings.h, string, string.h strings.h, string.h, asm/string.h
	3	lib, unistd.h, asm/unistd.h, 'unistd.h
	4	lib, netinet/if, ether.h, netinet/ip, udp.h, linux/if, ether.h, netinet/ip.h, netinet/ip, tcp.h, netinet/tcp.h, netinet/in.h, netinet/in, systm.h, netinet/ether.h, netinet/tcp, timer.h
	5	lib, sys/cdefs.h, sys/ucred.h, sys/exec, elf.h, sys/types.h, sys/times.h, sys/filedesc.h, sys/procfs.h
	6	lib, sys/resource.h, sys/queue.h, sys/socket.h
	7	lib, netwib.h, net/bpf.h, netdb.h
	8	lib, windns.h, winuser.h, wininet.h, win.h, windowsx.h, winbase.h, winsock.h windows.h
	9	lib, errno.h, err.h, error.h, sys/errno.h
	10	lib, arpa/nameser.h, arpa/inet.h
Library Functions	1	libFunc, text, addtext, exit, atexit, next
	2	libFunc, strlen, nstrlen
	3	libFunc, memset
	4	libFunc, htonl, htons
	5	libFunc, memcmp, tmemcpy, memcpy
	6	lib Func, printe, dprintf, ip, print, printk, printit, printred, swprintf, pointer, asprintf, gzprintf, wsprintf, printgreen, vfprint, vprintf, vfprintf
	7	libFunc, socketadd, procgetadd, socketpair, 3dsocket, closesocketadd, socketsend, socket, nsocket
	8	libFunc, 3datoi, atoi
	9	libFunc, strcmpi, strncpy, strncmp, strnicmp, strcasecmp, lstrcmpi, strcmp stricmp, stricmp, lstrcpy, strcpy, strlcpy
	10	libFunc, dlerror, perror, ferror, error, herror
User Functions	1	UserFunc, wmain, main tmain, winmain
	2	UserFunc, pre, usage, prcode, usage, printusage, print, usage, x, fp, rm, usage, usage
	3	UserFunc, getesp, getsp, getip, fgets, get, esp, getreply, geteip, zgets, get, sp
	4	UserFunc, std, err
	5	UserFunc, get, shell, gen, shellcode, get, shelladdr, revshell, gotshell, get, server, hello, putshell, do, shell, getshell, entershell, shell, getshell, conn
	6	UserFunc, connectz, connectm, connect sockconnect, rdp, connect, iso, connect, connectzboard, bgp, connect, dsi, connect, connex, udpconnect
	7	UserFunc, resolv, host, resolvehost, resolv, resolve, host
	8	UserFunc, showbanner, banner
	9	UserFunc, timeout, timeout2, net, rtimeout, timeout, read
	10	UserFunc, cksum, chksum, in, chksum, checksum, in, cksum, csum
Variables	1	Var, bsd, shellcode, shellcodelen, freebsd, shellcode, irix, shellcode, shellc0de, ab, shellcode, dual, shellcode, deplshellcode, shellcod2e, trap, shellcode
	2	Var, shocke, shocks, sock, des, msock, csock, sock, usock, socket1, nsock, ssock, socketfd, shloc, sock, fsock, socket, x, socket, sockt, sockset, hsock, hsocket
	3	Var, buffrecv, buffer, env, buffer, buffread
	4	Var, xorport, i2oport, r, port, itoport, pexport, $rport, orig, port, shortaport, srcport, xport, srvport, xoredcbport, port, rport, export
	5	Var, saddrin, srvaddr, padding, addr, min, saddr, in1, saddr, in3, saddr, in2, s, addr, in, addr, hints, addrlen, csaddr, symaddr, addr, saddr, in, addr, in, lsaddr, su, padding
	6	Var, offset, ra, doffset, offset, offset, addr, offset0, offset1, offset2, offset3, offsets, roffset, loffset, dwoffset
	7	Var, uoff, woff, soff, offs, buff
	8	Var, ihost, myhost, pthost, sphost, hostip, ip, rhost, a, host, rhost, uhost, ircd, host, thost, cbhost, xhost, sin, rhost, host, lphost, phost, hosta, bindhost, lhost, hoste, hostm, hostp
	9	Var, size, c, size, fsize, tsize, midsize, ulsize, bofsize, tmpsize, bufsize, insize, sizeloc, fhsize, pktsize, bsize, retsize, sizev, sizew, sizes, sizex, sizey, sizez, ...
	10	Var, hwsadata, wsadat, wsadata

Due to a lack of time, we focused on Linux and Windows platform based compilations. After a long process of filtering errors 1285 instances were successfully compiled into ASM code (998 via Linux and 287 via Windows). From the research in the paper [10], the authors showed that an effective feature extrac-

Table 3. Sample of Top 10 Op-code pairs ordered by document frequency (most common across the collection)

Op-code pair	Total global occurrences
(movl, movl)	33165
(movl, call)	22411
(call, movl)	14811
(pushq, movq)	2715
(movq, movl)	15134
(leave, ret)	2909
(call, movq)	6604
(movq, subq)	2018
(movq, movq)	15930
(movl, movq)	10302

tion would be as follows. Over the Op-code sequences of each file, the n-grams algorithm was performed with a size of 2. For each of the possible Op-code pairs, a frequency count was given for each file. Since this resulted in too many features, the top 1000 most frequent Op-code pairs (by df) were taken as the final feature set (Table 3). The final dataset was then row normalized (across each feature's attributes). The final LLF dataset contained 1285 instances with 1000 features. The targets were either the 4 exploit types or the respective HLFs from the corresponding instances in the HLF dataset.

3.2 Single Stage Classifier of Machine Code

Our intent was see how much the HLFs help the classification of the LLFs. However, before building this model we needed a way to determine whether including the HLF would improve the results at all. In order to do so, it was necessary to build a second model which directly classified the exploit type from the LLFs. This single stage classifier was trained on the LLFs (2-gram OP-codes) to predict the class type (exploit type). In order to proceed we had to choose which machine learning algorithm was best for the dataset. At first we were interested in using an artificial neural network (ANN) because we believed that there exists strong nonlinear relations within our data. Our initial evaluations showed that a decision tree (DT) was a faster and more accurate classifier than the ANN for the given datasets. In order to be certain, we performed several cross validation on different ANN sizes (see Fig. 4).

Since the ANN was not a good option we used a DT as the single stage classifier (1S DT). The model of the 1S DT can be seen in Fig. 5. The evidence that drew us to our conclusions are available in Fig. 7 where the 1S DT out performed a 500 node single hidden layer ANN. The DT algorithms we used were those that were packaged with MATLAB [4,6].

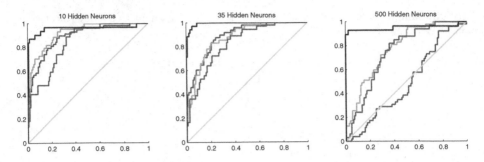

Fig. 4. The Receiver Operating Characteristics from training a single hidden layer artificial neural network with different sized hidden layers.

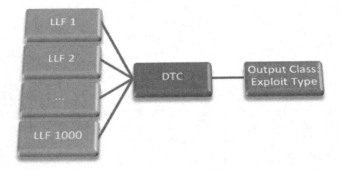

Fig. 5. The single stage DT learning model (1S DT). A classification decision tree is trained on the LLFs to predict the exploit type of the instance

3.3   Two Stage Meta-Classifier on Machine Code and High Level Features

The intent of this model is to show how HLFs can be used as a means for boosting the classification accuracy. To test this we built the two stage DT model (2S DT) shown in Fig. 6.

The idea behind the model is that since the HLFs hold abstract information about the exploit type they can assist in the classification. In other words, when the 2S DT is presented with a new instance's OP-codes, it attempts to first determine what the HLFs were. Afterwards, these predictions are used to "construct" the abstract picture of "the exploit type". For both the S1 and S2 DTs, we trained them on 85 % of the dataset, and then evaluated them based on the remaining 15 %. The results on the test set can be found in Fig. 7.

3.4   Comparing Results

The results present several interesting points. First of all, the 2S DT does not perform as well as the 1S DT. However, it still performs well as a predictor in general. This indicates that there is a strong connection from the LLFs to the

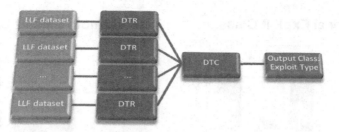

Fig. 6. The two stage DT learning model (2S DT). For each HLF, A single regression decision tree (DTR) is trained on the entire LLF dataset (an expert in predicting that HLF). The HLF predictions of these DTRs are the inputs to the decision tree classifier (DTC) trained to classify the instance's exploit type

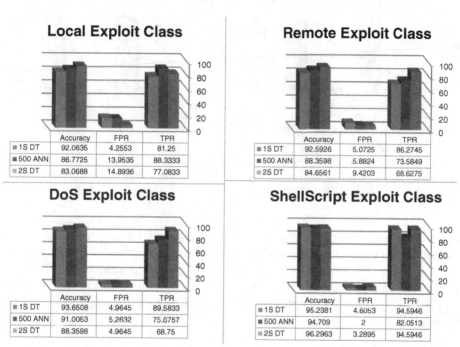

Local Exploit Class

	Accuracy	FPR	TPR
■ 1S DT	92.0635	4.2553	81.25
■ 500 ANN	86.7725	13.9535	88.3333
■ 2S DT	83.0688	14.8936	77.0833

Remote Exploit Class

	Accuracy	FPR	TPR
■ 1S DT	92.5926	5.0725	86.2745
■ 500 ANN	88.3598	5.8824	73.5849
■ 2S DT	84.6561	9.4203	68.6275

DoS Exploit Class

	Accuracy	FPR	TPR
■ 1S DT	93.6508	4.9645	89.5833
■ 500 ANN	91.0053	5.2632	75.6757
■ 2S DT	88.3598	4.9645	68.75

ShellScript Exploit Class

	Accuracy	FPR	TPR
■ 1S DT	95.2381	4.6053	94.5946
■ 500 ANN	94.709	2	82.0513
■ 2S DT	96.2963	3.2895	94.5946

Fig. 7. The results of the classification models on the test set. Displayed are the models' evaluations separated by targeted class

HLFs in terms of the exploit type. Another interesting result presented itself. The best performance the 2S DTC could provide should be the same accuracy as a DTC trained on the HLFs directly. However, contrary to this notion, the results (Fig. 8) show a DTC trained on predicted HLFs performed better than a DTC trained on the original HLFs. The reason for this is because although the DTRs in the 2S DT had a degree on error in their predictions, they included extra

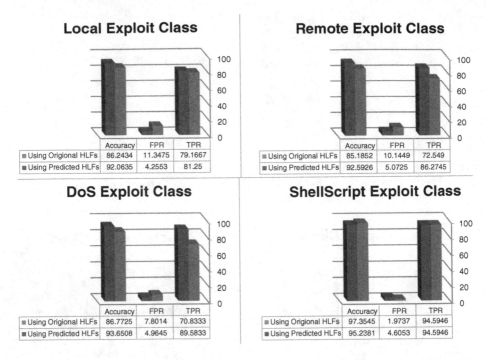

Fig. 8. A comparison between performing classification using a model trained on the original HLFs and a model trained on predicted HLFs. Note that the predicted features offer better performance (Color figure online)

information from the LLFs. Therefore, the predicted HLF which the DTC was trained on were actually "boosted" in their information (classification) content.

In summary, although the 2S DT is not as good as a simple 1S DT, there is a benefit to including the HLFs as a part of the processes. Further research should be considered on improving and capitalizing on fusing HLF into LLF models (Fig. 9).

4   Applying Unsupervised Learning

In this section we apply unsupervised learning in order to find patterns and corrections between instances on exploits. In particular, we use a SOM to seek out new classes of exploits and interesting unseen relations between groups of instances. The use of a SOM for this task is desirable for the following reasons. A SOM is an unsupervised machine learning algorithm that finds correlations between instances' features by positioning the instances on a 2D topological map. This means that instances which are found close together in a cluster are considered to be of the same "class". Furthermore, by investigating the distance and order of different clusters to one another can reveal further insights. Lastly, overlapping clusters indicate shared interests, yet dissimilar personalities.

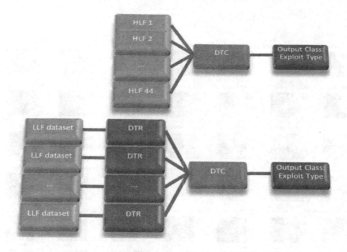

Fig. 9. The two classification decision trees (in red) compared in Fig. 8. The primary difference is that the top DTC has been trained on the actual HLFs while the bottom DTC has been trained on "predicted" HLFs (Color figure online)

4.1   Creation of the Dataset

The dataset used was the same HLF dataset used in Sect. 3. The only difference was that the label "exploit type" was not included in the training process and additional information from the database in Sect. 2 was used during the evaluation. This extra information includes: the year of submission and the target platform. Furthermore, the data was normalized in order to assist the SOM in finding correlations between instances. The normalization method used was the well-known mean over standard deviation method.

4.2   Applying the SOM

The SOM used was a 900 neuron map in a staggered square formation. The training process consisted of 200 iterations over the entire dataset. It can be seen that the HLFs (such as the number of libraries and function name groupings) were more than enough for the SOM to distinctly find the correlations between the instances. In Figs. 10 and 11 the neuron weights can be seen to show distinct patterns in the dataset.

4.3   Observed Patterns and Results

There are many ways to find interesting information about existing known classes. One method is that after training a SOM on unlabeled data, we plot the fallout of all the instances onto the SOM's 2D map. Afterwards, we *ask* all instances which have some particular trait to *raise their hand*. By plotting the densities of the selected instances we can see patterns emerge. In general, these

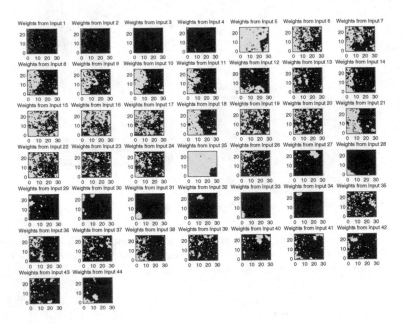

Fig. 10. The neuron's neighboring weights (biases) for each of the 44 HLF inputs. Overlapping strong weights indicate a strong correlation between the features.

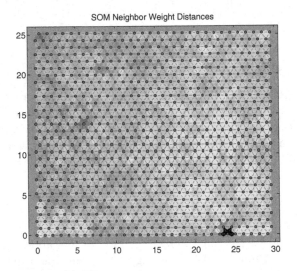

Fig. 11. The SOM neighboring weights altogether.

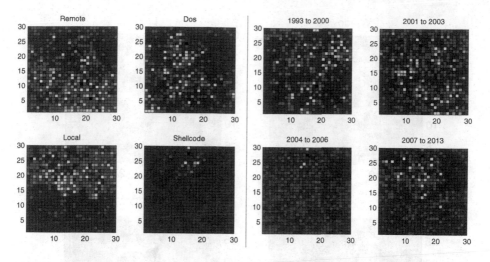

Fig. 12. Left: The fallout by density of the instances for each "exploit type" on the SOM. Right: The fallout by density of the instances by year of submission. The year ranges are balanced bins based on the histogram from Fig. 1

traits are the labels we left out of the training set. For this reason, we expect the SOM not only to find the correlation between these labels by itself, but also learn out new ones that we haven't seen before.

There are many interesting correlations and patterns which are evident in the results. Focusing on the left side of Fig. 12, note the differences between the instances of each exploit type. For the most part, the personality of remote exploits is disjoint to that of the local exploits. However, there is a small cluster of remote exploits at (22,20) which merges with the local exploits. It is clear that these exploits are neither DoS or shell-code types, so the question arises, "what is the cause of this unique cluster?". Upon further speculation, we can note that from Fig. 13 the majority of that cluster is target for the Windows platform. This may indicate a new class of exploit that is a mix of both remote and local existing primarily on the Windows operating system. Having another look at the left side of Fig. 12, other clear distinctions arise between the exploit types. For instance, Shell-code and local exploits are clearly disjoint yet favor being located in the northern hemisphere of the map. By merging these patterns we can tell that although shell-code exploits are disjoint to remote ones, they are far more similar to them than local exploits. This gives a nice indication of what behaviors to look for when classifying an exploit's type. Moving the focus over to Fig. 13, note that there is a distinct hole within the Windows instances at (15,16). This is particularly interesting since this correlates to the same gap found in the remote exploit types (left side of Fig. 12). This indicates that there is a definitive grouping of correlated local and DoS exploits that are not found on Windows platforms. It would be very interesting to investigate what these local and DoS exploits have in common. Moreover, note that the Linux platforms

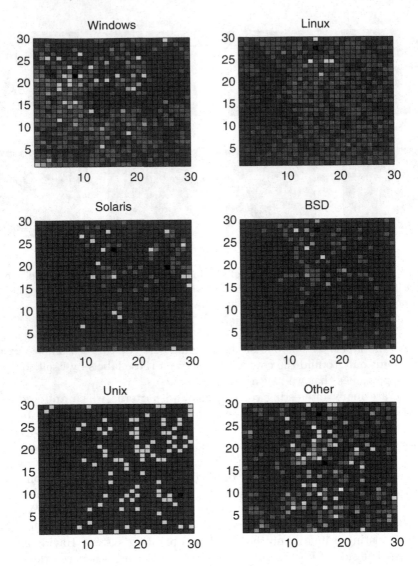

Fig. 13. The fallout by density of the instances for each "targeted platform" on the SOM

mostly favor the right while the DoS exploits favor the left. Although there is an overlap between these instances, it is clear that the usage of DoS type exploits (or exploits that have the same behavior) is not common on Linux platforms. Another interesting fact about the Linux platform is the correlation between Linux based exploits and shell-code exploits (15,25). This connection apparently is not only popular in general, but in particular during the years 2004–2006 (right side of Fig. 12). While this cluster is a highly active until today, it is notable that it was less so prior to the year 2001. Lastly, note the similarity between Linux and BSD. It would appear that their exploit personalities are very similar. Shifting the focus now onto the right side of Fig. 12, note how the popularity of using particular exploits have changed over time. It would appear that there were favoured trends that were picked up by the exploit DB community and then later dismissed. By using these results it is possible to determine what "old exploits" are and therefore where a new classifier should put its focus. In other words, the results here, show the concept drifts over time, and can be used to pick up on the new trends (an catch them in the act) while dismissing the old ones. Including this information into active learning algorithm could improve its accuracy. One example of a trend is the correlation between the remote exploits and the recent years. It is clear by their overlap that not only has remote exploits been less interesting to in the past, but now they are the "hottest" item (2006–2013). Another example is that Shell-code type exploits have been popular from year to year, while other exploit types such as DoS and remote have come and gone. Lastly note that over the years 2006 to 2013 there has been less interest in exploit types falling out in the right and bottom sides of the map (a backwards "L"). There is a clear relation between this pattern and the patterns in the DoS and local exploits. There we can see that the upper right and lower left quadrants have an inverse existential relation, while the overlapping upper left quadrant is populated by both of them. When merging this pattern with the 2006–2013 instances, we can tell that the diagonal disjoint clusters indicate that in the past, DoS and local exploit have behaved as very different "animals" and have been kept distinct in terms of their code. However, as evident from their overlap in the upper left quadrant, today their behaviors have becomes merged. This new class of behaviors that has appeared in the recent years is incredibly intriguing a more time should be invested into analyzing this trend.

5   Conclusion and Future Work

The practicality of using metadata and high level features, found in certain databases, as a means for classifying exploit-types has been widely overlooked. In particular, community pooled resources such as Exploit DB. In this article we have shown how the application of supervised and unsupervised machine learning algorithms to high level features can provide insightful contributions to classification of low level features. In the case of supervised learning, although the inclusion of HLFs to classify LLFs did not provide a direct improvement, insight was gained in the connection between the two. In the case of unsupervised learning, many patterns were uncovered and possible unknown exploit classes were discovered as well. This information could be highly beneficial in designing strong specialized classifiers. For future work, we recommend investing time into a deeper analysis of the SOM mappings in order find new class types. Furthermore, it would be interesting to use SOMs as a means for detecting and predicting concept drifts as they come up. Lastly, the dataset used in this article was incomplete with respect the total number of instances available in Exploit DB and others. More accurate results may be achieved if these instances are included.

Acknowledgements. This research was supported by the Ministry of Science and Technology, Israel.

References

1. Bayer, U., Comparetti, P.M., Hlauschek, C., Kruegel, C., Kirda, E.: Scalable, behavior-based malware clustering. In: NDSS, vol. 9, pp 8–11. Citeseer (2009)
2. Bellman, R.E.: Adaptive Control Processes: A Guided Tour, vol. 4. Princeton University Press, Princeton (1961)
3. Breiman, L.: Random forests. Mach. Learn. **45**(1), 5–32 (2001)
4. Breiman, L., Friedman, J., Stone, C.J., Olshen, R.A.: Classification and Regression Trees. CRC Press, Boca Raton (1984)
5. Christodorescu, M., Jha, S.: Static analysis of executables to detect malicious patterns. Technical report, DTIC Document (2006)
6. Coppersmith, D., Hong, S.J., Hosking, J.R.: Partitioning nominal attributes in decision trees. Data Min. Knowl. Disc. **3**(2), 197–217 (1999)
7. Kohonen, T.: The self-organizing map. Proc. IEEE **78**(9), 1464–1480 (1990)
8. Patcha, A., Park, J.-M.: An overview of anomaly detection techniques: existing solutions and latest technological trends. Comput. Netw. **51**(12), 3448–3470 (2007)
9. Ritter, H., Kohonen, T.: Self-organizing semantic maps. Biol. Cybern. **61**(4), 241–254 (1989)
10. Shabtai, A., Moskovitch, R., Feher, C., Dolev, S., Elovici, Y.: Detecting unknown malicious code by applying classification techniques on opcode patterns. Secur. Inform. **1**(1), 1–22 (2012)
11. Sung, A.H., Xu, J., Chavez, P., Mukkamala, S.: Static analyzer of vicious executables (save). In: 20th Annual Computer Security Applications Conference, pp. 326–334. IEEE (2004)
12. Wagner, D., Dean, D.: Intrusion detection via static analysis. In: Proceedings of the 2001 IEEE Symposium on Security and Privacy, S&P 2001, pp. 156–168. IEEE (2001)
13. Walenstein, A., Venable, M., Hayes, M., Thompson, C., Lakhotia, A.: Exploiting similarity between variants to defeat malware. In: Proceedings of the BlackHat DC Conference (2007)
14. Wespi, A., Debar, H.: Building an intrusion-detection system to detect suspicious process behavior. In: Recent Advances in Intrusion Detection (1999)

Detecting Computers in Cyber Space Maliciously Exploited as SSH Proxies

Idan Morad and Asaf Shabtai$^{(\boxtimes)}$

Department of Information Systems Engineering,
Ben-Gurion University of the Negev, Beersheba, Israel
idanmora@post.bgu.ac.il, shabtaia@bgu.ac.il

Abstract. Classifying encrypted traffic is a great challenge in the cyber security domain. Attackers can use the SSH protocol to hide the nature of their attack. This is done by enabling SSH tunneling to act as a proxy. In this study we present a technique for matching (encrypted) SSH incoming sessions with corresponding (encrypted) SSH outgoing sessions through a series of SSH servers. This is an indication of suspicious activity and therefore an important step in order to identify SSH servers that are potentially used as a stepping-stone in a chain of proxies.

Keywords: Encrypted traffic · SSH · Cyberattack · Machine learning

1 Introduction

Secured Shell (SSH) is a client-server protocol that is used for remote login and remote command execution [1]. It provides authentication and secured (encrypted) communications over an insecure channel. SSH is also used for tunneling, i.e., corresponding a port on the client machine with a port on a machine that resides within a private network over TCP/IP communication (also known as port forwarding). The tunnel is established between the SSH client and the SSH server, and the communication within the tunnel is encrypted.

Unfortunately, the SSH protocol may be maliciously exploited by hackers in order to hide the source, destination and nature of an attack. This can be done by enabling SSH tunneling acting as a proxy through which the malicious traffic will be transmitted (e.g., leaking sensitive data, command and control communication). As a case in point, the Flame virus detected in 2012 used SSL and SSH for stealing sensitive information [2] and the Duqu virus detected in 2011 used SSH port forwarding to hide the command and control traffic and the IP of the control application [3]. Wahlisch *et al.* [4] implemented a mobile device honeypot. While analyzing suspicious access via the Internet to smartphones, manual attacks that first established SSH connection and then targeted the address book and stored photos were identified.

Figure 1 illustrates a legitimate and malicious use of an SSH server. A *benign client* connects to the *destination* server over an unsecured network via the SSH server. The communication between the client and the SSH server is encrypted

© Springer International Publishing Switzerland 2015
I. Bica et al. (Eds.): SECITC 2015, LNCS 9522, pp. 201–211, 2015.
DOI: 10.1007/978-3-319-27179-8_14

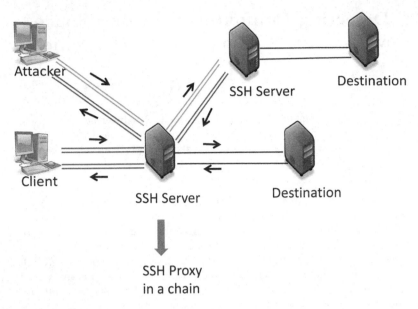

Fig. 1. Illustrating an attack scenario using an SSH server as a proxy (Color figure online)

(marked in double red lines). The communication between the destination server and the SSH server is not protected (i.e., encrypted) by the SSH protocol.

An *attacker*, on the other hand, may connect several SSH servers in a chain (in an onion routing approach) in order to forward the attack traffic to the next SSH server (marked in red and yellow lines). In this case an incoming session and a correlated outgoing session are encapsulating the same traffic (encrypted). Thus, if one can correlate incoming encrypted traffic with an outgoing encrypted traffic, both containing the same content, we can indicate that the server is being used as an SSH proxy in a chain, which might be illegitimate.

The contribution of this study is a simple method for classifying and correlating incoming and outgoing sessions in SSH servers. This is an important step in order to identify SSH servers that are potentially used as a stepping-stone in a chain.

The rest of the paper is structured as follows. In Sect. 2 we describe the related works. Section 3 presents the proposed method. In Sect. 4 we present the evaluation of the proposed method and Sect. 5 concludes the paper and suggests ideas for future work.

2   Related Works

Previous works have applied machine learning techniques for analyzing SSH network traffic. The first class of studies attempted to distinguish regular (non-tunneled) SSH traffic, such as regular remote interactive logins or secure copying activities, from encrypted tunneled SSH traffic across network boundaries. Dusi *et al.* [5] presented the "Tunnel Hunter" as an efficient solution based on statistical classification techniques (Naïve Bayes) that can provide a behavioral characterization of an application layer protocol to detect tunneling activities. The legitimate behavior of application protocols is modeled using statistical features extracted from the TCP sessions carrying them. During the classification phase, each session is assigned with an anomaly score. If the anomaly score is smaller than a given threshold, it is considered as a legitimate session.

Another class of works investigated the use of machine learning in identifying the protocol transmitted across an SSH tunnel. Alshammari *et al.* [6] used two supervised learning algorithms, AdaBoost and RIPPER, for classifying the different services/applications running over the SSH traffic. The features used in [6] include Stdev/Mean/Max/Min of packets' interarrival time, Stdev/Mean/Max/Min of packets' length, number of bytes, duration of the inspected flow and more. The classification task was divided into two phases: The first phase focused on the identification of SSH traffic in a given traffic log file. The dataset used in this phase was composed of traffic traces captured on real networks of four classes (SSH, MAIL, DNS, HTTP). According to the reported results of the first experiment, the RIPPER algorithm outperforms AdaBoost in terms of classifying SSH traffic with over 99 % detection rate and an approximate 1 % false positive rate. The second phase concentrated on identifying the different services/applications running over an SSH session. The dataset used in this phase was composed of packets of flows of 11 classes (1,000 flows from each class) including Shell over SSH, SFTP over SSH, Telnet, and FTP. The results for the second phase showed that the RIPPER algorithm can classify the different running services with detection rate over 97 % and with false positive below 0.3 %.

Dusi *et al.* [7], also used machine learning algorithms, specifically GMM and SVM, for identifying the application being forwarded inside the SSH tunnel. SSH sessions are represented using size and direction. Evaluation was conducted using a training set containing 1,000 flows for each the following protocols: HTTP, POP3, POP3S and EMULE (representing most common traffic classes: Web, P2P and mail) and a test set containing more than 500 encrypted flows for each protocol (including "unknown" protocols over SSH - MSN, HTTPS and BitTorrent). Results showed that the SVM outperformed the GMM algorithm while providing an accuracy of over 86 %. The above mentioned studies mainly focused on classifying the type of encrypted traffic. Since tunneled traffic may be legitimate, we are interested in identifying cases in which the traffic is tunneled encrypted to another SSH server with different layer of encryption.

Hellemons *et al.* [8] focused on detecting malicious SSH traffic. They presented the SSHCure, a flow-based SSH intrusion detection system. SSHCure analyzes traffic flows (i.e., sequence of packets) in order to identify three phases of an attack: the scanning phase, brute-force phase and die-off phase. During the scanning phase the attacker scans an IP address block in order find hosts that are running an SSH daemon. In the brute-force phase, the attacker attempts to login to the detected hosts using a large number of username and password combinations. Once the attacker gains access to an SSH server, the die-off phase begins. This is the actual attack which includes commands being executed by the attacker on the target host. In order to avoid blocking legitimate traffic, the SSHCure can detect the die-off phase assuming that the previous phase of the attack, the brute-force phase, was detected. Hellemons *et al.* [8] attempted to identify the phase of attacking an SSH server while we focus on the next step–maliciously using a compromised SSH server and using it as a stepping stone in a chain of SSH proxies.

3 Proposed Method

The goal of our research is to link incoming tunneled streams with outgoing streams of the same traffic. Finding such correlations between encrypted incoming and outgoing streams indicates that the SSH server is used to forward a tunnel and is acting as a proxy in a chain. The assumption is that some similarity of properties is being preserved between the incoming encrypted traffic and outgoing encrypted traffic of an SSH server (e.g., time between packets).

We propose and evaluate two methods: a *machine learning* approach and an *attribute ranking* approach. In the machine learning approach we generate for each incoming session, a profile, and match it with the most similar outgoing (encrypted) session. In the second approach, we rank the attributes of each session and match incoming and outgoing encrypted sessions based on the ordering of the attributes.

3.1 Extracted Attributes

Each incoming/outgoing session is represented by a chronologically ordered instance. Each instance was generated by aggregating a predefined amount of packets (in our experiment we used 10 consecutive packets) and computing a set of contextual, network-based attributes proposed by Alshammari and Zincir-Heywood [6]. The list of features is presented in Table 1.

3.2 Machine Learning-Based Approach

In the machine learning approach we used two anomaly detection approaches. In the first approach we applied the Ensemble of Feature Chains (EFC) anomaly detection algorithm [9] with an underlying REPTree classifier. First, a model was generated for each incoming session. The correlation process was performed as follows: Given a test set containing the instances of an outgoing session, each anomaly detection model (representing the behavior of a specific incoming session) was applied to the test set. The incoming session is labeled as correlated with the outgoing session with the lowest average anomaly score.

In the second approach the feature vectors of incoming session instances were considered as a cluster, and a centroid was computed and used for representing the session. The centroid was generated by computing the average of each feature over all the instances of the incoming session.

Table 1. Computed set of features.

Feature Name	Description
active_time_avg	The average active time period in the instance
active_time_max	The maximal active time period in the instance
active_time_min	The minimal active time period in the instance
active_time_stdev	The standard deviation of the active time period in the instance
idle_time_avg	The average idle time period in the instance
idle_time_max	The maximal idle time period in the instance
idle_time_min	The minimal idle time period in the instance
idle_time_stdev	The standard deviation of the idle time period in the instance
inter_arrival_time_avg	The average of inter-arrival times of the packets
inter_arrival_time_max	The maximal inter-arrival time of the packets
inter_arrival_time_min	The minimal inter-arrival time of the packets
inter_arrival_time_stdev	The standard deviation of inter-arrival times of the packets
packet_length_avg	The average length of packets in the instance

In order to correlate incoming and outgoing sessions we computed the distance of each incoming session centroid from the instances of an outgoing session. An outgoing session with the closest instances is likely to be correlated with the incoming session, while "closeness" is determined according to some distance function. In our experiments we evaluated using Euclidean distance and Cosine similarity. An incoming session was determined to be correlated to the outgoing session with the highest number of closest instances according to the selected distance matric.

3.3 Matching Attributes Approach

We hypothesize that the order of the incoming sessions, when sorted by the average value of a given feature, should be preserved also for the outgoing sessions (the average value is computed for all the instances of an incoming session). Based on this assumption, we proposed the following method which assigns a similarity score for pairs of incoming and outgoing sessions based on their rank in the sorted lists.

The proposed method is presented in Fig. 3. The input to the algorithm is the list of features F, a matching factor k, a list of incoming sessions and a list of outgoing sessions. Incoming and outgoing sessions are represented by its centroid (i.e., the vector of averaged feature values).

First, we initialize all possible pairs of incoming and outgoing sessions with a score of 0 (line 1). Then, for each feature $f \in F$, we sort the sessions' centroids (both incoming and outgoing) by the value of the feature f (lines 2-2.2). Given the ordered lists of incoming and outgoing sessions (according to feature f) we update the score of each pair using to the `CalculateScore` function (lines 2.3-2.3.1.2).

The `CalculateScore` function uses the indexes of the sessions' centroids and the matching factor k. The score of the $i - th$ inSession and $j - th$ outSession is set according to the following equation:

$$calculateScore(i, j, k) = \begin{cases} i - j = 0, & k \\ |i - j| < k, & k - |i - j| \\ |i - j| > k, & 0 \end{cases}$$

If the indexes of the inSession and outSession are equal, the function assigns the score k. If the distance is smaller than k, the function scores with the difference between k and the distance of the indexes. Finally, if the difference is bigger than k, the function scores with 0. In the example in Fig. 3, the matching factor k is set to 3 and the centroids are sorted by feature f. The outgoing session that is located in the same place, respectively in their lists, with the incoming session is given the maximum score k. The outgoing sessions that are located with the distance of 1 from the index of incoming sessions are given the score 2, and so on. When the distance between the indexes is bigger than k, the given score is 0 (Fig. 2).

```
Input:
    F - a list of features
    k - the matching factor
    inSessions - a list of incoming sessions' centroids
    outSessions - a list of outgoing sessions' centroids
Output:
    scores - an array of scores for each pair of inSession and
             outSession
Procedure: MatchByAttributes
    1. for each inSession ∈ inSessions and outSession ∈ outSessions do
        1.1 initialize scores(inSession, outSession) ← 0
    2. for each feature f ∈F do:
        2.1 sort inSessions by feature f
        2.2 sort outSessions by feature f
        2.3 for each inSession ∈ inSessions do:
            2.3.1 for each outSession ∈ outSessions do:
                2.3.1.1 i ← index of inSession in inSessions
                2.3.1.2 j ← index of outSession in outSessions
                2.3.1.1 scores(inSession,outSession) += calcuateScore(i,j,k)
    3. return scores
```

Fig. 2. Procedure: match by attributes

4   Evaluation

4.1   Evaluation Environment

The proposed method was evaluated using evaluation environment. The evaluation environment allows network traffic transmission (e.g., HTTP) through SSH

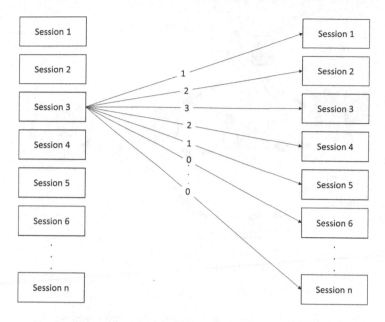

Fig. 3. An example of the scoring technique

tunnel, chaining SSH tunnels, adding noise/background traffic, and simulating attack traffic.

The traffic generated was tunneled using the SSH protocol and forwarded via a chain of three stepping stones (SSH servers). The traffic was recorded on every hop in the chain, and on the client machine as well using Wireshark [10]. Data was collected using five Linux AMI instances residing in different geographic locations on the Amazon cloud. The chains were automatically created using Python scripts running on the client machine.

Each chain established consisted of three servers. While the second and third servers remain the same (Servers 2 and 3 in Fig. 4), the first server of the chain is selected each time to be one of the servers 1, 4 and 5. We refer to each chain as a scenario, which is named after the servers constructing it. For example: 'scenario 123' refers to the chain in which its first server is "Server 1", its second is "Server 2", and the last is "Server 3".

For the evaluation we collected encrypted traffic that passes through the three SSH servers. Each server in the chain removes one layer of encryption until the last server in the chain (Server 3) forwards the traffic in plaintext to the destination. The traffic that was generated for the evaluation included various protocols and activities, such as downloading files or filling out a form. Table 2 presents the list of types of protocols and activities, and the number of sessions generated for each scenario (i.e., chain). There were a total of 807 incoming and outgoing sessions of all protocols.

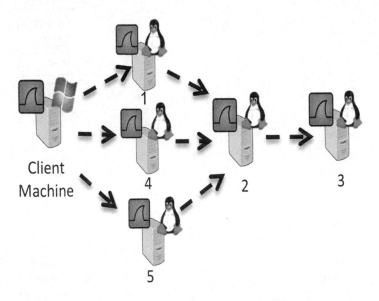

Fig. 4. Stepping-stone chains setup on Amazon cloud servers

Table 2. Protocols' sessions statistics

Type	Scenario 123	Scenario 423	Scenario 423
HTTPdownloadFile	15	12	13
HTTPfillForn	19	10	14
HTTPRandomLink	8	16	12
HTTPSclickRandomLink	22	16	18
HTTPSdownloadFileFromDropboxSite	38	20	6
HTTPSenterToGmail	38	36	32
HTTPSfillForm	50	46	46
HTTPSuploadFileToDropboxSite	26	24	34
HTTPuploadFile	8	8	22
HTTPwatchVideo	4	6	4
IMAP	9	8	4
IRC	10	8	10
Plain SSH	4	15	4
POP3	8	8	12
SKYPE	6	4	6
SMTP	16	2	16
TORRENT	6	4	4
XMPP	6	8	6

4.2   Results

In order to evaluate the proposed method we conducted experiments as described in the following sections. We tested the correlation only on Server 2 because it is the only server which had encrypted SSH ingoing sessions and encrypted SSH outgoing sessions (the other servers had plain text as incoming sessions or outgoing sessions). In the experiments, the metric selected to evaluate the algorithm is *hit rate* which is the percentage of correctly matched sessions (out of the total number of sessions).

Machine Learning-Based Approach. The machine learning-based approach yielded a low success rate where the EFC algorithm succeeded to correlate 5 out of the 807 sessions (i.e., hit rate = 0.62 %) and the centroid (clustering) approach could not detect any correct match.

In attempting to understand such unsatisfying results, we hypothesized that the SSH Server manipulation of the traffic (i.e., removing one layer of encryption) was effecting the ability to profile the session behavior through the extracted feature and match the profile with the outgoing sessions. This conclusion led to the proposal of the next approach.

Matching Attributes Approach. In the matching attribute approach we assume that a similarity of properties was being preserved between the ingoing encrypted traffic and outgoing encrypted traffic of an SSH server, only for this approach, we suggested that the order of average value of a given feature (the average value is computed for all the instances of a session), should be similar (or preserved) also for the outgoing sessions.

To evaluate the matching attribute approach we defined the following research questions:

1. What is the minimal, optimal subset of features that maximizes the hit rate? This is important in order to avoid a lengthy computation time. There are 17 attributes, meaning a 2^{17-1} was a valid combination to score (choosing *none of the attributes* was considered invalid).
2. What is the matching factor k which maximizes the hit rate?
3. What is the overall hit rate of the proposed method?

In order to answer the first question we tested all possible combinations of the feature subset with matching factor $k = 8$. On the chain of 123 servers the best hit rate was 6.83 %, for the chain of 423 the best hit rate was 11.55 % and for the chain of 523 the best hit rate was 8.37 %. The common features over all the best feature subsets were:

- active_time_ avg
- inter_arrival_time_max
- inter_arrival_time_min
- inter_arrival_time_stdev
- session_duration

To answer the second question, we used the five features (listed above) and the matching factor k was set to 1, 3, 5, 8, 15, 20, 30 and 50. The highest hit rate was achieved for $k = 16$, with hit rates of 4.44 % in chain 123, 9.97 % in chain 423 and 8.37 % in chain 523.

In order to evaluate the overall performance (hit rate) of the proposed method we conducted a series of experiments that would show what the average hit rate was, without dependence of the matching factor nor the features. For each experiment, the matching factor was between 6 and 44, and the attributes in the features were both chosen randomly. The experiments were performed 10, 50, 100, 200 and 500 times. The average hit rate was 4.3 %. The results are presented in Table 3.

Table 3. Experiment 3 results

# iterations/dataset	10	50	100	200	500	
123	3.55 %	3.06 %	2.93 %	2.91 %	2.99 %	
423	5.34 %	5.86 %	5.89 %	5.71 %	5.61 %	
523	4.37 %	4.48 %	4.18 %	4.29 %	4.19 %	
Avg.	4.37 %	4.39 %	4.26 %	4.25 %	4.20 %	4.3 %

To conclude, the matching attributes approach showed a better performance than the machine learning approach and with only a small set of features. The hit rate was better and although it is still a low hit rate (8.9 % on average) it still provides an indication that there are correlated sessions, which could indicate that the server was being used for malicious purposes.

5   Conclusion and Future Work

In this paper, we presented a simple yet efficient method for correlating sessions of encrypted ingoing and outgoing traffic in an SSH server which could indicate that the server is used as a proxy in a chain, and thus could be suspected as being malicious traffic.

In future work the method should be tested on a large-scale network (more than a few stations) and with normal (legitimate cases) of SSH port forwarding sessions. In addition, we are planning to evaluate the ability to classify the protocol or service that is encapsulated in the encrypted SSH session using machine learning techniques, and use this information in order to improve the correlation hit-rate.

Acknowledgment. This research was sponsored by the Captain Cyber Consortium, funded by the Chief Scientist of the Israeli Ministry of Economy under the Magnet Program.

References

1. Barrett, D.J., Silverman, R.E., Byrnes, R.G.: SSH, The Secure Shell: The Definitive Guide. O'Reilly Media, Inc., Sebastopol (2005)
2. Kaspersky Labs, The Roof Is on Fire: Tackling Flame's C&C Servers (2012). http://www.securelist.com/en/blog?print_mode=1&weblogid=208193540/
3. Kaspersky Labs, The Mystery of Duqu: Part Six (The Command and Control servers) (2011). http://www.securelist.com/en/blog/625/The_Mystery_of_Duqu_Part_Six_The_Command_and_Control_servers
4. Wählisch, M., Vorbach, A., Keil, C., Schönfelder, J., Schmidt, T.C., Schiller, J.H.: Design, Implementation, and Operation of a Mobile Honeypot. arXiv preprint arXiv:1301.7257 (2013)
5. Dusi, M., Crotti, M., Gringoli, F., Salgarelli, L.: Detection of encrypted tunnels across network boundaries. In: 2008 IEEE International Conference on Communications, pp. 1738–1744. IEEE (2008)
6. Alshammari, R., Zincir-Heywood, A.N.: A flow based approach for SSH traffic detection. In: 2007 IEEE International Conference on Systems, Man and Cybernetics, pp. 296–301. IEEE (2007)
7. Dusi, M., Este, A., Gringoli, F., Salgarelli, L.: Using GMM and SVM-based techniques for the classification of SSH-encrypted traffic. In: 2009 IEEE International Conference on Communications, pp. 1–6. IEEE (2009)
8. Hellemons, L., Hendriks, L., Hofstede, R., Sperotto, A., Sadre, R., Pras, A.: SSHCure: A flow-based SSH intrusion detection system. In: Sadre, R., Novotný, J., Čeleda, P., Waldburger, M., Stiller, B. (eds.) AIMS 2012. LNCS, vol. 7279, pp. 86–97. Springer, Heidelberg (2012)
9. Tenenboim-Chekina, L., Rokach, L., Shapira, B.: Ensemble of feature chains for anomaly detection. In: Zhou, Z.-H., Roli, F., Kittler, J. (eds.) MCS 2013. LNCS, vol. 7872, pp. 295–306. Springer, Heidelberg (2013)
10. Wireshrk 1.8.6 (2015). http://www.wireshark.org/

On a Lightweight Authentication Protocol for RFID

George-Daniel Năstase and Ferucio Laurenţiu Ţiplea[✉]

Department of Computer Science, "Alexandru Ioan Cuza" University of Iaşi,
700506 Iaşi, Romania
{george.nastase,fltiplea}@info.uaic.ro

Abstract. This paper focuses on the lightweight mutual authentication protocol for RFID systems proposed in [7]. The randomness of the non-linear feedback shift register sequences used in the protocol is reconsidered, a new technique for generated better such sequences is proposed, and the security and privacy of the protocol is formally argued.

1 Introduction

An RFID system is typically composed of three elements: an RFID reader (transceiver), a number of RFID tags (transponders), and a back-end database (or server). The reader and the back-end database may be viewed as a single entity as they communicate through a secure channel. However, the communication between reader and tag is insecure and, therefore, it is subject to eavesdropping. As a conclusion, the (mutual) authentication between reader and tag becomes one of the most important problems in this context.

Many authentication protocols for RFID systems have been proposed. They are usually classified according to the computational power of the tag. If the tag has strong computational capabilities, then it can implement protocols based on strong cryptographic primitives [2,3,8,14,18]. Of course, such tags can be too costly to be adopted in most retailer operations which are envisioned as major applications of the RFID technology. A large number of authentication protocols proposed so far are based on hash functions, hash function chains, pseudo-random functions, and random number generators [1,9,15,16,18,27,32]. A third class of authentication protocols is the class of lightweight and ultra-lightweight authentication protocols. They only require to perform primitive operations such as random number generation, arithmetic bit-wise operations, cyclic redundancy code checksum, or even light hash or pseudo-random functions [4–6,11,12,18–23,30]. There is a widespread view that the lightweight and ultra-lightweight authentication protocols will be the best candidate technology for securing the future low-cost RFID systems.

F.L. Ţiplea — Author partially supported by the Romanian National Authority for Scientific Research (CNCS-UEFISCDI) under the project PN-II-PT-PCCA-2013-4-1651.

© Springer International Publishing Switzerland 2015
I. Bica et al. (Eds.): SECITC 2015, LNCS 9522, pp. 212–225, 2015.
DOI: 10.1007/978-3-319-27179-8_15

Contribution. In [7], a lightweight authentication protocol has been proposed. The main idea is to use non-linear feedback shift register (NLFSR) sequences generated by the position digit algebra function (PDAF) [24,25,28,29]. Unfortunately, some of the main properties of the PDAF, as described in [29] are flawed and, as a consequence, the NLFSR sequences used in [7] might have short periods. We discuss this weaknesses in this paper and we propose better NLFSR sequences. Based on these NLFSR sequences we improve the protocol in [7] and, moreover, we provide formal arguments for its security and privacy.

Paper Organization. The paper is organized into six sections. The next section discusses two wrong results proposed in [29] regarding the PDAF. The third section proposes a new technique to generate NLFSR sequences with long periods by using the PDAF. Our new authentication protocol is discussed in Sect. 4, while the next sections focuses on its correctness, security, and privacy analysis. We conclude in the last section.

2   Remarks on the Position Digit Algebra Function

We recall first a few basic concepts used throughout this paper. $\mathbb{Z}$ ($\mathbb{Z}_r$) stands for the set of integers (integers modulo r, with $r > 0$). The addition in $\mathbb{Z}_r$, denoted $\oplus_r$, is also called the *r-XOR operation*. That is, $x \oplus_r y = x + y \mod r$. When $r = 2$, this is the standard XOR operation, whose notation is simplified to $\oplus$.

In this paper, $r \geq 2$ denotes a number base and $\mathbb{Z}_r$ is the set of the r-ary digits. Given $n \geq 1$, the elements $x \in \mathbb{Z}_r^n$ will be written in the form $x = x_0 \cdots x_{n-1}$, where x_i is the ith r-ary digit of x, for all $0 \leq i < n$.

The *position digit algebra function* (PDAF) [24,25,28,29], also called *the combining function* [24–26], is the function

$$PDAF : \bigcup_{r \geq 2, n \geq 1} (\mathbb{Z}_r^n \times \mathbb{Z}_r^n) \to \bigcup_{r \geq 2, n \geq 1} \mathbb{Z}_r^n$$

given by

$$PDAF(x, y)_i = x_i \oplus_r x_{i \oplus_n y_i},$$

for all $r \geq 2$, $n \geq 1$, $x, y \in \mathbb{Z}_r^n$, and $0 \leq i < n$. x is called a *value key* and y an *offset key*. We will further refer to $PDAF(x, y)$ as $x[y]$.

Two r-ary n-digit numbers $x, x' \in \mathbb{Z}_r^n$ are called *value key equivalent* [29], abbreviated *VK-equivalent*, if $x[y] = x'[y]$, for some $y \in \mathbb{Z}_r^n$. Two r-ary n-digit numbers $y, y' \in \mathbb{Z}_r^n$ are called *offset key equivalent* [29], abbreviated *OK-equivalent*, if $x[y] = x[y']$, for some $x \in \mathbb{Z}_r^n$.

Proposition 1 ([29]). *Let x, x', y, y' be four r-ary n-digit numbers.*

1. *If r is even and $x'_i = x_i + r/2 \mod r$, for all $0 \leq i < n$, then x and x' are VK-equivalent.*

2. *The probability of generating at random two VK-equivalent r-ary n-digit numbers is*

$$\frac{1}{(r-1)^n} + \epsilon$$

for some negligible small number ϵ.

3. y *and* y' *are OK-equivalent if and only if, for all* $0 \le i < n$, *one of the following holds:*

  – $y'_i = y_i + jn$, *for some* $1 \le j \le \alpha_i$, *where* $\alpha_i = \left\lfloor \dfrac{r-1-y_i}{n} \right\rfloor \ge 1$;

  – $y'_i = y_i - jn$, *for some* $1 \le j \le \beta_i$, *where* $\beta_i = \left\lfloor \dfrac{y_i}{n} \right\rfloor \ge 1$;

  – $y'_i = y_i$.

4. *If* $n < r$, *then the probability of generating at random two OK-equivalent r-ary n-digit numbers is*

$$\frac{\prod_{i=0}^{n-1}(\alpha_i + \beta_i + 1) - 1}{r^n}$$

Remark 1. One more property of the PDAF is mentioned in [29], namely that the probability of generating two OK-equivalent r-ary n-digit numbers is 0 if $n \ge r$.

Unfortunately, this property is false as the following example shows ($r = 16$, $n = 24$, and the numbers are written in hexadecimal):

$$x = 41\,CD\,69\,39\,AF\,A8\,F0\,55\,86\,82\,F1\,67$$
$$y = 1C\,F9\,F7\,BC\,B9\,52\,5B\,22\,7C\,52\,8E\,69$$
$$y' = 1C\,F6\,F4\,BC\,B2\,42\,5B\,2D\,7C\,56\,8E\,69$$

Clearly, $y \ne y'$; however, a simple computation leads to $x[y] = x[y']$.

Remark 2. It is mentioned [29] that the PDAF can be used to define *non-linear feedback shift-register* (NLFSR) *sequences* with long average period lengths, as follows:

– choose initially at random two r-ary n-digit numbers x_0 and x_1;
– define $x_{i+2} = x_i[x_{i+1}]$, for all $i \ge 0$.

For such NLFSR sequences, [29] estimates the average period length to $(r-1)^n$. For instance, if $r = 16$ and $n = 32$, the average period length is 4.31×10^{37}, which is large enough for cryptographic purposes. Unfortunately, our computer tests do not confirm the estimates in [29], as the chart in Fig. 1 shows. We have used $r = 16$ and $n = 32$. On average, the first 188 elements in the sequence are all pairwise distinct, but then they repeat themselves quite heavily. The test was repeated 10^5 times and the chart in Fig. 1 illustrates the average number of repetitions.

The above idea was used in [7] to generate three NLFSR sequences, as follows:

– choose at random three r-ary n-digit numbers c_0, c_1, and c_2;

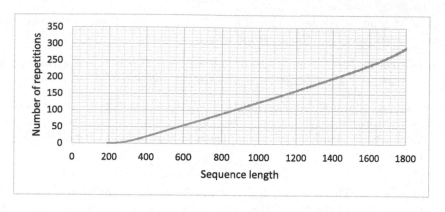

Fig. 1. Repetitions in the sequence $x_{i+2} = x_i[x_{i+1}]$

- compute new values for c_0, c_1, and c_2 as follows:
  - save the old values of these numbers: $c_{k,aux} := c_k$, for all $0 \leq k \leq 2$;
  - compute the new c_0 by $c_0 := c_{1,aux}[c_{0,aux}]$;
  - compute the new c_1 by $c_1 := c_{0,aux}[c_{1,aux}]$;
  - compute the new c_2 by $c_2 := c_{i,aux}[c_{2,aux}]$, where i is randomly chosen from $\{0,1\}$.

The three sequences thus generated are α, consisting of c_0's, β, consisting of c_1's, and γ, consisting of c_2's. Unfortunately, as these sequences are based on the same idea discussed above, they have quite short periods as the chart in Fig. 2 shows (the test was repeated 10^5 times with $n = r = 16$ and the chart in Fig. 2 illustrates the average number of repetitions).

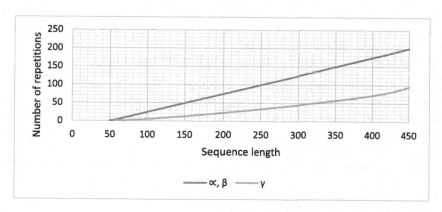

Fig. 2. Repetitions in the sequences α, β, and γ

3   OK-equivalence and PDAF-based NLFSR Sequences

We are interested to know what properties should an r-ary n-digit number x satisfy such that, given x and $x[y]$ one can uniquely extract y. Proposition 1(4) shows that y might not be unique if $n < r$, and Remark 1 shows the same for $n \geq r$. However, we have the following result.

Proposition 2. *Let x be an r-ary n-digit number. If $n = r$ and x consists of pairwise distinct r-ary digits, then $x[y] = x[y']$ if and only if $y = y'$.*

Proof. Assume that $n = r$ and x consists of pairwise distinct r-ary digits. Clearly, if $y = y'$ then $x[y] = x[y']$.

Conversely, the relation $x[y] = x[y']$ leads to $x[y]_i = x[y']_i$, for all $0 \leq i < n$. That is,

$$x_i \oplus_n x_{i \oplus_n y_i} = x_i \oplus_n x_{i \oplus_n y'_i}$$

for all $0 \leq i < n$. This equation leads to $x_{i \oplus_n y_i} = x_{i \oplus_n y'_i}$, for all $0 \leq i < n$. As x consists of distinct digits, it follows that $y_i \equiv y'_i \mod n$, for all $0 \leq i < n$. As y_i and y'_i are n-ary digits, it follows that $y_i = y'_i$, for all $0 \leq i < n$. Therefore, $y = y'$. $\qquad\qquad\square$

Remark 3. The requirement $n = r$ in Proposition 2 is crucial for the conclusion of the Proposition. Indeed, take for instance $r = 16$, $n = 8$, $y_0 = 7$, $y'_0 = 15$, and $y_i = y'_i$, for all $1 \leq i < 8$. Then,

$$x[y]_0 = x_0 \oplus_{16} x_{0 \oplus_8 y_0} = x_0 \oplus_{16} x_7$$

and

$$x[y']_0 = x_0 \oplus_{16} x_{0 \oplus_8 y'_0} = x_0 \oplus_{16} x_{0 \oplus_8 15} = x_0 \oplus_{16} x_7$$

which show that $x[y] = x[y']$, although $y \neq y'$.

In what follows assume that $MakeUnique$ is a deterministic algorithm that, on an input $x \in \mathbb{Z}_n^n$, outputs an n-ary n-digit number x^* whose digits are pairwise distinct. There are many ways to design such an algorithm. For our purposes is not important to know how such an algorithm works; that is, we may assume that $MakeUnique$ is publicly known.

Define now five sequences of n-ary n-digit numbers as follows:

– choose at random five r-ary n-digit numbers c_0, c_1, c_2, c_3, and c_4;
– compute new values for c_0, c_1, c_2, c_3, and c_4 as follows:
   • save the old values of these numbers: $c_{k,aux} := c_k$, for all $0 \leq k \leq 4$;
   • compute the new c_0 by $c_0 := c_{1,aux}[c_{0,aux}] \oplus c_{3,aux}$;
   • compute the new c_1 by $c_1 := c_{0,aux}[c_{1,aux}] \oplus c_{4,aux}$;
   • compute the new c_2 by $c_2 := c_{i,aux}[c_{2,aux}]$, where i is randomly chosen from $\{0, 1\}$;
   • compute the new c_3 by $c_3 := Rev(c_{3,aux})[c_{4,aux}]$;
   • compute the new c_4 by $c_4 := Rev(c_{4,aux})$,
   where Rev is the reverse function which mirrors the number.

Consider now the same sequences α, β, and γ as defined in Remark 2. We have computed $25 \cdot 10^6$ elements in each of these sequences, and no repetitions were encountered (the test was repeated 10^5 times). Therefore, these sequences have much better behavior than those in Remark 2.

Consider now γ^* as being the sequence obtained from γ by replacing each element x of it by x^* ($x^* = MakeUnique(x)$). In this case, our tests (for $n = r = 16$) show sporadic repetitions in γ^* after the first $2.5 \cdot 10^5$ elements (see the chart in Fig. 3).

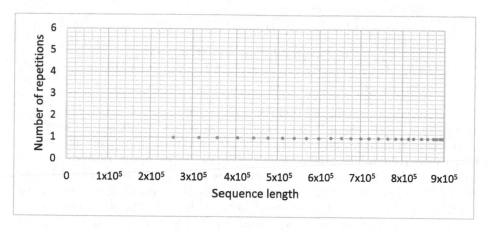

Fig. 3. Repetitions in the sequence γ^*

If c_4 is computed in a different way at every $2.5 \cdot 10^5$th iteration, namely

– $c_4 := a[c_{4,aux}]$, where a is randomly chosen,

then γ^* has a similar behavior to α, β, and γ.

These sequences will be used in the next section in order to propose a new RFID authentication protocol.

4   The Protocol

The RFID authentication protocol we propose in this section is only slightly changed from the original one in [7]. However, the changes are vital for its security. The protocol is based on the sequences described in the above section. As the only operations performed by tags are base r additions for some radix r, the protocol can be regarded as a lightweight or even a ultra-lightweight protocol.

The protocol includes three parties: a reader R, a tag T, and a back-end server S equipped with a database which maintains information about tags. We assume that the channel between the reader and the back-end server is secure, while the one between the reader and the tag is insecure.

The initialization phase, which is to be described below, sets the basic elements needed for the protocol to be run.

Protocol initialization

1. An integer $r \geq 2$ and a hash function are chosen and made public;

2. A private key K_R of some symmetric cryptosystem (such as AES) is chosen uniformly at random and securely distributed to the reader R;
3. For each tag T, the following steps are performed:
    (a) sets $n = r$;
    (b) seven values $K_{ST}, c_0, c_1, c_2, c_3, c_4, LT \in \mathbb{Z}_r^n$ are chosen independent and uniformly at random;
    (c) the value $P(T) = h(\{ID(T)\}_{K_R} \| K_{ST})$ is computed ("$\|$" denotes concatenation);
    (d) $P(T), K_{ST}, c_0, c_1, c_2, c_3, c_4, LT$ are stored in the tag T;
    (e) $P(T), \{ID(T)\}_{K_R}, K_{ST}, c_0, c_1, c_3, c_4, LT, c_{4,prev}$ are stored in the server's data base, where $c_{4,prev} = c_4$.

A pictorial view on the distribution of these parameters is provided in Fig. 4, and a short description of them is in order. The server cannot see the identities of the tags it manages because the they are encrypted by the key K_R known only to the reader. The random numbers c_0, c_1, c_2, c_3, c_4 act as seeds for four sequences α, β, γ, and γ^*, as in the previous section. The parameter LT (*last transaction*) is used to count the numbers of queries executed on the tag by readers, and to synchronize the database and the tag. The parameter $c_{4.prev}$ stores the previous value of c_4 and it is used by the server when the tag was not able to authenticate it at the previous query. More precisely, the search in the database uses first c_4. If the search fails for all database records, then it starts again with $c_{4,prev}$. If it succeeds now, the server learns that during the previous query the tag was not able to authenticate it.

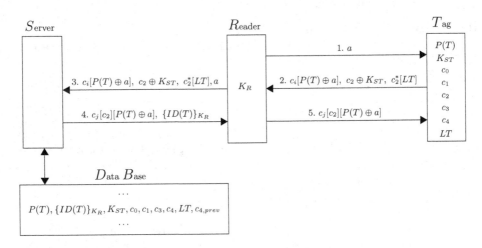

Fig. 4. The protocol

Protocol description

1. $R \longrightarrow T$: The reader R chooses uniformly at random $a \in \mathbb{Z}_r^n$ and sends it to the tag T;

2. $T \longrightarrow R$: The tag T chooses uniformly at random a bit $i \in \{0, 1\}$, and then computes and sends

$$c_i[P(T) \oplus a], \ c_2 \oplus K_{ST}, \ c_2^*[LT]$$

to the reader R. Finally, the tag increments LT by 1 and updates c_0, c_1, c_2, c_3, and c_4 as follows:
- $c_{k,aux} := c_k$, for all $0 \le k \le 4$;
- $c_0 := c_{1,aux}[c_{0,aux}] \oplus c_{3,aux}$;
- $c_1 := c_{0,aux}[c_{1,aux}] \oplus c_{4,aux}$;
- $c_2 := c_{j,aux}[c_{2,aux}]$, where j is the binary complement of i;
- $c_3 := Rev(c_{3,aux})[c_{4,aux}]$;
- $c_4 := Rev(c_{4,aux})$;
3. $R \longrightarrow S$:   The reader forwards the received message together with the random a to the server;
4. $S \longrightarrow R$: On receipt of the reader's message which we will further denote as "x, y, z, a", the server searches the database to find the record row associated to the tag. For each record row

$$P(T'), \{ID(T')\}_{K_R}, K_{ST'}, c_0', c_1', c_3', c_4', LT', c_{4,prev}'$$

of the data base, the server does the following:
  (a) extracts c_2 from y (by using $K_{ST'}$) and then obtains LT from z;
  (b) if $LT < LT'$ then it goes to the next record row;
  (c) if $LT \ge LT'$ then
      i. temporarily updates c_0', c_1', c_3', c_4', by $(LT - LT')$ times, in the same way as the tag did. Let $c_0'', c_1'', c_3'', c_4''$ be the results;
      ii. computes $c_0''[P(T') \oplus a]$ and $c_1''[P(T') \oplus a]$, and checks if either of them equals x. If false, then it proceeds to the next record row; otherwise, the server draws the conclusion that this is the record row corresponding to the tag which was queried by the reader (more specifically, $T' = T$); it also obtains the bit i. Afterwards, it replaces LT' by LT, (c_0', c_1', c_3', c_4') by $(c_0'', c_1'', c_3'', c_4'')$, and sends

$$c_j'[c_2][P(T') \oplus a], \{ID(T')\}_{K_R}$$

to the reader (j is the binary complement of i). Then, the update process is repeated one more time for c_0', c_1', c_3', c_4', and LT' is incremented by one. Finally, the servers does:
        - $c_{4,prev}' := c_4'$;
        - $c_4' := a[c_4']$;
  (d) if all record rows were searched and the property from the item above failed for all of them, then it restarts the search, this time using c_{4_prev}' instead of c_4'. If the process fails again then the server signals an error message to the reader;

5. $R \longrightarrow T$:   When the reader receives the message, it extracts the tag's identity from $\{ID(T')\}_{K_R}$, and forwards

$$c_j[c_2][P(T') \oplus a]$$

to the tag;

6. On receipt of the reader's message, the tag computes $c_2[P(T) \oplus a]$ by using its own memory-stored a, c_2, and $P(T)$, and compares it with the received message (recall that the tag updated c_2 after answering to the reader). If they are not equal, an error message is signaled; otherwise, the authentication succeeds and the tag performs the same update of c_4 by a as the server did (without storing the previous c_4).

The first five steps of the protocol described above are pictorially represented in Fig. 4.

Remark 4. A few remarks about the protocol correctness and efficiency are in order.

1. The extraction of a unique LT from $c_2^*[LT]$, when c_2 is known (step (4) in the protocol description), is based on Proposition 2 (remark that $n = r$).
2. The term $c_2 \oplus K_{ST}$ in the steps (2) and (3) hides c_2 which is needed to compute LT at the server side (from $c_2^*[LT]$). If c_2 is random, then $c_2 \oplus K_{ST}$ is random too (although K_{ST} is fixed for the tag).
3. The only operations performed by the tag are base r additions and comparisons, which can efficiently be implemented in the tag's logic.

Remark 5. Our protocol was designed for the case $n = r$. It can be modified to work for the case "$n > r$" in several variants. For instance, the algorithm $MakeUnique$ could be changed such that, on the input c_2 it outputs $c_2^* \in \mathbb{Z}_r^r$ with pairwise distinct r-ary digits. Moreover, in such a case, LT should be in $\mathbb{Z}_r^r$.

Another option to deal with the case "$n > r$" would be to choose $n = \ell r$ for some $\ell > 1$. Then, decompose c_2 and LT into ℓ pieces of size r, namely $c_1 = c_{21} \cdots c_{2\ell}$ and $LT = LT_1 \cdots LT_\ell$ respectively, and compute $c_2^*[LT]$ by

$$c_2^*[LT] = c_{21}^*[LT_1] \cdots c_{2\ell}^*[LT_\ell],$$

where $c_{2i}^* = MakeUnique(c_{2i})$, for all i.

Remark 6. The protocol we proposed can be run even if the tag did not authenticate the server (reader) at the previous session. However, it is customary to assume that some upper bound t on the number of successive incomplete sessions is necessary to impose. This upper bound is also necessary to avoid the overflow of the parameter LT. If the upper bound t is exceeded, the tag may signal an error.

5   Correctness, Security, and Privacy Analysis of the Protocol

The analysis of a RFID protocol usually takes into consideration three aspects: correctness (no false negatives), security (no false positives), and privacy [10,17,31].

Correctness. Following [10], a RFID authentication protocol is correct if, executing it honestly, the identification of a legitimate tag only fails with negligible probability.

A simple inspection of the protocol, in the view of Remark 4, shows that false negatives are not possible (in the absence of an adversary).

Security is the property that an illegitimate tag is not authenticated by the server, except for a negligible probability.

Assume that a tag T (legitimate or illegitimate) answers to some query a by

$$c_i[P(T) \oplus a'], \ c_2 \oplus K_{ST}, \ c_2^*[LT]$$

and the reader sends

$$c_i[P(T) \oplus a'], \ c_2 \oplus K_{ST}, \ c_2^*[LT], \ a$$

to the server.

According to the protocol description, the server looks in its database and, for each tag T' checks the equality

$$c_b'[P(T') \oplus a] = c_i[P(T) \oplus a']$$

for some bit b (see the step 4(c) in the protocol description). If this equality holds, the server identifies the tag T as being the tag T' (although T' might not be T, but the server does not know this).

As $c_i[P(T) \oplus a']$ and $P(T') \oplus a$ are fixed given values for the server, the problem is to estimate the probability of c_b' to fulfill the equality above. More generally, given two random numbers $y, v \in \mathbb{Z}_r^n$, we are interested in estimating the probability of finding x such that $x[y] = v$. Or, in other words, we are interested to estimate the maximum number of solutions in x to the equation $x[y] = v$. This equation is equivalent to the system

$$
\begin{cases}
x_1 \oplus_r x_{1 \oplus_r y_1} = v_1 \\
\cdots \\
x_n \oplus_r x_{n \oplus_r y_n} = v_n
\end{cases}
\tag{1}
$$

The first remark is that if $i \oplus_r y_i = j$ and $j \oplus_r y_j = i$, for distinct indexes i and j, then:

1. if $v_i \not\equiv v_j \mod r$, then the system (1) does not have solutions;
2. if $v_i \equiv v_j \mod r$, then any solution to x_i leads to at most one solution to x_j (and vice versa).

(if i and j are as above, we will say that the ith and jth equations are *paired*).

Our second remark is that a variable x_i for one of the system's equations is substituted into another equation, the resulting equation still has at most two variables.

These two remarks leads to the conclusion that the worst case regarding the number of solutions to the system (1) is that when the variables are paired two by two as above. In such a case the maximum number of solutions to the system is upper bounded by $r^{n/2}$ (the variables are paired two by two and for each pair, a solution to one of the pair components leads to at most a solution to the other pair component).

Therefore, the probability of getting a solution to the equation $x[y] = v$ is at most

$$\frac{r^{n/2}}{r^n} = \frac{1}{r^{n/2}}$$

For large n, this is negligible.

Privacy. The protocol we have proposed is lightweight and, therefore, it is improper to use a privacy model as the one in [10,17] which is suitable for protocols based on pseudo-random functions or random oracles. However, we have identified a protocol in [17] which can be considered as a generalization of our protocol and allows us to reason about the privacy of our protocol.

In [17], the following protocol is considered, based on two random functions $F : \{0,1\}^{\alpha+k+1} \to \{0,1\}^k$ and $G : \{0,1\}^k \to \{0,1\}^k$

1. the initial state of the tag is set to a random k-bit string K_0;
2. the protocol rules are:
    (a) the reader picks a random α-bit string a and sends it to the tag;
    (b) the tag in state K sends the value $c = F(0, K, a)$, stores $d' = F(1, K, a)$ in its temporary memory, and refreshes its state K to $G(K)$;
    (c) the reader searches its database for a pair (T', K') with the property $c = F(0, G(K')^i, a)$ for some $i < t$. If it finds such a pair then it sends $d = F(1, G(K'), a)$ to the tag, and updates K' by $G(K')^i$;
    (d) the tag checks $d = d'$.

It is shown in [17] that this protocol is narrow-destructive private in the random oracle model, if k and t are polynomially bounded (in the security parameter) and 2^{-k} is negligible (the reader is referred to [17,31] for privacy models for RFID protocols; the limited space does not allow us to recall them here).

Our protocol follows the same line as the protocol above. The internal state of the tag is the vector

$$P(T), K_{ST}, c_0, c_1, c_2, c_3, c_4, LT$$

The function F is the one which gives the answer to the reader's query (see step 2 in the protocol), while G is the function used by the tag and the server to update the internal state. The tag performs one more update of its state when it authenticates the reader but this does not make much difference between our protocol and the one described above. We have not included an upper bound on the number of incomplete sessions, but this can be added as mentioned in Remark 6. Therefore, we may think that our protocol is an instance of the protocol described above and, as a conclusion, it may be thought of as a lightweight candidate to the narrow-destructive private class of mutual authentication RFID protocols.

The protocol does not achieve forward security. If a tag is corrupted and the adversary gets the internal state of the tag, then the adversary can impersonate the tag if it does not miss any complete session (a session is complete if the tag authenticates the server and, in such a case, it randomizes its state by the nonce received from the reader). However, if the adversary misses some complete session, then he can impersonate the tag with negligible probability. This property is common to many other authentication protocols such as [13,15]. In fact, reaching forward security without public key cryptography is an open problem, already mentioned in [31].

6   Conclusions

We have revisited the lightweight authentication protocol for RFID systems in [7] and we have proposed an improved one. The improvement takes mainly into consideration the randomnesses of the NLFSR sequences used in the protocol. Moreover, formal analysis of its security is provided. As with respect to privacy, it is argued that the protocol can be viewed as an instance of a narrow-destructive private protocol proposed in [17].

References

1. Avoine, G., Oechslin, P.: A scalable and provably secure hash-based RFID protocol. In: Third IEEE International Conference on Pervasive Computing and Communications Workshops, pp. 110–114, March 2005
2. Batina, L., Guajardo, J., Kerins, T., Mentens, N., Tuyls, P., Verbauwhede, I.: An elliptic curve processor suitable for RFID-tags (2006)
3. Batina, L., Guajardo, J., Kerins, T., Mentens, N., Tuyls, P., Verbauwhede, I.: Public-key cryptography for RFID-tags. In: Proceedings of the Fifth IEEE International Conference on Pervasive Computing and Communications Workshops, pp. 217–222. IEEE Computer Society, Washington, DC, USA (2007)
4. Burmester, M., de Medeiros, B.: The security of EPC Gen2 compliant RFID protocols. In: Bellovin, S.M., Gennaro, R., Keromytis, A.D., Yung, M. (eds.) ACNS 2008. LNCS, vol. 5037, pp. 490–506. Springer, Heidelberg (2008)
5. Chien, H.-Y., Huang, C.-W.: Security of ultra-lightweight RFID authentication protocols and its improvements. SIGOPS Oper. Syst. Rev. **41**(4), 83–86 (2007)
6. Chien, H.-Y., Huang, C.-W.: A lightweight authentication protocol for low-cost RFID. J. Signal Process. Syst. **59**(1), 95–102 (2010)
7. Ţiplea, F.L.: A lightweight authentication protocol for RFID. In: Kotulski, Z., Ksiopolski, B., Mazur, K. (eds.) CSS 2014. CCIS, vol. 448, pp. 110–121. Springer, Heidelberg (2014)
8. Feldhofer, M., Dominikus, S., Wolkerstorfer, J.: Strong authentication for RFID systems using the AES algorithm. In: Joye, M., Quisquater, J.-J. (eds.) CHES 2004. LNCS, vol. 3156, pp. 357–370. Springer, Heidelberg (2004)
9. Henrici, D., Muller, P.: Hash-based enhancement of location privacy for radio-frequency identification devices using varying identifiers. In: Proceedings of the Second IEEE Annual Conference on Pervasive Computing and Communications Workshops, pp. 149–153, March 2004

10. Hermans, J., Peeters, R., Preneel, B.: Proper RFID privacy: model and protocols. IEEE Trans. Mobile Comput. **13**(12), 2888–2902 (2014)

11. Juels, A.: Minimalist cryptography for low-cost RFID tags (Extended Abstract). In: Blundo, C., Cimato, S. (eds.) SCN 2004. LNCS, vol. 3352, pp. 149–164. Springer, Heidelberg (2005)

12. Juels, A., Weis, S.A.: Authenticating pervasive devices with human protocols. In: Shoup, V. (ed.) CRYPTO 2005. LNCS, vol. 3621, pp. 293–308. Springer, Heidelberg (2005)

13. Kardaş, S., Çelik, S., Arslan, A., Levi, A.: An efficient and private RFID authentication protocol supporting ownership transfer. In: Avoine, G., Kara, O. (eds.) LightSec 2013. LNCS, vol. 8162, pp. 130–141. Springer, Heidelberg (2013)

14. Lee, Y.K., Sakiyama, K., Batina, L., Verbauwhede, I.: Elliptic-curve-based security processor for RFID. IEEE Trans. Comput. **57**(11), 1514–1527 (2008)

15. Lim, C.H., Kwon, T.: Strong and robust RFID authentication enabling perfect ownership transfer. In: Ning, P., Qing, S., Li, N. (eds.) ICICS 2006. LNCS, vol. 4307, pp. 1–20. Springer, Heidelberg (2006)

16. Ohkubo, M., Suzuki, K., Kinoshita, S.: Cryptographic approach to "privacy-friendly" tags. In: In RFID Privacy Workshop (2003)

17. Paise, R.I., Vaudenay, S.: Mutual authentication in RFID: security and privacy. In: Proceedings of the 2008 ACM Symposium on Information, Computer and Communications Security, ASIACCS 2008, pp. 292–299. ACM, New York, NY, USA (2008)

18. Pantelić, G., Bojanić, S., Tomašević, V.: Authentication protocols in RFID systems. In: Zhang, Y., Kitsos, P., (eds.) Security in RFID and Sensor Networks, pp. 99–120. Auerbach Publications, April 2009

19. Peris-Lopez, P., Hernandez-Castro, J.C., Estevez-Tapiador, J.M., Ribagorda, A.: EMAP: an efficient mutual-authentication protocol for low-cost RFID tags. In: Meersman, R., Tari, Z., Herrero, P. (eds.) On the Move to Meaningful Internet Systems 2006: OTM 2006 Workshops. LNCS, vol. 4277, pp. 352–361. Springer, Heidelberg (2006)

20. Peris-Lopez, P., Hernandez-Castro, J.C., Estevez-Tapiador, J.M., Ribagorda, A.: M^2AP: A minimalist mutual-authentication protocol for low-cost RFID tags. In: Ma, J., Jin, H., Yang, L.T., Tsai, J.J.-P. (eds.) UIC 2006. LNCS, vol. 4159, pp. 912–923. Springer, Heidelberg (2006)

21. Peris-Lopez, P., Hernandez-Castro, J.C., Tapiador, J.M.E., Ribagorda, A.: Advances in ultralightweight cryptography for low-cost RFID tags: gossamer protocol. In: Chung, K.-I., Sohn, K., Yung, M. (eds.) WISA 2008. LNCS, vol. 5379, pp. 56–68. Springer, Heidelberg (2009)

22. Peris-Lopez, P., Hernandez-Castro, J.C., Estevez-Tapiador, J.M., Ribagorda, A.: Lightweight cryptography for low-cost RFID tags. In: Zhang, Y., Kitsos, P., (eds.) Security in RFID and Sensor Networks, pp. 121–150. Auerbach Publications, April 2009

23. Piramuthu, S.: Protocols for RFID tag/reader authentication. Decis. Support Syst. **43**(3), 897–914 (2007)

24. Relevant Security Corp., Denver, Colorado, USA. Real Privacy Management^{TM} (RPM). Reference Guide Version 3.1 (2009)

25. Relevant Security Corp., Denver, Colorado, USA. Real Privacy Management^{TM} (RPM). Cryptographic Description Version 3.2 (2010)

26. Sherman, A.: An initial assessment of the 2factor authentication and key-management system, May 2005

27. Song, B., Mitchell, C.J.: RFID authentication protocol for low-cost tags. In: Proceedings of the First ACM Conference on Wireless Network Security, pp. 140–147. ACM, New York (2008)
28. Tanaka, H.: Security-function integrated simple cipher communication system. In: Proceedings of the 2006 Symposium on Cryptography and Information Security (2006)
29. Tanaka, H.: Generation of cryptographic random sequences and its applications to secure enchipering. In: Proceedings of the 2007 Symposium on Cryptography and Information Security (2007)
30. Vajda, I., Buttyn, L.: Lightweight authentication protocols for low-cost RFID tags. In: In Second Workshop on Security in Ubiquitous Computing Ubicomp 2003 (2003)
31. Vaudenay, S.: On privacy models for RFID. In: Kurosawa, K. (ed.) ASIACRYPT 2007. LNCS, vol. 4833, pp. 68–87. Springer, Heidelberg (2007)
32. Weis, S.A., Sarma, S.E., Rivest, R.L., Engels, D.W.: Security and privacy aspects of low-cost radio frequency identification systems. In: Hutter, D., Müller, G., Stephan, W., Ullmann, M. (eds.) Security in Pervasive Computing. LNCS, vol. 2802, pp. 201–212. Springer, Heidelberg (2004)

Spam Filtering Using Automated Classifying Services over a Cloud Computing Infrastructure

Alecsandru Pătraşcu$^{(\boxtimes)}$, Ion Bica, and Victor Valeriu Patriciu

Computer Science Department, Military Technical Academy, Bucharest, Romania
alecsandru.patrascu@gmail.com, ibica@mta.ro, victorpatriciu@yahoo.com

Abstract. Together with the increase in size of Internet technologies and coped with the need for instant communication between people, unsolicited messages or spam messages represent a serious problem for most system administrators and users. This problem permits the usage of various technologies and techniques in order to solve it and filter volumes of thousands of email messages per day.

In this article we present a new solution for spam detection and classification, based on a Cloud supported infrastructure of a service oriented architecture. Our implementation is able to scan and classify a large stream of emails. We also prove that the architecture is scalable across multiple datacenter nodes and it is able to handle a continuous flux of emails, keeping users configuration a top priority.

Keywords: Spam analysis · Cloud computing · Bayesian filtering

1 Introduction

Currently any mail server for a large enough domain is constantly bombarded with spam messages. This hinders the daily activities and congests the traffic on the server and in relatively short time it can lead to a total paralysis of its stored information and thus will not be accessible.

The current paper has the goal of filtering spam messages so that they cannot reach the users Inbox. In this way the server will become more manageable and less congested. Our application is intended to be used in a distributed environment, which has the advantage of high computing power and thus being able to offer a good performance management system for all mail in high traffic conditions. It will continuously communicate with a mail server for a large domain, will interact with it, will process incoming messages and save the results into a local database. Users can also interact with the system and provide feedback constantly, depending on the settings they want. The system should take account of these settings in order to increase its efficiency and maintain the number of false alerts to the minimum.

The spammer the one who sends spam - needs a list of email addresses to send messages. These can be obtained legally or illegally. It is considered that an address is obtained illegally when the spammer uses various search engines to find

© Springer International Publishing Switzerland 2015
I. Bica et al. (Eds.): SECITC 2015, LNCS 9522, pp. 226–241, 2015.
DOI: 10.1007/978-3-319-27179-8_16

valid addresses on the Internet, or when using special programs. The spammer uses different combinations of the previous two to get possible addresses.

What is the purpose of searching these email addresses? The spammer, who may be a normal or legal person, sends emails advertising, commercial or pornographic content to these addresses in their own interest, in return for money or for the benefit of another person, to determine the recipient to purchase various products or services.

In this way, before the adoption of anti-spam laws, there were accounted by different Internet Service Providers (ISPs) around 30 billion spam messages a day [1]. Detecting spam is still a very difficult challenge, due to the dynamic nature of spam. Over time, any anti-spam filter is ineffective in blocking the new techniques of sending spam.

In this paper we propose a novel method of spam detection focused on scalability through a service oriented architecture. The paper is structured as follows. Section 2 of this paper presents other research related to the contributions of this paper and general antispam detection methods. Section 3 describes the Bayes Filters and the other algorithms used in this paper. The main contribution of this paper is presented in Sect. 4 which contains the description of the antispam architecture and the used cloud infrastructure. Section 5 presents test cases and experimental results used to validate this model and demonstrate its performance while Sect. 6 presents the conclusions and outlines the areas for further research.

2   Related Work

To distinguish a legitimate email from a spam message is a hard job. It is very difficult to realize if a message is authentic or not just by looking at the sender and subject fields. But why does it matter if a message is authentic or not? Because if the message is authentic, we can contact the company involved and ask to be removed from the email lists, or if they didn't want, to add their address in order to filter our emails so that messages will arrive in the spam folder and not in the inbox, and even complain to consumer protection. However, if spammers hide the origin of the message, or forge the sender address by sending the email through a compromised server, filters used to classify the message header will also be inefficient and will not be able to forward a complaint against them. So in order to effectively combat this kind of messages, a series of filters must be created in order to detect such messages using other criteria than the email address. To determine whether a message is authentic, the message header must be verified. Although many parts of the header can be forged, the field that shows the last mail server that the message went through to reach the recipient is genuine.

On the market are a lot of software solutions for fighting spam messages such as SpamAssassin, SpamCop or K9. There are also numerous research projects focusing on this subject. In the article [2] the authors underline in their study about spam, the need for a reliable solution to fight this threat. They also used a

Bayesian filtering algorithm, but implemented on a single monolithic machine in a naive way. They also focus on their research on measuring different performance parameters of such algorithms and comparisons with keyword pattern spam analysis tools.

Another related publication is [3] which studies the impact to the enterprise levels of such anti-spam solutions in large ESP's (Email Service Providers). They analyze different approaches to scanning email that arrive in each user inbox. One is pushing the scan to the user's computer and the other one is implementing centralized spam filtering. Their paper describes the issues encountered if a large-scale spam filtering implementation on a fixed budget is needed.

Kang et al. [4] also focus on statistical based anti-spam analysis. They also studied the problem of scaling to large enterprise-level of mail servers. Their implementation and observations reflect the problem of using a dictionary based look-ups and how these problems can be avoided in order to increase the total speed of the system. Their solution was to use an approximation method, but in our opinion, although they obtained a good speed-up for the look-up process, the data loss in this method can be vital to understanding the spam messages, especially the new, not previously analyzed before.

Beow et al. talk in [5] about the opportunity of using Cloud computing technologies in spam filtering. They present how using regular software applications designed for regular networks are a bad idea in Cloud and they present a high level view of a Cloud based anti-spam framework. Salah et al. take this matter to a different level in their work [6] and present a Cloud based security overlay network that can provide antispam services.

In this direction, we cannot exclude also in-cloud antispam solutions available on the market, such as those from Symantec Hosted Service [7] and Zscaler [8], combine multiple commercial AV and antispam engines, resulting in a multi layered defense to protect the client from email-based attacks. They detect embedded suspicious URLs in emails by the "following link" capability and block Web link emails when necessary.

On the hardware devices area, we find solution providers such as Fortinet with the FortiGuard Antispam Service [9], which uses both a sender IP reputation database and a spam signature database, along with sophisticated spam filtering tools on Fortinet appliances and agents, to detect and block a wide range of spam messages. An alternative is offered by Check Point with their Anti-Spam and Email Security Software Blade [10], which uses the same basic pattern matching as FortiGuard, and provides highly accurate anti-spam coverage and defends organizations from a wide variety of virus and malware threats delivered within email.

Our approach is a hybrid one, using spam signatures for known spam messages and using automatic checking with probabilities if a certain message is not found in the signature database. We explain next how the internal mechanism of our approach work.

3   Bayes Filters for Spam Detection

The filtering system used in the application is based on Bayesian filters. Over time it has been proven that they have a very good detection rate and can adapt easily to different mechanisms invented by spammers. The implemented filter is based on a calculation of conditional probabilities, depending on the frequency of occurrence of a word, both in a spam context and in a non-spam one.

Bayes theorem represents a first mean to determine the probability of an event A_i (the component of a partition), in the situation in which you know that it's appearance is influenced by the happening of another independent event B. The formula of this theorem is:

$$Pr(A_i|B) = \frac{Pr(B|A_i) \times Pr(A_i)}{\sum\limits_{j=1}^{k} Pr(B|A_j) \times Pr(A_j)}$$

The A_i events are independent and the a priori probabilities $Pr(B|A_i)$ are estimated [11]. Furthermore, these factors cannot remain static, meaning that at certain time intervals the a priori probability must be updated. This computation can be made in several modes, but in the scope of email filtering we will use block mode processing, with some fixed points: the a priori probability is equal to the greatest a posteriori probability, the a priori probability is equal to the a posteriori probabilities average and the a priori probability can be equal to the a posteriori probability.

When new email arrives, it is divided into tokens, and the most "interesting" words are used to calculate the probability of being spam. By interesting for a token, we understand the difference between the mean probability of being spam and a neutral average of 0.5. In this calculation we take into account the existing values in the database. If a token is found, it is given a probability of 0.4 because we assume, for beginning, that it is a non-spam word. We consider a mail spam if we get a higher probability than 0.9.

For greater efficiency, we used several schemas in order to split into tokens, based on content analysis. First, there is a basic tokenizer, which extracts the tokens in a raw way. It understands HTML elements, as well as Base64 encoding type. It's permitted the use of a small set of characters '.', ',', '+', '−', within a token, the rest being seen as separator characters. Tokens made only from numbers are ignored, while tokens formed from numbers and punctuation are not ignored, as they can hold valuable information, such as IP addresses. For example, the token "23" is ignored, while the token containing the IP address "23.81.154.68" is not. To keep a database as compact and as small in size and to keep the number of false positives to a minimum, we converted each letter of each token to lower case.

Also, we did not take into account tokens that have length 1 or 2, because we noticed that they load unnecessarily the database and effective analysis and tokens formed exclusively of characters '.', ',', '+', '−' were ignored.

One of the most important decisions taken in order to improve the performance of the filter was ignoring HTML tags. We decided to do this, because after a series of tests, we concluded that the HTML tags do not offer any valuable information in our decision taking process. Firstly, the filter should generate as few false positives as possible. After analyzing the data used in the database, we noticed that tokens which were more likely to be considered as spam, were HTML tags and attributes. After implementing this solution we observed a reduction in false positives. The list of the most interesting terms has become more accurate, because now contains conclusive tokens, unlike HTML tags and attributes, hex color codes, etc.

In the intermediate tests we noticed, when analyzing whether an email is or not spam, a predilection for the "select" requests in the database. To make a more rapid implementation, but also to improve performance of the module connected to the database, we optimized the database by putting indexes on columns frequently required, and by increasing cache space of the Sql Server. Also, whenever we could, we've used a local word cache, implemented as a hash tables for extra speed. The word cache was used only in the first instance, in the process of raw email processing. After this point, the database was used exclusively in order not to affect the overall stored information.

4   Service Based Antispam Architecture

The usage of Cloud Computing technologies in spam analysis in order to better filter email messages is not a new idea. Nevertheless, in our paper we will use our custom Cloud framework, that is fully described in [12], on top of which we built our software modules that are responsible with spam filtering. In Fig. 1 we can see that the top view of a cloud computing framework contains two main layers: a virtualization layer and a management layer.

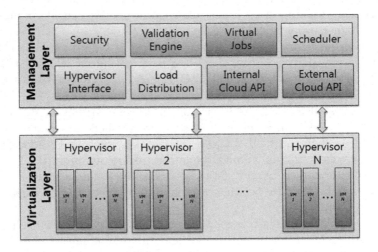

Fig. 1. Cloud Computing framework as base for spam analysis

In the *Virtualization layer* we find the actual platforms/servers that host the virtual machines and have virtualization enabled hardware. In the *Management layer* we find the modules responsible for enabling the entire operations specific to the cloud. These modules are, in order: **Security** (responsible with all security concerns related to the cloud system - intrusion detection and alarming module), **Validation engine** (receives requests to add new jobs to be processed), **Virtual jobs** (creates an abstraction between the data requested by the user and the payload that must be delivered to the cloud system), **Scheduler** (schedules the jobs to the virtualization layer), **Hypervisor interface** (acts like a translation layer that is specific to a virtualization software vendor), **Load distribution** (responsible with horizontal and vertical scaling of the requests received from the scheduler), **Internal cloud API** (intended as a link between the virtualization layer and the cloud system), **External cloud API** (offers a way to the user for interacting with the system).

Our Cloud Computing architecture makes use of the concept of *leases*, in which we can specify the amount of time the job must run, or specify between what hours in a day it is running. To achieve our goal, we created a lease that during the day, when the datacenter is mostly occupied by the users, uses a minimum number of nodes and during the night, when the datacenter is almost entirely free, it automatically scales up to use a maximum number of nodes. In order to store the emails we have also used several nodes from the datacenter so that the entire data will be accessible from the machine RAM.

The application contains five modules which work together, as can be seen in Fig. 2, each having its well defined role. These components are: DataBase Layer, Dummy Email, Message filter, Message analyzer and Processed data backup.

The logic of the application is as follows. First, the module responsible with interaction with the database must be started so that the whole system will have the possibility to connect to the underneath database using this supplementary layer. This is an essential component, and in order for it to work, a database server must be installed on the host machine. Secondly, the registration of the dummy email to different spam generating sites is necessary so that the system will benefit from the accelerated learning. For this module to work, a mail system must be provided on the host machine. The message filtering module is an important component for the system because it can filter each user's message and separate the spam from the non-spam. An email server must exist on the host machine so that this module should work efficiently. The next step is to start the analysis system. This is the critical module from the application because it is responsible for taking the decision that an email message is spam or not, according to its content. It can only work if there is an email system on the host machine. The entire process can be viewed also in Fig. 3.

For testing we used the Apache James mail server. We chose this solution because it is a mature software project, used in industry. Communication with it is made through "Matchers" or "Mailets". They allow users to write their own handlers for emails, such as storing in a database, filtering them, etc. In addition, it is written entirely in Java and fits perfectly on the project specifications.

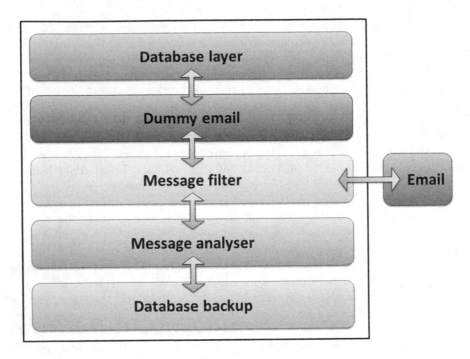

Fig. 2. Components of the antispam solution

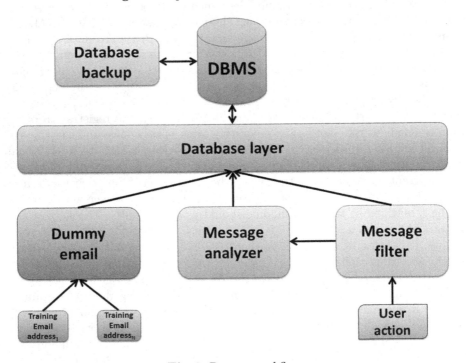

Fig. 3. Process workflow

The current software solution was designed as a combined architecture model. This has benefits both from the advantages of "client-server" model, but also a "distributed-computing" model, because the system is composed from a series of software components running on different machines that communicate over a network to provide a response to user requests as soon as possible. The server component consists from the module that interacts with the database and it provides "services" via a Web Service and also in the module that analyzes messages.

4.1 DataBase Layer

As depicted in Fig. 4, this module doesn't have a graphical user interface by itself, the module being implemented as a Web Service that control actions such as CRUD (Create-Read-Update-Delete) to the database. These operations will be performed by the server component of the module. It receives requests from online connected customers. The module is a client-server component responsible for connecting to and communicating via the database. We chose this way for maintaining transparency between the application and database used, and to increase the security offered [13–15].

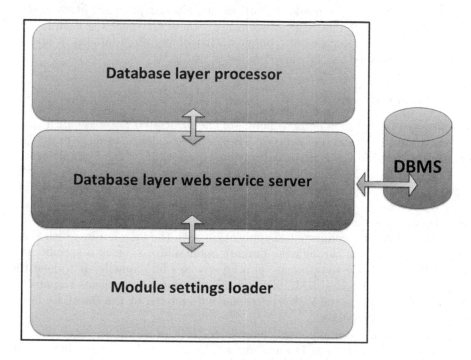

Fig. 4. DataBase layer structure

The database itself contains the following tables: *header_ht* (keeps the hash for the message headers), *body_ht* (keeps the hash for the message body.

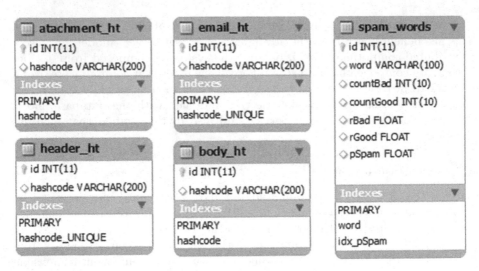

Fig. 5. Database schema

This data, along with the header is used for the filtering process), *atachment_ht* (keeps the hash for the message attachments), *email_ht* (keeps the hash for the entire message) and *spam_word* (contains a list of keywords labeled as spam). The database schema can be viewed in detail in Fig. 5.

4.2 Dummy Email

The purpose of this module is to populate the associated database with spam content to aid the detection process. They will be indexed using a hash algorithm. This module has a graphical user interface itself, which is implemented as a daemon to "listen" changes made by the email application, more exactly receiving emails on a dummy address, indexing and introducing the data into the database used by the entire system. The module will only insert values into the database. Inserts are made through an appropriate Web Service.

This module also connects the application with the location in which spam messages are received through the dummy email address, using a specific daemon. It's also notable the presence of a layer who's functionality is to load the necessary settings from an XML file, and the existence of two clients responsible with the connection to the Web services and sites offered by the DataBase Layer and the messages analyzer.

In order for the dummy email module to work properly, an email account must be created in advance. The account will be used solely for receiving and filtering spam. It is the duty of the application manager to register on different sites that generate spam (such as those with pornographic content, gambling, etc.) to improve the overall performance of the entire system. In addition, this action may be made on multiple email addresses, or even on the actual workstation.

In the latter case, after populating the database with hash values, those can be injected into the database in use.

When receiving an email in this account, the daemon that listens and which is responsible for that task is alerted and begins the process of scanning and analysis. For the entire message a hash is calculated. This hash is then compared with the values existing in the database. If it is found, it means that the message has already been received before and will not proceed further through the process of analysis. If it is not found, it will proceed to the next step, the analysis in which the calculated hash is stored in the database. In addition, the message is sent to the message analyzer which splits the message into a header, body and an attachment and saves all relevant data in the database. It uses the fact that the message received and going to be analyzed is 100 % spam.

4.3   Message Filter

The purpose of this module is to achieve a first filtering of emails from the incoming mail server. It uses the saved data from the previous module. It doesn't have a graphical user interface by itself, and it is implemented as a daemon which "listens" changes made by the email application, namely the receipt of emails on an address associated with each profile, their analysis and filtering.

The filtering module also monitors certain areas on the disk where a user receives a message. When this event has occurred, it starts the process of analysis. First, it calculates the hash of the whole message and compares it with the existing database. If found, the message is automatically classified as spam and a particular action is performed. If it's not found, the message is sent to the analyzer. It will respond with a probability that indicate if the message is spam, and according to the application settings and user settings for each filter module, a particular action is performed or determines that the message is legit.

This step takes into account user intervention. If they decide that they received a particular message which is spam or offensive in any way, this module is responsible for capturing these requests. The message will be automatically sent to the message analyzer and analysis result is stored in the database.

4.4   Message Analyzer

The purpose of this module is to analyze incoming messages and depending on the operation required, to achieve effective filtering or analysis of the message. This module can be seen in a graphical way in Fig. 6.

The module also performs the calculation to determine if an incoming message is spam or not. To this end, according to data received and from the existing data in the database, a probability is computed based on it. It can be noticed the existence of a Web Service responsible for receiving messages. They may come from the module or from the dummy email filtering module. In the case of message filtering, this message can be chosen by the user, in which case the analysis result will be stored in the database, along with other user settings. This Web Service has triple use, depending on how it is invoked.

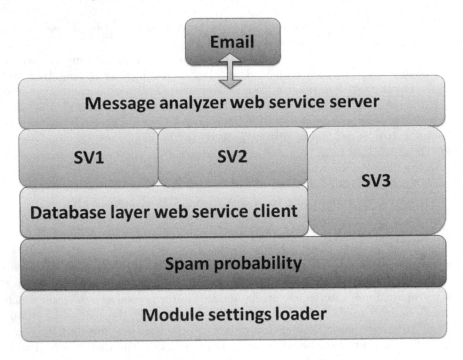

Fig. 6. Structure of the message analyzer

The sub modules SV1, SV2 and SV3 represent the services responsible with scanning and analysis of a certain part from the message. **SV1** will be responsible with the analysis of the header of an email. According to the addresses found, it is determined whether they are or aren't authentic. **SV2** will be responsible for analyzing the actual content of the message. Before analysis, the message's hash is compared with the existing ones in the spam database. If we detect a Base64 encoding, the message is automatically decoded and then analyzed. If the analyzer finds keywords that can be spam (such as words with obscene meaning, use of pure colors, the replacement of A with 4, etc.), the result is stored in the corresponding database table, respectively spam_words and body_ht. In case of body_ht, the content will be encoded in Base64 and then stored in the database. Saving words will be made in clear-text. **SV3** will be responsible for analysis of email attachments, if any. Before analysis, the attachment's hash is compared with the existing ones in the spam database. If it's not found there, it moves to the actual scanning. If we detect a Base64 encoding, the attachment is automatically decoded and then analyzed. If a multi-level archive is detected, it will be analyzed layer by layer. Detecting a banned file (e.g. executable files with multiple extension), leads to cataloging as spam and the analysis results are saved in the corresponding database table.

Each of the three sub modules is easily scalable. Each SV is composed from a "MASTER" processes and several "SLAVE" processes. Master process will achieve load-balancing among all slave processes to prevent network congestion or the use of only one process while others sit idle.

To this end, we used a technology similar to JavaSpaces, called SqlSpaces [16–18]. The solution chosen is an implementation of the concept of "Tuple Space", but provides as a back-end a database. The idea is to have a client-server communication performed exclusively by tuples. Customers can write and read tuples from the server without even knowing about the existence of other clients. Tuples search mechanism is performed by making templates that are then interpreted as wildcards.

In parallel with the analysis of spam, the SqlSpaces server is started. It creates a common area for all customers who will participate in the analysis. When the analyzer receives a message to process, regardless of operating mode, it splits the message in the three component parts and from each creates a "job" that is injected into the common area. Workers of a certain kind, which are also connected to the area, listen for specific jobs and when it appears, they are processed and the result is also put on the common area. The analyzer detects the presence of responses for injected jobs, downloads and processes them.

4.5   Processed Data Backup

The purpose of this module is to create a backup of the database at predefined intervals, chosen by the user. It does not use temporary data structures, nor assume an important role in consumption of memory resources, because the module uses the existing CRON utility in the host operating system.

5   Experimental Results

We tested our proposed architecture in order to prove the scalability and performance claims. Our focus was on demonstrating the fact that this is a usable architecture and that a service oriented approach is possible for spam filtering.

In the intermediate tests we noticed, when analyzing whether an email is or not spam, a predilection for the select requests in the database. To make a more rapid implementation, but also to improve performance of the module connected to the database, we optimized the database by putting indexes on columns frequently required, and by increasing cache space of the Sql Server. Also, whenever we could, we've used a local cache, implemented as a hash tables for extra speed.

When implementing this architecture we replaced calls to String.split() with the methods of the StringTokenizer class. Although it offers little flexibility, we preferred this implementation because it offered a faster response time. As illustrated in Fig. 7, calls for StringTokenizer runs three times faster than calls for String.split(), because the method split() receives as a parameter a regular expression that requires a recompilation whenever it is used. You can use a variant of this method, in which the regular expression is compiled only once, but without significant increases in speed.

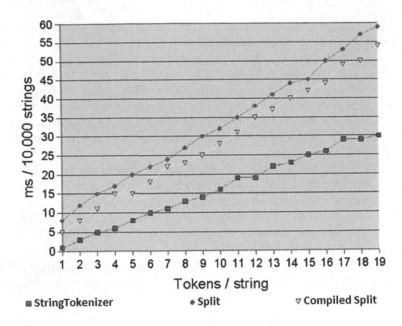

Fig. 7. Matching speed for random traffic data

Another part that we optimized was the distributions of workers for every component. The initial tests were made on five computer systems, using three workers for the message analyzer, one for each part of the email. But in this case we saw that the rest of the modules were running hard and slow because they were split across the two remaining systems. After taking the system configuration to different states, we found one in which our system performed the best. At this stage, the system was fully functional and optimized. Tests followed the response time and the accuracy of the results.

The first testing phase was made on a single computer, having a single physical CPU and 4 GB of RAM. In the first step we analyzed a single email and got a response time of 4 s. In the second step, we analyzed batches of 100 emails, each of about 100 relevant tokens, in a single thread and got a response time of 220 s, which means an average of 2.2 s for a single email, on a single CPU core.

The second testing phase consisted in running using our custom Cloud Computing framework [12]. At each of the computing nodes we implemented container based virtualization [19]. In Fig. 8, you can see our servers testbed configuration. We have used 12 server racks, split as follows: two server racks were used to install the modules of ReC2S, and the remaining nine racks were used as worker nodes each having a single module running. Each of the ten worker nodes racks contained eight physical servers, each server having a total of 32 physical cores and 64 GB or RAM. The racks used for the management frameworks contained only two physical servers, each having a total of 8 physical cores and 16 GB of RAM. The entire topology was interconnected using Gigabit

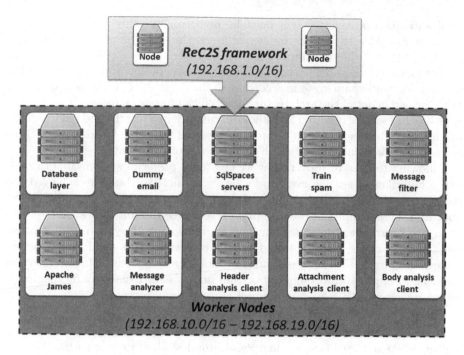

Fig. 8. Testbed configuration

connectivity. The phase was conducted by analyzing batches of 100 emails, using a total of 32 threads. To reduce the influence of the centralized database in the overall running time, we implemented the database across all eight servers, using the "MySQL Cluster" software. We obtained a response time of about 8 s, which means an average of 0.08 s for a single email.

We also compared our implementation to the others. The main difference is that they tested in a single-way environment. We didn't found any mention in they work to the other modules, resembling the ones we have implemented. Also, we observed that mainly, they are focusing only on the Bayesian filtering algorithms and don't mention details about the system as a whole. We found in our experiments that taking care only of the filtering system is not the best way, because all the modules have a great overall impact. Because our system is specially designed and implemented in such way that it can scale to very large number of systems, thus being a fully distributed platform, it is hard to compare our results, which are presented in a batch manner, in a mail by mail approach, with the ones that others give us.

6   Conclusions and Future Work

Spam messages are and will be a great problem for the existing email servers. A large quantity of them can block any email server in a short time. Thus, an email anti-spam filtering system must be used to solve this problem. Because in a big network, with a large number of users, the spam emails are received in huge quantities, a different approach must be taken.

Our focus on this paper was on presenting a novel design and implementation of a complete anti-spam system, according to the initial specifications and claims. We described in detail the architecture of an efficient system, designed within the scope of a full service oriented architecture, running in a distributed environment that has the advantage of high computing power. The actual filtering algorithms are based on Bayesian filters, which are known to be efficient.

Following tests have proven that we created a powerful system able to cope with a high flow of emails, even under heavy traffic. We therefore achieved the goal of providing scalability to our anti-spam architecture. Moreover, due to the replicated service approach we also provide a degree of fault tolerance.

In the future we intend to continue working on this system and improve it by using multiple interconnected database servers. This shall give a better performance, but also a high redundancy. Another direction for future research would be to improve the configuration and deployment capability by making it able to interface with a large number of current email servers.

Acknowledgment. This paper has been financially supported within the project entitled "Horizon 2020 - Doctoral and Postdoctoral Studies: Promoting the National interest through Excellence, Competitiveness and Responsibility in the Field of Romanian Fundamental and Applied Scientific Research", contract number POS-DRU/159/1.5/S/140106. This project is co-financed by European Social Fund through the Sectoral Operational Programme for Human Resources Development 2007–2013. Investing in people!

References

1. Spam Messages Report. http://www.symantec.com/content/en/us/enterprise/other_resources/b-istr_main_report_v19_21291018.en-us.pdf
2. Androutsopoulos, I., Koutsias, J., Chandrinos, K.V., Spyropoulos, C.D.: An experimental comparison of naive bayesian and keyword-based anti-spam filtering with personal e-mail messages. In: Proceedings of the 23rd Annual International ACM SIGIR Conference on Research and Development in Information Retrieval, Athens, Greece (2000)
3. Kolcz, A., Bond, M., Sargent, J.: The challenges of service-side personalized spam filtering: scalability and beyond. In: Proceedings of the 1st International Conference on Scalable Information Systems, Hong Kong (2006)
4. Li, K., Zhong, Z.: Fast statistical spam filter by approximate classifications. In: Proceedings of the Joint International Conference on Measurement and Modeling of Computer Systems, Saint Malo, France (2006)
5. Aun, M.T.B., Goi, B.-M., Kim, V.T.H.: Cloud enabled spam filtering services: challenges and opportunities. In: Sustainable Utilization and Development in Engineering and Technology (2011)
6. Salah, K., Calero, J.M.A., Zeadally, S., Al-Mulla, S., Alzaabi, M.: Using cloud computing to implement a security overlay network. IEEE Secur. Priv. **11**(1), 44–53 (2013)

7. Check Point Anti-Spam & Email Security Software Blade, Symantec Hosted Service. https://hostedendpoint.spn.com
8. Zscaler Web Security Service. http://www.zscaler.com/product-cloud-security/web-security.php
9. FortiGuard Antispam Service. http://www.fortinet.com/support/fortiguard_services/antispam.html
10. http://www.checkpoint.com/products/anti-spam-email-security-software-blade/
11. Murphy, K.P.: Machine Learning: A Probabilistic Perspective. MIT Press, Cambridge (2012). ISBN: 0262018020, 9780262018029
12. Pătraşcu, A., Leordeanu, C., Dobre, C., Cristea, V.: ReC^{2}S: reliable cloud computing system. In: European Concurrent Engineering Conference, Bucharest (2012)
13. Gregory, P.H., Simon, M.: Blocking Spam and Spyware For Dummies. Wiley, Indianapolis (2005). ISBN-10: 0764575910, ISBN-13: 978–0764575914
14. McGregor, C.: Controlling Spam with SpamAssassin. Linux Journal, Vol. 153 (2007)
15. Spamcop.net - beware of cheap imitations. http://www.spamcop.net/
16. Blanzieri, E., Bryl, A.: A survey of learning-based techniques of email spam filtering. Artif. Intell. Rev. **29**(1), 63–92 (2008)
17. Weinbrenner, S., Giemza, A., Hoppe, H.U.: Engineering heterogenous distributed learning environments using tuple spaces as an architectural platform. In: Proceedings of the 7th IEEE International Conference on Advanced Learning Technologies (2007)
18. Schneider, K.-M.: A comparison of event models for naive bayes anti-spam e-mail filtering. In: Proceedings of 10th Conference of the European Chapter of the Association for Computational Linguistics, Budapest, Hungary (2003)
19. Linux Containers. https://linuxcontainers.org/

Contributions to Steganographic Techniques on Mobile Devices

Dominic Bucerzan[1]($\boxtimes$) and Crina Raţiu[2]

[1] "Aurel Vlaicu" University of Arad, Arad, Romania
dominic@bbcomputer.ro
[2] "Vasile Goldis" Western University of Arad, Arad, Romania
ratiu_anina@yahoo.com

Abstract. In modern information and communication systems, information security is becoming an increasingly important issue due to the threats from all different types of attacks. The network security is becoming more important as the number of data being exchanged on the Internet increases. Therefore, the confidentiality and integrity of data requires protection against unauthorized access and use. This reality is the base for the study conducted in this paper regarding the field of Digital Steganography, in order to provide solutions for confidential communication between computers and mobile devices. The authors propose a new solution in order to provide confidentiality and secrecy of digital data that is transferred through todays available platforms for communication. The study is based on the SmartSteg application and consists of a package of steganographic and cryptographic applications that works both ways on Android and Windows platform.

Keywords: LSB steganography · Cryptography · Android · Windows · SmartSteg

1 Introduction

Steganography techniques are used since antiquity for covert communication. Despite this, digital steganography is an emerging area and has a growing trend. Today, along with cryptography, the two techniques are the main methods used to ensure digital information security [2].

The main goal of steganography is to communicate securely in a completely undetectable manner and to avoid drawing suspicion to the transmission of hidden data. Steganography hides the existence of the information in different carrier files (often in media files), protecting it against detection and removal. An important feature of a stegosystem is to make the carrier file difficult to be distinguished from an ordinary file [7].

Cryptography is used to ensure especially confidentiality and integrity, by making the information indecipherable to an eyedropper.

© Springer International Publishing Switzerland 2015
I. Bica et al. (Eds.): SECITC 2015, LNCS 9522, pp. 242–252, 2015.
DOI: 10.1007/978-3-319-27179-8_17

The open environment of nowadays available networks for communication is full of threats and risks. In order to enhance the security of digital information, specialists propose, as a method, the combination of the above mentioned techniques.

This solution has been developed, implemented, studied, researched and has generated complex dedicated algorithms in personal computers environment.

Regarding mobile devices, few and light research were made in this field and the threats for digital information security grew more severe. Mobile devices support complex applications, however they neglect the security of the data they use, thus favoring potential attackers, giving them the opportunity to alter sensitive data [2].

One of the major issues that occur in this environment is the fact that almost all platforms have dedicated application. This is in contradiction with one of the characteristic of digital information, namely availability. This fact is sustained by some aspects regarding: several physical differences between the devices; every type of device has its own type of operating system. Every type of device has different performances regarding calculations speed.

In this paper we present a reliable and robust solution that ensures confidential and private digital data communications through Internet and Mobile Networks. Based on SmartSteg application developed for Android, we propose a solution to provide confidential communication between computers and mobile devices.

The goals that we want to achieve in the proposed study are:

- to design an algorithm that allows embedding a lager quantity of digital data in a digital image;
- to design an algorithm that consumes minimal time and hardware resources;
- to minimize the steganalysis detection issues.

2   Related Works

The steganographic applications available on the market and in the literature, designed for smart phones that work with Android Operating System, have major limitations regarding:

- their functionality on different devices;
- the capacity of embedded secret information;
- the imperceptibility of the embedded data;
- the computational complexity, that refers to the computational cost of embedding and extraction;
- the lack of a correspondent application that works on computers;
- the lack of information about the performance of steganographic methods: capacity, security, imperceptibility, computational complexity [6].

We consider that the main disadvantage of the steganographic applications that are designed for Android smart phones is the fact that they embed only a small quantity of data (short sequence of characters). This excludes the possibility to secretly traffic images or large documents [1]. Here we discuss some of the steganographic applications available today on mobile platforms, applications that we have tested:

- T.F.M. White and J.E. Martina developed an application that uses steganography to hide a short text message in an audio message. The user can share that message [3]. The same idea is retrived in StegDroid Alpha (2011).
- The following applications embed only *short text messages* in images: Stegosaurus (2015), Stegano IMessAGE, Pocket Stego, Stegos, Kryfto, Photo Hidden Data, Steganography Image, Steganography Master, EstegApp (2014), Steganografia, Secret Letter, StegDroid Alpha VipSecret, PixelKnot: Hidden Messages, PtBox FREE, SecureMessage, Stegan (2013), Da Vinci Secret Image, Stego Message, StegoLite, Camopic (2012): *embeds short text messages*;
- MoBiSiS, MobiStego (2013) are using Multimedia Messaging Service (MMS) to send the image that covers the secret message. This means that the size of the cover image with the secret message embedded must be less than 30 KB [3]: *embeds small quantity of data*;
- Steganography (by Jan Meznik, apr.2014) makes the resulted file shorter than the original one; this means that a user can embed a smaller quantity of data. The same idea is used by Secret Tidings (2014); the resulted image with message embedded is corrupted, the user may see changes: small sequence of characters and image files; does not permit multiple saving; *does not maintain the original type of the support image; modifies the length of the original file*;
- Steganography Application (by Preethi Natarajanl, dec.2012) does not work. It returns a blank screen with "unfortunately steganography application has stopped" on it. Also StegDroid Alpha (2013), Crypsis (2012): *does not work*.

These are the main reasons that led us to develop a new version of SmartSteg, which is able to encode and embed files up to 2 megabytes (MB), using minimal time resources and still be resistant to steganalysis attacks.

3   Proposed Solution and Implementation

In the literature [3], steganographic methods are divided into three main categories: pure steganography, secret key steganography, and public key steganography.

In our proposed project we choose to work with secret key steganography algorithm. The security of the stego-system relies on the stego-key which consists of secret information exchanged between the sender and the intended receiver using other secure channel. Only the sender and the intended receiver should be able to reveal the secret data.

At this stage of the project, SmartSteg provides confidential communication between computers that run on Windows Operating System and devices that run on Android.

In our research we focused on the embedding algorithm, cryptographic algorithm, quantity of secret information that can be hidden without distinguishable changes in the cover file and obtain minimal processing time.

The proposed algorithm has reached a very good processing speed. For example a cover file of 16 MB can embed approximately 2 MB of secret information in less than 1 s. The processing and the necessary changes occur in this short time, which is significant considering that it is working on different Android version on Smartphone.

3.1 Design of the Application

SmartSteg is designed to contain three main modules: cryptographic algorithm, random function, embedding process.

Figures 1 and 2 shows the design chosen for the two versions of SmartSteg.

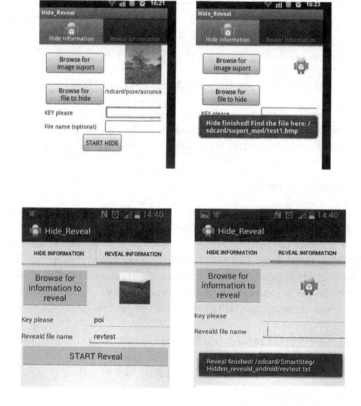

Fig. 1. Design for the application that runs Android

The visual design of SmartSteg is minimal; it is not a complex one because this was not a target for our study. We used few defined objects from JAVA

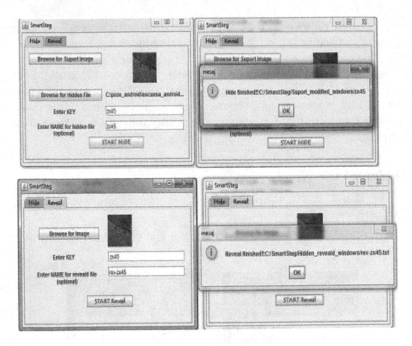

Fig. 2. Design for the application that runs Windows

and we built every control that was needed. This decision was taken to avoid conflicts in accessing the original cover files on different Android versions.

3.2 Cryptographic Solution

SmartSteg uses secret key steganography combined with secret key cryptography to ensure confidential and private communication.

We use a stream cipher algorithm to encode the secret information. The result of this step is an array of scrambled bits of secret information. The stream cipher we used is a proprietary one. Stream ciphers are characterized by small size, high speed execution and minimal consumption of computing resources. Given these characteristics, stream ciphers can optimize applications running on mobile devices [8].

Regarding the cryptographic module of SmartSteg, the proposed solution works with symmetric key. The modularity of the application allows the symmetric key solution to be changed with a public key algorithm.

3.3 Embedding Solution

Figure 3 shows details about the embedding process. In this process we use an improved LSB (least significant bit) technique combined with a random selection function.

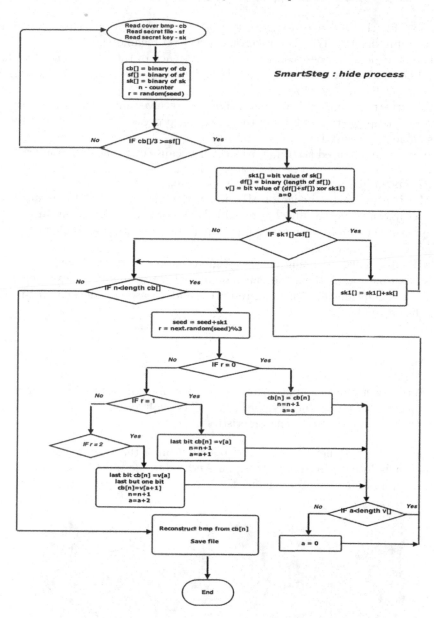

Fig. 3. SmartSteg scheme of the embedding process

LSB technique, known as noise insertion, uses raster image as a cover, mainly bitmap format files (BMP).

SmartSteg algorithm proposes an improved solution of LSB technique that may embed 0, 1 or 2 bits of secret information in a byte of the cover file using a random function. The random function defines the number of bits of a byte from the cover file that are selected to carry the secret information. The embedding rate is approximately 1/8 like in conventional LSB technique.

The embedding process continues until the reach of the end of the cover file even if the end of the secret file is reached. This happens to conceal the length of the secret file to a possible attacker.

To extract the embedded information the receiver must enter the correct key and the application will start the revealing process. After the secret file is reassembled, it is saved on the device.

In our study we used BMP files as a cover because of the next characteristics:

- this type of files are proper for LSB technique;
- BMP files are raster image of MB dimension, this favoring the quantity of secret information that may be embedded. The proposed algorithm can embed a quantity of secret information approximately that equals to an eight part of the size of the cover file;
- BMP files allows to maintain the original cover file type, dimension, pixel distribution and in the same time to conceal a reasonable quantity of data with minimal time and hardware resources and a reasonable level of distortion of the cover file.

3.4   Results

Figure 4 presents an example of image that we used in tests with SmartSteg, both on Android and Windows platforms. The resulted image with secret data embedded has the following characteristics:

- keeps the type, dimension and pixel distribution of the original cover image;
- the resulted image from SmartSteg on Android is the same with the resulted image from SmartSteg on Windows.

Original cover image   Resulted image

Fig. 4. Original cover image, resulted image, BMP-type, 2.14 MB, 1000 × 750 pixel distribution

Figure 5 is the binary representation of Fig. 4. One can see the following:

- the header of original cover image equals with the header of resulted image. This means that the dimension and the type of the files are the same;
- in red there are the different bytes between the original cover image and the resulted image;
- no relevant differences in terms of pixel values between the original cover image and the resulted image after processing with SmartSteg.

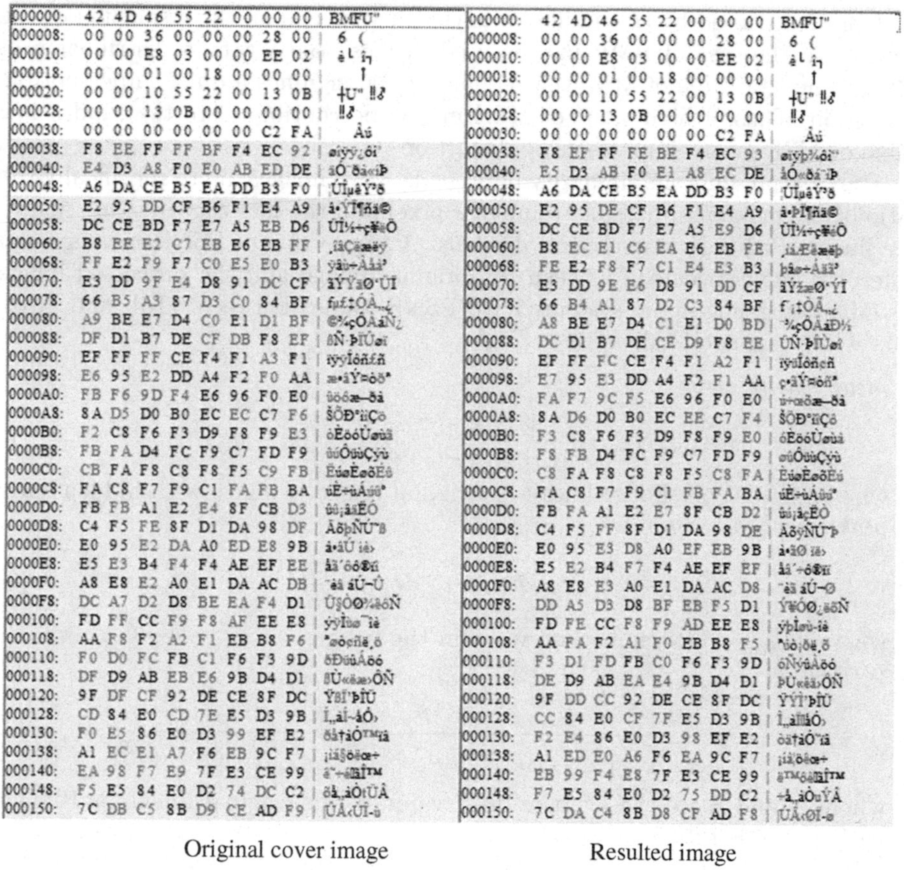

Original cover image   Resulted image

Fig. 5. Binary differences between original cover image and resulted image

4   Steganalysis

Steganalysis is the science that deals with the detection of steganography, the estimation of the length of secret data and with its extraction [5].

In the literature there is not a widespread procedure to evaluate the performance of steganographic systems. It is proposed to measure the characteristics of the compared systems and of the resulted image with information embedded. The emphasis is on the quantity of secret information which may be embedded and on its difficulty to be detected.

The indicators recommended by researchers to determine the quality of digital images are PSNR (peak signal-to-noise ratio) and MSE (mean squared error) [9]. MSE is the difference between the two images, more precise it represents the statistical difference between the pixels value of the original image and the pixel values of the resulted image with secret information embedded.

One issue raised by this indicator is that it depends on the resolution of the images. In the case of BMP images used in this study, with a distribution of 24 bits/pixel, a value of MSE that equals to 100 signifies a quite imperceptible distortion. Thus, a high value of MSE means perceptible distortion and a low value of MSE means imperceptible distortion [9].

PSNR represents the similarity between the two images, more specifically the ratio of the maximum possible value of a pixel and the intensity of distortion to the image. PSNR is measured in decibels. A high value of PSNR means small differences, unnoticeable, between the original image and the processed image [9]. Most steganographic systems have PSNR values between 30 db and 40 db [10], which is a good value.

– *mean square error*

$$MSE = \frac{1}{M \times N} \sum_{i=1}^{M} \sum_{j=1}^{N} (p_{ij} - q_{ij})^2 \tag{1}$$

where: $M \times N$ pixel distribution, p original image, q image with hidden data;
– *peak signal-to-noise ratio*

$$PSNR = 10 \times log_{10} \frac{C_{max}^2}{MSE} \tag{2}$$

where: C_{max}^2 - maximum pixel value in the image;
– *correlation*

$$r = \frac{\sum_{i=1}^{M} \sum_{j=1}^{N} (p_{ij} - \bar{p})(q_{ij} - \bar{q})}{\sqrt{(\sum_{i=1}^{M} \sum_{j=1}^{N} (p_{ij} - \bar{p})^2) \times (\sum_{i=1}^{M} \sum_{j=1}^{N} (q_{ij} - \bar{q})^2)}} \tag{3}$$

where: $\bar{p}$ and $\bar{q}$ are the average pixel value in the original image and image with embedded data.

The PSNR obtained values are over 50 % (test value: 53.52 dB), a very good value compared to other steganographic applications [10].

Fridrich *et al.* [4,7,11] introduces RS Steganalysis as a powerful method of LSB steganographic detection. Beside this technique, Benchmark test is also a well known technique in this field. According to these techniques, the relevant parameters used to measure the differences between original cover image and the resulted image with embedded data is given by the formulas (1), (2) and (3), [7].

In our project the recorded values of the color percentages (RGB) obtained after running RS Analysis are between 70 % and 90 % which are good values [7].

Table 1. SmartSteg properties

Properties	SmartSteg	Android application
Compatibility		
with different devices and operating systems	Compatible with any Android and Windows mobile devices	Most of them work only on Android smart phones
Capacity		
of embedded information	Large variety of files	Short text messages
Availability		
of performance information	Providing performance information	No performance information
Changes		
to the original cover image: dimension or type	Keeps the original cover image: dimension and type	Most of them change the original cover image: dimension or type

5 Conclusions and Future Work

SmartSteg is a new solution in steganography technique on mobile devices. The project proposed in this paper has major advantages like:

- low degradation of cover image associated with large volume of hidden data and large variety of hidden files;
- it is based on secret key cryptographic algorithm and on the random selection of the bits with secret information, fact that ensures high level of security;
- high processing speed;
- works on Windows and on all versions of Android.

SmartSteg has no limitation raised by other steganographic application on Android, like shown in Table 1.

The modularity of the application allows the symmetric key solution to be changed with a public key algorithm. This is a future issue for us.

In our future research we intend to develop an improved version of SmartSteg that can use PNG files as cover image for steganography, due to the popularity of this type of image. Also, we intend to develop a version of SmartSteg that runs under IOS operating systems.

References

1. Wang, Z., Murmuria, R., Stavrou, A.: Implementing and optimizing an encryption filesystem on android. In: 2012 IEEE 13th International Conference on Mobile Data Management (MDM), pp. 52–62. IEEE (2012)
2. Muttik, I.: Securing Mobile Devices: Present and Future. http://www.ingrammicro.com/healthcare/McAfee_MobileSecurity.pdf

3. Bucerzan, D., Raţiu, C., Manolescu, M.J.: SmartSteg: a new android based steganogrphy application. Int. J. Comput. Commun. Control 8(5), 681–688 (2013). http://univagora.ro/jour/index.php/ijccc/article/view/642
4. Fridrich, J., Goljan, M.: Practical steganalysis of digital images state of the art. Proc. SPIE 4675, 1–13 (2002)
5. Wolfel, U.: Efficient and provably secure steganography. Doctoral Dissertation, Universitat zu Lubeck, Institut fur Theoretische Informatik (2011)
6. Swain, G., Lenka, S.K.: Classification of image steganography techniques in spatial domain: a study. Int. J. Comput. Sci. Eng. Tech. (IJCSET) 5(3), 219–232 (2014). Swain, G. (eds)
7. Fridrich, J.: Steganography in Digital Media: Principles, Algorithms, and Applications. Cambridge University Press, New York (2009)
8. Paar, C., Pelzl, J.: Understanding Cryptography: A Textbook for Students and Practitioners. Springer Science & Business Media, Heidelberg (2009)
9. Veldhuizen, T.: Measures of image quality. http://homepages.inf.ed.ac.uk/rbf/CVonline/LOCAL_COPIES/VELDHUIZEN/node18.html
10. Cole, E., Krutz, R.D.: Hiding in Plain Sight: Steganography and the Art of Covert Communication. Wiley, New York (2003)
11. Fridrich, J., Goljan, M., Du, R.: Reliable detection of LSB steganography in color and grayscale images. In: Proceedings of the 2001 Workshop on Multimedia and Security, Ottawa, Canada (2001)

Secure Implementation of Stream Cipher: Trivium

Dillibabu Shanmugam[✉] and Suganya Annadurai

Hardware Security Research Group, Society for Electronic Transactions and Security,
Chennai, India
{dillibabu,asuganya}@setsindia.net
http://www.setsindia.org/hardware.html

Abstract. Trivium is a hardware oriented synchronous stream cipher designed by Christophe De Cannière and Bart Preneel [7]. Trivium is one of the eSTREAM final portfolio cipher. Regardless of the security of the cipher in theory, implementation attacks like Differential Power Analysis (DPA) attack [10,12,18] and Fault attack [9] on Trivium were observed. DPA attack of Trivium exploits the re-synchronization phase of the algorithm to reveal the key.

In this paper, we analyse various implementation techniques as countermeasures for Trivium stream cipher against DPA attack. First, we present Threshold Implementation (TI) of Trivium using random mask value. Second, we propose algorithm level changes (Modified Trivium) to counteract the attack, which introduces negligible resource overhead to the implementation. Third, random accelerator concept is introduced for parallel architecture along with combined techniques of TI and algorithm level changes to further increase the attack complexity. Finally, we present comparative study on the performance of Trivium for the proposed techniques.

Keywords: Trivium · Differential power analysis attack · Threshold implementation and algorithm level countermeasure

1 Introduction

Stream ciphers are efficient in hardware that can be realised in constrained area and consumes less power. They are very useful for streaming encryption, for example, live streaming video or audio encryption. Also found useful in RFID, Bluetooth, NFC and LTE applications. To promote the design of efficient and compact stream ciphers, eSTREAM [1] project was initiated in 2004. The eSTREAM final portfolio was announced in 2008, where seven stream ciphers (Four for fast encryption in software and three for efficient implementation in hardware) were selected. Trivium is designed to be more efficient in hardware. Vulnerability of Trivium against Differential Power Analysis (DPA) attack were proposed in [10,18]. A detailed study on correlation power analysis attack on Trivium was presented in [12]. Though the attack is explored in the

© Springer International Publishing Switzerland 2015
I. Bica et al. (Eds.): SECITC 2015, LNCS 9522, pp. 253–266, 2015.
DOI: 10.1007/978-3-319-27179-8_18

re-synchronisation stage of the cipher, the attack is trivial if the attacker has access and control over the device. Therefore, it is important to implement the cipher with proper countermeasure against DPA attack. Countermeasure is a process of breaking the correlation between secret information processed and its leakage characteristics. At the same time, the countermeasure should not burden the resource requirement of the cipher. Hence, it's a need of the hour to have an efficient countermeasure with affordable area, speed and cost overheads.

Related Work: Countermeasures can be implemented at various levels of design flow, such as algorithm level, architecture level and cell level. To protect cryptographic device from DPA attack, countermeasures at all possible levels have been suggested. Algorithmic level countermeasures like random delay [6], insertion of dummy instructions that executes at random time [5] were proposed to resist implementations from side-channel attack. In [8], the authors cryptanalysed the random delay implementation of AES in an Atmel microcontroller using pattern recognition and Hidden Markov Model techniques. Architecture level countermeasures focus on varying the power pattern from the original power pattern. This can be done by the change of clock frequency [2], by noise insertion and instruction stream randomization [11]. Though these countermeasures succeed in changing the algorithm's power consumption pattern, it is quite possible for an attacker to retrieve the original pattern [14] with little more effort. Hiding intermediate values at cell level, such as sense-amplifier based logic (SABL) [19], simple or wave dynamic differential logic (SDDL/WDDL) [20] have been published. In SABL the input logic structure is designed to balance all internal node capacitances for constant power consumption under all input conditions and for every clock cycle. WDDL achieves an important reduction in the power variation, but their drawbacks are the increased area, computation time and power consumption. Most of the countermeasures have been implemented and evaluated in block ciphers.

Few papers were published on countermeasure for stream ciphers. In [4], it is suggested to maximize the switching activity in each cycle. Though the pattern of power consumption changes considerably, increased switching activity consumes more power and area. Mansouri et al. further optimised the approach in [13], which reduces the power overhead by averaging the switching activity. Incorporation of suppression circuit to suppress information leakage through power supply pin was proposed in [16]. In [3], Sense Amplifier Based Logic (SABL) is used to decrease the power variations. But these approaches increase overall power consumption and area.

In this work we propose secure implementation techniques against DPA attack of Trivium stream cipher.

Our Contributions: First, we present threshold implementation of Trivium using random mask values generated using Pseudo Random Number Generator (PRNG) or Physically Unclonable Function (PUF) circuit and discuss the resistivity against DPA attack. Second, we share our observation in the initialization phase of algorithm structure and describe algorithm level changes as modified Trivium to increase the complexity of the attack with negligible overhead.

Third, we explore random acceleration of parallel architecture (Algorithm executes n bits at a time) based on the process variation of the silicon chip using PUF to vary the power consumption of Trivium. In addition, we explore the incorporation of combined countermeasures (TI and algorithm) in parallel architecture to increase the complexity of the attack further. Finally, we compare the performance of the proposed implementation techniques.

Outline of This Paper: In Sect. 2, we give a brief description about structure of Trivium hardware implementation and power analysis attack on Trivium. Countermeasure is detailed in the Sect. 3. Section 3.1 describes threshold implementation of Trivium stream cipher and its DPA resistance. In Sect. 3.2, we discuss algorithm level changes (modified Trivium) in initialization phase of the cipher and architecture level countermeasure. Performance of these countermeasures are compared in Sect. 4 and the paper is concluded in Sect. 5.

2 Hardware Implementation of Trivium

The implementation of Trivium [7] consists of a 288-bit shift register and few boolean operations (AND and XOR). We use VHDL (Very High Speed Integrated Circuit Hardware Description Language) for implementation, SASEBO (xc2vp7-fg456-5) evaluation board for experiment and power measurement and MATLAB tool for statistical analysis.

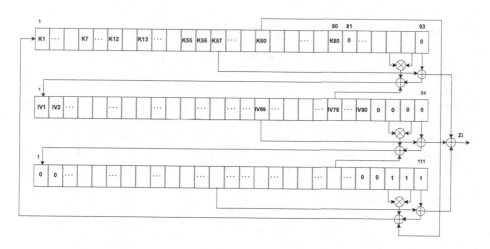

Fig. 1. Hardware implementation of Trivium Initialization Phase

Figure 1 describes hardware implementation of initialization phase of Trivium. It Initializes the key, Initialisation Vector (IV) and constant values that are loaded on single 288-bit register. First 80 bits are loaded with key, then 13 bits of zeroes, followed by 80 bits of IV and again zero for all bits, except the last three bits, which are set to one. During initialization phase, boolean operations are performed on values of certain position of the register, then the entire register is shifted left by one position, and output of boolean operations are updated on relevant position in the register. The initialization phase is iterated for 1152 rounds, after that the key streams are generated for encryption.

2.1   Power Consumption of Trivium

Dynamic power consumption is the main source of leakage information for CMOS circuits. Trivium implementation consists of Feedback Shift Register (FSR) and logic gates. FSR has flip-flops connected in series with a feedback on the first flip-flop. Consequently, flip-flops changing its state from 0 to 1 or 1 to 0 leaks dynamic power consumption.

Hamming distance power model suits very well to describe the power consumption of the hardware implementation of Trivium. Hence, power consumption of Trivium for each clock cycle is modeled as follows:

$$P^i = \Sigma_{j=1}^{288}(s_j^i \oplus s_j^{i-1}),$$

where P^i denotes the power consumption of ith iteration and S_j denotes the state value of jth position.

2.2   Attack on Trivium Hardware Implementation

Trivium is vulnerable to DPA attack, because the initial loading of register has consecutive zero values. These values are used along with the key bits to update the register. In some instances, the key bit alone is updated with the IV value. By observing the power consumption, the attacker can easily guess the key value with the known IV value. In Trivium, 94th position of register is the target of the attack, where the known IV bit is updated with the unknown key bit.

In round 1, all values of the register from position 94 to 288 are known and K_{66} being the only exception as shown in the equation.

$$(S_1, S_2, .., S_{93}) \quad \leftarrow (K_{69}, K_1, .., K_{79})$$
$$(S_{94}, S_{95}, ., S_{177}) \quad \leftarrow ((K_{66} \oplus IV_{78}), IV_1, ..)$$
$$(S_{178}, S_{179}, .., S_{288}) \leftarrow (IV_{69}, 0, 0, .., 0)$$

Calculating two hypothetical power consumption using both possible values $K_{66} = 0$ and $K_{66} = 1$, the correct key bit can be determined using correlation power analysis. Using the same method, all the key bits can be retrieved as presented in [12, 18].

3   Countermeasures

In this paper we present the countermeasure for Trivium stream cipher at algorithm and architecture level. We propose two algorithm level countermeasures, threshold implementation (TI) and changes at algorithm level to have modified Trivium. Though TI is not a new concept, we attempted to implement and analyse the performance of TI in Trivium stream cipher. In algorithm level changes, modifications are done in algorithm itself to minimize the leakage of the secret information by increasing other bits dependency. Architecture level countermeasure hides the leakage of information, by implementing the algorithm in parallel. The success rate of countermeasure is based on how much valid information leakage has been reduced on the particular intermediate state. We analyse the possibility of information leakage with these countermeasure techniques and show that the level of security has been increased. Hence, the attack complexity is also increased.

3.1   Threshold Implementation

The Threshold Implementation (TI) countermeasure was proposed by Nikova et al., in [15]. Threshold implementation is the process of decomposing the secret information function as shares of function, process the shared functions separately and then reconstruct to form a original information. The following three properties need to be fulfilled for secret sharing implementation such as Correctness, Non-completeness and Uniformity.

- *Correctness:* The sum of the output shares gives the desired output.

- *Non-completeness:* Every function is independent of at least one share of each of the input variables.

- *Uniformity:* If the input shares are uniformly distributed, the output shares must also be uniformly distributed.

By these properties even if the adversary does not know the value of one share, it will be difficult to reconstruct the information.

DPA attack of Trivium in Sect. 2.2, exploits the non-linear function AND operation to mount DPA attack. Therefore, the main focus of TI of Trivium is sharing the nonlinear function (AND) that satisfies the properties of TI. In [15], multiplication of two input variable is elaborated as $Z = N(x,y) = xy$ with the number of shares $n = 3$ and defined the 3 functions f_i as follows:

$$Z1 = f_1(X2; X3; Y2; Y3) = X2Y2 \oplus X2Y3 \oplus X3Y2$$
$$Z2 = f_2(X1; X3; Y1; Y3) = X3Y3 \oplus X1Y3 \oplus X3Y1$$
$$Z3 = f_3(X1; X2; Y1; Y2) = X1Y1 \oplus X1Y2 \oplus X2Y1$$

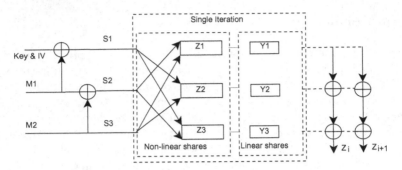

Fig. 2. Shared functions

Above share functions are used in Trivium with random bits M1 and M2 as depicted in the Fig. 2.

Here M1 and M2 are 288-bit random masks that can be generated using any Pseudo Random Number Generator (PRNG) or secure Physically Unclonable Function (PUF) circuit along with implementation of Trivium. For each re-synchronisation phase of Trivium, random mask will be generated for shared functions. The implementation details for shared circuit of Trivium is described in the Algorithm 1. After 1152 iterations of Trivium, specific bits from three registers S1, S2 and S3 are xored to generate key stream output (Z_i).

Security Analysis. Threshold implementation of Trivium maintains three 288-bit register, namely S1, S2 and S3. Attack on any one of the register (share) could not reveal the secret information. However attack on all the shares becomes tedious and obviously increase the attack complexity. The point of attack is same as normal Trivium implementation, that is 94th bit position. Therefore, Hamming Distance has to be taken at the 94th bit position of initial state of three registers S1, S2 and S3 with the present state of three registers S1, S2 and S3. The dependency of key bits after the first iteration is derived in the following equations. It is assumed that the random masking bits are unknown to the attacker.

Initial state:

$$t_1 = S1_{94} \oplus S2_{94} \oplus S3_{94}$$

$$= (IV_1 \oplus M1_{94}) \oplus (M1_{94} \oplus M2_{94}) \oplus M2_{94}$$

After first iteration :

$$t_2 = S1_{94} \oplus S2_{94} \oplus S3_{94}$$

$$S1_{94} = S2_{66} \oplus S2_{93} \oplus S2_{171} \oplus (S2_{91} \ \& \ S2_{92}) \oplus (S2_{91} \ \& \ S3_{92})$$
$$\oplus (S3_{91} \ \& \ S2_{92})$$
$$S2_{94} = S3_{66} \oplus S3_{93} \oplus S3_{171} \oplus (S3_{91} \ \& \ S3_{92}) \oplus (S3_{91} \ \& \ S1_{92})$$
$$\oplus (S1_{91} \ \& \ S3_{92})$$

Algorithm 1. Threshold Implementation of Trivium Initialisation Phase

Input: 80-bit Key, 80-bit IV, 288-bit M1 and M2 random mask
/* Initialization */
/* Key, IV are masked with random bits S1 */
$(S1_1, S1_2, \ldots, S1_{93}) \leftarrow (K_1, \ldots, K_{80}, 0, \ldots, 0) \oplus (M1_1, M1_2, \ldots, M1_{93})$
$(S1_{94}, S_{95}, \ldots, S1_{177}) \leftarrow (IV_1, \ldots, IV_{80}, 0, \ldots, 0) \oplus (M1_{94}, M1_{95}, \ldots, M1_{177})$
$(S1_{178}, S1_{179}, \ldots, S1_{288}) \leftarrow (0, \ldots, 0, 1, 1, 1) \oplus (M1_{178}, M1_{179}, \ldots, M1_{288})$

/* Random bits M1, M2 are Xored */
$(S2_1, S2_2, \ldots, S2_{288}) \leftarrow (M1_1, M1_2, \ldots, M1_{288}) \oplus (M2_1, M2_2, \ldots, M2_{288})$

/* Random bits M2 */
$(S3_1, S3_2, \ldots, S3_{288}) \leftarrow (M2_1, M2_2, \ldots, M2_{288})$
- -
for $i = 1$ to 1152 do

/* Share function 1 */
$t_{21} \leftarrow (S2_{66} \oplus S2_{93} \oplus S2_{171} \oplus (S2_{91} \ \& \ S2_{92}) \oplus (S2_{91} \ \& \ S3_{92}) \oplus (S3_{91} \ \& \ S2_{92}))$
$t_{22} \leftarrow (S2_{162} \oplus S2_{177} \oplus S2_{264} \oplus (S2_{175} \ \& \ S2_{176}) \oplus (S2_{175} \ \& \ S3_{176}) \oplus$
$\quad\quad (S3_{175} \ \& \ S2_{176}))$
$t_{23} \leftarrow (S2_{243} \oplus S2_{288} \oplus S2_{69} \oplus (S2_{286} \ \& \ S2_{287}) \oplus (S2_{286} \ \& \ S3_{287}) \oplus$
$\quad\quad (S3_{286} \ \& \ S2_{287}));$

$(S1_1, S1_2, \ldots, S1_{93}) \leftarrow (t_{23}, S1_1, \ldots, S1_{92})$
$(S1_{94}, S1_{95}, \ldots, S1_{177}) \leftarrow (t_{21}, S1_{94}, \ldots, S1_{176})$
$(S1_{178}, S1_{179}, \ldots, S1_{288}) \leftarrow (t_{22}, S1_{178}, \ldots, S1_{287})$

/* Share function 2 */
$t_{31} \leftarrow (S3_{66} \oplus S3_{93} \oplus S3_{171} \oplus (S3_{91} \ \& \ S3_{92}) \oplus (S3_{91} \ \& \ S1_{92}) \oplus (S1_{91} \ \& \ S3_{92}))$
$t_{32} \leftarrow (S3_{162} \oplus S3_{177} \oplus S3_{264} \oplus (S3_{175} \ \& \ S3_{176}) \oplus (S3_{175} \ \& \ S1_{176}) \oplus$
$\quad\quad (S1_{175} \ \& \ S3_{176}))$
$t_{33} \leftarrow (S3_{243} \oplus S3_{288} \oplus S3_{69} \oplus (S3_{286} \ \& \ S3_{287}) \oplus (S3_{286} \ \& \ S1_{287}) \oplus$
$\quad\quad (S1_{286} \ \& \ S3_{287}));$

$(S2_1, S2_2, \ldots, S2_{93}) \leftarrow (t_{33}, S2_1, \ldots, S2_{92})$
$(S2_{94}, S2_{95}, \ldots, S2_{177}) \leftarrow (t_{31}, S2_{94}, \ldots, S2_{176})$
$(S2_{178}, S2_{179}, \ldots, S2_{288}) \leftarrow (t_{32}, S2_{178}, \ldots, S2_{287})$

/* Share function 3 */
$t_{11} \leftarrow (S1_{66} \oplus S1_{93} \oplus S1_{171} \oplus (S1_{91} \ \& \ S1_{92}) \oplus (S1_{91} \ \& \ S2_{92}) \oplus (S2_{91} \ \& \ S1_{92}))$
$t_{12} \leftarrow (S1_{162} \oplus S1_{177} \oplus S1_{264} \oplus (S1_{175} \ \& \ S1_{176}) \oplus (S1_{175} \ \& \ S2_{176}) \oplus$
$\quad\quad (S2_{175} \ \& \ S1_{176}))$
$t_{13} \leftarrow (S1_{243} \oplus S1_{288} \oplus S1_{69} \oplus (S1_{286} \ \& \ S1_{287}) \oplus (S1_{286} \ \& \ S2_{287}) \oplus$
$\quad\quad (S2_{286} \ \& \ S1_{287}));$

$(S3_1, S3_2, \ldots, S3_{93}) \leftarrow (t_{13}, S3_1, \ldots, S3_{92})$
$(S3_{94}, S3_{95}, \ldots, S3_{177}) \leftarrow (t_{11}, S3_{94}, \ldots, S3_{176})$
$(S3_{178}, S3_{179}, \ldots, S3_{288}) \leftarrow (t_{12}, S3_{178}, \ldots, S3_{287})$
end

$$S3_{94} = S1_{66} \oplus S1_{93} \oplus S1_{171} \oplus (S1_{91} \ \& \ S1_{92}) \oplus (S1_{91} \ \& \ S2_{92})$$
$$\oplus (S2_{91} \ \& \ S1_{92})$$

Values of S1, S2 and S3 can further be expanded to,

$$S1_{94} = (M2_{66} \oplus M1_{66}) \oplus (M2_{93} \oplus M1_{93}) \oplus (M2_{171} \oplus M1_{171}) \oplus$$
$$((M2_{91} \oplus M1_{91}) \ \& \ (M2_{92} \oplus M1_{92})) \oplus ((M2_{91} \oplus M1_{91}) \ \& \ M2_{92}) \oplus$$
$$(M2_{91} \ \& \ (M2_{92} \oplus M1_{92}))$$
$$S2_{94} = M2_{66} \oplus M2_{93} \oplus M2_{171} \oplus (M2_{91} \ \& \ M2_{92}) \oplus (M2_{91} \ \& \ M1_{92}) \oplus$$
$$(M1_{91} \ \& \ M2_{92})$$

$$S3_{94} = (K_{66} \oplus M1_{66}) \oplus M1_{93} \oplus M1_{171} \oplus (M1_{91} \mathbin{\&} M1_{92}) \oplus$$
$$(M1_{91} \mathbin{\&} M1_{92}) \oplus ((M1_{91} \oplus M2_{91}) \mathbin{\&} M1_{92})$$

Since unknown random mask values are used in xor operation, the mask value can be combined and t_1 and t_2 can be written as

$$t_1 = IV_1 \oplus M_w$$
$$t_2 = M_x \oplus M_y \oplus (K_{66} \oplus M_z)$$

$$HD = HW(t_1 \oplus t_2)$$
$$HD = HW(IV_1 \oplus M_w \oplus M_x \oplus M_y \oplus (K_{66} \oplus M_z))$$
$$HD = HW(IV_1 \oplus K_{66} \oplus M)$$

Here, IV_1 is a known input and key bit K_{66} is unknown and constant for all encryptions. Random mask M is unknown value and it varies for each encryption. Therefore, in order to reveal the secret key by power analysis, the attacker needs to compromise the PUF or PRNG circuit to get masking value, which is generated for each encryptions. Therefore the hypothetical key guess possibly not give high correlation without guessing the random mask value.

3.2 Modified Trivium

Trivium has vulnerability in its initialization phase, since thirteen zeroes are initialized (S_{81} to S_{93}) continuously in its design. This vulnerability is exploited, when algorithm is executed in the initialization phase. To avoid such an exploitation with minimal overhead, those thirteen consecutive zeros are to be distributed among 80 bits of the key, which certainly increase the complexity of the attack.

The feed forward paths involving the AND operation are crucial for the security of Trivium as they prevent cryptanalysis that exploit the linearity of the cipher. The AND operation is equal to modulo 2 multiplication. If we multiply two unknowns, the result contains product of two unknowns. If one input to AND operation is fixed to zero, then the output is fixed to zero. If the value of one input to AND operation is fixed to zero, the influence of the other bit is neglected, in the case of Trivium the other input bit is key bit. Therefore, key bit will not propagate and diffuse for randomization. On the other-hand, if one input is fixed to one, then output has the dependency on the other input (key bit), which will propagate and diffuse quickly for randomization. Hence, to have quick randomization, we chose to incorporate thirteen ones in the initialisation phase. However, if the thirteen ones are continuous in any position within the register, then the same vulnerability (part of state value becomes vulnerable) as in the case of zero exist. Consequently, it should be distributed uniformly among 80 bits. Hence, incorporating one at every seventh bit would be ideal. In the distribution of ones, AND operation yields key bit output at every seventh position. For these reasons, we chose ones that are distributed among 80-bit key value, instead of zeros. The key stream output after incorporating the proposed changes (modified Trivium) will be different from the original algorithm. However, the structure, the tap positions and the functions are same. Therefore, the security analysis of the Trivium claimed

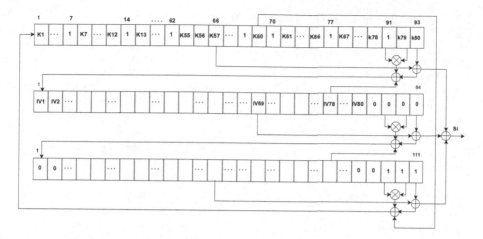

Fig. 3. Architecture of algorithm level changes for Trivium

in [7] believed to be the same for the modified Trivium, irrespective of the initial loading values. The proposed structure of Trivium is as shown in Fig. 3.

The idea here is to use different initialisation values which has better resistance against DPA than the one chosen by the designers. To confirm the randomness of key streams generated using our approach, 1000000 (one million) bits of output key stream of the modified algorithm is tested for randomness using NIST test suite [17]. The results are presented in Table 1. The results of modified Trivium is compared with the original version of Trivium and first one million bits of Π for the test vector.[1] This shows that the modification of the algorithm in the initialisation phase does not affect the randomness of the key stream, perhaps it increases the randomness.

Security Analysis. The point of attack is similar to the DPA attack [12], whereas the number of unknown values are increased in the hypothetical intermediate values. For the first round, the state register is given as follows:

$$(S_1, S_2, .., S_{93}) \quad \leftarrow (K_{60}, K_1, .., K_{79})$$
$$(S_{94}, S_{95}, ., S_{177}) \quad \leftarrow ((K_{57} \oplus IV_{78} \oplus 1.K_{79} \oplus K_{80}), IV_1, ..)$$
$$(S_{178}, S_{179}, .., S_{288}) \leftarrow (IV_{69}, 0, 0, .., 0)$$

As discussed in Sect. 2.2, the first register values (S_1 to S_{93}) can be omitted during the Hamming distance computation. In round 1, the leading bit of the second register can be calculated by:

---

[1] Modified Trivium, Key:0x9999999999, Initialization vector: Random. Every seventh bit is incorporated as one in the loading of initialization phase.

Table 1. NIST Randomness test for modified Trivium

Tests	π	Trivium [7]	Modified Trivium
Frequency	0.578211	0.458087	0.586441
Block Frequency (m = 128)	0.380615	0.260054	0.386992
Cusum-Forward	0.628308	0.044979	0.948586
Cusum-Reverse	0.663369	0.247113	0.879794
Runs	0.419268	0.088652	0.155112
Long Runs of Ones	0.02439	0.330619	0.759176
Rank	0.083553	0.698237	0.327832
Spectral DFT	0.010186	0.783087	0.755036
Non-overlapping Templates (m = 9, B = 000000001)	0.165757	0.180413	0.17198
Overlapping Templates (m = 9)	0.296897	0.220271	0.257452
Universal	0.669012	0.033668	0.71509
Approximate Entropy (m = 10)	0.361595	0.923856	0.337823
Random Excursions (x = +1)	0.844143	0.645253	0.681384
Random Excursions Variant (x = −1)	0.760966	0.737837	0.755118
Linear Complexity (M = 500)	0.255475	0.589581	0.801023
Serial	0.143005	0.111355	0.776755

$$S_{94} = S_{66} \oplus S_{91}.S_{92} \oplus S_{93} \oplus S_{171}$$
$$S_{94} = K_{57} \oplus 1.K_{79} \oplus K_{80} \oplus IV_{78}$$

As there are three unknown key bits, the hypothesis need to be the combination of these bits. It is to be noted that the three unknown bits are given to the linear function, which will not helpful to uniquely determine the correct key bits using DPA attack. Therefore, the key hypothesis will not provide high correlation for correct key guess and the DPA attack on initial rounds is not feasible with more unknown key bits. Further, implementation of the proposed countermeasure is evaluated using SASEBO evaluation board. There is no unique peak for the correct key guess upto 100,000 encryptions, whereas the implementation of Trivium without countermeasure can be attacked with 10,000 encryptions. The area requirement and other metrics are presented in Sect. 4.

Parallel Architecture. Parallel architecture of Trivium computes and updates n (say 64) bits for each clock cycle. Therefore it executes n (64) times faster but consumes more power and area when compared to normal execution. Further intermediate state are always in multiples of n, this means in order to attack an intermediate state the power model should be designed in multiples of n. Therefore point of attack should be multiples of n bits. These parallel mechanism would be useful for applications were parallel bits of streaming is needed. This approach will strengthen the initialization phase against chosen IV attack, slide attack, specific state attack and DPA attack. Further, we implemented algorithm

---

Algorithm 2. Random Accelerate design using PUF/PRNG circuit

Input:Secret key $K = (K_1, .., K_{80})$;Initialization vector $IV = (IV_1, .., IV_{80})$;
Output:Intermediate state update$(S_1, ..., S_{288})$
initialization : K_1 to $K_{93} = (K_1, .., K_{80}, 0, 0, 0, 0, 0, 0, 0, 0, 0, 0, 0, 0, 0)$;

/* Incorporation of one in every seventh bit */
for $x \leqslant 93$ do
   | If $(x \bmod 6 == 0)$ then
   | Right shift K_{x+1} to K_{93} by 1
   | $K_{(x+1)} \leftarrow 1$;
   | $x + +$;
End
$(S_1, ..., S_{93}) \leftarrow (K_1, ..., K_{93})$;
$(S_{94}, ..., S_{177}) \leftarrow (I_{V1}, ..., IV_{80}, 0, .., 0)$;
$(S_{178}, ..., S_{288}) \leftarrow (0, ..., 0, 1, 1, 1)$;

/* Module $t_{K_{1,2,..,N}}$ to be called */
$K = 1, 2, 3$: K (Describes corresponding equation number)
Module $t_{K_{1,2,..,N}}$ then
$i \leftarrow N - 1$;
$t_{1_N} \leftarrow (S_{66-i} \oplus S_{91-i}S_{92-i} \oplus S_{93-i} \oplus S_{171-i})$;
$t_{2_N} \leftarrow (S_{162-i} \oplus S_{175-i}S_{176-i} \oplus S_{177-i} \oplus S_{264-i})$;
$t_{3_N} \leftarrow (S_{243-i} \oplus S_{286-i}S_{287-i} \oplus S_{288-i} \oplus S_{69-i})$;

/*If process variation is low then algorithm execution triggers for parallel architecture/
if $PRNG$ or PUF output $= 0$ then
   | accelerate circuit **begin**
   | | $N \longleftarrow 64$;//64 bit parallel architecture
   | | $X \longleftarrow 18$;//18 clock cycle for initialization phase
   | | $j \longleftarrow 0$;
   | | for $j \leqslant X$ do
   | | | $(S_1, .., S_{93}) \leftarrow ((t_{3_N})\&(t_{3_N-1})\&...\&(S_1, .., S_{92-N}))$;
   | | | $(S_{94}, ., S_{177}) \leftarrow ((t_{1_N})\&(t_{1_N-1})\&...\&(S_{94}, .., S_{176-N}))$;
   | | | $(S_{178}, .., S_{288}) \leftarrow ((t_{2_N})\&(t_{2_N-1})\&...\&(S_{178}, .., S_{287-N}))$;
   | | End
   | **end**
   | End
End /*If process variation is high then algorithm executions normal architecture*/
else
   | $t_1 \leftarrow S_{66} \oplus S_{91}S_{92} \oplus S_{93} \oplus S_{171}$;
   | $t_2 \leftarrow S_{162} \oplus S_{175}S_{176} \oplus S_{177} \oplus S_{264}$;
   | $t_3 \leftarrow S_{243} \oplus S_{286}S_{287} \oplus S_{288} \oplus S_{69}$;
   | $(S_1, .., S_{93}) \leftarrow (t_3, S_1, .., S_{92})$;
   | $(S_{94}, ., S_{177}) \leftarrow (t_1, S_{94}, .., S_{176})$;
   | $(S_{178}, .., S_{288}) \leftarrow (t_2, S_{178}, .., S_{287})$;
End

---

level countermeasure with parallel architecture to increase the complexity of the attack. The area utilization is presented it the Table 2.

Random Acceleration Design. The size of n in parallel architecture of Trivium can be varied between 1, 4, 8, 16, 24, 32, 48 and 64. We used three input multiplexer to choose the size of n between the eight ranges. The multiplexer chooses the number of parallel bits n to be generated depending on random value generated using PRNG or PUF circuit. This will rapidly varies its power consumption and mis-align the power traces based on process variation of circuit. Moreover, intermediate state differs from each and every power traces. So, it is not easy to identify specific round and align in each and every traces. This makes chosen IV attack difficult to do. For instance, Algorithm 2 describes random accelerate of 1 bit or 64 bits based on PUF or PRNG circuit output. In order to attack the above example, we need twice the number of traces and should able to differentiate the power traces (whether each power trace belongs to 1 bit or 64 bits execution power consumption) for each and every bit attack. This will be difficult and non-trivial. Similarly, more choices can be implemented with other parallel architectures such as 4, 8, 16, 24, 32, 48 or 64 to make the algorithm execution more random. But it increases the area requirement very high.

We would like to discuss pros and cons of PUF and PRNG circuit. PRNG requires additional storage space to store and maintain the key or seed. Moreover, PRNG is a deterministic algorithm and will not vary from device to device. Hence, there is a possibility of pattern formation as well. Whereas, PUF circuit produces output based on the process variation of the chip. PUF can be designed to produce output based on the challenge given as input or without giving any input. PUF extracts unique feature of silicon chip, hence it is specific for the device. In general PUF shows significant progress in security related applications. However one needs to take care of the trade-off on selecting the critical components. In addition, we implemented 8-bit parallel architecture combined with TI and algorithm level countermeasure. Further, the algorithm can be executed n times faster than normal algorithm execution and also increases the complexity of the attack. However, this approach increases the area.

4   Performance Comparison of Implementation Techniques

Performance and area overhead of the proposed countermeasure techniques are presented in Table 2. We have taken FPGA, xc2vp7-fg456 as target device. From

Table 2. Implementation results of Trivium

Implementation	Update Register(s)	Clock Cycles	Area (slices)	Flip Flops	LUTs
Unprotected Trivium	1 bit	1152	362	371	483
	8 bit parallel	144	421	380	760
	16 bit parallel	72	443	379	807
	24 bit parallel	48	470	380	859
	32 bit parallel	36	492	378	903
	48 bit parallel	24	540	379	1001
	64 bit parallel	18	585	377	1093
Modified Trivium	1 bit	1152	366	372	484
	8 bit parallel	144	451	373	805
	16 bit parallel	72	468	372	855
	24 bit parallel	48	497	373	899
	32 bit parallel	36	515	371	936
	48 bit parallel	24	557	372	1020
	64 bit parallel	18	593	369	1099
Threshold Implementation	1 bit	1152	885	947	1631
Combined (TI and Modified) Implementation	8 bit parallel	144	1421	946	2623

the comparison table it is understood that algorithm level changes (modified Trivium) of Trivium requires only few additional gates as overhead with reasonable security. Threshold Implementation takes 2.5 times area as overhead when compared to unprotected implementation. Though 64-bit parallel algorithmic countermeasure consumes 1.6 times additional areas compared to single bit (modified) Trivium implementation, but it operates 64 times faster. The 8-bit parallel architecture of combined (TI and Modified) countermeasure consumes 3.15 and 3.3 times additional area when compared to modified Trivium and unprotected implementation of Trivium respectively.

5   Conclusion

In this paper, we presented both Threshold Implementation countermeasures and modified Trivium implementation to protect against DPA attack of Trivium stream cipher. We elaborated TI implementation of Trivium and its security analysis. Then we had shown algorithmic level changes as modified Trivium very less area requirement with reasonable security enhancement. Also we proposed PUF based random acceleration to randomize the power consumption. In future, we plan to focus on countermeasures for other possible light weight ciphers.

Acknowledgments. This Research work was funded by Department of Atomic Energy (DAE), Govt. of India under the grant 12-R&D-IMS-5.01.0204. We would like to thank our team members for their assistance in this work and anonymous reviewers for their useful comments.

References

1. The ECRYPT Stream Cipher Project. http://www.ecrypt.eu.org/stream/. Accessed 15 December 2014
2. Akkar, M.-L., Bévan, R., Dischamp, P., Moyart, D.: Power analysis, what is now possible... In: Okamoto, T. (ed.) ASIACRYPT 2000. LNCS, vol. 1976, pp. 489–502. Springer, Heidelberg (2000)
3. Atani, R.E., Mirzakuchaki, S., Atani, S.E., Meier, W.: On DPA-resistive implementation of FSR-based stream ciphers using SABL logic styles. Int. J. Comput. Commun. Cont. **4**, 324–335 (2008)
4. Burman, S., Mukhopadhyay, D., Veezhinathan, K.: LFSR based stream ciphers are vulnerable to power attacks. In: Srinathan, K., Rangan, C.P., Yung, M. (eds.) INDOCRYPT 2007. LNCS, vol. 4859, pp. 384–392. Springer, Heidelberg (2007)
5. Clavier, C., Coron, J.-S., Dabbous, N.: Differential power analysis in the presence of hardware countermeasures. In: Paar, C., Koç, Ç.K. (eds.) CHES 2000. LNCS, vol. 1965, pp. 252–263. Springer, Heidelberg (2000)
6. Coron, J.-S., Kizhvatov, I.: An efficient method for random delay generation in embedded software. In: Clavier, C., Gaj, K. (eds.) CHES 2009. LNCS, vol. 5747, pp. 156–170. Springer, Heidelberg (2009)
7. De Canniere, C., Preneel, B.: Trivium specifications. eSTREAM. ECRYPT Stream Cipher Project, Report 2005/030 (2005)

8. Durvaux, F., Renauld, M., Standaert, F.-X., van Oldeneel tot Oldenzeel, L., Veyrat-Charvillon, N.: Cryptanalysis of the CHES 2009/2010 Random Delay Countermeasure. Cryptology ePrint Archive, Report 2012/038 (2012). http://eprint.iacr.org/

9. Dutta, A., Paul, G.: Deterministic hard fault attack on trivium. In: Yoshida, M., Mouri, K. (eds.) IWSEC 2014. LNCS, vol. 8639, pp. 134–145. Springer, Heidelberg (2014)

10. Fischer, W., Gammel, B.M., Kniffler, O., Velten, J.: Differential power analysis of stream ciphers. In: Abe, M. (ed.) CT-RSA 2007. LNCS, vol. 4377, pp. 257–270. Springer, Heidelberg (2006)

11. Grabher, P., Großschädl, J., Page, D.: Non-deterministic processors: FPGA-based analysis of area, performance and security. In: Proceedings of the 4th Workshop on Embedded Systems Security, p. 1. ACM (2009)

12. Jia, Y., Yupu, H., Wang, F., Wang, H.: Correlation power analysis of Trivium. Secur. Commun. Netw. **5**(5), 479–484 (2012)

13. Mansouri, S.S., Dubrova, E.: An architectural countermeasure against power analysis attacks for FSR-based stream ciphers. In: Schindler, W., Huss, S.A. (eds.) COSADE 2012. LNCS, vol. 7275, pp. 54–68. Springer, Heidelberg (2012)

14. Messerges, T.S., Dabbish, E.A., Sloan, R.H.: Investigations of power analysis attacks on smartcards. In: USENIX Workshop on Smartcard Technology (1999)

15. Nikova, S., Rechberger, C., Rijmen, V.: Threshold implementations against side-channel attacks and glitches. In: Ning, P., Qing, S., Li, N. (eds.) ICICS 2006. LNCS, vol. 4307, pp. 529–545. Springer, Heidelberg (2006)

16. Ratanpal, G.B., Williams, R.D., Blalock, T.N.: An on-chip signal suppression countermeasure to power analysis attacks. IEEE Trans. Dependable Secure Comput. **1**(3), 179–189 (2004)

17. Rukhin, A., Soto, J., Nechvatal, J., Smid, M., Barker, E.: A statistical test suite for random and pseudorandom number generators for cryptographic applications. Technical report, DTIC Document (2001)

18. Strobel, D., Paar, I.C.: Side channel analysis attacks on stream ciphers. Ph.D. thesis, master thesis (2009)

19. Tiri, K., Akmal, M., Verbauwhede, I.: A dynamic and differential CMOS logic with signal independent power consumption to withstand differential power analysis on smart cards. In: Proceedings of the 28th European Solid-State Circuits Conference, ESSCIRC 2002, pp. 403–406. IEEE (2002)

20. Tiri, K., Verbauwhede, I.: A logic level design methodology for a secure DPA resistant ASIC or FPGA implementation. In: Proceedings of the Conference on Design, Automation and Test in Europe, vol. 1, p. 10246. IEEE Computer Society (2004)

Fast Searching in Image Databases Using Multi-index Robust Fingerprinting

Cezar Pleşca[1,2]($\boxtimes$), Luciana Morogan[1], and Mihai Togan[1,2]

[1] Department of Computer Science, Military Technical Academy,
Bucharest, Romania
{`cezar.plesca,morogan.luciana,mihai.togan`}`@gmail.com`
[2] Department of Research and Development, certSIGN, Bucharest, Romania

Abstract. Robust image fingerprinting seeks to transform a given input image into a compact binary hash using a non-invertible transform. These binary hashes exhibit robustness against common image processing and find their extensive application in multimedia databases where near neighbor index search is often employed. Unfortunately, robust fingerprinting length is usually longer than 32 bits which makes impossible to use them as direct indices in multimedia databases.

This paper analyses a theoretical approach that allows to map a r-neighbor search in Hamming space into a couple of direct index searches, using multiple hash tables built on fingerprinting substrings. We analyse the performances of this approach using a concrete perceptual fingerprinting scheme that we previously detailed in other paper. Experimental results conducted on a well known 4000 image dataset confirm dramatic speed-ups over a linear scan approach.

Keywords: Perceptual fingerprinting · Multimedia indexing · r-neighbor search · Multi-index hashing

1 Introduction

The emergence of the digital age necessitated the storing of large volumes of digital data such as personal photographs and videos. In this context, there is an emerging need of quickly retrieving a digital image from very large databases.

Content-based image retrieval (CBIR), also known as query by image content (QBIC) is the application of computer vision techniques to the image retrieval problem, that is, the problem of searching for digital images in large databases. "Content-based" means that the search analyzes the contents of the image rather than the metadata such as keywords, tags, or descriptions associated with

C. Pleşca and M. Togan—Author partially supported by the Romanian National Authority for Scientific Research (CNCS-UEFISCDI) under the project PN-II-IN-DPST-2012-1-0087 (ctr. 10DPST/2013). All the authors contributed equally to this work.

I. Bica et al. (Eds.): SECITC 2015, LNCS 9522, pp. 267–279, 2015.
DOI: 10.1007/978-3-319-27179-8_19

the image. The term "content" in this context might refer to colors, shapes, textures, or any other information that can be derived from the image itself.

Another image retrieval problem consist in finding a slightly modified image (e.g. compressed or affected by noise) inside a large image database. We have to stress out from the begining that this work consider the image retrieval problem in this context, rather than in the sense of CBIR systems. Given the size of the multimedia databases, such large-scale search demands highly efficient and accurate retrieval methods.

Traditionally, for binary content, hashing algorithms from the cryptographic field could be used to index large databases in order to speed-up the retrieval process. Such an algorithm produces a short binary output known as a checksum or hash. The hashing process is both compressive and non-invertible. Compression results in small checksums that can be easily compared, while non-invertibility means that the original input cannot be recovered from its checksum.

Traditional cryptographic hashing methods are designed to be used with non-changing digital data such as files, executables and passwords. In this manner, they are sensitive to even 1-bit changes into the input data. This is known as the "avalanche effect" as even the slightest change in the input will produce large changes in the resulting checksum.

However, there are certain types of digital data where small variations cannot be avoided. In digital imaging, many common transformations such as JPEG compression, scaling, cropping and enhancement do not alter the perceptual content of the image but do change the pixel values. The sensitivity of traditional hashing methods prevents their use on multimedia data. Large image and video databases such as Google Images or Facebook cannot take advantage of hash based retrieval, authentication and digital rights management.

To account for the specific properties of visual data, new techniques are required which do not assure the integrity of the digital representation of visual data but its visual appearance. One such technique is based on robust hash functions which are able to produce near identical checksums for two similar visual inputs whilst preserving the compressive and non-invertible properties.

One of the first perceptual hashing schemes was proposed by Fridrich [2], who obtained a hash by projecting the image on a set of zero-mean random patterns generated based on the random key (a password used as the seed for a pseudo-random generator). Since then, robust hash functions have been widely applied for image indexing and retrieval applications. Images are hashed to produce content dependent binary strings. These binary sequences are relatively short and can be much more efficiently compared than non-binary features.

Nevertheless, exhaustively comparing the image query q perceptual hash with each fingerprint from an database of N images is infeasible because linear complexity $O(N)$ is not scalable in practical settings. To cope with this problem, hashing based r-neighbor (binary codes that differs by at most r bits) techniques have attracted more attention in the last decade as they provide faster retrieval time. In this work, we build upon a fingerprinting method proposed in [1] to evaluate the speed-up performances of a multi-index approach [13].

2 Image Hashing Framework for Image Retrieval

It is generally known and commonly accepted that an image hashing scheme should comply some properties. Usually represented as a function $H = H(I, K)$, with I as the input image and K as the secret-key, we resume our representation to $H(I)$. Our choice is based on the targeted application (i.e. image indexing and retrieval) where the secret key K can be considered constant and is, therefore, no longer needed. The robustness and the collision-free properties are the properties needed to be satisfied for a perceptual hash, also known as the image fingerprint.

The **robustness** refers to the property of the hash to be invariant to common and minor image transformations such as noise, compression, geometric distortions, filtering and contrast enhancement. The **collision-free** property represents the sensitivity of the hash to different inputs displaying major differences. Moreover, two different hashes, obtained (with high probability) from two perceptually different images, must differ by a distance beyond a given threshold.

In general, there is a well-known four-stage process of the majority of the already proposed hashing methods: feature extraction, randomization, quantization and encoding [16]. Since we discuss our hashing scheme in the context of image retrieval, we only need the three-stage process described below:

1. *Feature Extraction.* This stage is essentially used in order for the robustness property to be satisfied. These extracted features should finely represent the input and they are often driven from the image color, its texture or its form. The output of this stage will be represented by a real-valued feature vector.
2. *Quantization.* The randomized features are discretized into a vector of quantized features. To achieve this, one can use the Lloyd-Max, the uniform or a random quantizer. The output data is not yet transform into a binary form, but quantized into discrete levels due to a set of thresholds.
3. *Encoding.* To each quantization level a unique bit-string is assigned. The length of the string is predefined. This assignation is provided by different encoding schemes usually using the standard binary representation or the Gray code. The advantage of the Gray code over the binary one is provided by the difference of only one bit between two consecutive integers.

At the end of the hashing chain there could also be a compression step, whose aim is the reduction of the hash length while still preserving the Hamming distance. Moreover, for the compression step, one can also integrate decoding stages of the error-correcting codes [4]. Through the image hashing methods, the feature extraction represents the most captious stage from the above presented ones [6, 11, 17]. Examples of such features include the block-based histograms [3], the image-edge information [14], the image feature points [12] or the relative magnitudes of the DCT coefficients [7].

One pioneer fingerprinting method was proposed by Fridrich et al. [2] where the perceptual hash is based on the projection of an input image over a series of random normalized smooth patterns. It was shown that their proposed technique is robust to both noise and filtering-based image modifications. Still, this technique was not invariant to scale and rotation. In [15], the authors proved the fact that the method is also collision prone. The collision prone refers to a statistic modeling of the hash bit generation process of an arbitrary image in order to be modified to output the same hash.

In order to generate an invariant to common gray-scale operations, Venkatesan et al. captured the principal values obtained after applying a wavelet transform over the image blocks [17]. Further, on the resulted array, the quantization and the compression processes are applied to obtain the perceptual hash. Some disadvantages of this method were shown by Meixner [10], concerning transformations like object insertion, gamma correction and contrast changes.

In [11], Venkatesan et al. introduced an image hash which was constructed in a iterative manner, based on thresholding and spatial filtering. The schemes from [2,11,17] proved a good resilience under the operations such as additive noise and common filtering. Nevertheless, regarding the desynchronization and the geometric distortions, the results were relatively poor.

Willing to pass these disadvantages, new methods were proposed that exploits features extracted from various transform domains. A first example is described in [6], based on the properties of the Radon transform. Other methods use Randlet transform coefficients [9] or the features extracted from the singular values decomposition of pseudo-randomly image blocks [5]. These methods proved good robustness especially against the rotation and the cropping attacks.

Based on a joinder of global and local descriptors, the authors of [18] proposed the image summarization. The global features were extracted making use of the luminance and the chrominance characteristics of an image (the Zernike moments). The local features were based on position and texture information of the image salient regions. For generating a shape-contexts-based image hash, the method from [8] was also based on some robust local feature points. The robust SIFT-Harris detector was manipulated in order to select the most stable SIFT key-points under various content-preserving distortions. Finally, the detected local features are embedded into shape-contexts-based descriptors.

3   Overview of Our Perceptual Fingerprinting Scheme

The scheme we proposed in [1] is based on the log-polar image representation. It is already known that such representation has interesting properties with respect to invariant geometric transformations. The choice we made in extracting the image features was based on a key that outputs a very robust perceptual hash. The log-polar representation space convert rotations and scaling operations applied in the original space into circular shifts and translation.

Let us consider the polar coordinate system (R, θ) where R denotes the radial distance from the image center (x_c, y_c), while θ represents the angle made with the horizontal axis. Any image pixel becomes actually one point in the polar system which is described by the equations below:

$$R = \sqrt{(x - x_c)^2 + (y - y_c)^2}, \theta = \arctan\left(\frac{y - y_c}{x - x_c}\right) \qquad (1)$$

The circles in the Cartesian space are mapped to horizontal lines in the polar coordinate space, as illustrated in the Fig. 1a and b below. The origin is considered to be in the upper left corner while θ and R lie along the horizontal and vertical axes, respectively. Moreover, the radial lines in the original image space are mapped to vertical columns in the polar coordinates space.

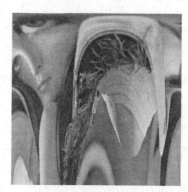

(a) Original Image   (b) Polar Image

Fig. 1. Polar coordinate transformations

One can easily observe that in the new polar coordinates system, rotations become vertical circular shifts while scalings imply changes of horizontal lines to other positions. In fact, scaling multiplies the R coordinate with the scaling factor ρ. Therefore, taking the logarithmic scale on the R axis will map the previous multiplication to an addition with a constant factor, namely a translation.

Putting in other words, the (R, θ) polar coordinates become $(r = \log R, \theta)$ in the new log-polar coordinates. The usage of the new coordinates translates the scale transformation applied to the original image into a vertical downward shift along the r axis in the log-polar transformed image.

Since after geometric transformations, the large majority of the horizontal lines remain unchanged, taking some aggregate metrics such as the mean or the standard deviation could be good candidates for robust features. Building on these observations, the basic steps of our fingerprinting algorithm [1] are:

1. *Preprocessing.* A Gaussian low-pass filter is applied to an input image I to provide robustness to noise addition. The resulted image J is then converted into log-polar coordinates to get an image denoted LP.
2. *Feature Generation.* A number of L horizontal random lines from the bottom half of the image LP are chosen and their mean is computed along the θ-axis. These average values are kept to obtain the image feature vector.
3. *Post Processing.* The resulting vector is uniformly quantized by representing each value on a number of b bits using the Gray encoding. The output binary hash sequence contains therefore a number of $n = L \cdot b$ bits.

4   Multi-index Hashing Approach

Perceptual hashing used to represent image data in terms of compact binary codes often facilitates fast neighbor search in image indexing and image retrieval applications. In this context, the most compelling reason for binary codes is their use as direct indexes (addresses) into a hash table, yielding a dramatic increase in search speed compared to an exhaustive linear scan.

Image hashing code lengths are often significantly longer than 32 bits in order to achieve satisfactory retrieval performance, thus making their use, as a direct index, impossible. Moreover, hashing codes of two similar images are not generally identical but rather in a Hamming distance of a few bits. To find all neighbors within a given Hamming distance of a query image, one needs to examine all hash table entries, a computation which requires a linear time in both the database size and the hash length.

To speed-up this computation, we build upon a theoretical approach proposed in [13] that presented a new algorithm for exact r-neighbor search on binary codes that is dramatically faster than exhaustive linear scan. Their approach is called *multi-index hashing*, as binary codes from the entire database are separated into m disjoint substrings which are used as indexes for m different hash tables.

Given an image query code, images that fall exactly in at least one such substring are considered neighbor candidates. These image candidates are then checked for validity using the full hashing code, to remove any non-r-neighbors. To be practical for large-scale datasets, the authors found, by means of simulation, that the substrings must be chosen so that the set of candidates is small, and storage requirements are reasonable.

The key idea resides in a simple observation, namely that with N binary codes of n bits, the vast majority of the 2^n possible entries in a full hash table will be empty, since $2^n \gg N$. Therefore, it would be expensive to examine all entries within r bits of a query code, since most of them contain no items. Instead, the idea was to create hash tables based on substrings of the full binary codes, thus merging many previous buckets together by marginalizing over different dimensions of the Hamming space.

4.1   Searching r-neighbor Hamming Codes

In this subsection we briefly discuss the details of the multi-index hashing approach analyzed in [13]. Each binary code h, comprising n bits, is partitioned into m disjoint substrings, $\{h_1 \cdots h_m\}$, each of length n/m bits. For now, we assume that n is divisible by m and that the substrings comprise contiguous bits, but this condition will be relaxed further.

The key idea rests on the following statement: when two binary codes h and g differ by at most r bits, then, in at least one of their m substrings they must differ by at most $r' = \lfloor r/m \rfloor$ bits. For example, if h and g differ by 3 bits or less, and $m = 4$, at least one of the 4 corresponding substrings must be identical.

The authors show that even it suffices to examine all buckets within a radius of r' bits in all m hash tables, generally a small number of hash tables need to be investigated. More precisely, given $r = mr' + a$, where $0 \leq a < m$, to find any image within a radius of r bits on n-bit codes, it suffices to search $a + 1$ substring hash tables to a Hamming radius of r', and the remaining $m - (a+1)$ substring hash tables up to a radius of $r' - 1$.

A special case is when $r < m$, hence $r' = 0$ and $a = r$. In this case, it suffices to search $r + 1$ substring hash tables for a radius of $r' = 0$ (i.e. exact matches), while the remaining $m - (r+1)$ hash tables can be ignored. Clearly, if a hash code does not match exactly with the hash query in any of the selected $r + 1$ substrings, then the code must differ from the query in at least $r + 1$ bits.

4.2 Multi-index Hashing for r-neighbor Search

From the previous section, it is clear that, given a set of method parameters, one can establish a threshold T such as, with great probability, hashes of similar images are within a Hamming distance of T bits while hashes for different images will lead to a distance beyond T. We put ourselves into the special case of multi-index hashing approach (i.e. $m > r$) and consider $r = T$.

First, one compute hash binary codes of length n for the entire database, and then build one hash table for each of the first $r + 1$ substrings of length s from the entire hash. Clearly, $(r + 1)s \leq n$, hence $s \leq \lfloor n/(r+1) \rfloor$. Each image from the database will be placed in its corresponding bucket in each of the $r + 1$ tables, with the average number of collisions depending of the value of r.

Then, given a query image having a hash g with the substrings $\{g_j\}$, $j = \overline{1, r+1}$, one investigates the j-th substring hash table for images that are placed in the bucket whose index is g_j. We obtain a set of candidates from the j-th substring hash table, denoted $C_j(g)$. As explained previously, the union of the $r + 1$ sets, $C(g) = \cup_j C_j$ is necessarily a superset of the r-neighbors of g. The last step of the algorithm computes the full Hamming distance between g and each candidate in $C(g)$, retaining only those codes that are true r-neighbors of g.

Algorithm 1 outlines the r-neighbor retrieval procedure for a query image hash g. The search cost depends on the number of lookups (i.e., the number of buckets examined) and the number of candidates tested. Not surprisingly, there is a natural trade-off between them. With a large number of lookups one can minimize the number of extraneous candidates. By merging many buckets to reduce the number of lookups, one obtains a large number of candidates to test.

5   Experimental Results

In this section, we evaluate the performance of the multi-index hashing approach described earlier on our fingerprinting scheme presented in the third section. First, we compute a confidence interval for the threshold T that allows us to distinguish between similar and distinct images on a 4000 image dataset. Second,

---

Algorithm 1. r-Neighbor Search for Query g

1: Compute query substrings $g_j, 1 \leq j \leq r+1$
2: Candidates $= \varnothing$
3: **for** $j = 1$ to $r+1$ **do**
4:     C_j = candidates at bucket g_j from j-th hash table
5:     Candidates = Candidates $\cup\ C_j$
6: **end for**
7: Remove all non r-neighbors from the Candidates set

---

we evaluate the speed-up rate for an image retrieval system by comparison with the linear scan of all hashing codes. In this context, we experimentally study the influence of the substring length used in the multi-index approach as well as the Hamming radius (i.e. threshold) in the r-neighbor searching. Third, we investigate the speed-up dynamics according to the size of the image database.

5.1 Database Experiment Setup

The metric we used to measure the distance between two images is the Hamming distance between their binary hashes, h_1 and h_2 respectively, normalized with respect to the length n of the hash:

$$d(h_1, h_2) = \frac{\sum\limits_{i=1}^{n} |h_1(i) - h_2(i)|}{n} \tag{2}$$

This distance is expected to be near 0 for similar images and close to 0.5 for dissimilar ones. Moreover, this distance should increase with the distortion between the manipulated and the original image.

For testing purposes, we used the Microsoft Research Cambridge Database that contains over 4000 color images, either in 640×480 or in 480×640 resolution, available at the address: http://research.microsoft.com/downloads. These images are grouped in different classes (e.g. cars, flowers), each class containing multiple content-related images, as shown in Fig. 2.

The robustness of our hashing scheme was first tested against a list of content-preserving operations shown in Table 1. For each such operation, we vary the corresponding parameter: for example, considering rotation, we vary the angle between $1°$ and $10°$. For each value of the parameter, we measure the normalized Hamming distance between the hashes of the original image and the manipulated image; the results obtained are averaged over the entire set of images.

As expected, the results obtained for these manipulations were very closed to the ones reported in [1], and we do not detail them here. The maximum normalized Hamming distance computed under content-preserving manipulations was around 3%, which means a radius of 9 bits from a hash length of 300 bits.

We also consider the Hamming distance between the hashes of dissimilar images, which indicates the discriminative capability of the hashing algorithm. For each pair of distinct images, we compute the normalized Hamming distance

(a)   (b)

(c)   (d)

Fig. 2. Database images from different classes.

Table 1. Set of content-preserving manipulations

Manipulation operation	Parameter of the operation
Gaussian Noise	Noise Variance from 0.0 to 0.2
Geometric Rotation	Rotation Angle from 1 to 10
Geometric Scaling	Scaling Factor from 1.0 to 2.0
JPEG Compression	Quality Factor from 10 % to 90 %

between their hashes. The minimum value of these distances is 7 %, meaning that two distinct images differ at least by 21 bits of their fingerprints. Therefore, any value in the confidence interval [9–21] could be set as a threshold, in order to minimize false positives and false negatives rates.

5.2 Speed-up Rate Evaluation

Next, the main metric we used is the **speed-up rate**, defined as the ratio between the linear scan time to search an image in the entire database and the time needed by the multi-index method for the same purpose. Linear scan refers to the classic approach where the hash of a query image is compared against the precomputed hashes of all database images, using the Hamming distance. Multi-index hashing search refers to the searching method described in the previous section and synthesized in Algorithm 1.

We first studied the influence of the substring length parameter, denoted s, used to build multiple hash tables. As explained before, for a given Hamming radius r and a total length of the fingerprint n, we should have $s \leq \lfloor n/(r+1) \rfloor$. For our first experiment, $n = 300$ bits and we fixed $r = 14$ (in the confidence interval [9–21], hence $s \leq 20$.

In the query process we used all images in the database, slightly modified by transformations described in Table 1 and we measured the average time taken by a search operation. For the linear scan procedure we obtained an average time of 20.13 ms while the multi-index approach average time varies between 70.23 ms (for $s = 5$) and 1.15 ms (for $s = 20$).

The gain ratios for different substring length are depicted in Fig. 3. As expected, the speed-up rate grows with the length of the substring used for hashing operation. Longer substring length reduces the number of collisions in the buckets of the hash tables, and since the number of hash tables is constant (i.e. $r + 1 = 15$), this contributes to a quicker retrieval.

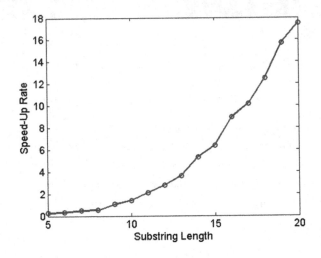

Fig. 3. Speed-up rate dynamics for different substring lengths

Next, we examined the influence of the threshold parameter r in the performance of the multi-index hashing approach. From the previous experimental analysis, it is clear that, given a threshold r, to maximize the speed-up rate, one should set the substring length at its maximum possible value, i.e. $s = \lfloor n/(r+1) \rfloor$. We experimented with different values of r in the interval [5–20] and the results are illustrated in Fig. 4.

Smaller radius implies a larger substring length, henceforth a better speed in the searching process; this came at the cost of a smaller tolerance against content-preserving transformations, therefore leading to more false negative alarms.

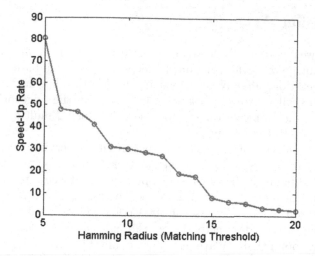

Fig. 4. Speed-up rate dynamics for different matching thresholds

The best trade-off seems to be for a minimum threshold inside the confidence interval (i.e. [9–21]; for $r = 9$, the substring length would be $s = 30$ and the multi-index hashing method is about 30 times faster than the linear scan search.

The last experiment we conducted concerns the scalability of this method. In this manner, we randomly select a subset of the entire image database and conduct the same searching process previously described to compare the two methods. In this case we set the threshold at its minimum value (i.e. $r = 9$) and the substring length at $s = 30$. One can notice from Table 2 that while the classical scan method involves a linear time complexity, the average time needed by the multi-index method increase very slow with the database size. Despite this encouraging results, larger image databases need to be considered in order to estimate the growth rate of the multi-index hashing method.

Table 2. Multi-index Hashing Performance Scalability

Database size	Multi-index (milliseconds)	Linear scan (milliseconds)	Speed-up rate
500	0.402	2.561	6.40
1000	0.435	5.112	11.88
1500	0.478	7.446	15.83
2000	0.506	9.918	19.82
2500	0.527	12.435	23.90
3000	0.573	15.137	26.54
3500	0.604	17.490	29.15
4000	0.653	20.130	30.97

6   Conclusion

In this paper, we investigated the practical performances of a multi-index hashing approach for image retrieval using our fingerprinting scheme based on log-polar image representation, already described in [1]. Multi-index hashing approach presented in [13] allows to map a r-neighbor search in the fingerprinting Hamming space onto a couple of direct index searches, using multiple hash tables built on fingerprinting substrings.

The good resiliency of this scheme to content-preserving operations (e.g. noise addition, compression and geometric transformations) together with its discriminative capability allows us to compute a confidence interval in which a threshold could be set. Starting from these observations, we conduct a series of experiments on a real database of 4000 color images in order to estimate the gain of the multi-index method over the classic linear scan approach. We experimentally found that the average time required by the multi-index method slowly increase with the database size and one can expect an improvement of up to a 30 times faster image retrieval.

In the future, we would like to investigate the performances of the multi-index hashing approach using state-of-the-art fingerprinting algorithms and larger image datasets. Further studies could also be oriented on the CBIR (Content Based Image Retrieval) systems coupled with the transformation of representative image features into binary codes, in which context the performances of k-nearest neighbor approach based on multi-index hashing need to be addressed.

References

1. Cezar, P., Luciana, M.: Efficient and robust perceptual hashing using log-polar image representation. In: IEEE International Conference on Communications, pp. 1–6 (2014)
2. Fridrich, J.: Robust hash functions for digital watermarking. In: International Conference on Information Technology: Coding and Computing, pp. 178–183. IEEE Computer Society (2000)
3. Jing, F., Li, M., Zhang, H., Zhang, B.: An efficient and effective region-based image retrieval framework. IEEE Trans. Image Process. **13**(5), 699–709 (2004)
4. Johnson, M., Ramchandran, K.: Dither-based secure image hashing using distributed coding. In: International Conference on Image Processing, pp. 751–754 (2003)
5. Kozat, S.S., Venkatesan, R., Mihçak, M.K.: Robust perceptual image hashing via matrix invariants. In: IEEE International Conference on Image Processing, pp. 3443–3446. IEEE (2004)
6. Lefèbvre, F., Czyz, J., Macq, B.M.: A robust soft hash algorithm for digital image signature. In: IEEE International Conference on Image Processing, pp. 495–498 (2003)
7. Lin, C.Y., Chang, S.F.: A robust image authentication method distinguishing JPEG compression from malicious manipulation. IEEE Trans. Circuits Syst. Video Technol. **11**(2), 153–168 (2001)
8. Lv, X., Wang, Z.J.: Perceptual image hashing based on shape contexts and local feature points. IEEE Trans. Inf. Forensics Secur. **7**(3), 1081–1093 (2012)

9. Malkin, M., Venkatesan, R.: The randlet transform: application to universal perceptual hashing and image identi cation. In: Allerton Conference (2004)
10. Meixner, A., Uhl, A.: Analysis of a wavelet based robust hash algorithm. In: Security, Steganography, and Watermarking of Multimedia Contents. SPIE, vol. 5306, pp. 772–783 (2004)
11. Mihçak, M.K., Venkatesan, R.: New iterative geometric methods for robust perceptual image hashing. In: Sander, T. (ed.) DRM 2001. LNCS, vol. 2320, pp. 13–21. Springer, Heidelberg (2002)
12. Monga, V., Evans, B.L.: Robust perceptual image hashing using feature points. In: IEEE International Conference on Image Processing, pp. 677–680. IEEE (2004)
13. Norouzi, M., Punjani, A., Fleet, D.J.: Fast exact search in hamming space with multi-index hashing. IEEE Trans. Pattern Anal. Mach. Intell. **36**(6), 1107–1119 (2014)
14. Queluz, M.: Toward robust, content based techniques for image authentication. In: IEEE Second Workshop on Multimedia Signal Processing, pp. 297–302 (1998)
15. Radhakrishnan, R., Xiong, Z., Memon, N.D.: On the security of the visual hash function. J. Electron. Imaging **14**(1), 013011 (2005)
16. Swaminathan, A., Mao, Y., Wu, M.: Robust and secure image hashing. IEEE Trans. Inf. Forensics Secur. **1**(2), 215–230 (2006)
17. Venkatesan, R., Koon, S.M., Jakubowski, M.H., Moulin, P.: Robust image hashing. In: IEEE International Conference on Image Processing, pp. 664–666 (2000)
18. Zhao, Y., Wang, S., Zhang, X., Yao, H.: Robust hashing for image authentication using zernike moments and local features. IEEE Trans. Inf. Forensics Secur. **8**(1), 55–63 (2013)

Author Index

Printed in the United States
By Bookmasters